*Preaching
the
Good News*

Preaching
the
Good News

GEORGE E. SWEAZEY

Princeton Theological Seminary

PRENTICE-HALL, INC., Englewood Cliffs, New Jersey

Library of Congress Cataloging in Publication Data

SWEAZEY, GEORGE EDGAR, 1905–
   Preaching the good news.

   Bibliography: p.
   Includes index.
   1. Preaching. I. Title.
BV4211.2.S93   251   75-4997
ISBN 0-13-694802-2

10 9 8 7 6 5 4 3 2 1

Prentice-Hall International, Inc., *London*
Prentice-Hall of Australia, Pty. Ltd., *Sydney*
Prentice-Hall of Canada, Ltd., *Toronto*
Prentice-Hall of India Private Limited, *New Delhi*
Prentice-Hall of Japan, Inc., *Tokyo*
Prentice-Hall of Southeast Asia (Pte.) Ltd., *Singapore*

ACKNOWLEDGMENTS

Countee Cullen, *Color* (New York: Harper & Brothers Publishers, 1925), p. 3. Reprinted by permission of Harper & Row Publishers, Inc.

A. E. Housman, from "Shot? so quick, so clean an ending?" from "A Shropshire Lad," Authorized Edition, from *The Collected Poems of A. E. Housman*. Copyright 1939, 1940, © 1965 by Holt, Rinehart and Winston, Inc. Copyright © 1967, 1968 by Robert E. Symons. Reprinted by permission of Holt, Rinehart and Winston, Inc. and the Society of Authors as the literary representative of the Estate of A. E. Housman; and Jonathan Cape Ltd., publishers of A. E. Housman's *Collected Poems*.

Hugh Kingsmill, *The Best of Hugh Kingsmill* (London: Victor Gollancz Ltd., 1970), p. 380. Reprinted by permission of Victor Gollancz Ltd.

Ogden Nash, "Ha! Original Sin!" from *Verses from 1929 On* by Ogden Nash. Copyright © 1931, renewed 1958 by Ogden Nash. Reprinted by permission of Little, Brown and Company, and J. M. Dent & Sons Ltd. Publishers.

Sara Teasdale, "Spirit's House," from Collected Poems by Sara Teasdale. Copyright 1917 by Macmillan Publishing Co., Inc., renewed 1945 by Mamie Wheless. Reprinted by permission of Macmillan Publishing Co., Inc.

To our children

Anne George Handy

Much loved teachers from whom I am still learning

Contents

MATERIAL

SUBJECTS

THE PARTICIPANTS

Preaching
the
Good News

Introduction

Can anyone be taught to preach? There is no standard style; every preacher must discover his own ways. What makes good preaching is not musty maxims of homiletics but a burning eagerness to say what congregations need to hear.

It must be recognized, however, that preaching is not a natural skill; the methods that will make it effective can be taught, and the mistakes that will spoil it can be pointed out. Even the most talented artists and craftsmen need instruction. Proficiency in public speech has been a respected subject for study ever since Aristotle's *Rhetoric;* knowledge of what to do and what to avoid has been accumulating across the years. Some of the skills are timeless, and new ones are needed for each generation. A preacher needs help with such matters as:

What preaching can do
How to use words effectively
Where to find enough material for sermons every seven days
How to draw a congregation together in love and trust
What makes people want to listen
How to use the Bible, and how not to abuse it
The ways to lessen resistance to what may be unwelcome
What makes a sermon march toward a worthy goal, and what gets it lost

A preacher who has an average of 280 listeners a week will have six thousand hours of time entrusted to him in a year. Anyone who claims all that human life for listening to his preaching has an awesome obligation. Integrity requires him to learn to preach as well as possible or to quit, since people come to the church and look up at the minister because they trust him to do his best to use that opportunity for God's great purposes.

This book is intended for students who are preparing to be preachers, and for preachers who need a fresh outlook. I have tried to deal with the basic matters preachers are supposed to know about, and also with the newer thinking and contemporary styles. I hope I have dealt with serious technical and theological subjects in a way that will be appropriate for lay readers, including first-year students. This book is also intended for lay church members who may wish to know more about a part of church life to which they give so much time, and which depends so much on them.

The table of contents shows that the chapters are grouped by purposes. A student who is starting a class which includes sermon making might need to go into the section on Technique before reading the rest of the book. A minister who is preaching every Sunday might wish to get at once to the Subjects section. Lay readers might begin with the last chapter, which is specially for them, and then go to the Basics. The sections are not, however, designed to be independent and none of them can be rightly understood without the others.

The superior preaching of the women in my classes reveals how very much the church is losing by not having more women ministers. My strong feeling about this made me try hard to use both feminine and masculine words to refer to preachers, but this put me into a losing struggle with the English language. It was simply impossible to keep saying "person," or "his and her," or "man and woman." I have had to accept the convention of using masculine terms for both sexes. This practice has been ascribed to male presumption, but perhaps it merely indicates that the male sex is the less specific.

Scripture quotations are from the Revised Standard Version unless there is such a notation as KJV (King James Version), NEB (New English Bible), or TEV (Today's English Version).

I

The Importance of Preaching

Five million sermons a year are preached in this country. In almost every neighborhood and crossroads people gather each week to hear about the Christian beliefs and way of living. Think of how any other organized movement could use a chance like that! A preacher knows that every Sunday he can have uninterrupted access to the attention of a room full of people for twenty-five minutes. But does he have it? Are all those people listening, or are they simply sitting out an ancestral rite which requires no attention? I have recently been able to attend a variety of churches and listen to many sorts of preachers. I try to sit where I can see the faces of the congregation. Some people are obviously tuned out during the sermon, but most are hearing it. Their eyes are on the preacher, they look interested, their expressions change to match what is said.

But is so much listening a good thing? Christianity is not something you talk about, it is something you do. Sitting through sermons can become the major Christian activity. With most of us being drowned by words—words on paper, words from radios, and talk shows, and commentators—the thought of all the talking that goes on in church may be disquieting.

The contrast of words with deeds, however, is a false one. Words *are* deeds. The ancient Greeks had the saying, "By words alone are lives of mortals swayed." The talkers are the doers, if what they talk about is important. The greatest doer of all was called "the Word," and words that start with him have changed men and nations. His spokesmen have their hands on the switches that control human destiny. If what the preacher says can even slightly alter the direction in which people are aimed when they leave the church, the effect can be beyond all calculation. What people think determines everything; that is why Joseph Conrad said that words "have set whole nations in motion and upheaved the dry, hard ground on which rests our social fabric. . . . Give me the right word and the right accent and I will move the world."

Preaching is certainly not the church's most important activity; nothing that takes place in the church building is. It is not when the church members are gathered, but when they are dispersed into the world, that they are most truly functioning as parts of the saving, healing body of Christ. But sermons can have a great deal to do with that. Good preaching can be at the heart of everything a church does, in its building and outside it. Ministers wonder whether they could not see more good from their efforts through other forms of ministry—counseling, or work with small groups, or community action. Indeed, they may; but these do not rival preaching, they interact with it. They build the sermons, and the sermons build them. A church's best forms of service are likely to get their inspiration, aims, and promotion from the pulpit. And the best sermons are likely to be extensions of all the church is doing. The conversations, therapies, and services to the distressed are continued in the pulpit.

A new church usually starts with a preaching service; and when a church quits, that service is the last thing to be given up. Those who want to move us into what they imagine the twenty-first century will be like while we still have a generation to go in this one may insist that preaching is becoming obsolete. All experience indicates that everything else will become obsolete before preaching does. And when a dying church comes back to life, that usually starts, not with new programs or activities, but with new life in the preaching.

Preaching can never be understood apart from worship. A sermon is not a public speech, it is an element in a worshipping experience. Preaching may be studied by itself, just as hymnology or the sacraments may be considered separately, but it must always be remembered that the sermon is just one part of an extended experience with God. From this it gets a power that, as a lecture, it could never have. All the deep human needs that make worship necessary make preaching necessary, because the sermon is one of the most powerful means for bringing about the encounter between God and men. Whether or not you think of preaching as a sacrament depends upon your private dictionary. It does use a material element, not wine or water but the spoken word, for a spiritual result. The crude, rough element of the preacher's thought may give the occasion for the miracle to happen. The Word makes the word efficacious. The sermon enunciates the faith that makes all worship valid. The liturgy conveys the timeless which the sermon then sets forth in timely terms, and applies to the contemporary scene. Worship without sermons could exploit God for each one's private fancies; sermons without worship could make the preacher the object of the service. John Calvin was vehement against those who minimize preaching to magnify the Eucharist. "Without the Word the Sacrament is but a dumb show; the word must go before." "Burying preaching, they do only charm the sacraments with magical enchantment." "If the visible symbols are offered without the Word, they are not only powerless and dead, but harmful jugglery."

There are reasons why the service where the word of God is preached is so important for the church. A religion whose key word is "love" requires fellowship. Other religions can center in solitary meditation, or ceremonial, or scholarship, or the keeping of laws. A religion of love, which is a personal relationship, can best be conveyed through a person in the company of persons. That is the point of Phillips Brooks' famous definition of preaching as "truth through personality." Communication through a living, breathing, present human being has a necessary element that truth from a printed page or a broadcast cannot have. James Stewart recalls how Jeanie, in Scott's novel, *The Heart of Midlothian,* is determined to go to London to plead before the King for Effie's life. She says, "A letter canna look, and pray, and beg, and beseech, as the human voice can do to the human heart." It has been suggested that modern technologies have made preaching obsolete. The invention that would seem most likely to do that came out in the fifteenth century. There was every reason to expect that printing would make preaching unnecessary. It enabled people to have Bibles and all the finest sermons to read when they pleased. But printing actually increased the number of hearers for the spoken word. When you read a speech, how poor the reading is compared to hearing it. The human voice, the human eye, and the human presence are the means of communication the human heart loves best.

Phillips Brooks' definition could be expanded to say that preaching is "truth through personality, *in the midst of personalities.*" People together are a different sort of creature from people alone. They may be more human or less human, but they think, feel, and respond differently.That is why Christians need both solitary worship and worship with others. Luther said, "At home, in my own house, there is no warmth or vigor in me, but in the church, when the multitude is gathered together, a fire is kindled in my heart." Some learning we get best by ourselves, but there is much we will never get except in company. That is why students go to schools instead of taking correspondence courses. There are inspirations and enjoyments we can never have in solitude. That is why recordings and broadcasts have not made concerts unnecessary.

If I want to learn about prison conditions, it may be better to stay at home and read a book than to attend a lecture. But I am far more likely to be moved to do something about those conditions if I am in a group, listening to a warden or an ex-convict, than if I am at home reading the same thing. Something electric is exchanged among clustered hearers which alters the way they operate. That is why the Psalmist said, "O magnify the Lord *with me,* and let us exalt his name *together.*" Quakers will go miles through rain or snow to sit together in silence because silence with others is totally different from silence alone. Even the distance separating people makes a difference. Speakers rightly dread empty front rows and spaced out hearers because people within reach of each other are far more responsive than the same people scattered out. Ministers dislike empty front pews, which separate them from the congregation like a psychological moat. Unneeded back pews and balconies had better be roped off. The sermon is nearer what a sermon ought to be when the listeners feel drawn to each other and to the preacher. A bond of common feeling among the worshippers is established when the sermon begins with something about which they all feel deeply or are enthusiastic. This organic sense of fellowship is necessary for real preaching and common worship; it is at the heart of Christianity. Through the years, educated Christians have left the great religious authors on their shelves and come to churches to listen to mediocre preachers because, from a person among persons, they were getting what they could never get alone.

The church needs to make a great deal better use of tapes, films, and broadcasts. These can have tremendous value. But they will never be rivals for the preaching service; they are a wholly different sort of experience. For lovers a telephone is a wonderful boon, but a poor substitute.

Preaching is at the heart of Christianity because it has been the chief means of imparting the saving truths. A person cannot give his heart to Christ until he is told who Christ is and what he taught. Christianity is not a feeling or an ecstatic state, it is the commitment of life to certain basic truth about God, and man, and right, and destiny, which then can be the source of ecstasy. A Christian needs to know about the mighty acts of God in history. Faith in Christ is a sublimely simple thing, but following him in every part of life is not a simple thing at all. The riches of Christianity are unsearchable. Preaching conveys and explains the saving truths, and help Christians to keep on growing.

The Christian life is free, but it is not improvised. It is not dictated by rules, but it does have guides. The Bible, and the record of 2000 years of trying, have a great deal to say about the life that is lived in love and loyalty to Christ. That is what sermons try to pass on to those who are trying to be Christians.

Christians have a mission. They are in the world to teach, to heal, to help, to condemn, to shatter, and to save. They come to their churches to learn what they should do by themselves and together. These are the matters with which sermons have to deal.

The imparting of truth through personality in the midst of personalities is required by the very nature of the biblical religion. From the Exodus to the end of the record, it was a powerful influence in the life of the Hebrew people. Jesus preached, and he commanded his disciples to preach. As the New Testament church matured, its reliance on preaching increased. The proclamation by a person to a group, whether it was called *kerusso, euaggelizo,* or *kataggelo,* was a primary way of bringing people to the Christian faith and of building them up in that faith. The Apostles were first of all preachers, not priests or administrators. Paul declares, "God did not send me to baptize, but to preach." He admits, "It would be misery to me not to preach," and he exhorts Timothy, "Preach the word!"

Across the centuries, whenever the Church has been vital, we find that same emphasis on preaching. Chrysostom, around the year 400, called it the "one vital medicine" for the sickness of the Church. Gregory the Great, about 1070, said that a minister who avoids preaching is as guilty of "fratricide" as a physician is if he fails to treat a wounded man, "thus causing his death." The low times in the history of the Church have invariably been those when preaching was neglected. It was almost displaced by pageant and ceremonial just before the Reformation. The minimizing of preaching today is not a sign of progress in communications but of regress in religious interest. When it is said, "People do not come to hear sermons like they used to," it must be added sadly, "and even less do they come for all the rest the church is doing." All the great upsurges of vigor in the church's history have been heralded by a new enthusiasm for preaching. This was seen with the Dominicans, the Franciscans, the Lollards in the Reformation, and with the Methodists. The flaming movements have been kindled and kept ablaze by preachers such as Ambrose, Augustine, Savonarola, Hus, Luther, Calvin, and Wesley. Protestantism has never found a substitute for preaching, and it never can. Its whole life is bound up with the personal communication of Christian truth and guidance within the fellowship of worship. The health and vigor of a church will always be related to the health and vigor of its preaching.

In every age it has been suggested that preaching may be out of date. Many in the Middle Ages believed that the Christian's life was sustained by the sacraments, so that preaching was not necessary. During the Reformation it was declared that the Holy Spirit enabled every Christian to interpret the Scriptures for himself so that there was no longer any need to listen to the clergy. The spread of literacy was expected to eliminate the regard for the preacher as the educated man. In 1880 the *London Times* started a great discussion with the question, "Why not be content to worship only, when we go to church?" In 1890 a New England periodical created a stir with a symposium on, "Shall we go on preaching?" In 1900 it was seriously questioned whether there would be any place for preaching in the new century. In the 1920s a prominent Episcopal minister made headlines across the nation by demanding "a moratorium on preaching." But now, in the last fourth of the twentieth century, committees looking for ministers for churches still usually list good preaching as the most hoped-for quality.

Old objections to preaching keep appearing as reasons why it is not suited to "our time." People today, it is said, resent authority. They find it insufferable for anyone to mount a pulpit to tell others how to think or act. The English philosopher, Bernard Bosanquet, early in this century declared, "I think all preaching has a certain affinity to bad manners." The very words, "preach," and "preachy" have a bad connotation. "Don't preach to me," is a sure put-down. This is a necessary warning against a superior, censorious, dogmatic style of preaching. But every human contact is manipulative. The participants in every conversation try to push each other around. Preachers from all sorts of pulpits work on us all the time—politicians, columnists, commentators, editorialists, playwrights, essayists, teachers, bosses, luncheon club oracles. It is well that with all these others there are some preachers who are trying to influence what happens by the Christian point of view. The modern minister does not claim any pipeline to heaven that is not available to others. His purpose is not to do other people's thinking for them, but to stimulate it. When someone says to him at the church door, "I did not agree with you today," the preacher knows, first, that the critic has had a profitable Sunday, and, second, that the criticism may be right.

A writer recently declared, "One-way communication is as outmoded as the Model-T." Apparently he has not seen the papers. There has not been a time in the history of the world when speakers to crowds were as influential as they have been recently. The Nazi movement was built by preaching. Its monstrous rallies were the setting for Hitler's pulpit. The Communists fought hard to outbid Hitler by preaching. When I was in Germany in the 1930s, the courtyard of our apartment in a workers' district was regularly invaded by Communist gospel teams. With their portable organs, hymns, and shouted sermons they were the Salvation Army with a different message. It was by endless oratory and public indoctrination that the masses in North Viet Nam, Cuba, and China were made Communist.

Most of the great movements in the Western World have been fired and sustained by preaching. Think of Demosthenes' Philippics, and Cato's cry, "Carthage must be destroyed!" and the spread of Christianity, the Crusades, the Reformation, the American and French Revolutions, abolition, the labor movement, the anti–Viet Nam protests, Martin Luther King, Malcolm X, and every political campaign. Churchill did much to destroy the Nazi movement, which was built by public speaking, not because he was a great strategist or administrator, for he was not, but because he was a great orator. It would be strange for the church to decide that its birthright of preaching is outmoded while everyone else is making so much use of it. As a matter of fact, almost all communication is "one-way." Whenever you read a book or newspaper, listen to a broadcast, attend a play, go to a meeting, or have something explained, you are getting one-way communication.

It is often the preacher who is most discouraged about preaching. It may be difficult for him to see the result of it. One hundred twenty years ago a famous preacher wrote, "I wish I did not hate preaching so much, but the degradation of being a Brighton preacher is almost intolerable . . . all I say and feel is that by the change of the times the pulpit has lost its place." But today we know that few men have ever influenced so many others for good as did Frederick W. Robertson.

Herman Melville said in *Moby Dick,* "The pulpit is ever this earth's foremost part; all the rest comes in its rear; the pulpit leads the world. . . . Yes, the world's a ship on its passage out, . . . and the pulpit is its prow." Human destinies are not determined in parliaments, factories, or laboratories; the course is fixed where human character is being formed. The future depends on people's attitudes, and these are the preacher's business. Lincoln said, "With public sentiment nothing can fail; without it nothing can succeed. Consequently, he who moulds public opinion goes deeper than he who enacts statutes or pronounces decisions." Judges, policemen, and statesmen must wring their hands in futility until the things a preacher works for are accomplished. Farmers and doctors keep people alive; the minister labors to make their lives worth living. I know that many a garage mechanic is a better minister of Jesus Christ than I am—but he does not have my opportunities!

Those twenty-five minutes of uninterrupted access to the minds of a crowd of listeners are the preacher's great chance to do what most needs doing. When there is anything he thinks is of overwhelming importance for people to hear, he gets to say it. He cannot preach from himself. But if there is a God who has revealed Himself to men, if there is a gospel that applies to our situation, then the preacher will not lack for things that must be said. What could be more important? When J. D. Jones was preaching at Bournemouth, England, he became widely respected for his influence on public affairs. One day he was visited by a political committee which proposed to have him elected to the House of Commons. Next day he sent them his reply. It quoted what Nehemiah said when he was up on the wall of Jerusalem, helping to rebuild it: "I am doing a great work, so that I cannot come down." Dr. Jones underlines those last two words, *"come down."* That is how important preaching is.

II

New Developments in Preaching

Preaching has to be as old as the ways of God with men, and as new as the morning paper. Many of its techniques remain valid through the centuries, and others scarcely last a decade. It must change to match the thought forms and vocabulary of every generation.

THE DECLINE OF ORATORY

One change in the modern mood that has affected preaching is the decline of oratory. The orator has suddenly vanished from our scene. Just yesterday there were Winston Churchill and Martin Luther King; today there is a silence as startling as that when a foghorn quits blowing. Has the oldest of the arts really played out? The skillful use of eloquence to move crowds predates history. Primitive people provide some of the finest examples of it. Oratory is the art that has had most to do with statecraft and religion; gifted public speakers had an honored place in every ancient culture. Oratory has had a powerful influence on our country's history. To say that it has been given up is like saying that painting or drama has disappeared.

Great crowds still assemble for political conventions or campaign speeches, but can you recall any recent platform masterpieces? Who is there in the present Senate whose intention to speak will fill the galleries? Only athletes can now sell out an auditorium the way a Russell Conwell or a Robert Ingersoll used to do. William Jennings Bryan, William E. Borah, and John L. Lewis have no successors. The golden voices of the Chautauqua circuit are stilled.

Yet there is no giving up of public speaking. Attorneys still deliver summaries to juries; sales managers exhort their forces; the chief activity of luncheon clubs is hearing speeches; attenders at conventions of all sorts spend most of their time listening to someone at the mike. But speakers now do not risk soaring much above the commonplace. This is not just a change of styles; styles of oratory have always gone out of date with every generation. Rather, it is the shunning of any art at all that marks the modern mood.

Perhaps oratory could not survive the present tendency of the arts to veer away from obvious form and feeling. When my daughter returned from college I learned that the poems I loved were doggerel. Tennyson, Browning, and Shelley were rhymsters who used rhythms and said things. When did you last see poems which did that in any high-class magazine? Why did our forefathers love to have their "nobler emotions" worked on, while we scorn it as manipulative? It is all right for TV commercials and smash-hit movies to stir up our cheap sentiments by the most crude devices, but an appeal to anything above that level we discount as schmaltz. Imagine the derision of a modern audience if a Patrick Henry were to plunge an imaginary dagger into his bosom as he whispered, ". . . or give me death!"

A concomitant of the decline of oratory is an unconcern about who writes the speeches. There is no doubt that Lincoln wrote his Gettysburg Address, but a modern presidential speech is openly a team product. When a corporation mails you the speech its board chairman made to an important audience, you can assume only that it was he who read it. He may have known as little about it as did the executive who groped to his soaring climax with "So let us face tomorrow in the spirit of one seven seven six!"

The waning of oratory in the United States is reflected in contemporary preaching styles. The old argument about whether or not sermons are an art form is settled for the present—they are not. Perhaps there has never been better preaching than there is now—preaching that is plain, informative, helpful. But few sermons are distinguished literature. By the definition of oratory as "the art of stirring emotions by oral exhortation," there is not much oratory on Sunday mornings. The tradition of the hero-preacher still lingers in the South, but it is flickering.

What guest preacher could you count on to bring out an audience today? Billy Graham is about the only one who gets big crowds. With him as with many of the noted evangelists, it is not the power of what he says but the appeal of his personality and the settings that fill the colosseums. Until recently, the delegates at denominational assemblies looked forward to a chance to hear famous preachers. Now the evening meetings are more likely to be given over to rock festivals (religious, of course), multimedia presentations, or simulation games.

What this is doing to the average preacher is both good and bad. The good result is that ministers are speaking in the way best suited to modern Americans. Just as our present senators do not aspire to the toga of Henry Clay, so most ministers preach their own sort of sermons and do not try to be Spurgeons. The theatrical gesture, the throbbing poetry, the elaborately polished phrases are no part of the weekly fare. Though there is only a quarter-spectrum emotional range, there is likely to be the hard impact of plain earnestness, the straight facing of dreadful facts, and a realistic assurance of the grounds of hope. At its best, contemporary preaching is carefully designed to be clear, relevant, and simple. At its worst, it tries self-consciously to be of the "now" generation, to use the fad phrases of the pseudo-sciences, to be adroitly obscure.

A bad result of minimizing the art of public speech is carelessness. The feeling sometimes seems to be that it does not matter how you do it. Many, who know that congregations will be listening to them every Sunday for years to come, still have little interest in learning how to preach. In this they show a defective sense of the shortest line to the greatest distance.

Learning to preach is more complicated than it used to be, and more exciting. My seminary instruction was based on a textbook written sixty years before. There was still a standard way to preach. There isn't now. Some of the old and new books give valuable help, but they cannot say, "This is how to do it." Each preacher has to try for himself a wide variety of styles, thinking of his own peculiar makeup, of different audiences and situations, and of the need for a widely varied change of pace. A "free" preaching style requires much more than ordinary thought and work, which a good many preachers have not understood. When disappointed hearers say, "These young ministers just don't know how to preach," they may be thinking of the stream-of-consciousness style that begins nowhere, ends nowhere, and leaves nothing behind.

Although in this decade oratory is in eclipse, we can be sure it is not finished. There have been other periods in Western history when there were almost no orators, in the church or out of it. In cultures whose religions impart passivity, the arts of public speech have never flourished. There will be oratory wherever there is fervent belief and the certainty that it matters what each person does. Oratory needs a shared storehouse of heart-stirring material. When most educated people knew the classics, and even the uneducated knew the Bible, speeches in parliaments and lecture halls rang with references to Greek and Roman heroes, and to Hebrew kings and sages. When neither the classics nor the Bible are generally known, and popular literature is not a rich source of allusions, orators are hard up for what will unite and move a crowd.

The revival of great preaching must be joined with renewal in the Church. It takes hearers who can be kindled to make burning preaching possible. There must be people who can care with a passion about what the preacher says. Strong preaching builds strong faith, and strong faith enables strong preaching; the spiral goes up or down. The American Church's last great orator had the advantage of being identified with the one theme about which American Christians in large numbers were "under conviction." When Martin Luther King declared, "I have a dream," or "I've been to the mountain top," he reached the hearts of Christians who were black and white, Baptist and Episcopalian. Great public speaking does not grow from barren soil.

When American Christians work through their confusions to life-gripping convictions which they share with glowing intensity, then a new generation of pulpit masters will appear. But, after all, we do not have to have them. The unadorned, down-to-life clarity of modern preaching is what the present generation of Americans needs most. It may not be art but, at its best, it is very, very good.

NEW TRENDS IN THE CHURCH AND
IN THE WORLD

Theology and hermeneutics are the two disciplines on which preaching most depends. In both of them there are exciting new concepts in methodology and theory. Their purpose is to make the language of faith and the Biblical witness intelligible to thoughtful modern minds. There are many sorts of new theology and new hermeneutics. Some of them are, indeed, attempts to ride in the religious bandwagon without God, but others are rigorously and brilliantly doing the necessary job of relating the timeless truth to the modes of expression and the forms of thought of the best minds of our time. The preacher who does not take the help this offers him may be preaching to the sort of people who are no longer there. The preacher's temptation is to leave the new developments to the specialists, while he busies himself making a simple faith relevant to the congregation. One problem is that he himself may not be that simple; as a religiously sophisticated child of his time he may have an aching need for God-talk and Bible-talk that can speak to him. He has to be able to present Christianity in the concepts that belong in the mental world of the better-educated members of his congregation. Even those who have no taste for scholarship will recognize it if their minister has not kept up with what is happening in his own field.

Preaching today will be strongly affected, and perhaps rocked, by new understandings of the Church. What is the Church? We may think we know, but when we see stately cathedrals and store-front meeting places, ancient hierarchies and wild sects, floating prayer groups and the Anti-Church for Christian Radicals, it is not easy to be sure. John Calvin's definition was, "Wherever we find the word of God purely preached and heard, and the Sacraments administered according to the institution of Christ, there it is not to be doubted is a church of God." Some theologies have defined the Church by an apostolic succession of palms on scalps, which makes a valid clergy the guarantors of a true Church. It has been customary to think of the apostolate and the preaching in terms of the ordained clergy. The present tendency is to think of them in terms of the laity. It is the whole Church membership that has the apostolic function, so why does it not have the apostolic succession? Because the preaching is designed to equip the laity for mission, and because the Church exists in mission, why is it not the hearers, instead of the speaker, who define the Church? Or, because it is the gospel that makes the preaching valid, why not define the Church, not by the preaching or the hearing of the word of God, but by obedience to it? Then the Church's identifying activity is not the preaching service, but it is every act by which the gospel is made manifest.

The question "What is the Church?" leads inevitably to the question

"What is a minister?" Denominations, through study groups and committees, are doing some new thinking about that. New understandings of the Church may dramatically change the role of the preacher. Preaching, as the act that constitutes the Church, may be thrown out one door and brought back in another as the activity that is essential in the formation of the people of God.

Church people today are intent on personal relationships. *Relational theology, relational worship, relational forms of church life* have become familiar new terms. This follows the growing understanding of the basic human need in terms of lack of self-esteem, of identity, of belonging, of acceptance, and of reconciliation. Christ put his Church on earth to save people from that lostness. The Church must therefore make people open to each other. It should be a community of love and trust where there is always someone to listen and care. It must make the unsure know that they are loved.

A preacher in the pulpit might seem too remote to have much part in relationships, but the fact is that the relational conception is having a great deal to do with the content and mood of modern preaching. The Sunday service is the radiating center where Christians learn to be accepting of each other. The very feel of a church service can rescue people from a sense of insignificance and send them out more warm and loving. Modern preachers are not assuming the bearing of the spellbinder, the man of letters, the scholar, the Moses on Mount Sinai, or the dying man to dying men. They are trying rather to create the impression of friendship, and caring, and being with their hearers in a common quest.

The same new styles of thought that have their theological expression in "process theology" have also produced new conceptions of preaching. These do not count on the pulpit masterpiece as a finished product, but rather on the "sermon event" as an unfinished happening. The sermon is not what is transferred from the mind of the preacher to the minds of the hearers, it is something that is going on between them. Letting God into the process makes the sermon a three-party transaction. God uses the preached word as the occasion for another stage in the experiencing of the Divine Word. The whole experience goes far beyond what the minister says, both in content and in time. Long after the preaching is over, the sermon is still coming into actuality in the hearer's life and thought.

Preaching must take account of new modes of consciousness and new bearings to life. Contemporary assumptions are in many ways different from those of a few years ago. Innovative services have held in the church some for whom old rituals had gone stale, and they have made worship a new discovery for others. The very unconventional services may remain valuable for only a minority in most congregations, but they have made some important discoveries. They have pioneered ways of preaching and worship that are now being used in the major services.

Preachers are trying some creative new ways. The use of aids to preaching and unprecedented forms will be considered in Chapter X. The Old

Testament prophets used visual aids, and they would have understood the modern use of sight and sound equipment to enrich preaching. Some ministers attempt to give the feel of a common enterprise by moving out of the pulpit and into the congregation when they preach. This may not work; a preacher magnifies himself when he goes into the aisle. Preachers are letting others help them. A dance group may be used. Someone from the congregation may be asked to make a comment. After the sermon is ended, the people in the pews may be asked to cluster informally to discuss it, and some of them may be invited to come forward to report on the discussion.

New ways of making preaching a cooperative enterprise will be described in later chapters. Periodically the minister may explain to the congregation his theory of preaching, and say what he hopes they will be doing while he is speaking and afterward. They need to understand that they and the preacher and the Holy Spirit work together to produce what happens in their minds and hearts. Many people do not know that there are supposed to be as many sermons in a preaching service as there are people in the congregation.

III

The Purpose of Preaching

The church entrusts its pulpit to a minister for a very special purpose. He is not there to indulge his whims. Hearers come because they expect him to perform a unique function. Everyone who goes into a pulpit runs hard into the questions, "Why am I here? What should I be doing?"

The preacher in the pulpit of the Iona Abbey in Scotland is given no chance to miss that question. Straight in front of him, protruding from the side of an arch, is a hideous face. It is the face of a soul in torment. The medieval architect put it there to remind the preacher that his task is to save that soul. The sermon is to bring to people what their souls need most:

1. *The Bible.* The preacher's task is to close the gap between what the Bible offers and the people's needs. Those who differ widely in their views of the Bible still regard it as the unrivaled source for sermons. *"The Confession of 1967 of the United Presbyterian Church,"* says "The one sufficient revelation of God is Jesus Christ, the word of God incarnate, to whom the Holy Spirit bears unique and authoritative witness through the Holy Scriptures, which are received and obeyed as the word of God written. The Scriptures are not a witness among others, but the witness without parallel."

Karl Barth, in his little book *The Preaching of the Gospel,* declares that a sermon should contain nothing that is not in the Bible. His statement is extreme and forceful: "Preaching is the word of God which he himself has spoken; but he makes use . . . of a man who speaks to his fellowmen, in God's name, by means of a passage from Scripture. . . . It is this man's duty to proclaim to his fellowmen what God himself has to say to them by explaining in his own words a passage from Scripture." "Preaching has one single point of departure, which is that God revealed himself." "The Church is a community placed under Revelation. . . . In this context then, but only there, can one speak of educating men, of giving moral and spiritual help to humanity." "There is nothing to be said which is not already found in the Scriptures . . . if he feels that . . . he must add some practical instruction, then his trust is not complete." Barth says that "if preaching is faithful to the Bible, it cannot be tedious." In that he is wrong. There is a style of preaching which attempts to paraphrase a Bible passage, with no comments or embellishments. It can be painfully turgid. I remember an expectant congregation that had come to hear a famed European churchman. We were looking forward to the inspirations he could have given from his vast ecumenical experience, but he was true to his Barthian principles. His entire sermon was the detailed retelling of an Old Testament story that had been familiar to us since childhood. It was dull. Barth even said that a sermon should have no organization beyond that of the Bible passage it expounds; its structure must come from following the Bible sequence. He never repudiated these early instructions to preachers but, fortunately, when he preached he was not a Barthian. Many of his sermons are skillfully constructed, and they say a good deal that is not directly from the Bible.

Barth's exaggeration is useful in reminding us that the preacher is not in the pulpit to give his own ideas or his gleanings of the wisdom of mankind. The preacher trusts that God has inspired many writers, possibly including himself, but he knows that his task is to apply to human needs the Biblical revelation. What he preaches is not a free-form Christianity in general, but the specific Christianity that is presented in the Scripture.

2. *God's Saving Acts.* During the past decades it has become increasingly popular to declare that the one purpose of preaching is to proclaim the mighty acts of God for man's salvation. Thus, unless this is at least a part of a sermon, it cannot be considered Christian preaching. This is a needed corrective to the tendency of preachers to talk about anything that seems important. Apart from the saving acts of God, all our good advice about morals, love, joy, and right relationships plays out in futility.

Reinhold Niebuhr, in his article "Moralistic Preaching," defined moralizing as "holding up high ideals of brotherhood and love to men and nations on the supposition that nothing more than their continued reiteration will ultimately effect their realization." There is no use preaching genial race relations to those in whom the vicious pack impulses that make races problems for each other are still raging. We will not deactivate the nuclear bomb by church pronouncements. For a preacher to exhort the normally self-centered, licentious, and foolish to behave themselves is like a doctor's commanding his patients to be well.

Right living is the church's business, but you cannot have the gospel's fruits without the gospel's roots. The church must labor for more wholesome environments, but I once heard a rural pastor tell a national church assembly, "If you put a pig in a parlor, it isn't the pig that gets changed." What God has done in Christ to produce the new person is the source of everything the Church is hoping to accomplish.

We may question the insistence that the proclamation of what God has done for man's salvation has to be in every sermon. It could be in some other part of the worship service. It might still be in mind from preceding Sundays. To tell the congregation every Sunday that God has saved his people by his stretched-out arm might be a little like announcing before every session of the Congress that the Constitution has been ratified. It is heartening to know that the Children of Israel have been delivered from their bondage in Egypt, and we must always have in the front of our minds the consciousness of our redemption through Christ's death and resurrection, but to require a reference to these in every sermon might become conventional. For a good marriage, a husband and wife have to express their love often enough to keep a lively awareness of it, but there does not have to be a declaration of love before every discussion of household affairs.

The sermons and instructions about sermons in the New Testament make it clear that the basic theme of preaching is the declaration of what God has done through Jesus Christ, with the call for personal acceptance and repentance (Acts 2:14–40; 3:12–26; 3:16–21; I Cor. 1:17) This is called the *kerygma,* which means "proclamation." English translations simply call this the "preaching." When modern sermons have their source in this, then in relation to it they may properly take up many other matters—predestination, the life of Augustine, the structure of Lamentations, urban ministries, the financial canvass, sex, Church and State, marriage. The depressing effect of such a list is our clue. The prospect of a long future of listening to subjects like those is dreary until we think of them in connection with the good news of the grace of God. Detached from the heart, they are like severed limbs lying around loose.

The proclamation of salvation, apart from its implications for daily living, can be a pious sham. John Wesley, an ardent evangelist who gave his life to calling people to be saved, was also a practical realist. So it is not too surprising to hear him saying, "Let [someone] that has neither sense nor grace bawl out something about Christ, or his blood, or justification by faith and his hearers will cry out: 'What a fine Gospel sermon!' I find more profit in sermons on either good tempers or good works, than in what are vulgarly called Gospel sermons."

3. *An Encounter with Christ.* When the minister from the pulpit tells of Jesus Christ, he is not talking of someone who is dead and gone, he is offering an encounter with the living Lord. Jesus Christ is present in the church, coming down the aisle, moving along the pews, entering into the consciousness of the people, ready to reconcile them with God and with each other, to give new life, joy, beauty, and strength, ready to make their minds like his. Christ can be the trademark on an institution that was named in grateful tribute to his memory, but with no more real connection with what happens in the church than Chief Pontiac has with the automobile factory, or William Penn has with the Penn Central railroad. It is the business of the sermon, not to remind people of what Christ once did, but to tell them what he is ready to do now. The implied text of every sermon is "Behold, I stand at the door and knock."

It is the real presence of Christ in the church service, and the real work of Christ in the people there, that the sermon proclaims. Professor

H. H. Farmer said, "The necessity of preaching resides in the fact that when God saves a man through Christ he insists on a living, personal encounter with him here and now." (*The Servant of the Word*, p. 27.) Roman Catholics find Christ literally present in the consecrated element, renewing His redeeming work when the mass is celebrated. (Father Ronald Knox, the witty Catholic scholar, said he had heard many an argument about the "real presence," but when he went into St. Paul's Anglican Cathedral, he had no doubt at all of the real absence.) Protestants have their experience of the actual presence and the renewed redemption. To preach Christ rightly is to make Him present for the hearers. His redeeming act is extended on that day to all who will receive it. As Dr. P. T. Forsyth put it, "The Gospel is an eternal, perennial act of God in Christ, repeating itself within each declaration of it. . . . It is this act that is prolonged in the word of the preacher, and not merely proclaimed. . . . A true sermon is a real deed." (*Positive Preaching and the Modern Mind*, pp. 6 and 22.)

In the Bible a word is not just a semaphore that signals a meaning from one mind to another. A word is also a performer; it does things. Christ is the Word of God, not just because He translates the language of heaven into a language mortals can understand, but because He does the work of God. The word of the preacher participates in this action of the Divine Word; it not only says something, it does something. Protestants are too likely to misunderstand the sermon as a discourse to be thought about; it should, rather, be the occasion for an event that is experienced.

When the preacher thinks of his congregation he has to wonder whether what the theologians talk about really happens. How many people in the average church service really have that transforming experience with the present Christ that this view of preaching calls for? How many preachers really expect it? As I think of the people I see in the church on Sunday mornings, I doubt whether many of them have been aware of having experienced a recapitulation of the atonement. They have tried to follow the prayers, sing the hymns, and listen to the sermon. I hope they will go out with some inspirations and some good ideas; occasionally some of them may have been deeply touched, but it is not likely that many of them will have had anything that even approaches a mystical experience with a present Christ.

But the encounter with Christ for which sermons call does not have to be felt as a mystical experience. Many Christians have at some time had a strong and vivid sense of the presence of Christ, but not as a weekly event. He is more likely to come to us at such a depth of personality that we have not been aware of his coming. It is only afterward that we know we have a poise, a kindness, a joy, and a clarity that could only be his doing. In my years of church-going I have rarely experienced, while listening to a sermon, anything I could identify as an encounter with Christ, and I cannot count on having it happen to others when I preach. But, as I reflect, I am convinced that it has happened; it has not been known in ecstatic experiences, but in times of growing illumination and accumulating certainty.

It is heartening to know that even Bernard of Clairvaux experienced Christ's presence only in this way. Saint Bernard said, "The Lord has visited me, and that many times. And although he has often entered into me I have never known when he came. . . . He did not enter by the ears, for he is without sound. . . . How then, you ask, when his ways are thus altogether unsearchable, could I have known that he was present? In the flight of vices and the restraint of carnal affections I have perceived the power of his virtue. . . . In the amendment, however small, of my ways I have experienced his goodness and gentleness. In the renovation and reformation of my mind and spirit . . . I have seen the fashion of his beauty. And as I have reflected on all these things, I have been overwhelmed by his greatness." That is what the minister can hope will be happening as he preaches.

4. *Teaching.* Bible scholars argue over what, on the basis of the New Testament vocabulary, preaching should be. C. H. Dodd in 1937 created a minor sensation by insisting that "much of our preaching in the church at the present time would not have been recognized by the early Christians as *kerygma.*" (*The Apostolic Preaching and Its Development.*) If only the proclamation of salvation is preaching, then the pulpit is being largely misused. The Greek verbs most often translated "preach," *euaggelizo* and *kerusso,* both mean to announce the good news of salvation. But Dr. Ozora Davis insists that to heal *(therapeuein),* to exhort *(parakalein),* to admonish *(nouthetein),* to confirm *(episterizein),* and to edify *(oikodomein)* can, by the New Testament example, also be included in preaching.

The decision on what may properly be said from the pulpit during a church service will not be settled by this sort of word scrutiny. The right use of a congregation's assembly for worship must be determined by whatever will best serve God's loving purpose, for the people present, and for the world. Both immediate and final needs must be considered.

We learn more about the purpose of preaching from the New Testament practice than from the vocabulary. We find three sorts of public discourse. The evangelistic type was addressed to those outside the church. It told what God has done in Christ and called for acceptance of it. The second sort was addressed to the catechumens to prepare them for baptism. The third sort was for the members of the Christian community. It was intended to improve their knowledge of the Christian faith, to exhort them to holiness, and to instruct them in the Christian life. The New Testament epistles are our fullest guide to how sermons should be used. Most of these were intended to be read to assembled Christians; they are sermons by an absent preacher. As we study the New Testament epistles we are getting the early church model of what sermons should contain.

The imparting of information is an essential part of preaching. The acceptance of Christ requires a knowledge of who he is, what he said, what he did, and what he does. Christianity does not require scholarship, but we never know all we need to know. What the Bible has for us is inexhaustible. Through the centuries the Church has accumulated a wealth of insights, inspirations, and practical experience in how to live, which is to be passed on as a birthright to every generation.

We cannot rigidly distinguish the evangelist from the teacher, the *kerygma* from the *didaskalia*. The proclamation of the gospel must include the imparting of information, and the church's education must never leave out the appeal for commitment. Those who have accepted Christ must through a lifetime be instructed in the implications of the gospel, and along with this they must repeatedly be summoned to renewed and higher dedication to him.

A minister who preaches in a church is not allowed to be a specialist. He dare not think of himself as primarily an evangelist, an educator, an inspirer, a counselor, or an enabler of social action. His congregation will be deprived if he is not all of these, and more.

It is interesting to see how American preaching has swung back and forth between proclamation and teaching. In the early part of the last century the emphasis was on revivals; the purpose of preaching was to save souls. By the middle of the century Horace Bushell was leading a reaction against this which called for a teaching ministry. In 1871, Henry Ward Beecher, in his Yale Lectures, indicated a new trend by his belittling of teaching and his emphasis on the minister as "herald." In 1908, the Yale Lectures were again typical of a reverse swing when President Faunce of Brown University took as his theme "The Educational Ideal in the Ministry." That was the theme also in most Protestant churches until World War II. At present there is more concern for commitment, involvement, and relations than for knowing. Enthusiasms bring extremes which must periodically be corrected. The parish preacher needs a sense of history that will save him from being captured by every passing fashion.

The end result, toward which preaching looks, is the person in Christ. A conversion is not a leap, it is a turning; the new convert is standing where he was before, but now facing in a different direction. From then on he has to move in that direction to become what a Christian ought to be. Preaching is intended to help that happen. We are told that Christ gave "teachers, to equip God's people." (Eph. 4:12–13 NEB) The Church is an assembly line where saints are equipped.

5. *Sustaining.* A preacher who nurtures his hard-beset people will try to bring them to the sources of strength. Ian Maclaren was told, "Your best work in the pulpit has been to put heart into men for the coming week." He believed that "the chief end of preaching is comfort." A minister's sermons must be inspired by his precious chance to help those who are finding life grindingly hard. He will be thinking of the father with a fine engineering background who is selling door to door because he has exhausted himself and his finances trying to find work in engi-

neering, and of the parents whose beloved daughter will always have to be with them or in an institution. He expects to see next Sunday the wife who knows her husband's weekends away are spent with another woman, and the family that has just received word that their son has been gravely injured. The minister who literally believes that God's mercy still heals the broken-hearted and lifts up those whose burdens are too great to bear will be awed and grateful for his chance to offer it. Dr. James Black of Scotland told an audience of ministers in New York, "When I think sometimes of the puzzled and burdened hearts in every congregation whose hurt perhaps is concealed under a twisted smile . . . I cannot but think that some of our smart, flashy sermons are as thoughtlessly cruel as they are impertinent. Get down deep, gentlemen. Get down deep." (*The Mystery of Preaching*, pp. 43–44.)

6. *Emotions.* Thomas Aquinas, following Augustine, gave the preacher three tasks: to instruct the intelligence, to kindle the emotions, and to form the will. Emotion is life's driving power. Making people feel more deeply about what they already know is an essential goal of preaching. Life depends not only on *what* people believe, but on *how* they believe it. The preacher tries to make people care intensely; he wants them to know joy, pathos, passionate indignation, and burning zeal. He hopes to melt the ice that encrusts cold hearts. Preaching that did not intensify the emotions would be as barren as preaching that did nothing for minds or wills.

Bernard Berensen, the famous art critic, said that the aim of art is to make us feel with an intensity of 4 some loveliness which before had been felt only with an intensity of 2. That is precisely what preaching is to do for religious feelings. It is to make people more sensitive, more responsive, more emotionally alive.

7. *Judgment.* Preaching must declare God's judgment on private sin and social wrong. The office of prophet must be exercised. The church, as the body of Christ, is in the world to condemn what he would condemn, and to heal what he would heal. The church must protest against what poisons character, breaks hearts, and stunts lives. Where there is oppression, injustice, and corruption, where God is mocked by heartlessness, God's church, through its pulpit, must cry out.

8. *Decisions.* Sermons are intended to change people. John Donne said, "For Publication of Himselfe He Hath Constituted a Church. And in this church . . . His ordinance of preaching batters the soule, and by that breach, the Spirit enters." Sermons must pound on closed hearts until they open up to change. A sermon is a failure if the person who leaves the church is the same one who entered.

Jesus asked for decisions from the Samaritan woman, the rich young ruler, Matthew, and all whom He called. He was constantly pleading, "Come," "follow me," "believe." The preacher never knows what issues are in the balance. Some hearer may be like a saturated salt solution, which a slight tap will cause to crystalize. Whenever a minister talks of faith or duty, he must not be a mere juggler of abstract concepts. He has to be like a lawyer before a jury, pleading for a verdict. In preaching to the members of the church, the purpose is not so much to tell them what they do not know as to get them to respond as they have not responded. We have accepted and assented to many Christian truths which we have not incorporated into our lives. We have looked at them without seeing them. The preacher's weekly task is to get seasoned Christians to begin to live in a new way by such familiar truths as the reality of the Holy Spirit, the joy of service, and the need to forgive.

9. *Action.* When other orators finished, people said, "What a magnificent oration," but when Demosthenes ended, they said, "Let us go and fight Phillip!" The test of a sermon is what happens afterward. A common complaint from congregations is, "It was all very impressive, but he never told us what we are supposed to do. It is often well for the minister to make a definite proposal. "Decide right now the hour in which you are going to open up your Bible and start reading." "Your checkbook stubs are the real confession of your faith; can you think now of some checks you are going to write that will say what you believe?" "Call to mind someone with whom you have a bad relationship, and do something today that can help to make it right." "Tell me after church that you will look after a parolee." Often, after a moving appeal, people are left wondering, "But how?" "How can I do anything about the migrant workers?" "How can I help others to know Christ?" Many an otherwise important sermon is left hanging in mid-air because the preacher never connects it with real living.

Peter Berger has said that ministers are mistaken in assuming that what they say on Sunday has any connection with what the hearers do on Monday. He believes that the person who listens on Sunday is a completely different person from the one who is making decisions the next week; the pew and the office desk are in two entirely different worlds, with no bridge between them. The separation is not really that complete. Some of the Sunday mood will linger; Sunday thoughts come to mind on other days. But preachers surely need to do everything they can to relate their sermons to what happens afterward.

It is the purpose that distinguishes an essay from a sermon. The treatment of a religious topic is not a sermon unless it is designed to have a result. Preaching is never intended to give the hearers some information and leave them where they were before. An essay looks at ideas; a sermon looks at people. A pulpit discourse can have essay sections, but until it looks toward having something happen to people, it is not a sermon. Ministers with academic tastes are constantly tempted to march generalities up and down when what people need is reality. A theme on a religious subject can be fascinating for a reader, and deadly dull from the pulpit. The Christian cause urgently needs the products of the hard intellectual labor of ministers with good minds. Both pure and practical reasoning are essential. But the test question for a sermon still must be, "Will it make tomorrow different for the people out in front?"

Students in my preaching classes are asked to state the purpose of their written sermons. It is significant that many of them do not distinguish a purpose from a topic. They may put the purpose as "an exposition of the book of Jonah," or "to give a modern view of evangelism," which does not say why they are talking about Jonah, or about evangelism. A good many of us waste our sermons because we think they have a purpose, when all they really have is a topic. Then, with all our earnest efforts, we are likely to fall into the old error of "aiming at nothing and hitting it hard."

Sermons need an altar call. The response may not be to come down the aisle and grasp the preacher's hand while the last verse is sung one more last time. But the finest sermon is likely to drift away with the breath that uttered it unless some way of responding to it is proposed.

The purpose of preaching is incalculably great. That does not mean that all sermons must be solemn. Samuel Baxter's famous saying, "I preached as never sure to preach again, and as a dying man to dying men," can be misleading. The minister of a congregation has a wider choice of topics than does the chaplain of a sinking ship. The characteristic note of Christianity is gladness. The most serious sermons can be joyful; but they cannot be trivial. The Christian preacher has no time to waste. Someone has said that if a congregation could preach to the minister its text might be "Our souls loathe this light bread." There is too much at stake for a preacher to be diverted from the great purposes of preaching.

IV

The Preacher's Authority

Why should a preacher expect anyone to listen to him? Is there any reason why a sinful mortal should stand before others and talk to them in an authoritative way about God and righteousness? This Man of God role can seem like the survival of the medicine man in civilized society. It is the preacher who is hit hardest by these doubts. Others may take his function for granted—he never can. When he sees in the pews the battle-scarred veterans for Christ, whose spiritual maturity he looks up to with awe, he has to wonder, "Why am I up here?"

It can be reassuring to know that even the Bible's preachers had this same misgiving. Moses backed off, saying, "They will not believe me or listen to my voice, for they will say, 'The Lord did not appear to you.' I am not eloquent . . . but I am slow of speech and of tongue." (Ex. 4:1, 10) Isaiah protested, "I am a man of unclean lips." (Is. 6:5) Jeremiah said, "I am only a youth." (Jer. 1:6) Paul's detractors denied his authority. It is encouraging for modern preachers to believe that the reassurances given to the Bible preachers still apply. Moses was told, "Who has made man's mouth? . . . Go, and I will be with your mouth and teach you what you shall speak." (Ex. 4:11–12) Isaiah's lips were cleansed. The Lord said to Jeremiah, "I have put my words in your mouth." (Jer. 1:9) Paul declared, "Not that we are sufficient of ourselves to claim anything as coming from us: our sufficiency is from God, who has qualified us to be ministers." "For what we preach is not ourselves, but Jesus Christ as Lord." "We are ambassadors for Christ, God making his appeal through us." (II Cor. 3:5–6; 4:5; 5:20)

The historic old Reformed church in Debrecin, Hungary, has an interesting way of using the Bible to nerve trembling preachers. The very high center pulpit is reached by going through a door in back of the Communion table, climbing a winding stairway, and coming into the pulpit through the front wall. On his way up the preacher's self-doubts can be quieted by Scripture. At the foot of the stairs are the words, "You shall be my witnesses." (Acts 1:8) On the first landing is the verse, "God, be merciful to me a sinner!" (Lk. 18:13) On up there is lettered on the wall, "I am praying . . . for those whom thou hast given me." (Jn. 17:9)

At the next landing the preacher faces the promise, "Every one who acknowledges me before men, I also will acknowledge before my Father who is in heaven." (Mt. 10:32) The double door into the pulpit has on its right and left panels the words, "We preach Christ—Crucified." (I Cor. 1:23)

The modern minister is bound to wonder how these promises apply to him. He wonders as he goes to the church door, depressed by the sense that his sermon was a failure. He wonders as he toils at his sermon preparation, and knows that it does not feel greatly different from any other writing in the groping for something to say, and the revising and crossing out. He wonders when he looks at his old sermons, and when he disagrees with what other preachers say.

If a preacher did nothing more than paraphrase the Bible, he might claim to be God's spokesman. But he has to try to apply the Bible to every part of human life, which seems to force him to play the wise man who makes pronouncements on art, manners, politics, business, and child psychology. A minister is sure to color his understanding of the gospel with the biases of his class and nation, and he is constantly tempted to present the mixture as the Word of God. This was kindly pointed out to me one Sunday by a wise Elder. I had preached on "Christian Burial," with some very explicit statements on what funeral practices were Christian and what were not. The Elder told me, "You weren't talking about Christian burial; you were talking about middle-class, rational, inhibited burial. What you happen to like would be entirely wrong for most of the Christians of the world." A century ago Phillips Brooks said, "The preacher is no longer the manifest superior of other men in wit and wisdom." We are still not pulling ahead.

The preacher has no source of divine wisdom that is not available to other Christians. When his sermons imply that those who disagree with him are resisting God, they are entitled to be irritated. The people in the pews read the same Bible he does, and pray as earnestly for guidance. There is nothing in ordination that creates an oracle. We can hope that the qualities of a preacher's mind and heart make him worth hearing, but just as they do anyone. Then what authority does a preacher have?

WHERE THE MINISTER GETS HIS AUTHORITY

1. *He has the authority of his commission.* He has been assigned to preach. Others might be just as able, but the Church has ordained him to the task.

The word "preach" has two meanings. When it means, "to tell," then all Christians must be preachers. They all are called to tell what Christ can do for men. Wherever they are, they are to witness to Christ by their words and by their lives. In this sense, the most effective preachers are the laity, who all week long are out in the world telling and demonstrating what God wants men to know.

But the word "preach" has the other meaning, "to speak to a group of people on religious subjects." Jesus commanded that his truth be proclaimed, and from his time until today one of the best ways has been public proclamation. When a preacher wonders what right he has to stand up and talk to people about God and righteousness, the answer is simply that this vastly important duty has been given to him. The preacher is assigned by other Christians to lead them in their quest for better Christian knowledge and living. He is not to give their answers, but to help their search. A preacher is to be listened to because he has been asked to speak. It is that which makes him special. Luther said, "We are all priests, but we are not all clergymen."

Jesus has never since his incarnation been physically absent from the earth. He transferred his work from the body of bones and tissues that served him in Palestine to the bodies of his followers. They are in their communities to be doing what Jesus would be doing if he were there in the flesh. "You are the body of Christ," Paul said to Christians collectively, and immediately pointed out that Christ's various ministries are now assigned to specific human bodies—doctors heal, friends comfort, lawyers defend, preachers speak in public in Christ's behalf. (I Cor. 12:27–30) Paul Scherer told of being suddenly assigned to preach to a congregation that had gathered to hear Toyohiko Kagawa, who had missed the appointment. Dr. Scherer knew that as soon as he stood up to preach a pall of disappointment would fall on the people who had gathered to hear the famous Christian from Japan. He said, "I think I could have stammered and given it up had not a thought blazed suddenly in my mind, that after all I was not taking the place of Kagawa but of Jesus Christ . . . That flash of realization gave me my freedom." He did not mean that he became infallible, but that, like the Christian physician or comforter, he was acting in Christ's stead.

What preachers say will be Christ's speaking, as long as they are quoting or paraphrasing his words. When they are interpreting, they can still hope that they are true to his intention. This will always be imperfect, of course. What is transmitted by intercontinental short-wave amateur radio is likely to be broken up with fading and squeals and static, but it can still be a precious message from home. No performer ever gives the music just as the composer intended, but we listen with gratitude.

There are two sorts of Christian preaching, and both hearers and preachers need to recognize the difference. Sometimes the preacher is like Moses at Mount Sinai; his declaration is, "Thus says the Lord!" When he is preaching on the elemental truths of the Christian faith he does not have to say, "It is possible that we are saved by grace," or "I would like to suggest that God may be love." There are many matters on which the minister can say with no uncertainty, "This is eternal truth." But there are other times when the minister is like Moses in the wilderness, searching with the people for the right way without being sure it has been found. Sermons have to deal not only with ultimate truth and goodness, but with how to live by them. That can never be settled. The church is where people search together for Christian solutions to the practical problems they are facing. Sermons are important in this. Even those that are tentative are more than just one man's opinions; they are opinions that are rooted in acceptance of the Christian faith. The preacher does not need to step out of the pulpit or remove his robe when he is giving his own views, but his two roles have to be distinguished. Most listeners know which is which.

Are preachers called? Every Christian has been called by Christ, with a call that says both, "Come," and "Go"—"Come unto me," and "Go minister for me." Every follower of Christ—every teacher, office worker, musician, preacher—has been called to "full-time Christian service." And with every call there is a commission and a promise.

The call to the ministry of preaching can take many forms. It comes in terms of each one's unique personality and situation. It was when Isaiah was deeply distressed by a national crisis that he was sure he heard God say, "Whom shall I send?" and he answered, "Here am I! Send me." Jeremiah believed he had been appointed before he was born. The shepherd Amos was following his flock when he was called to preach. Peter Marshall was alone on a Scottish moor at night when he felt God's hand upon his shoulder. One of the most effective preachers was first a salesman. He was driving to an appointment when he become so sure God was calling him that he pulled off the highway out of heavy traffic to get it settled. Such dramatic calls are exceptional. When they are right, they are probably the sudden projection into consciousness of a certainty that has long been taking shape.

God always gives us guidance when we ask for it, and he always makes us work for it. In finding our calling, there usually has to be an ordeal of purely rational calculation. We consider our opportunities, our abilities, and our temperament. These have to be measured against a hard-thought-out evaluation of what is needed most. The great purposes we have in Christ must be clearly before us. Prayer helps to clarify them. Out of all this, the sense of the rightness of a calling can emerge.

A powerful element in this for the preacher may be an overwhelming longing to tell what people most need to hear. Nietzsche described this longing as like that of a bee so overloaded with honey he has to deliver it. Jeremiah said, "There is in my heart as it were a burning fire shut up in my bones, and I am weary with holding it in, and I cannot." (Jer. 20:9) Paul exclaimed, "I cannot help myself; it would be misery to me not to preach." (I Cor. 9:15 NEB) He begged the Colossians, "Include a prayer for us, that God may give us an opening for preaching, to tell the secret of Christ." (Col. 4:3 NEB) When we see all around us the broken hearts, the broken homes, and the broken lives, all our love and compassion may make us ache to tell people what Jesus Christ can do for them. When we see a world that is lurching and staggering through massive miseries toward more dreadful horrors, we may be overwhelmed by a desperate urgency to proclaim the way of life, for men and for mankind.

This does not mean that there is always joy. A person who feels overpowered by the importance of preaching may still shrink from it. Karl

Barth said, "Preaching is an act of daring, and only the man who would rather not preach and cannot escape from it ought ever to attempt it." A person who delights in preaching may be enjoying mostly the chance to perform in public; he may "have an itch that only an audience can scratch." In the early church a man who was consecrated as Bishop was required to say as part of the rite, *"Nolo episcopari"*—"I do not want to be a Bishop." A reluctance to be a preacher may be one of the qualifications. It might be said, "Never become a preacher unless you are strongly impelled to do something else." One might better say, "Never become a preacher unless there are a dozen other things you would rather do." The deep-down happiness at being allowed to give people what they need most of all will be there, of course. But on the surface a distaste for the image and a dread of the responsibility may be the first reactions to the call.

Many young people first turn toward the ministry purely out of theory, with no real desire or sense of being called. They want to serve their fellow men, and are convinced that the great needs are spiritual. They have no hope in materialism, and they see in Christ the only way. What the Church is supposed to do seems to them what most needs doing, though they have no real enthusiasm for the Church. Those can be splendid reasons for turning toward a preaching ministry. The love affair with the Church can develop later. Many a minister first receives his call through a congregation. His love for his people convinces him that he is where he ought to be. When he is sure he is doing what is important for them, he feels God's hand upon his shoulder. When a preacher finds that his all too human words are being used to bring people to the blessings of the life in Christ, then he knows he has been called. Then, that late, he may first understand Dr. Jowett's famous saying, "In all genuine callings to the ministry there is a sense of the divine initiative, a solemn communication of the divine will, a mysterious feeling of commission, which leaves a man no alternative but sets him on the road." *(The Preacher.)* He may even understand Paul's reference to "that purpose for which Christ Jesus grasped me." (Phil. 3:12 Phillips)

2. *The preacher has the authority of special training.* There is a tribe of nomad sheep herders in Turkestan which has no schools, so one boy is picked in every generation to go off to learn to read and write. He becomes the source of information for the tribe. The Church trains someone to be a special source of Christian knowledge for each congregation. He has more chance than do the others to learn what the Bible says and how to understand it. The accumulated wisdom and experience of the past is mediated to the others through him. His studies are supposed to equip him to be for his congregation a theologian, a dispenser of the best of Christian thinking, and an advisor in private difficulties and public problems.

The priesthood of all believers does not mean that everybody knows as much as everybody else. The Christian politician, school teacher, and musician have Christian insights others lack. The Church gives its ministers special schooling and continuing opportunities for learning. The congregation's formal call to a minister in my denomination says, "That you may be free from worldly care and avocations, we promise and oblige ourselves to pay you the sum of . . ." meaning that the minister is to have a chance for religious study which those with worldly care and avocations do not get.

3. *The preacher has the authority of the Church.* When he stands in the pulpit to preach, he is not alone. The whole Church is speaking through him. With him, and informing what he says, are the fathers of the early Church, the medieval mystics, the giants of the Reformation, and the Christian thinkers of our day. Jesus said, "I have yet many things to say to you, but you cannot bear them now. When the Spirit of truth comes, he will guide you into all the truth." (Jn. 16:12–13) Through the centuries, the Spirit has been leading Christians into fuller understanding. It is from the pulpit that the wisdom the Church has acquired across the years is transmitted to the people.

The point of view from which the preacher speaks has been formed within him by the Church. The Church made him what he is by baptism and by its nurture of his childhood and youth, by sermons, church books, magazines, prayers, hymns, the Lord's Supper, church fellowship, seminary training, contacts with other ministers, meetings, conventions. All these help shape his sermons. The Church's ancient creeds and modern declarations are in the preaching. The whole people of God, from Abraham to the present moment, are heard through the sermons.

A Protestant preacher does not have the Roman Catholic belief in a tradition of continuing infallible revelation that has been given through the Church and validated by it. He does not have the Orthodox reliance upon a changeless interpretation of Scripture that comes from the early Church. He does not even have the assurance that he can speak for his denomination, or his congregation. But he does know that the Church instructs him in what he says and authorizes him to say it. However much he tries to make a sermon entirely his own, it will still be a group product. The whole Church is in the preaching.

4. *The preacher has the authority of the Bible.* A Peter Arno cartoon shows a preacher saying to the congregation, "According to the word of God—and I quote . . ." Such modesty is the preacher's only hope. People come to church to hear what God says to man through the Scriptures. When there is no Bible in the pulpit, there will be no people in the pews. Russell Davenport put it bluntly in an editorial in *Fortune* magazine. "The voice of the church today we find is the echo of our own voices. . . . Unless we hear a voice, men of this generation will sink down a spiral of depression. There is only one way out of this spiral. The way out is the sound of a voice; not our voice, but a voice coming from something not ourselves in the existence of which we cannot disbelieve. It is the earthly task of the pastors to hear this voice, to cause us to hear it, and to tell us what it says. If they cannot hear it, or if they fail to tell us, we as laymen are utterly lost. Without it we are no more capable of saving the world than we were of creating it in the first place." The Bible is that voice from

outside. Christians believe that the Creator did not wind up the universe and go off to let it run itself. He has intervened in human thought by the revelation of himself. One who speaks from that revelation is literally speaking from above the human level. As Augustine said, "Every man who preaches the word is the voice of God."

The Bible says that it is not God's only revelation: "The heavens declare the glory of God." (Ps. 19:1) The Gentiles "show that what the law requires is written on their hearts, while their conscience also bears witness." (Rom. 2:15) But the Scriptures are the revelation on which the Church bases its communication of God's saving truth. As one confession puts it, "The church has received the books of the Old and New Testaments as prophetic and apostolic testimony in which it hears the word of God and by which its faith and obedience are nourished and regulated. . . . God's word is spoken to his church today where the Scriptures are faithfully preached. . . . *(The Confession of 1967)* This view of the Bible as the source of the Church's proclamation has been unchanged across the centuries. In 1647 the *Westminster Confession* said, "The whole counsel of God, concerning all things necessary for his own glory, man's salvation, faith, and life, is either expressly set down in Scripture, or by good and necessary consequence may be deduced from Scripture." In 1561 the *Second Helvetic Confession* said, "In this Holy Scripture, the universal Church of Christ has the most complete exposition of all that pertains to a saving faith, and also to the framing of a life acceptable to God." "In order to instruct men in religion and to remind them of divine things and of their salvation, the Lord commanded the preaching of the Gospel." Or, to go still further back, "All Scripture is inspired by God and is useful for teaching the truth, rebuking error, correcting faults, and giving instruction for right living." (II Tim. 3:16 TEV) The most eloquent and learned preacher will find there are few who want from him an interpretation of the wisdom of mankind, much less a weekly exposition of his views.

This answers the question with which this chapter started: "Why should a preacher expect anyone to listen to him?" The answer is, "He shouldn't." They come to hear the gospel preached as it is found in the Bible. As I mounted the steps to the pulpit in the old church in Komarno, Czechoslovakia, the congregation rose. I ended my greeting and paused, and they stayed standing. I went on into the topic of my sermon for a few minutes and paused, and still they stood. So I turned to the translator and asked, "Don't they want to sit down?" He looked puzzled and spoke to the people; they hesitated and then took their seats. I learned later that it is their custom to stand until the preacher gives his text. Perhaps the congregation is unwilling to settle down to listen until they are sure they will get to hear the Bible. In another minute they might have sadly headed for the doors.

V

Understanding the Bible

The preacher's authority comes from the Bible. This raises the hard question, "What is the Bible?" Is it a miraculous communication from God to men, or is it the response of men in olden times to the thought of God? With so much uncertainty about the Bible, it might seem impossible to use it as a source book for Christian truth. In this we need the guidance of Biblical scholarship and hermeneutics. A minister can know that his preaching is firmly grounded in eternal truth when it is supported at four levels:

1. *Theology.* First of all comes the understanding of God and of God's relationship to man. Is God It, or He (He-She), or Thou? If Thou, then what sort of communication is there between God and the spiritual beings he has made? If the Doctrine of Revelation allows for some sort of God-man communication, then we must determine the Bible's place in God's whole plan of self-disclosure.

2. *Hermeneutics.* Here hermeneutics takes over. It shows us how to understand what God is saying to us through the Bible. It helps us answer such questions as: What qualifies a writing to be considered Holy Scripture? In what sense were the authors inspired? How do we distinguish eternal truth from ancient Hebrew folk lore and first-century Christian legends? Is there a unifying message in the Bible, or is it an assortment of disconnected messages? What is the relation of the Old Testament to the New, and of the Gospels to the Epistles? Is there a developing revelation in the Bible, or is every paragraph God's final truth? How do we determine what a passage meant to the people to whom it was first addressed, and how much of that applies to us?

The word "hermeneutics" can be traced to Hermes, the divine messenger who interpreted what the gods said to mortals. It refers to the principles by which any sort of communication is interpreted. A recent expansion of the term makes hermeneutics the study of the whole idea of the transmission of thought, which combines with linguistic theory to make a new sort of epistemology. In the usual sense, hermeneutics tells how to understand something that comes from a strange era, culture, language, or mentality. Shakespeare scholars use hermeneutics. It is needed to interpret Ikhnaton, Heraclitus, Marx, Picasso, Brecht. Our concern is with biblical hermeneutics. It tells us how to understand what the Bible is saying to us, as we try to translate from very different languages, cultures, and ways of thinking, into our terms. We need to know how the Bible people expressed themselves, and the precise meaning of the words they used. We need to know whether a passage is history, poetry, or fiction, whether it is hyperbole or plain fact.

Hermeneutics offers us (1) *laws*—e.g., "Look for only one main point per parable," (2) *principles*—e.g., "A passage must be interpreted in the light of what it was intended to mean to its first recipients," and (3) *assumptions*—e.g., "God spoke in a special way through Jeremiah." Homiletics uses the laws and principles as though it were a science, but the assumptions keep it from being one.

3. *Exegesis.* Hermeneutics tells us how to get God's message from the Bible; exegesis is the process of getting the job done. Hermeneutics tells us the sort of research we have to do—theological, historical, linguistic—to get the meaning from a text. Then exegesis opens up the books and does it.

This might seem to be an impossible weekly task—but it is not as bad as it looks. A preacher works out his hermeneutical understandings early, and he keeps developing them bit by bit. The same principles apply to many sermons. Exegesis also accumulates. What the preacher learned about conditions in Ephesus for a sermon from Ephesians will be as useful for all his other sermons from that book.

Besides, only a very scholarly preacher will go back to the original sources for his hermeneutical and exegetical work. Most will find much of the work already done for them in commentaries, Bible dictionaries, and word books. These are likely to be chosen to match the preacher's hermeneutics. That saves much plowing through material the preacher will not want to use, but it cuts off the growth he could have by exposure to various points of view.

A preacher might hope to escape any labor on hermeneutics and exegesis because the Bible means what it says, and it is addressed to every congregation. Such a preacher, sharing the anti-war revulsion of the early 1930s, might have told his congregation that a Christian cannot bear arms because the Bible says, "Thou shalt not kill." Caught up in the war fervor after Pearl Harbor this same preacher might have declared that it is private killing that is forbidden, and a state may sanction taking life to defend the innocent against malefactors. Later, when consciences became sensitive about capital punishment, this minister might have preached that it is wrong for the state to destroy a malefactor's life because the Bible says, "Thou shalt not kill." When the abortion question comes along, the minister may find that the private ending of a life can be permitted. With euthanasia, there may be another new understanding of the Sixth Commandment. Thus the Bible can be made to support anything the preacher wants to say. So protean a book could scarcely give much guidance.

A serious use of that commandment would require, first, a decision about whether or not the Ten Commandments apply to modern Christians. The precise meaning of the Hebrew word *ratsach*—"kill"—should be investigated. The acts forbidden and permitted by this commandment in Bible times should be determined. The teachings about killing in the rest of the Bible and the implications of the gospel must be studied.

New astronomies keep appearing because: (1) The stars can be depended on, (2) the tools for studying them keep improving, (3) understandings about them keep developing. For somewhat the same reasons, new sorts of hermeneutics keep appearing. In neither astronomy nor hermeneutics are the most recent theories sure to be the best ones. What is now called the "new hermeneutic" has developed in Europe since World War II. It grew from Rudolf Bultmann's view of the supernatural in the Bible as truth-revealing myth. With clues from Heidegger and existentialist assumptions, it has become an inclusive theory of Bible interpretation that is also a philosophy. Fuchs and Ebeling have written from this point of view in Europe, and the book *The New Hermeneutic,* by Robinson and Cobb, presented it in English in 1964. At the opposite pole are the various conservative approaches to the Bible which recognize recent scholarship but still hold to direct inspiration.

4. *Application.* The fourth level in joining sermons to divine authority is the application of the timeless word to present needs. The listener has not received the revelation until he knows, not just what the Bible says, but what it says *to him.* The light of Scripture is not illuminating me until it has shone into some darkened corner of my life. The Bible people at their nearest are six thousand miles and two thousand years from where I live, and often a Bible sermon gets no closer to me. Many a fascinating sermon presents a colorful exegetical performance, and then quits. Thus a congregation may go home with a new understanding about what went on in Philippi, but with no new understanding about themselves. The preacher may assume that the implications are obvious—but are they? When the minister preaches about the healing of the lepers, will the congregation connect that with donations to the cancer drive? Just before Joshua led the people across the Jordan to face the terrors of an unknown land, God told him, "Be strong and of good courage; be not frightened, neither be dismayed; for the Lord your God is with you." That was just what Joshua needed, and it may be just what is needed by the man who is twisted with fear at the thought of losing his job. But that man may never see how words that were meant for Joshua apply to him unless the preacher makes the connection. The woman who is in constant panic over what may happen to her children may not see how a quaint story from a strange sort of people has any meaning for her life. The preacher does not have to know the very fears, sins, and problems that harass the various members of the congregation. He does have to apply the ancient message in such vivid modern terms that the hearers will be thinking of themselves.

Ministers with widely diverging views of Scripture still find in it the authority and basis for their sermons. Its treasures for the preacher are inexhaustible, whether he considers himself conservative or liberal. It is surprising to see how much alike are the teachings that both sorts of preachers find in the Bible. The same lessons are drawn from a story, whether it be considered an instructive historical event or a meaning-filled myth. The sublime truth we get from the twenty-third Psalm or the fourth chapter of First John does not depend on who wrote them. Students who wonder how they can preach before they have settled their nagging questions about the Bible may be astonished. They discover it has a great deal they are burning to tell about, which is not at all affected by their uncertainties.

VARIOUS VIEWS OF THE BIBLE

The simplest view is that the Bible is word for word inspired, and that it means what it seems to say. There would be no benefit from an infallibility that is not available, so it is also held that the manuscripts and translations we have are also infallible. The Roman Catholic Church insisted that Jerome was divinely kept from error when he translated the Bible into Latin. Those who regard the Bible as infallible are quite aware of the difficulties. They cannot explain how a circular vessel that was ten cubits across could be thirty cubits around (I Ki. 7:23)—a circle's circumference is 3.1416 times its diameter. They know that Mark says, "It was the third hour when they crucified him," (Mk. 15:25) while John says that Jesus was still with Pilate at the sixth hour. (Jn. 19:14) But they find it easier to believe that their understanding is faulty than that the Bible is wrong. They say that if we can choose what we will believe in the Bible, then none of it is certain. If the Bible is wrong when it says, "the sun stood still" (Josh. 10:13) then it may be wrong when it says, "God is love." (I Jn. 4:8) If the story of Jonah is an allegory, then the story of Jesus' resurrection, or even of his birth, might also be an allegory. The cover-to-cover literalist takes the Bible as a first-year Latin student takes Caesar—getting the gist of it and assuming that what does not seem to make sense probably does. He does not have to think that the Holy Spirit took over the Bible authors like zombies. The Spirit could respect their personalities and use them as a musician can use various instruments to communicate his music.

Most Christians across the centuries have believed that the Bible is infallible—at least in matters of faith and practice. This permits the preacher to say with assurance, "Hear the word of God," and it attracts congregations who are eager to learn more of the unquestioned truth.

Ministers who have a much less rigid view of how the Bible is inspired also have it as the basis for their preaching. They see that the nearest to the "real" Bible we can get is not a black-bound book, but hundreds of ancient manuscripts in many languages, scattered in libraries and museums around the world. Though the textual uncertainties are mostly minor, they will always keep us from having a flawless Bible. But those who believe that God never intended his communication to be as mechanically simple as the literalists would like to have it may still be sure that the divine revelation is in the Bible.

Some see God revealed in the Bible not just in static texts, but in what he is doing. They see him lifting the religious understandings of the Hebrew people from the primitive ideas of the early Old Testament to the exalted spiritual purity of the later prophets. They see God moving the Apostle Paul from the views on women and marriage of a once bigoted Pharisee to those that were incredibly advanced and unconventional for his time and place. What he said was spoken from a way station in this progress; it was not God's final word. But what the spirit of Christ was doing to this former ultrareactionary surely reveals God in action. One Bible book is called "The Acts of the Apostles," but the whole Bible could be called "The Acts of God."

If Paul could be wrong in his opinions about women's hair styles, and when the end of the world was coming, how can we trust him when he says, "Love never fails?" Paul himself answers that. He attributes what he says about eternal matters to "a revelation of Jesus Christ." (Gal. 1:12) But on temporal matters he admits, "I have no command of the Lord, but I give my opinion." (I Cor. 7:25) We are not left to choose what we like. It is an old rule that Scripture is the interpreter of Scripture. Those who doubt that God sent the she-bears to tear the children who made fun of Elisha's bald head doubt it on the authority of Scripture. God in the Bible is not a graven image, a frozen concept—he is being understood at even higher levels. The understanding of himself to which God finally brings his people in the Bible is not on a monotonous flat plain; it mounts up to the summit where Jesus is. All else in the Bible is to be judged by him.

Luther said that God revealed himself in Christ in the weakness of human flesh, and he revealed himself in the Bible in the weakness of a human book. If the Bible, unlike all other ancient books, were completely free from error in the beginning and had been transmitted across the centuries through thousands of copyists without the slightest inaccuracy, then it would be not so much a holy book as a magic book. Faith would be short-circuited if we were forced to believe in the Bible's more-than-human origin by a mechanical trick. It would be not a source of worship, but an object of worship. The real evidence that the Bible is God's word is not its form but its effects. Except for the incarnation, there is no miracle in the Bible as startling as the Bible itself. You may be uncertain about whether the walls of Jericho fell flat, but there is no doubt at all that this collection of ancient writings has toppled thrones, upset governments, and transformed human lives. We can watch it blasting evil institutions, exploding arrogant pretensions. A minister who preaches the Bible has incredible power in his hands.

In India, an articulate villager would be told one Bible story and then sent out to tell it to his neighbors. He would then be taught another story, and another, until much of the gospel was transmitted. That is the way

a preacher has to preach. Whatever be his theory about plenary inspiration, in practice he preaches only from the parts of the Bible in which he
has found Divine Truth. If there is only one verse in the Bible that is
God's word for you, you have a Bible—a one-verse Bible. If there is a
chapter that is for you wisdom from outside this world, you have a one-
chapter Bible. As long as we live, our working Bible keeps enlarging. We
do not have to worry too much about why some passages that have not
so far said much to us are in the Bible. The canon from which we preach
is the expanding circle of what has come blazing into light. The Holy
Spirit is the witness to his word. As the *Westminster Confession* puts it,
"Our full persuasion and assurance of the infallible truth, and divine
authority thereof, is from the inward work of the Holy Spirit, bearing
witness by and with the Word in our hearts." The Spirit probably never
bears witness to all sixty-six books at once.

Those who have this attitude are in danger of judging the Bible, instead of letting it judge them. They can consider as temporal the sayings
of Paul they do not like. They may leave out of the circle of what has
become luminous for them the very parts they need the most because
these hit them hardest. Everyone who evaluates the Bible from his own
hermeneutical angle—which may be revivalism social revolution, or patriotism—can end up being his own Bible-maker. He may look into the Bible
to find Jesus, and be delighted to see a face very like his own looking back
at him. But if we believe that there is a Holy Spirit who witnesses to his
word, then these dangers of subjective judgments diminish. The Spirit
will not leave us free to follow our own tastes; He will make us accept in
the Bible what we desperately wish we could escape. There is a point to
the old doctrine that only believers can be trusted with the Bible. Those
whose judgments are under the influence of the living Christ can be allowed some freedom.

At a stage farther from the old orthodoxy are those who insist that
questions of fact and historicity are unimportant. Those who regard the
creation story as fact and those who see it as inspired allegory get from it
exactly the same truths. Why does it matter whether the Ten Commandments came down from Mount Sinai or up from the worshipping community as long as they are regarded as God's law? Whether a writing was
first sent to a church or came out of a church, what it says to us is the
same. Much that is miraculous in the Gospels might have been created by
the early Church as it reflected on Jesus and tried to find some way to
represent what he meant. Would that not also tell us what we need to
know about him? Just as "sitteth on the right hand of God the Father
Almighty" is not a literal seating arrangement, so what is represented by
the virgin birth, the ascension, and the resurrection can be true without
being factual. Indeed, the whole question about the historical Jesus is
unimportant, according to this view. Whether he ever lived or not, what
we have in the Gospels is a figure of such unutterable love and majesty
and beauty that every life can be judged by whether it inclines toward him

or away from him. Jesus Christ, whether literally born in Bethlehem or born from imaginations that were open to God's Spirit, has been God's means of salvation for all who let their lives be dominated by him. Perhaps God could convey His truth better through the exalted conceptions of poets and myth-makers than through actual biographies. We picture inspiration as guiding the stylus of a scribe. Could it not also be given to a minstrel chanting in a village circle, or to his grandparents from whom he heard the tales, or to priestly editors who worked over material they were given? Does it matter whether a Gospel was produced for a church by one man, or by a church for all men—whether an epistle is the burning outpouring of a Christ-kindled apostle or the accumulated insights of a Christ-kindled fellowship? Indeed, some feel that freeing the Bible from confinement to history releases its spiritual treasures. As long as theology was based on a history, every new attitude to that history forced agonizing reappraisals in theology. If we permit God to communicate through myth and invention, then spiritual truth can be more adequately expressed.

But if we go far enough upon this line we come to where every religious concept disintegrates. Sin, forgiveness, morality, salvation, the life to come, God, and man glimmer out, and we are left with nothing but philosophical word games and speculations about the psyche. The demythologizers' road disappears finally in the fog. Far short of that, there is a point where a Christianity of truth without fact, whose creeds can be sung but not said, becomes esoteric and out of reach for nine-tenths of the human race. A religion that is not available to common people, but only to those of specially subtle intellect, could not be Christianity. When a preacher's private belief is too recondite for most of the people in the pews, he has the wrong religion for a Christian church. Christ came for rag-pickers and Nobel laureates. Cover-to-cover literalists fear that if a rent is made in the fabric of infallibility the whole Bible will ravel out, and with it the Christian faith. That possibility is there. There's a point beyond which the minister would have no source for preaching. But short of that, there are many different views of the Bible which provide the preacher with authority and confidence.

How much should a preacher tell the congregation about Bible difficulties? He must, of course, be honest. The Bible does not need to be defended by being presented as something it is not. In the later dynasties in Egypt there were two religions in the temples. There was a secret, hidden religion for the priests; and there was a quite different religion the priests practiced in public and offered to the people. We do not want in our churches a religion of the professionals who have been exposed to advanced religious views, and another religion for the common folk. A minister must not conceal his scholarly reservations when they make a difference. As Rudolf Bultmann said, "The preacher must not leave his hearers in the dark about what he secretly eliminates, nor must he be in the dark about it himself." (*Kerygma and Myth,* p. 9) If all a minister reveals to his congregation is a simple, artless faith, many who are not simple and artless may give up. A bright person, who sees the difficulties in accepting the Bible, needs to know that the preacher sees them too.

On the other hand, there is no use to needlessly disturb people, or to introduce difficulties with no chance of working them through. Honesty does not require a minister to say, "Let us pray the Lord's Prayer, adding at the end those words that are not his." It is not necessary in a Scripture reading to explain, "Another Gospel tells this in a different way." Demythologizing is not what old people need when they hear the well-loved words. Preachers have to beware of parading their pedantry in the name of honesty.

Seminary study will in some ways change a student's view of what the Bible is. What is more, his views will keep changing if he has a live and growing faith. There may be transition stages in which the minister fears he has lost his authority for preaching because he has come to see the Bible in a different way. He may need to remember that across history there have been many astronomies—from Ptolemy, Copernicus, and Galileo, to today's. The succession of astronomies does not make the stars doubtful; it shows that they are always there. Dr. Coffin told of the problems of handling all the trains and the tens of thousands of passengers that went through each day when the old red-brick Grand Central Station in New York was being replaced. But amidst dust, plank walks, barriers, and temporary props the traffic was uninterrupted. A minister may have to work it out like that in periods when his theology or hermeneutics is changing. But, above all, he cannot refuse to move from what has been outgrown. He must not dishonor the Bible by pulling back from devoting to it all the best powers of his mind and heart.

Through all the old and the new hermeneutics the Bible still has the answers to man's deepest needs. It does not answer everything. We have to remember two Protestant principles: "Where the Bible speaks, we speak; where the Bible is silent, we are silent"; and "The Bible tells us enough to satisfy our needs, but not enough to satisfy our curiosity." There is much more we would like to know, about such matters as heaven, psychic phenomena, and the spirits of animals. The Psalm says only that "Thy word is a lamp to my feet and a light to my path." It gives us the light we need for where we have to go, but there are wide reaches on either side of the path it does not illuminate. By showing the path, it saves us from getting lost out in the mysteries. On our journey across the years the Bible reproves our sins and sustains our hopes. It is our passport to the grandest realms of the human spirit. Above all, the Bible tells us who Jesus is, and what he did and said, and what he has for us. The Bible has the more than human truth a troubled world is seeking. It is the Book that makes our preaching valid.

VI

The Power of God in Preaching

Familiarity makes us miss the wonder of a strange thing that happens every Sunday. Out of their homes come housewives, bankers, mechanics. These people, who have been busy with practical affairs all week long, are on their way to church. They are going because they expect to make a special contact with Almighty God. There has never been anything else as romantic in all the adventure stories of the human race. The quest for the Holy Grail and the Argonauts' search for the Golden Fleece become commonplace in comparison with this weekly event. But do these seekers find what they are looking for? If not, theirs is a peculiarly persistent mistake, with fifty-two chances a year for two thousand years to find out that the encounter with God does not occur.

I went straight from seminary to a pastorate in a college town. There, every Sunday, I saw in the congregation the professors of Bible, philosophy, history, and Greek—the sort of people who just the year before had been examining my knowledge of those subjects without being at all impressed. It is scarcely likely that they left their well-stocked shelves because of anything I would tell them. But they were there every Sunday, grateful and happy for what they were getting. It did not happen because of me but in spite of me. It was an authentic miracle—that is, an event beyond all earthly causes.

This miracle is the preacher's only hope. Could anyone expect to be able to do what a minister is supposed to do—to introduce people to Jesus Christ, to persuade them to accept the Christian faith, to show people how to live as Christians, to comfort, reprove, strengthen, inspire? Every minister's claim to power would make a field marshall blush. An honest man is sure to conclude, "I am not cut out for this sort of thing. It is not in my line." But over against our self-doubt is the knowledge that this is done every Sunday by preachers who do not have what it takes.

This is the wonder, the absurdly impossible wonder, that keeps happening in church work. A cartoonist could have a field day putting captions which describe what church people think they are doing under pictures which show how they look. Here is a shy gentleman with his best tie tucked in, perched on someone's sofa, making a call for the church. The title of this picture is "The Soul Winner." Think of a picture of some nice church ladies, with their teacups pushed aside and their heads bowed. The Spiritual Life Group is meeting. Under this picture put the caption "The Future is Controlled from this Power Station." Here is a picture of a distraught church school teacher harassed by a wild class. Its title is "Setting Little Feet on the Golden Stairs." Another picture might show a rumpled preacher, in a welter of books and notes, disgustedly ripping the paper out of a typewriter and hurling it on the floor. Under this one put the words, "The Holy Spirit Having Transmission Difficulties." But the strange fact is that those titles may be literally true. The most convincing evidence of the miraculous we are likely to witness is what happens from such obviously inadequate human causes. Church people have to count on it. Every minister has the experience of going to a home where disaster has struck, dragging himself up the walk, trying to think of how to help, and coming up with nothing. So he mumbles some banalities—"So sorry—he was a wonderful boy— God will help you—don't get too tired," and goes off, knowing he has failed, wishing he could be one of those people who radiate strength and comfort. Later, the person he went to help tells him, "Your coming was just what I needed. It made me know I could go on living." The minister wonders, in astonishment, "Who, I?" And the answer would have to be, "No, not you."

We need to identify where this more than human help comes into preaching. Inspiration is mysterious, but it is not vague.

1. *The help is given during the preparation of the sermon.* Praying along with this can determine what sort of process it is. The difference is more in the feel for the job, in the mental bearing, than in any unexpected wisdom. It is true that the preacher does get some good ideas that he does not seem to generate within himself; he may be surprised by flashes of insight that come to him. But to ascribe these to the Holy Spirit amounts to saying that, because he does not know where they came from, they must have come from God—and that is dangerous. Bad and foolish thoughts may also come mysteriously from some hidden chambers of the mind. No doubt a crooked lawyer who is contriving ways to get a guilty client freed may also have unexpected illuminations. A little girl, watching her father prepare a sermon asked, "How do you know what to say?" "God tells me," he answered. "Then why do you keep crossing it out?" she asked.

A minister, who is grinding away at the job of sermon preparation, may not feel like a channel of the Holy Spirit. He is more likely to feel like a dull hack as he pounds his head and looks for texts that are not in the Bible. He may strain all week for the good ideas that will not come. But with all this something more may be happening. Prayer puts the great purposes more clearly in sight. With a God-conscious bearing, the choice of what to say is more likely to be right, and mistakes are more likely to be avoided. God helps only those who are straining and suffering, but prayer brings understanding that will direct the hard strivings in the right directions.

The sort of help Jesus promised His disciples has not ceased—"It is not you who speak, but the Holy Spirit." (Mk. 13:11) "I myself will give you power of utterance and wisdom." (Lk. 21:15 NEB) Paul recognized that "we impart this in words not taught by human wisdom but by the Spirit." (I Cor. 2:13)

God gives understanding to the preacher through the insights that come to him all through his life; all of his experiences are interpreted from the standpoint of his faith in Christ. Everything that happens to him thus builds up in him a wisdom that is greater than his own. All this slowly acquired understanding is at his disposal as he prepares his sermon.

2. *The help is given during the preaching of the sermon.* At the Fourth Presbyterian Church of Chicago I saw a card attached to the inside of the door through which the preacher goes from the robing room to the pulpit. It had been put there by a former pastor, Harrison Ray Anderson. On it was God's promise to Moses, "My presence will go with you," and Moses' reply, "If thy presence will not go with me, do not carry us up from here." (Ex. 33:14–15) A minister is often gratefully aware of results from his preaching he cannot account for. On many a Saturday night it may take a strong resolution to keep him from skipping town. He knows that all he has for the congregation is dull and clumsy. The next morning, with a heavy heart, he goes into the pulpit. Then, to his astonishment, he may see that, instead of resentful boredom, there is a lively interest. What he is advocating is accepted with enthusiasm. People leave with shining faces. This surprising result may sometimes be traced to what has happened to the minister's manner. If a preacher out of desperation has been begging God for help, he may show an earnestness and spiritual intensity that are appealing.

There are times when a preacher's inner state is completely wrong. Then, also, something mysterious may rescue the congregation. The preacher may be in a time of spiritual dryness. He may come into the pulpit poisoned by an argument, or brooding over a rebuff. Sometimes a preacher is not with his sermon; he is not being hypocritical, he is just not there. I have suspected that a preaching robe can join the processional and conduct a church service without having a man inside. God and the robe read the prayers and preach the sermon while the minister looks on. This could not become habitual, of course. On most Sundays, the minister in person must be very much participating, but there are bad times when he discovers how much can be done without him.

3. *A more than worldly help is given to a sermon by its more than worldly subject matter.* A car salesman has only the attraction of the car working with him; what the preacher is offering has a sublime appeal. The great advantage in talking about the promises of God is that the promises are true. Even those who reject "the supernatural" may still feel a reverence for Jesus, and a regard for the Bible as a special sort of

authority. A minister who preaches from the Bible gets a hearing he could not expect for himself.

Anyone who pleads with the city council about bad housing has to make his own case. But when a preacher in a Christian congregation condemns tenements in which rats bite babies and lives are blighted, he is seen as having heaven on his side. He can condemn exploitation and corruption, not just as heartless and disgraceful, but as denounced in eternity.

The minister has the power of God to help his preaching, because it is the things of God he talks about. The Bible shows that when bad men preach the truth, even from wrong motives, it can still be effective. Jonah did not want to preach to Nineveh, and he did not want Nineveh to heed his preaching, but the power of the message he was required to give made Nineveh repent in spite of him. Paul tells of those who "proclaim Christ in a jealous and quarrelsome spirit." They, "moved by personal rivalry, present Christ from mixed motives, meaning to stir up fresh trouble for me." Then he comes to the startlingly cheerful conclusion, "What does it matter? One way or another, in pretence or in sincerity, Christ is set forth, and for that I rejoice." (Phil. 1:15, 17, 18 NEB) Even hypocritical preaching can bring a blessing if it tells the truth about Jesus Christ. We can count on more than human help with more than human subjects.

4. *The power of God is given to preaching through what the Holy Spirit is doing in the hearers' hearts.* A preacher would be astounded to know what is going on in people's minds while he is preaching. Even when they are giving full attention, what he is saying is probably not a tenth of what they are thinking about. Moreover, the best of them will take off from something that is said on excursions of their own. Listeners do not follow a sermon, they keep bouncing from it and coming back. We do not encourage minds to wander, but sermons can do their greatest good by stimulating people to pursue their own thoughts. Because the sermon comes within a worship service, the private thinking will be colored by the mood of worship, responding to the thought of God, taking off from sermon words—"love," "mercy," "forgive," "anger," "hope." This is altogether different from mere woolgathering.

The sermon is a catalyst for the Holy Spirit. Dr. Samuel Moffett of Korea told of the visiting professor who asked to preach in a Korean church. With some misgivings, an engagement was made with a village congregation. The professor began his sermon: "In the history of human thought there are two categories, the inductive and the deductive." The Korean pastor who was translating looked at the speaker in horror. He looked out at the congregation of gnarled farmers, toil-worn women, and children rolling on the floor. Then he began his translation: "I have come today to tell you what Jesus Christ means to me." Thus they went on, with the professor preaching his sermon and the translator preaching his until they finished together. That is what happens in every church every Sunday. While the minister is preaching his sermon, the Holy

Spirit is preaching his, and his is the one that matters. This is the "sermon event" that overflows the preached sermon on all sides.

5. *The power of God can be found in what happens after the sermon has been preached.* One day the remarkably gifted preacher, Peter Marshall, said to his friend, Wilbur LaRoe, "I preach, and preach, and preach, and *nothing happens!*" Mr. LaRoe, a Washington lawyer, answered, "How dare you say, Peter, that nothing happens! The gospel of Jesus Christ is so valid and the principles set forth in the Bible are so eternally sound that it is impossible to preach the gospel without something happening. The result may not be visible immediately, but an impression is made on the hearts of the people." He then told Dr. Marshall how he was helped through a crisis in his life by a sermon he had heard twenty years before. (*The Church We Love,* pp. 21–22)

Every preacher who has been at it long enough has had people tell him of something he said long ago which in time became of great importance for them. A garage owner told me that something I said in his church when he was young saved him from folly when he was going through a spell of middle-aged delusion. I had said that sulphuric acid and adultery both have to be corrosive because that is the way things operate. That does not seem very memorable, but time made it so. When Frederick W. Robertson in England was having his time of deep discouragement about preaching, a storekeeper showed a customer his back room, where he had a picture of Dr. Robertson on the wall. He said that whenever he was tempted to give shoddy goods or short measure he went back there to look at that picture. A preacher never knows the postponed good his sermons do.

If the power of God in preaching were not a fact, preaching would never have survived. By definition, the usual church cannot have an unusual preacher. Just ordinary, mediocre ministers will be in most pulpits. Many of the people in most congregations listen to a preacher who is their mental inferior. There is no hope for preaching unless there is something that can make an average minister inspiring. An obvious solution might be to encourage mediocre ministers to borrow more from the masters. But a lusterless person does lusterless borrowing.

A century ago William Arthur wrote, "If the preaching of the Gospel is to exercise a great power over mankind, it must be either by enlisting extraordinary men or by the endowing of ordinary men with extraordinary power." (*Tongues of Fire*) There will never be enough extraordinary men to go around, so the only hope is the endowing of the ordinary men. It is that which has kept preaching going in the past. We can count on it today.

There are conditions for getting this extraordinary power. One requirement is humility. Brains and eloquence can handicap a minister if they give him an illusion of competence. The gifted often wear thin. It is those who out of desperation and discouragement beg for help who get it. When a preacher thinks, "I am going to ring the bell today," that is the day when no bells ring.

A second condition for getting God's help is hard work. In no branch of church work is the Divine power given to those who have not done their best. The old saying is, "Inspiration is nine-tenths perspiration." It is only to those who have strained and struggled to the end of their resources that the supplement is given. Dr. Paul Scherer told of the young minister who explained to a parishioner that, in order to leave a place for inspiration, he always wrote only the first half of his sermon, and left the last half for God. The man answered, "Sir, I congratulate you! Your half is invariably better than God's."

A third requirement for receiving the divine supplement is to believe in it and ask for it. It is never automatic. It is only when we are in a state for receiving it that the help is given.

We bring the crude product of our agony and straining and offer it to God. And just as God can, if necessary, take very rough bread and poor grape juice and make them the bearers of the holy, so he can take our commonplace, faulty, inadequate words and, by a miracle of grace, make them a source of endless blessing. That is what we have to count on. James Stewart says, "Every Sunday morning when it comes ought to find you awed and thrilled by the reflection—'God is to be in action today, through me, for these people: this day may be crucial, this service decisive, for someone now ripe for the vision of Jesus.'" (*Heralds of God,* p. 47)

VII

Preaching as Communication

COMMUNICATION THEORY

Modern studies of communication promise to be of great significance for the Church. Communication is the church's business. The Church is called to proclaim, to evangelize, to teach; its health depends on how well its members communicate with each other; its Lord is the Word. The Church must therefore stay in close and grateful contact with the vast amount of new study and research that is being devoted to communication.

The philosophers of the communications movement are searching through linguistics for their ontological and epistemological *pou sto;* at the other extreme are the practicing psychologists, with their stop watches and slide rules. At the philosophers' end are the older students of consciousness, like Bergson, and the newer language theorists, like Fuchs and Ebeling. Martin Heidegger has explored what language can and cannot do; Wittgenstein has made even nonphilosophers aware of linguistic analysis.

A stage closer to the preacher's needs are the communications theorists who work in such fields as semiotics, semantics, psycholinguistics, and neurophysiology. Many educated people have become aware of their warnings of loose thinking and loose practice, but their influence on nonspecialists has not been large. That isolation ended when the writings of Marshall McLuhan exploded into popular interest. Here was a communications thinker of vast learning, whose books fascinated ordinary readers. He has been hailed as the herald of a revolution like Galileo's, and as a sensationalist whose novel style conceals capricious thinking. He may be widely misunderstood, but that is not of great concern to him. True to his principles, his books are not intended to convey understanding to the readers' minds, but to produce effects there. He judges all communication, including his own, by participation, involvement, and commitment. Media, as McLuhan uses the term, are "extensions of our physical and nervous systems" by which communication takes place. These have been vastly enlarged and their relationships altered by modern technology. A medium which uses all of a person's sensory faculties, and which leaves a chance for immediacy (that is, for participation, involvement, and commitment) is "cool." A medium which concentrates on one form of perception and which does not allow for much immediacy is "hot." It may seem strange that a man who endures Canadian winters would have "cool" mean live, loose, direct, while "hot" means devitalized, rigid, and confined. McLuhan believes that modern technologies make minds less receptive to linear communication, where word follows word and paragraph follows paragraph in print or speech. There is now more dependence on simultaneous perception. The sights and sounds from a television broadcast get to us all at once, and wrap us around in meanings. Its messages are not communicated unit by unit; they hit us from all sides at the same time. As they come, we are not simply receiving—we are interacting with them. As McLuhan puts it, "Insight is a kind of mental involvement in process." This sort of perception has changed the way we think. We are no longer as accustomed to sequential thinking, which corresponds to learning from print. Thought processes now have an all-at-once quality. Thus there is a new mode of human consciousness. This has brought speculation about a new sort of preaching that will reach people "through all the senses at once."

The Jesuit scholar, Walter J. Ong, writes learnedly on the same subjects. He considers a word to be properly transmitted by sound, and only secondarily by sight. Man communicates through all his senses (his "sensorium"), but different cultures use them in different proportions. What is in print is "devocalized," "depersonalized," "devitalized."

There is much in all this for a preacher to think about. At its best a sermon can be "cool," but it may be deplorably "hot." A sermon cannot be an object, a production; a real sermon has to be an experience. McLuhan delights in the possibility that the electronic extension of the senses can make the world a "global village," united by communications that do not depend entirely on words. This has for the preacher both alluring possibilities and warnings. A fragmented, parochial Christianity will become increasingly anachronistic.

Prophets have been promising for some time that the new communications philosophies and theories were about to produce a revolution that would transform all communication, including preaching. So far the revolution has not appeared. It may be that we are in the interval that has to come between advances in pure science and their utilization in applied science.

PRACTICAL COMMUNICATION STUDIES

At the practical level, however, there is a great deal in the new communication studies that is important for the preacher. There has been an explosion of interest in those studies in the past few years. Much has been called for by the demands of those whose work depends upon communication—advertisers, political campaign managers, broadcasters, educators. By a systematic study of communication processes, including laboratory research and surveys, new knowledge has been gained. The diagrams and technical terminologies are presenting what most people have already thought about, but this does not mean they are not needed. When Aristotle declared that public speaking has speaker, speech, and audience, he was not revealing a startling discovery, but he was identifying the elements through which what goes on could be studied. The communication experts look at what is happening in each part of the process so it can be understood and improved. This is no new science. The ancients were fascinated with it. Modern studies depend heavily on classical rhetoric. Through the years, scholars have tried to find out how people are persuaded, informed, and motivated, so they could master the skills. The oldest known writing on communication theory was addressed to the son of the Pharaoh in about 3000 B.C. The oldest book that has been preserved is the *Precepts* on effective communication that were assembled in Egypt about 2675 B.C. Important contributions to the understanding of communication were made by the Greek Sophists, Plato, Aristotle, and Quintilian. Augustine was a teacher of rhetoric. Not much more was added until the upsurge of interest in the subject during the Renaissance. Two centuries ago, the elocution teachers introduced a new approach to oral communication. Modern experimental psychology has attacked the problems from a fresh angle. Semantics has brought a new sophisticaion in the use of words.

Recent studies have produced various ways of representing what goes on when people communicate. Some of these "models" use charts in which squares, circles, triangles, solid lines, dotted lines, and arrows are arranged with considerable complexity. By these, the various components can be identified and their operation and relationships considered. The model used here is almost the same as the Shannon-Weaver model, which was based on research done at the Bell Telephone Laboratories:

Whoever is the Source has a message he wants to give to the Receiver. That mysterious kinship by which people are connected permits what is in one mind to be put into another. There must be some sort of container in which the message can be transported; it can be a word, gesture, pantomime, or symbol. The Source puts the meaning he wants to convey into such a code, or into several of them which share in the conveying. The message can be encoded into Morse Code, hand signals, vocal sounds, print. There must be the assumption that the code will have the same significance to the Receiver that it had to the Sender. What is encoded must then be transmitted—by sight, sound, postman, mutual friend. The Receiver must then decode the signals to extract the message. Differences in the meaning of the code to the two parties, or distortion in transmission, will produce at least a slight difference between the message that was sent and the message that is received.

COMMUNICATION FOR THE CHURCH

The understanding of this process is of the utmost importance to the church, for most of the things the church exists to do depend upon communication. Our interest here is with that special part of the church's communicating that takes place in preaching.

Preaching is just one link in the proclamation of God's truth. We may think of the whole process of that proclamation as a series of linked communication events. It may be helpful to see these as a kerygmatic chain. At each stage, communication concepts have a direct bearing on the primary questions. At link 1, these questions are theological; at 2, they are hermeneutical; at 3, exegetical; at 4, homiletical; at 5, educational and evangelistic.The kerygmatic chain has these elements:

<pre>
    1   2   3   4   5
  God—Seer—Contemporary—Preacher—Hearer—Neighbor . . .
</pre>

The numbered links can be studied in terms of our communication model —Source, Encoding, Transmission, Decoding, Receiver.

1. It all begins with a God who, Christians believe, communicates with the creatures he has made and loves. The philosophic scandal here is obvious: There are no possible thought forms that could be shared by an infinite God and finite beings. Christians accept this scandal with an awe that transcends reason. Having experienced the unexplainable transfer of thought and feeling from one human being to another, we accept the far deeper mystery of communication between God and man. Christianity believes that "God created man in his own image," so that there is a likeness which lets man in his tiny way share the infinite understandings. Because of this likeness, we can speak the same language, though man can spend all eternity learning more of the divine vocabulary. We are not nameless waifs; our minds and spirits are not detached and solitary fragments. We have the best of all connections. God is not an abstract "It"—God is a "Thou."

God has many channels by which he communicates with humanity. One of them uses Seers—special persons who are chosen, individually or collectively, to receive a message and transmit it to others. The Bible preserves the messages that have been given through these Receivers, from the Seer of Sinai to the Seer of Patmos. The message must be encoded into signals which will convey to the Seer what God says. The code may be laws, songs, raptures, stories, the record of events. It may be transmitted by visions, dictation, tradition, arranged experiences. The Receivers must then decode the message in terms of their own comprehensions. These are human, so they must limit the scope of the message that can be retained. The Receiver's personality will color the images and concepts in which he presents the message to himself.

2. The Seer must now take up his task of giving the message to his

Contemporaries. He may use the same code in which the message came to him, or he may reencode it in signs that are more appropriate for the comprehension of the Contemporaries. The prophets made symbolic use of current events, they used pantomime, they declaimed. The Psalmists put their messages in rich imagery. Paul had a wide range of literary devices. The messages, thus encoded, were transmitted by speeches to crowds, by stern personal confrontations, by written scrolls, by being acted out before spectators. The Receivers then had to decode the messages in terms of their own understanding.

Much of what God wants to say to humanity he has encoded in his mighty acts of creation, preservation, deliverance, and redemption. He encoded his Word in Jesus Christ, who both spoke the message and dramatized it upon our stage. God's communication through these acts was given first to Contemporaries, and then to us.

3. The Contemporaries have passed the message on to us through the Scriptures. Sometimes they have recorded it in the terms in which they received it; sometimes they have reencoded it for the written record. The Bible is the Source from which the preacher receives, and then decodes for his own comprehension.

4. The Preacher then encodes what he has received from the Bible so that he can pass it on to the congregation in a sermon. He uses such semaphores as words, gestures, vocal intonations. The figures of speech and thought forms he uses are part of his code. The members of the congregation decode the sermon in terms of their needs and understandings. The point of the whole process is in what happens to the Hearers. Will there be, in communication terms, acceptance, persuasion, attitude change, internalization, and response? Or will there be noncomprehension, distortion, resistance, and rejection?

5. The whole New Testament makes it plain that no Receiver is to be a dead-end street. We are given the message for two purposes: first, for our own good and, second, so that we may pass it on. The only commandment that is recorded as being given in each of Jesus' last appearances to his disciples is the commandment to tell others the good news. That is how the gospel got across oceans and centuries to come to us. To the extent that we break the chain, it all ends with us. Many sorts of signaling devices are available to communicate Christ's message—conversations, print, the way we live, the witness of the Christian fellowship. These can be well or poorly used. Communication studies are important for the church because all Christians are divinely commissioned to be communicators.

THE APPLICATION OF COMMUNICATION STUDIES TO PREACHING

Now let us look at the fourth link to see how communication understandings can throw light on the preacher's task.

Communication is not an act, it is a *process*. It is what is happening in minds when meanings are being shared through a common system of symbols. At the moment of preaching, most of the communication is one-way, but it is the product of an exchange of messages that has been taking place in many forms. A sermon is an experience. It is not an entity which the preacher can hand over to the congregation, or which can be poked at and examined like an object. (See Chapter XXVIII.)

1. *Source.* Communication theories always assign primary importance to the qualities of the Source of the message. That is obviously true with preaching.

Aristotle said that the *ethos,* the character, of the speaker has most to do with the results of public speech because "we believe good men more fully and readily than others." He added, "It is not true, as some writers assume in their treatises on rhetoric, that the personal goodness revealed by the speaker contributes nothing to his power of persuasion; on the contrary, his character may be called the most effective means of persuasion he possesses." (See Chapter XXVII.)

His *skills* enable the speaker to be effective. They are the subject of most of Aristotle's writing on public speaking, and of communication studies ever since. They have an important part in most books and classes on homiletics. Learning how, from the best minds of the past and present, is just as important for preaching as it is for all the other arts and sciences. (See Introduction.)

The Source's *knowledge* is his equipment. People look to him for information, so he must be well-informed. The preacher has to decode the messages in the Bible, so he has to have a knowledge of theology, hermeneutics, and exegesis. (See Chapter V.) He must be an alert decoder of the messages from all sides that are telling him about human nature. He must have a broad general knowledge.

The *attitudes* of a speaker determine how well he can form and convey a message. His culture may make him put his message into codes the audience cannot decode. He may be inhibited by those he looks to as his "opinion leaders"—almost as though he expected to see the favorite teacher he once had, his current hero, or Martin Luther on the back pew. He may be limited by the influence of his primary groups—family, professional associates, cronies. Much has been said about the dangerous polarization of the church because the clergy and the laity cannot communicate with each other. As the sociologist, Jeffrey K. Hadden, put it, "Clergy and laity are on a collision course. In a very real sense, the laity have one church and the clergy have another." (*The Gathering Storm in the Churches,* p. 222) Preachers must try in many ways to get free of their confinements so they can enter into the world of those with whom they are trying to communicate. A speaker's emotional problems may block communication. If the hearers sense that he is resentful, carping, or arrogant, they will resist anything he says.

Empathy is essential for communication. The Source must be able to feel what the Receivers are feeling, to look at life from their eyes. That is why a minister's pastoral experiences are so necessary to his preaching.

(See Chapter XXVII.) A preacher has to be so close to his people that he can talk their language, know how words will affect them, and understand their needs and interests. He must have the sense of talking to people who are with him as he prepares his sermons. He dare not talk down or up to people—this will miss them either way. He needs to talk with them while he is preaching, as a friend talks with friends.

The minister counts on *prayer* to make him a more effective Source.

2. *Encoding.* The Preacher has to put his thoughts into containers that can convey them from his mind into the minds of the Hearers.

A preacher chiefly counts on words to deliver what he wants to say. Communication specialists have brought some surprising insights into the effects of the words we use. Words have "denotative" and "connotative" meanings which speakers commonly confuse. S. I. Hayakawa and other semanticists find that words convey a great deal that dictionaries do not mention. Preachers, who are professional users of words, need to learn from such scholars what words can and cannot do. Words are signals that can mean anything the Source and the Receiver agree on. Meanings are very private, and the same word will not have exactly the same significance and emotional effect for any two people. Even slight differences can be important, as with the foreign student who said of his convalescent wife, "She is not as painful as she was, but she is still very tiresome." A preacher uses the coloration of his words to signal the subtle nuances of his thoughts and feelings, so he has to be a connoisseur of words. (See Chapter XV.) Not only the words, but the way they are put together determine their meaning and effect. (See Chapter XIV.)

A great deal of study has been given to thought processes so that communicators can lead the Receivers' minds down paths that will bring them to the knowledge, beliefs, or inspirations the Source is trying to transmit. (See Chapters IX and X.)

Encoding has to do not only with the signals that are used but also with the thought packages in which the message is delivered. Will the preacher use metaphors, stories, logical constructions? (See Chapter XVIII.)

Words are not the only signals a preacher uses. His facial expression, body, and manner communicate. He may use symbols, banners, pictures, song, or drama to transmit his message. (See Chapter X, Example 19.)

Every sermon is a multimedia communication. The preacher is by sound and sight transmitting over multiple channels. While he is preaching, parallel messages may be going out from a picture window, candles, or liturgical vestments. These affect what people are getting from the sermon. This is one way to provide the "redundancy" which communication specialists insist increases the effect. Think of a Communion Service in which the sermon theme is "Sacrifice." People can be led to think of sacrifice by the hymns, anthem, readings, prayers, offering, bread, wine, and sermon. Whether or not a minister unifies the worship service around the sermon theme, there will be much that can add to the message. Any biblical sermon will be reinforced by the sight of the cross and the sense of the worshipping community. We do not have to wait for Youth Sunday to have an experience of multimedia communication.

3. *Transmission.* The signs into which the message has been encoded have to be carried from the Source to the Receiver. In church, these go directly by sound and sight. The improved use of the channels of voice and gesture was the concern of the old elocutionists; delivery is literally that. Whether or not the Receivers get the message depends on how well it is carried to them. Speech training is essential for all vocal communicators. It is specially needed by those who have been preaching for five years, and for ten. The bad habits they have fallen into need to be identified; the weaknesses that come with experience have to be corrected.

Good transmission requires attention to the communication situation. Different methods are required for morning and evening. It makes a difference whether the hearers are a loving fellowship or have no interest in each other. Their physical distance apart affects the way a sermon is received.

Contact is important in communication theory. Contact is not assured where the transmitted signals have reached the sense organs of the Receiver; they must also penetrate his consciousness and be taken up by his apperceptive faculties. This requires getting and holding attention. (See Chapter XI, *The Introduction,* and Chapter XIV, *Interest.*)

Noise, in communication terms, is anything that blocks, distorts, or diminishes transmission. For preaching, it can be a passing fire engine, the minister's new purple robe, distracting mispronunciations, or the hearer's prejudice against Dylan Thomas.

4. *Decoding.* Decoding and Encoding require much the same qualities. The Receiver's *ethos* determines his openness to a communication. Good listening requires very special *skills.* (Chapter XXVII.) If the sermon is beyond the hearer's range of *knowledge,* he will miss much of it. His *attitudes* color his interpretation of the signs. We are all inclined to hear what we want to hear; we read our own meanings into the message. Prejudice distorts perceptions. Our opinion leaders and primary groups set limits to our receptiveness; our culture defines the words we hear. "Pious" means "saintlike," to one person, and to another it means "hypocritical." The Receiver needs *empathy* with the way the Source thinks and feels in order to interpret rightly what he says.

5. *Receiver.* The whole purpose of any communication is to make something happen for the Receiver. He is to be persuaded, informed, trained, motivated, entertained, inspired. Communication looks to a change in emotions, attitudes, knowledge, abilities. (See Chapter III.) The message is to be not only accepted, but also internalized—which is to say that mental agreement has to be worked into the fibers of one's whole being. The young rector who visited Paris and was bitterly sorry he had not gone there before he was converted had not internalized his conversion.

Communication research tries to discover the methods that will achieve these results. Advertisers study motivation; educators study the learning process; lawyers study persuasion; politicians are eager for new insights on how attitudes can be changed. Preachers need to know about all of these. The various purposes of preaching (Chapter III) require a wide gamut of special communication skills.

The use of special skills to do things to people could raise some ethical questions for a preacher. Should he decide what is good for the members of the congregation, and use the tricks the experts have developed to make it happen to them? Thought control and brainwashing cannot be excused by a good purpose.

We can test our methods by whether they increase or decrease human freedom. Communication skills can be used in a way that lessens people's freedom to be fully functioning human beings who can make their own decisions. But good communication is designed to open up the whole process by which human beings relate to each other. It clears the blocked channels. It gives release from the frozen attitudes and misunderstandings that inhibit thought. It makes free decision possible. ("You will know the truth, and the truth will make you free.") In good communciation, Sources are not working on Receivers—rather, they are providing Receivers with the information and impulses they need in order to work on *themselves*. Good preaching is not the minister working on the congregation; it is the preached word releasing the congregation so that God can work on them. The Source sends out the signals, but the Receiver's response to them is what makes it communication. The hearer's part is all that really matters. (See Chapter XXVIII.)

Resistance blocks response. It has many sources. A chief one is self-advantage. A butcher could scarcely hear the reasons for vegetarianism. Communication breaks down between researchers, who find cigarettes injurious to health, and cigarette manufacturers, who may be sure they are giving the arguments against smoking fair consideration. The techniques for getting a message past built-in resistance are not coercive, they are liberating.

The ethical problem is not manpulation. Any contact between two people—a wave to a friend, the sending of a postcard—is manipulative. Whenever you become aware of another person, you have lost your independence; you can no longer be a perfect circle—which is why Sartre said, "Hell is other people." But so is Heaven. The real problem is exploitation—taking advantage of another person. A preacher who uses mass hysteria, morbid fear, or cheap sentiment for his own purposes is abusing his communication skill.

Feedback. Feedback is a message that goes back from the Receiver to the Source. In a conversation, the expression on the other person's face lets the talker know the effect of what he is saying. Newspapers get feedback from letters to the editor. Advertisers get it from how well the products sell. Authors get it from the book reviews. Preachers get it from the evident reaction of the congregation, and from what happens afterward. The performance of the Source depends on the signals that come back.

The feedback follows the same pattern—Source, Encoding, Transmission, Decoding, Receiver—that the primary message does, with the direction reversed. Feedback can come back to the preacher from the people in the pews by their frowns, squirming, looking at their watches, laughter, and Amen's.

There are two kinds of feedback: information feedback, and reinforcement feedback.

1. A thermostat gives *information feedback*. When the furnace raises the temperature of a room above a certain point, the thermostat turns the furnace off. Then, when the temperature goes below a certain point, the thermostat turns the furnace on again. Communication from the Room (the Receiver) to the furnace (the Source) tells the furnace what it is doing and what it needs to do.

Feedback from the congregation to the preacher tells him the effect of what he is doing, and whether he needs to change it. Some people are impassive, but there are others whose faces clearly reveal their thoughts, and these are likely to be the bright, concerned people whose opinions count for most. Their expressions show when they are pleased, puzzled, approving, doubtful, or amused. People signal by nodding agreement, looking at each other, slumping in their pews. A minister may sense the mood of a congregation without any evident signs.

Feedback is both immediate and delayed. People's words and attitudes at the church door are important; so are notes they write or chance comments. (See Chapter XVII, *Criticism*.) Ministers can get very practical help from sermon reaction meetings. Their immediate purpose may be the good of the participants, but they also let the minister know what he is accomplishing.

Sermon reaction meetings are of many sorts. In the simplest form, everyone is invited to stay after church to talk about the sermon. Specific people, whose opinions the minister wants, may be asked to make up a "talk back" group. Wallace E. Fisher had meetings for "Coffee and Conversation with the Clergy" one Sunday evening a month in which the morning sermons preached during the previous month were discussed. Gerald Jud had his sermons mimeographed each Sunday during Lent. The next week they were discussed at Colony (district) meetings in homes. Reuel Howe believes that sermon discussion is freer when the preacher is not present. If a tape recording is made of the discussion, he can listen later to what was said. Sometimes the participants are given mimeographed copies or outlines of the sermon to study in advance. Some meetings go through a prepared set of questions, such as: "What was the preacher trying to accomplish? What difference will it make to you? What would you have said? Do you disagree with any of it? What further thoughts has it aroused for you? Those who come to such meetings get an exciting sense of active participation in the sermon event. They are confronted with the preached word in a way that is not possible while they are sitting in the pews. Their thinking is expanded and clarified.

Feedback groups cannot well be permanent. They are usually set up for a limited time, perhaps for Lent or Advent, or in connection with a special series of sermons.

2. *Reinforcement feedback* is illustrated by what happens when the microphone, in a public-address system, is put too near the loudspeaker. Then the output is fed back into the input which builds up the output which increases the input until there is a screech whose volume is restricted only by the limitations of the system.

A preacher who gets immediate or delayed reinforcement feedback from his congregation can have a power he would never have without it. The congregation's responsiveness increases his ability to transmit which increases the responsiveness until it can become a very moving experience. There can also be negative feedback, by which a congregation drains a preacher's force.

Interaction is essential to good communication. It is needed before communication starts. Advertisers spend vast sums on market surveys. Preaching to strangers often seems unreal. There must be interaction during communication, which is why television studios make such elaborate provision for live audiences, and warm them up before the program starts, and why "eye contact" means so much to public speech. There must also be interaction after the overt communication has concluded. What is said in the pulpit should be just one part of a continuing relationship. The effect of a sermon should be shared, as the preacher and the people live, work, and think together.

VIII

What to Preach About

When Louis XVI heard the court preacher, he scoffed, "If the abbé had spoken a little about religion he would have spoken a little about everything." Many fascinating subjects have no place in the pulpit. Every real sermon has just one subject, *The Life God Offers Us Throuh Jesus Christ,* but that subject is inexhaustible. No preacher could get to all the fresh and necessary things that should be said about it. That is why Paul exclaimed, with a baffled exultation, that he had been told to preach "the unsearchable riches of Christ," and to make known "the manifold wisdom of God." (Eph. 3:8,10)

UNSEARCHABLE RICHES

The subject cannot be exhausted, but the preacher can. I have a recurring nightmare which I have learned also troubles other ministers. I find myself in a pulpit, with a roomful of faces looking up at me, and I have no idea why I am there or what to do. I suspect this dream reveals the preacher's deep anxiety about running out of sermons. Panic may seize him as he thinks of having to come up with what is new and important on the same subject every seven days for years on end.

There is no limitation to what the congregation needs to hear or to what could be said; the limitation is in the preacher. He never understands more than a narrow segment of the Christian faith; his emotional range is narrow; he cannot think of enough interesting vehicles for conveying what he has to say. Expanding the preacher is the most important part of preaching.

John Henry Jowett had a beautiful picture of the work of the minister. During an early pastorate in the north of England he called on a cobbler who lived in a little house beside the sea. The cobbler's workroom, where they talked, was so tiny that Dr. Jowett asked his friend whether he did not feel imprisoned by so small a space. "Oh, no," the man answered, "if any feelings of that sort begin I just open this door," and he pushed wide a door in the back that opened up to a majestic view of the sea. The narrow room was glorified by the far-flung vista. That, said Dr. Jowett, "expresses my conception of our ministry as we encounter men and women in their daily lot. We are to open that door and let in the inspiration of the infinite." (*The Preacher,* pp. 195–96.) It is a true and ennobling conception, but what happens is never that complete. The minister can never reveal the whole view. He may offer a glimpse through the keyhole or force the door open to a slender crack. The sermon is the aperture through which the congregation sees the infinite. The greatness of the gospel is always scaled down to the preacher's personal limitations. The first task of the minister is to work on himself so that he may become able to open up a larger view.

New preachers, who may despair of ever finding enough sermons, need to know that the sermon source is like an unused spring. At first it may seem to fill up slowly, but the more that is taken from it, the larger is the flow. When we get into the habit of thinking homiletically, then all our reading, conversations, adventures and misadventures, prayers, and meetings produce material for our sermons. A preacher should always be ready to jot down, at any hour of the day or night, ideas he will transfer to his sermon file. A minister who has been for a time in a nonpreaching ministry, and then returns to preaching, usually finds that his springs are very dry until he can work back into the habit of thinking like a preacher.

Ezekiel was told to eat the scroll before he tried to preach. (Ezek. 2:8–3:3) If we are regularly nourished by the Bible, the material for our sermons will steadily increase. Charles E. Jefferson, who counted on intensive Bible study, wrote in the introduction to one of his books, "This is a book of sermons, although the sermons have never been preached. I find that my mind, as I grow older, can create more sermons than it is possible for me to preach." (*The Character of St. Paul,* Introduction.)

My file of sermon ideas, which started with one card, now has four drawers. It has help for Biblical or topical sermons. The file lists over a thousand subjects. The *A* section has cards entitled: Abortion, Absolutes, Acceptance of people, Acceptance of fate, Action, Adiaphora, Adventure, Aging, Alcohol, Altruism, Ambition, Ancestors, Angels, Anger, Animals, Art, Aspiration, Astronomy, Athletics, Atonement, Auto. With each of these the full title is understood to be, "The Christian Faith and . . ." The "Animals" notations are theological, not zoological. Under "Autos" there is nothing on care and repair, but there are thoughts on how the way we drive reveals our attitudes to people. Many of the topics have several subdivisions. In theory, that many subjects would provide a different sermon subject for all the preaching Sundays for years ahead. In fact, the store is too slender for that, but if I had known when I started preaching that there were so many subjects, it would have relieved some apprehensions.

NO TIME FOR THE UNIMPORTANT

Cecil Rhodes opened up a continent, but his dying words were, "So little done, so much to do!" That is every preacher's lament. There is so much that should be said, and so little chance to say it! Ministers may agonize over what they put in their sermons, but they suffer more over what they leave out. Every minor matter that gets into a sermon pushes out forever all the more important things that never will get said. We preachers often form too great an affection for minor matters; a minister may starve a congregation by giving it too many good secondary things. If he delights in Palestinian archaeology, denominational doings, or Reformation history, his congregation may suffer for it. Thomas Merton told how, as a confused student hungry for faith, he started attending a Protestant church in New York. "The minister of the church was very friendly and used to get into conversations about intellectual matters and modern literature, even men like D. H. Lawrence with whom he was thoroughly familiar. It seemed that he counted very much on that sort of thing—considered it an essential part of his ministry. That was precisely one of the things that made the experience of going to his church such a sterile one for me. It was modern religion and politics that he talked about; not religion and God." *(The Seven Storey Mountain.)* The comment on English preaching just before the Wesleyan revival was, "Moonlight ripens no harvests."

The one subject for all sermons, *The Life God Offers Us Through Jesus Christ,* can make almost everything we do or think a proper topic for the pulpit. There are clear Christian implications in organic foods, punctuality, congregational expenses, and Latin hymnody, but these merit a place in sermons only if there is nothing else more pressing. It takes stern self-discipline to bar our passing enthusiasms from the pulpit —the exciting new book, the novel format for a sermon that everyone will find diverting. But such discipline is a necessary part of preaching.

On the eve of the American Revolution, with the British Parliament faced with having to find new measures if the loss of the colonies was to be avoided, King George III used his address to the Parliament to give his views on how cattle could be kept healthy. So it is with some of our preaching on lesser matters. How many tears and agonized expressions we would see if people revealed what is behind their pleasant Sunday-morning faces. How heedlessly callous some of our minor sermons seem in the light of the help we might have given! This does not mean that every sermon should be deadly serious. A sermon that is fun to listen to may sometimes be what is needed most, but there must always be a calculation of the best use of precious time.

Talks outside a church—at graduations, conventions, luncheon clubs— tempt a minister to display his virtuosity with nonreligious themes. He will be wise on such occasions to depart widely from a sermonic style, but he cannot throw away such a chance to say what most needs to be said to those who have little chance to hear it. The only restraints are strategic. If an astronaut were invited to make a speech, people would be disappointed if he talked on gardening, and when a minister is put on a program, it is almost always because of the hope that he will give some insight into the most important matters.

A BALANCED PREACHING PROGRAM

Sermon subjects could be classified: (1) Great Beliefs, (2) Individual Morality, (3) Social Morality, (4) Personal Problems, (5) Christian Disciplines. Each subject could use many styles—expository, topical, dramatic, or biographical.

The rule that a sermon should have a single purpose will usually confine it to one sort of subject, but not always. A Pentecost sermon might get to all five sorts of subjects. An exposition of I John 4:7–21 might go from Great Belief—"God is love"—to Christian Discipline—"he who abides in love abides in God"—to Personal Problem—"there is no fear in love"—to Individual Morality—"he who loves God should love his brother also"—to the Social Morality that all of this implies.

A congregation needs all these subjects. A preacher has to be a general practitioner. A specialist may be invited to the pulpit to deal with something that requires expert help, but week by week the congregation needs a family doctor. All preachers are inclined to indulge their tastes and aptitudes; we like to do most what we do best. Ministers even type themselves, and glory in it—"I am a doctrinal preacher," "Mine is a healing ministry." Ministers may hope that they can stress what their predecessors missed, and that their successors will make up what they lack. But congregations cannot wait that long. In the church every Sunday are people with a wide variety of needs. There are the lonely, the parents who are distraught, those who are cringing from a medical death sentence, the spiritually dry, those who can find no satisfying purpose, those who hate themselves, those who are heathen in some of their relationship, those who are groping for a faith. They must not have to wait too long to get what they are needing.

A preacher must try hard to give his congregation a balanced diet. There is no simple formula for this. The various sorts of sermon subjects do not necessarily deserve equal time. Their relative importance will depend on changing conditions in the lives of the people and in the world. The amount of time to be given to each subject must depend on the pastor's sympathetic perception of what his people need. This should not be improvised. There must be long-range planning. A minister who regularly decides on the spur of the moment what to preach about will present a reasonless assortment that is distorted in favor of his hobbies.

"That parson person, the consistently reasonable man," might dream of wholly rational sermon planning. He might classify the sorts of sermon subjects, and assign to each the proportion it should have. Thus, every ten weeks there would be a sermon of the ten-percent category. Even better, the minister might list all the possible sermon themes he can think of, perhaps several hundred of them, and give each a weight according to its importance. Then he could run the list through a computer and find whether a theme should be used three times a year or once a decade. I have preached sermons which I suspect a computer would allow only once in several lifetimes. It may be just as well that our planning cannot be so systematically programmed, but there must be some rationality to our choice of sermon subjects.

A minister's annual sermon planning helps him see what is needed most. Summer is the usual time for this. Planning looks in both directions. It starts with a review of the last year's themes, and then with the years before that, to see what has been neglected. Then the subjects for the year ahead are designed to correct any imbalance. Of course the designation of sermons will depend on what the minister is prepared to preach about. If the congregation has been hearing too little about prayer, and the minister has no ideas for any sermon on that subject, he knows he will have to order his reading and his thinking to get ready for it. Sermon planning reveals the minister's deficiencies. If a minister keeps a notebook with hoped-for sermons accumulating on each page, some will have to be marked for special attention because their subjects are most needed.

As I reviewed my last year's preaching, I found I had dealt most often with personal problems such as courage, enmity, sex, forgiveness, and depression. There were almost as many sermons on basic beliefs—incarnation, hope, life's purpose, death, prayer. Sermons on group morality were the next most frequent, dealing with such matters as war, democracy, communism, race, and mechanized culture. There was an unusual number of sermons on the Church—renewal, ecumenism, agencies, John Huss. There were glaring omissions; not once had I preached on family life, missions, stewardship, evangelism, poverty, or violence. The next year's plans should try to stress what had been slighted.

Planning for at least a year at a time keeps better balance also in other parts of the service. If the year's hymns and sermon topics are selected at the same time, hymns that have been sung too much, or too little, can be located. Matching these with the sermons is not always necessary. An opening hymn can have its own purpose in lifting hearts in worship. Ministers differ about the importance of having the sermon theme dominate the readings, anthems, prayers, and hymns. That gives a service a unified impact, but there may be advantages in saying several sorts of things. An anthem that is not used to help the sermon may do its own good. It is inconvenient if an anthem, hymn, or reading cannot be used until an appropriate sermon theme comes up, and it may inhibit quality. A minister may wish to change his sermon topic after the anthem schedule has been laid out. An obvious clash of themes and moods should be avoided, and some correspondence can be helpful, but a completely matching ensemble may not be necessary. Some hymns and scripture readings should be used more often than others, which complicates the planning. Planning for a year in advance takes only a fraction of the total time that will be used in the harried working out of choices week by week.

Some denominations specify special themes for more than half the Sundays. This is convenient if the minister wants to preach on that subject on that Sunday. It gets a sermon off to a good start to say, "Today is National Bible Sunday," or "This is Foreign Missions Day." Otherwise, a minister may reasonably assume that he knows what his people need better than do those who make up calendars.

The Venerable Bede is said to be the one who, in the eighth century, first arranged his sermons according to the seasons of the ecclesiastical year. His example was widely followed until, before the Reformation, it was the rule. Many of the Reformers rejected the practice, along with all the feasts, saints days, and fasts that crowded the church calendar. They saw these as pagan practices the church took over when it tried to convert the heathen masses by converting their celebrations. The imposed observances were rejected as hindrances to the Christian's life with God. The Puritans condemned all "observance of days" as "popish superstition"; they insisted that the Sabbath was the only special day God has approved.

It is quite true that the ecclesiastical year cannot be regarded as divinely appointed, but it can be accepted as a man-made device that has great benefit for Christians. We do not get the most from a life that has only the flat monotony of week after week with no variety. We need high points, great occasions, to make the landscape interesting. It is spiritual dullness that keeps people from seeing that birthdays, anniversaries, and religious celebrations are important.

We need reminders. Thanksgiving is not the day for giving thanks; it is the day that makes us aware all year of how much there is for which we should be thankful. Mother's Day is not the day for being nice to mothers; it should make us more appreciative every day. We can be kept aware of the great realities our faith by the recurring reminders of the Christian year. Without Christmas, we would give less thought to the wonder of the Incarnation. Without Lent, we would be less likely to do the soul-searching and repenting that we need.

The church calendar is a teaching instrument. Though its dates were inserted with no plan, the good sense of the church through the years has seen to it that what Christians most need to think about is emphasized. The basic elements of the Christian gospel have their liturgical seasons. The major events in the life of Christ are celebrated. The *kerygma* is proclaimed, the plan of salvation is reviewed in the cycle of the Christian year. The church calendar protects congregations from their preachers' moods and hobbies; its use keeps the choice of what to preach about from being just a personal selection.

The Jewish church used, and uses, the holy seasons to keep the central religious teachings lively. When the early Church decided that, through Christ, it had graduated from the instructions of the Jewish law, the old dates were largely left behind. The New Testament does not have much indication of any special days except the Sabbath. But as the centuries passed, the good and bad reasons for using time symbolically cluttered the hours, days, weeks, and seasons with pious designations. So many conflicting observances were crowded into the same times that dutiful Christians were hard put to know what God required. The eight daily hours of the divine office were fixed for private devotions. Thus the joy at Lauds, and the penitence at Compline, and the rest were assured for every day.

The value of such ordering is clear. So is the danger of making it a substitute for Christianity. The seamy side of it can be seen in the perturbation of the person who cannot worship because the pulpit hangings are the wrong color for the season. The feeling is not just that a custom has been overlooked, but that God has been offended. Some who criticize the giving of a party during Lent could never believe that Paul never heard of Lent, much less that he might have been thinking of such scruples when he condemned recent converts who still "observe days, and months, and seasons, and years! I am afraid I have labored over you in vain." (Gal. 4:10–11) Delight in medievalism may come from the recovery of our heritage, but it can come from the dark recesses of our being. Baptists and Presbyterians are enjoying delicious Gothic shivers at words and dates they just found out about. The printed calendar the United Presbyterian Church supplies its congregations has All Souls' Day on November 2. This date was established when a hermit on a rocky isle came upon a deep cleft from which he could hear the groans of the souls in purgatory. He was told that prayers could hasten their release. If we Presbyterians are remiss in offering such prayers, it is not because we have not been reminded.

There are charts that list the sermon themes that are appropriate for each season of the year. They probably cannot be controlled that closely. It would be too bad for a minister to have to say, "There have been so many depressing things happening lately; I just wish it were the season for me to preach on joy," or "Our groups are getting interested in the work of the Holy Spirit; next June I will get to preach about it."

The proportions of the liturgical year do not fit the needed emphases. The life of Christ and the great beliefs are commemorated from Advent through Pentecost, while the other half of the year has only numbered Sundays and minor celebrations. The calendar recalls what Christ did, but it slights what he said. It gives only one week, Holy Week, to the events to which the Gospels devote a third of their attention. The calendar has no Sunday for the atoning death of Christ. Most church members skip from the Hosannas of the Triumphal Entry to the joy of the Resurrection. We wish they would come to the Good Friday services, but we know quite well that only a small minority ever do, so for most worshippers the liturgical year ignores the cross. If preachers were to follow the lectionary, their Sunday congregations would not be told about the crucifixion. We might wish that some worldwide conclave of theologians would redesign the church calendar so that it might better proclaim the gospel, recapitulate the life of Christ, connect us with our history, and honor the right saints. That does not seem to be impending, but we still have the church calendar as a very useful source of wisdom and beauty, even though it requires a good deal of adaptation.

An ancient method of giving the congregation a broadly representative acquaintance with the Scripture, and with the sermon themes that are based on it, is the use of a lectionary, or pericope. This prescribes the readings for every Sunday of the year and for the major week-day celebrations. The selections are fitted to the chief events of the liturgical year. They are given for one or more years, and are to be repeated. It is felt that a preacher who picks out his own readings is not likely to give so well-proportioned a sampling of the whole sweep of the Bible and its teachings. Thus the texts for the worship and the preaching are decided by the long wisdom of the church, and not by one person's arbitrary choice. The minister is spared the ordeal of deciding what to preach about.

Some branches of the Christian church require their preachers to follow a lectionary; for others it is customary, but not required; for still others it is never heard of. Denominations that use a lectionary testify to the wonderful sense the congregations have of being together, which they get from having the same readings and the same subjects. The church members can get ready for the next Sunday's sermon by following the lectionary in their private and family devotions. Exegetical helps can be supplied to all the preachers. To be backed up by the lectionary is said to give a feeling of stability and a release from fretting.

Those who do not use a lectionary believe that the pastor of a church is better able to know what his people need than are strangers from remote eras and situations. Most of the traditional lectionaries have been modernized, but they still reflect the attitudes of those whose theology and view of Scripture were very different from ours. Selections made by committees in the past have no more claim to represent the traditions of the holy catholic church than do selections that are made today. To get the Bible readings and helps from a denomination is as impersonal as it would be to get them from a publication that offers "Fifty-Two Great Sermon Outlines for the Year." A congregation does not really get an acquaintance with the Bible from hearing the little bits that can be read in church, even if they listen to them. Those with this view question the assumption that a preacher cannot be trusted to give a congregation a good overview of the Bible or a well-balanced sermon diet. A minister who has a reasonably good knowledge of the Bible and who is a conscientious planner should, over a few years, give what his congregation needs far better than can the far-off lectionary makers.

Moreover, say these independents, the best preaching is not prescribed, it springs from life—from what is happening to people, from recent experiences, from felt needs, from current questions. It comes hot from the preacher's mind and heart. This is so necessary that ministers who use the texts they are given are likely to show much ingenuity in getting from them to the sermons they know should be preached. Chrysostom was an early and shining example. The calendar called for him to preach on the transfiguration on a Sunday when he was indignant over the cruel interest the money lenders were charging. He spoke of the great hope of seeing the Lord in his glory. But, he said, if that rapture is to be yours you will have to flee sin—such sin, for example, as exorbitant interest. The rest of the sermon was on usury.

My questions about preaching from a lectionary can be understood as coming from someone who has never done it. I was reared in a denomination where the lectionary is little used, so my uncertainties may come more from an accident of birth than from good reason. My limitations are revealed by my having no explanation for the fact that some of the best preaching comes from ministers who use a lectionary.

Any minister might do well to try preaching from a lectionary for a while. This might open up a new and rewarding approach to preaching. A lectionary is also a valuable checklist. It is likely to show a preacher parts of the Bible he is neglecting. A minister who studies several good lectionaries may discover many passages he knows he ought to use.

I wonder about the practice of taking the Scripture reading from the same sections of the Bible every Sunday—Old Testament and New Testament; or Old Testament, Gospel, and Epistle. For the year as a whole there needs to be some balance, but for any particular Sunday the readings that would best provide a rewarding service might be the Law and the Prophets, or a parable, with an echo of its message from Paul, and another from the Revelation. Sermons often set one Bible passage over against another, which structurally specified readings might not do. A service that has responsive, Old Testament, and New Testament readings is likely to give the Old Testament double time.

On the Friday when President Kennedy was shot, most ministers put aside their sermon plans for the next Sunday and started over. Long-range sermon planning is important, but it often imposes too wide a time lag. No one could have known in advance that the Attica riot would provide a good time for laying prison conditions on Christian consciences. People jest about preachers who have to read the morning paper to find out what they are going to preach about, but current interests and sermons should be related. The best sermons are often extended conversations. As the minister thinks of all the things he wishes he had said, it builds into a sermon. A problem in the church, or in someone's life, or something he reads may impel the minister into such a creative new appreciation of Christian truth that he is on fire with eagerness to bring it to his congregation. He thinks about it when he exercises and it is subject matter for his prayers. Sermons that can come hot from this state are likely to be the most useful ones.

The minister cannot always know months in advance how his thinking will develop. Outlines that looked exciting when the plans were being laid end up in dead-ends. The theme that was designated may be the very one in which the preacher is least interested when that Sunday approaches. It may be good discipline for him to master his moods and work on a subject he knows is important until he gets caught up in it. It is something he has to learn to do for a good many Sundays when the choice is limited—Christmas, Easter, Stewardship Sunday. But a minister should not feel forced to preach a weak sermon on a theme for which he is not ready because some months before he prescribed it for himself. Most of the sermons in a year's plan will probably be preached on their appointed dates, but many will not be. When this upsets the proportion of time that had been intended for the various sorts of subjects, that can be corrected during the year ahead.

CHOOSING THE SERMON SUBJECT

Within the broad outline of a properly balanced sermon program, the choice of which particular sermon to preach must be made. This choice can be determined by three considerations:

1. *The minister should try to please himself.* With all that must be said about avoiding hobbies and providing well-balanced preaching, it still is true that a minister's best sermons will be in the field of his greatest interest. There is no such thing as a well-rounded person—fortunately—and every minister will be naturally stronger in some areas than in others. All who are growing go through phases. There may be a period when a minister is most intent on theological interests; there may be a period when he is so heartsick and indignant over social evils that nothing else seems so important.

Phillips Brooks wrote, "You cannot think of people listening with pleasure or vivacity to a sermon on a subject which they knew the minister thought they needed to hear about, and thought the time had come to preach about, but which they also knew that he did not care for, and did not want to preach upon." (*On Preaching*, p. 155.)

The best sermons start with a conception so engrossing that it keeps racing through the minister's mind when he should be working on other things. Exciting ideas for it keep coming until he suffers over what he has to leave out. Such sermons are not painfully carpentered; they spring into being like prefabricated houses whose builders are out to break a record. Such sermons are exhilarating for the minister and, usually, for the congregation.

But not all sermons can be like that. There are not enough of them, and they are not on all the needed subjects. People have daily problems that cannot wait for help; they will be defrauded by a minister who preaches only on what most grips his interest. There are duty sermons that have to be preached. The minister puts painstaking work into them, not because he is on fire, but because this is a job he knows he ought to do. Strong and useful preaching comes from that. Sometimes, in the midst of hard labor on a duty sermon, the excitement begins to mount. Then, as Phillips Brooks put it, "your sermon shall be like the leaping of a fountain, and not like the pumping of a pump."

The preacher himself most needs to hear sermons on the matters in which he is weakest, and the only preacher he is likely to hear very often is himself. The first beneficiary of any sermon should be the preacher. We all try to make virtues of our weaknesses. Someone who is spiritually retarded will tell himself that he is not the mystical type; someone who is theologically incompetent will pride himself on being practical. A conscientious minister is forced to try to become a whole person. He cannot have a big brain and a shrivelled heart. A minister who would like to avoid preaching about prayer may preach himself into a grateful appreciation of it. If a preacher finds doctrine dull, then doctrine is probably what he and his congregation most need to hear about.

The conclusion will have to be that in the choice of sermon themes a minister should please himself—but not always.

2. *A minister should try to please his congregation.* Periodically some magazine will publish a researcher's survey of what people want most to hear about in church. This is usually set in contrast to another survey of the most frequent sermon themes to show that preachers are not meeting people's needs. Should a minister care very much about that? He is not running a cafeteria. You could almost assume that what people most need to hear about is not what they most want to hear about. Most of us enjoy hearing what the Christian faith can do for us; we do not enjoy nearly as much hearing what it demands of us. We want to be told that God loves us; we do not want to be told that we are sinners. When a minister preaches on the mastery of fear, or on how to have a happy home, or on the constructive use of disappointment, he can expect to hear grateful appreciation from those who were wanting just such help. When he preaches on the evils of America he can expect criticism and unhappiness. A minister is called to do what may be hard and unpleasant. He is to summon the reluctant to duty, to rebuke the erring, to humble the proud, to make the complacent dissatisfied with themselves.

Crowd-pleasing preachers do not rate very high in the Bible. God's prophets were stoned; Jesus was crucified. The Bible is filled with scorn for preachers who tell people what they want to hear. Jeremiah thunders. "An appalling and horrible thing has happened in the land: the prophets prophesy falsely . . . ; my people love to have it so." (Jer. 5:30–31) The preacher may therefore believe that if he is pleasing the congregation he must be failing in his duty because to be faithful is to be rejected.

In this he may be miscalculating because he overlooks an essential fact —he is talking to his fellow Christians. They can be presumed to be just as eager for goodness, and just as indignant over sin, as he is. If his attitude is "It is up to me to tell these hypocrites what they hate to hear," he has forgotten who they are and who he is. On those Sundays when he fears he is offending some, he can know that there are others who in their hearts are urging him on, agreeing with him, praying for him, rejoicing in his courage. They may not rush to the door to say, "Nice sermon, Reverend," but he can know that he is standing taller in their regard. If a preacher is pleasing no one in a church that has any claim at all to be a church of Christ, there is a strong possibility that he is wrong.

A Christian preacher is supposed, among other things, to give Christians what they want and need. Some of the gifts of the Gospel are comfort, strength, reassurance, and joy. Those who scorn "peace of mind" preaching forget how often this is just what Jesus offered—"Go in peace," "Peace be with you," "Peace I give you."

So a minister should please his congregation—but not always.

3. *A minister should try to please God.* As Hugh Latimer was going toward the royal chapel he heard a voice within him say, "Be careful what you preach today because you are going to preach before the King of England." Then he heard another voice that said, "Be careful what you preach today because you are going to preach before the King of Kings." That is the final test the preacher has to pass. In the succession of decisions that go into sermon-making the preacher has to ask not just, "Is this good construction?" or "Will this hold attention?" or "Will this make people think?" but "Is this what God wants said?" That is why prayer is important. With God and his high purposes more clearly in view, the decisions are more likely to be right. In the choice of subjects, sometimes there is an uneasy sense that it is the preacher's sermon, and not God's. The preacher's conscience should give him some hard times. Post-sermon depression is often guilt.

In choosing which sermon to preach a minister should try to please himself—but not always; he should try to please the congregation—but not always; and he should try to please God—always.

A SERIES OF SERMONS

Sometimes it is well to choose a series of sermons, rather than one at a time. The sermons can be related in various ways. It may be a portrait gallery—"Faces Around the Cross," "Old Testament Mothers," "Heroes in the Book of Acts." There may be a series on the parables, the Beatitudes, the Apostles' Creed, or the titles given to Jesus.

There are advantages in a sermon series; often a subject cannot possibly be well presented in the time available for one sermon. It is not rare for a minister to find during his sermon preparation that he simply has to break off unfinished and announce the rest of his sermon for a later Sunday. It is better to plan in advance for several sermons when one would clearly be too scanty. A single sermon on such a subject as the Christian attitude to war, or how to understand the Revelation must be so incomplete that it may leave false impressions. Preaching is supposed to teach. It can be better pedagogy to have solid teaching through a course of sermons than to jump from one subject to another. On some matters, holding on to the interest and building the understanding week by week conserves what would be lost by starting over. Private reading, group study, and discussion can be better promoted with a series than with isolated sermons.

There are advantages for the preacher. When he has studied for and preached a series on Ephesians, prayer, or the early Church Fathers, he may have gained a grasp and a delight that will lastingly strengthen his ministry. A sermon series may be later used for a guest lectureship or a Bible course. If a minister enrolls in continuing education, or undertakes concentrated study by himself, it may give him material for a sermon series.

A course of sermons can be advertised, and interest may build up from week to week. This may increase attendance. People like to look forward to what they will be getting, and they may try not to miss a Sunday for fear of losing an important unit. The idea of having a series is usually welcome, unless it comes too often.

We must also recognize the difficulties with a course of sermons. One of these is lack of variety. Often the preacher and the hearers get thoroughly tired of a course that has to go on and on until the announced end is reached. A woman recently told me how enthusiastic her church had been when the minister began a series of sermons on the Pastoral Epistles, and how wearied they all became when it went on for most of the winter. It is much better to announce a brief series that can be returned to later if it seems too short. A season—pre-Thanksgiving, Advent, Lent—may give good limits. Sometimes a preacher has high hopes for a series because he is enthusiastic about one or two of the sermons, which turn out to be the only good ones. It then moves like a ten-mule team when half the mules are dead. A series monopolizes a section of the year for one sort of subjects, leaving too little time for sermons that are needed more.

The problems are not insurmountable. An occasional series of sermons can be of great value. A sequence on the life of Paul may be the one way that will get many members of the church beyond their vague ideas of who Paul was, and what he did, and where he went. A course on heroes of the Reformation might be a fascinating study of the great doctrines of the Church as these are made exciting through the lives of those who were willing to die for them.

New preachers can look forward happily to never having to run out of sermon topics, and never having to get into ruts. The more they preach, the more they will find to preach about. The New Testament describes the limitless richness and variety of the preacher's task. We are "stewards of the manifold grace of God." (I Pet. 4:10) We are to declare nothing less than "the whole counsel of God." (Acts 20:27) Paul gropes for words to express how much the preacher has to talk about. He is to help his congregation experience more of "the unsearchable riches of Christ," to comprehend "the breadth and length and height and depth, and to know the love of Christ which surpasses knowledge." (Eph. 3:8, 18–19) After 3500 of his sermons had been published, Charles Spurgeon declared, "After thirty-five years I find that the quarry of Holy Scripture is inexhaustible, I seem hardly to have begun to labor in it." (*The Shadow of the Broad Brim*, by R. E. Day, pp. 137–38.)

IX

Sermon Structure

THE NEED FOR STRUCTURE

The strength of a sermon depends on its structure. Let no illusions about the beauty of speaking "straight from the heart" obscure that truth. A girl complained that a young minister's proposal of marriage to her had an introduction, three main points, and a conclusion. We would discount carefully structured expressions of affection, and some ministers tell themselves that the painstaking planning and writing of a sermon make it artificial. But right here is the difference. No girl would want a man to propose as though he knew how, but every congregation wants its minister to preach as though he knows how. They hope he has thought long and hard about how best to convey to them what is on his heart.

If preaching is an art, can there not be free-form sermons? Contemporary arts are trying to escape from pattern and rational design. There is nonrepresentational painting, abstract sculpture, poetry beyond meaning, and music that is nonrhythmic and atonal. If there can be a theater of the absurd, should there not be a pulpit of the absurd? Some ministers have found a good deal of satisfaction in an awareness-evoking style of preaching that transcends the ordinary limits of reason and speech. It has attracted some attention, but not many hearers.

Some arts have their purpose in themselves, but others are means to an end. An attorney's presentation to a court could be art, but it could not be abstract art. A sermon is like an editorial, a speech to the Senate, or a football coach's pregame exhortation—it has a function and it must be carefully designed for just this purpose. It is to inform, to elevate, to reprove, to incite, to open a way for the Spirit who makes young men see visions and old men dream dreams.

The detachment from actuality, which is possible for purely fanciful art, is impossible for preaching, because real life, earthly or heavenly, is its subject matter. It uses abstractions only as labels for reality. A sermon is an organism that has to live and function. A Jacques Lipchitz human figure that is mostly holes has significance, but it would have some trouble breathing and digesting. Some art can have the same working as a Rorschach test—it is not designed to say anything specific but to rouse whatever meanings it can. Some contemporary religious writing and speaking is of this sort. It does not want to be intrusively specific; we are supposed to make of it what we want to. For it, God is not the Father of all love and mercy, but whatever one senses to be ultimate. Jesus is not that Savior who is so vividly described in the Gospels, but a baffling Christ-concept that may be man's response to something in the haze. Truth is not to be given but to be self-generated. Whatever its other uses, the religious Rorschach style is not suited to the pulpit.

Architecture is an art that is much like that of preaching. A limitless variety of styles is possible, but the design must fit the function. An architect can have great freedom of expression, but if he is too independent of blueprints and engineering, his building will fall down.

A sermon that is intelligently planned toward a purpose is not a limitation but a liberation because it enables the preacher to do what he most wants to do. Phillips Brooks put it clearly: "Liberty is the fullest opportunity for man to be and do the very best that is possible for him." Liberty is not looseness. A kite that is released from its tether gets its looseness, but loses its liberty to be a kite. A "free balloon" is the captive of every passing breeze. Jesus said that we discover real living not by wandering all over the map, but on the definite, narrow way. A pianist is not free when he plows the keyboard with his elbows, but when he submits to the requirements for making music. A singer does not release what is surging for expression by uninhibited screeching, but by hitting the notes precisely, with carefully controlled technique. A preacher does not find freedom by ignoring form and structure; these set him free to be a preacher. In the hours of working on a sermon, there is a kind of buoyancy in developing what is already outlined, but there is a wearisome feeling of heavy going in laboring out a sermon with no clear plan.

Ever since Aristotle said "Beauty depends on order," this has been a maxim for speakers. Order simply means "rightness"; it is the opposite of messiness. It means that everything in the speech is exactly where it is, not by accident, but for good reason.

A minister needs to have some design for his sermon in mind before he starts constructing it. If all possible ideas on a text or a topic were accumulated with the hope that an outline would emerge, the sermon might end up just a loose anthology of good thoughts, with only an artificial plan. Dr. James Black made fun of an acquaintance who told him, "I've got three dandy illustrations, and I am looking for a good text." (*The Mystery of Preaching*, p. 110.) A minister may overindulge his brain children; he permits them to go where they do not belong and lets them wreck his plan. Courage to keep intruders out is an essential virtue, and a painful one.

Often, as the material accumulates, the original plan gets modified.

The outline should not be distorted to permit whatever attractive ideas occur, but thinking about details often brings improvements in the big picture. An unexpected direction may appear. The first design for a sermon on the Prodigal Son might show him discovering true freedom through four stages: (a) The unrecognized freedom he had always had at home; (b) the false freedom he had when he left home; (c) the lost freedom in the bondage of the pigsty; and (d) the true freedom he recognized when he got back home. But as the work progresses, a better way of helping the congregation to be free might be seen. To be free the Prodigal Son had to have: (a) A *self* that could use the freedom (he "came to himself"); (b) the *discipline* freedom requires, which he lost in "loose living"; (c) room for free living and thinking—which the harsh confinements of the pigsty did not permit; and (d) purposes worth using freedom for. The second outline is not a desertion of the first one, but a refinement of it.

THE REASONS FOR AN OUTLINE

A minister can no more construct a sermon without an outline than a builder can put up a house without drawings. The sermon outline shows what goes where and why. Some preachers may be able to develop the outline in their heads and work from it. For most of us that would be like trying to play blindfold chess.

The outline is the container in which the sermon is transported. Its divisions keep the contents from sloshing around. In communication terms, it is part of the signal system into which the message is encoded by the Source, and from which it is decoded by the Receiver. (See Chapter VII.) Those who smile at simple sermon outlines may forget that, unless the outline is simple enough to be perceived by the congregation, it loses much of its usefulness. The reasons for a clear outline are compelling:

1. An outline enables a preacher to use his craftsmanship. The knowledge he has of how to hold attention, how to teach, how to stir, how to win agreement cannot be applied to a sermon that is put together by feel.

2. A sermon's faults can be recognized and corrected when a summary of what it says is visibly spread out.

3. An outline keeps the preacher on the track and moving toward the goal as he constructs the sermon.

4. An outline saves working time. It spares the frustrations of getting all snarled in confusing lines of thought which may lead nowhere. Thought flows more freely down marked channels.

5. An outline helps the collecting of material. Its sections are like containers to be filled. Whether the minister is at his desk, reading for his sermon, or thinking about it as he rakes the leaves, he can be assembling ideas if he has a framework in mind.

6. Only with an outline can the right amount of time be allotted to each portion of a sermon.

7. A good outline makes for a good delivery. It gives the preacher a plain path to follow. He knows that comes next because there is a reason for it. He can speak directly to the congregation without having to keep looking at his notes. He can speak with far more expression because he has a story to tell, not just scattered items to give out. A sermon that is a collection of spare parts cannot be delivered with much freedom.

8. Well-organized sermons are more likely to be remembered by the congregation. The ideas are delivered arranged on a framework on which they can be carried home and stored for later use.

9. The preacher's meaning will be far better understood if the sermon has a coherent design.

10. It is much easier to maintain interest in a sermon when its progress can be seen. Motion holds attention. It has some of the excitement of a story with a plot that unfolds toward its climax.

11. An audience needs definite segments, like the innings in a baseball game, the pieces in a concert, or the acts in a play. It is a weary road that has no mileposts. There is a rhythm in listening; if the preacher does not provide for it people will make their own. When he shows he is finishing one section and moving on to the next, hearers turn in their seats, inhale deeply, and are ready to go on again.

THE OUTLINE AND THE CONGREGATION

Should the congregation be told what the outline is? Opinions on this vary. At one extreme is the rule "Tell them what you're going to tell them, then tell them, then tell them what you told them." A preacher who does this will announce main points in advance, summarize what has been said as each one is finished, and at the end review the sermon. This is a good teaching method for some subjects. It helps in understanding and retention, and rescues those whose minds have wandered. At the other extreme is the rule "Don't dangle the skeleton." A "one, two, three" framework can seem pendantic and mechanical. It may suggest that the preacher has a tiresomely prosaic mind. It would contradict the surging, soaring mood of many sermons to try to pack their living truth into neat boxes. Here again we come to the rule for preachers: "Never do anything always." With some sermons the outline should be repeatedly exposed; with others it should not be seen at all.

A body is more beautiful if the bones are not too evident, but if there is good flesh on them, it is reassuring to know the bones are there. If there is a great deal of flesh, the evidence of bones is needed to prevent the impression of a gelatinous mass. Most congregations like to have the course of a sermon explained. The eye can take in the whole structure of a building or a literary composition and keep its parts in order; the ear cannot recognize relationships that well. What is heard will be retained only as a jumble of scattered parts unless the connections are pointed out, perhaps repeatedly. A preacher is often dismayed to find that all anyone got from what he assumed was a well-reasoned exposition of truth were some illustrations or isolated thoughts; this bits-and-pieces comprehension may add up to a complete misunderstanding of the total message. A preview of the course and purpose of a sermon helps people listen understandingly. In some sermons an unabashed recapitulation is appropriate; in others it should be disguised, perhaps as a closing flight of inspiration. But something that will draw a sermon together and make its meaning clear may save it.

Only major points are usually mentioned in a public speech, though hearers may understand subpoints. This differs from writing, where Roman, Arabic, and letter listings can take the subdividing as far as the content calls for. The outline of a sermon on specific matters is a great deal easier to follow than is the outline of a sermon on abstractions.

A sermon will be better grasped and remembered if the titles of its points have some sort of correspondence. They may have a similarity in sound, or in the first letter—"A life must have Purpose, Plan, and Power." The relation may be logical—Hear, Question, Accept—or pictorial—"first the blade, then the ear, then the full grain in the ear." Such devices might seem fatuous, but even the best speakers use them because they can make the difference between a speech being lost and its being followed and remembered. Playing games with the alphabet was not too childish for the Psalmist.

THE QUALITIES OF GOOD SERMON STRUCTURE

Purposiveness

There is an old rule that before a minister starts composing a sermon, he should write down in one terse sentence what its purpose is. It might be, "To bring the Christian faith to bear on family problems," or "To show the relevance of Amos to our time." Until the minister sees definitely what he is trying to accomplish, he cannot plan the structure or assemble the material. When the goal is clearly in view, then everything can be streamlined toward getting there. The great weakness of many sermons is their meandering. They travel in circles, reverse their paths, go off at angles into dead-ends, or take the long way instead of the direct line. If a minister has thought about his purpose until he is very sure just what it is, he may not need to write it at the head of his work sheet. But the exercise of writing out that purpose sentence in a final form that is clear, concise, and definite is useful, even for experienced preachers.

A sermon often accomplishes little because the preacher mistakes a topic for a purpose. (See Chapter III.) A topic tells what the sermon is about; a purpose tells what the sermon is trying to do. "An Explanation of the 23rd Psalm" is a topic; "To make people think of the Lord as their Shepherd" is a purpose. "A Study of Various Forms of Prayer" is a topic; "To help people pray better" is a purpose. This mistaking of topics for purposes is the reason for the many interesting and informative sermons which do not make any real difference to anyone. To explain, to instruct, and to arouse are not ends in themselves, they are means to an end. Sermons on David and Jonathan, the poetic forms in the Psalms, forgiveness, or the causes of crime are appropriate in a church only if they will contribute to the life in Christ or the doing of God's will. Therefore the stated purpose of the sermon, which should be so clear before the preparation starts, must say how the sermon will do something Christ wants done, in persons and in the world.

Unity

A sermon cannot serve two purposes; zig-zagging toward different goals will result in reaching neither of them. There may be secondary benefits. A sermon on the Sovereignty of God might say some important things about making one's nation an idol, or a sermon on nationalism as a false religion might exalt God's Sovereignty, but the useful secondary should be introduced only if it serves the major goal. When a sermon approaches some subject about which the preacher has strong feelings he is tempted to go off on an excursion. That always steals force from the purpose for that day. Sometimes the apparent purpose is not the real one—which may be subterfuge, or just good psychology. A minister who is trying to induce the church to buy new hymnals may get at it through a sermon on worship, but he, at least, knows what his purpose is.

A preacher may switch goals in mid-course without knowing he is doing it. A sermon on John 3:16, "For God so loved the world that he gave His only Son, that whoever believes in Him should not perish," can start out as a sermon on the incarnation and turn into a sermon on salvation. A sermon on Proverbs 20:27, "The spirit of man is the candle of the Lord," can begin by telling of enlightenment by the Holy Spirit and end by a summons to be burned out in the service of the Lord.

The sermon that turns out to be diffuse collections of useful thoughts, as the minister yields to the temptation to put in whatever he thinks is good, can be the result of starting work too late. As Sunday approaches, the preacher does not have enough to say about his topic, so he fills the time with what is related but not straight to the point. Sometimes each major division turns out to be a sermon in itself, so the whole is a series, with each sermonette distracting attention from the others. Each division of a sermon should be required by its author to be a subdivision of the single purpose, and to contribute to it. Congregations recognize and resent sloppy thinking—"I never could figure out what he was getting at."

Holding to a topic or text does not necessarily give unity. I heard a sermon on Christian hospitality that, with complete logic, dealt with church fellowship, xenophilia, the Christian home, and the Lord's Supper. A sermon on Rev. 14:3, "A new song before the throne," might properly deal with worship, heaven, harmony, and beauty. Those are not facets of a subject, they are separate subjects that need separate sermons.

A strong, clear statement of the sermon's major truth can come in again and again, like a refrain, and be used as the conclusion. No one who listens can fail to know what the sermon is about. Repetition can lodge the sentence in each person's memory, like a stake to which other recollections of the sermon will be tied. It might be such an assertion as "God will never let all the doors to happiness be closed," "Church membership is not a connection, it is a way of life," "There is no substitute for religion in the running of a church," or "Christ is either Lord of all, or He is Lord of nothing."

Progress

Anyone coming down the aisle can steal attention from the preacher, because what is in motion is more noticed than what stays in the same place. For the same reason people lose interest in a sermon that is not getting somewhere. A lecture can have a series of equivalent passages that can come in any order—front to back or back to front. A sermon has to move onward, from one passage to the next. Many a congregation will understand the irritation of the presiding officer of the Westminster Assembly; when the same speakers kept returning to the same points, he admonished them, "I desire that you would so order your debates as not to go backwards."

Too many sermons are static; they circle around the same idea so long that the congregation is begging, "Let's get on with it." Before the composition of the sermon starts, the preacher needs to know how it is going to move toward its goal. The plan for this is the sermon outline. The outline shows how the sermon starts and how it moves, stage by stage, to achieve its purpose. The outline shows how each part grows out of what came before and prepares for what comes after it. It is the lack of sequence that makes sermons boring and ineffectual. Often a sermon is just a random collection of odds and ends, more or less related to the same subject; it could just as well have started at the other end or in the middle. It is like the sermon John Oman described: "It was like seeing Eskimo dogs that had been tied all around the sledge, for the subject was not advanced, but merely pulled about."

Sometimes the problem comes from mistaking an index for an outline. An outline is a plan for development. It is like a blueprint which shows how the parts are related to each other, and why. An index is a classified list of items. A preacher with a neat, orderly mind may present his subject from the point of view of the Bible, theology, and contemporary thought, and regard that arrangement as his outline. But it is really only a set of pigeonholes. That plan would be useful for a cataloguer, but is useless for a congregation. An outline is dynamic; an index is static. An index sermon on Rev. 3: 316, "You are lukewarm," might tell how a church can be lukewarm in (1) faith, (2) worship, (3) fellowship, and (4) service.

An outline sermon on that text could tell: (1) What it is for a church to be lukewarm; (2) why it happens; (3) the ways in which our church is lukewarm; and (4) what can be done about it.

The sermon structure should be rational. Often it is obvious that the minister is not thinking clearly. Subordinate matters are presented as major points. A sermon on sin might have as its divisions: I. Personal Sin, II. Collective Sin, III. Lust, IV. Sins of Omission, V. David's Sin, VI, Racism. A little thought would show that those have to be: I. Personal Sin, (1) Lust, (a) David's Sin, II. Collective Sin, (1) Racism. Sins of omission would not belong here at all.

There are some natural sequences:

1. The negative normally comes before the positive, because the untruth prepares us to understand this truth. A sermon for Pledge Sunday might explain that Christians give to the church not to buy their way into heaven, nor to feel pleased with themselves, nor to help the church reach a percentage goal, but to make the church a stronger instrument for Christ to use. If the right motive were put first, the effect would be weaker.

2. The problem is stated before the solution: Remorse for wrongs we have done is a crippling burden, but we cannot easily get rid of it; "I just can't forgive myself" is dreadfully true. Then can we ever think of ourselves without cringing? Christ shows us how we may be free.

3. The abstract comes before the specific. A sermon on Grace might define the word as "God's unmerited favor," and discuss it theologically as the result of God's love and man's inability, and then go on to tell how we can experience it in our marriages, our jobs, and our inner upsets.

4. The remote comes before the immediate. A sermon on courage might move from examples in the Bible and Church history and the contemporary scene to show how we also can be heroes.

The sermon introduction is an important exception to (3) and (4). A sermon that begins with the abstract or remote may attract few listeners. It is better to start with something very real and definite which will show people why the abstract or remote, which may immediately follow, are so important.

The best sequence for a sermon depends upon its purpose. If the intention is to persuade, then the outline should be logical. Classical rhetoric was largely devoted to the art of persuasion, and a preacher needs to know its rules about building up an argument and avoiding fallacies. If a sermon is intended to teach, then the outline would be pedagogical, with provision for such devices as summary and repetition. If a sermon is intended to inspire, or motivate, then the plan should allow for a buildup of emotion. For this, a progression through main points and subpoints might not reach the goal. For this sort of sermon, the sequence may be more like the plot of a story than like a builder's diagram. The plan might be: When this has been said, then the hearers will be ready for this, and then I can go on to this, so that. . . . A blueprint and a plot both require scrupulous planning. Neither has any place for meandering.

It is very important for the preacher to make his sequence clear. When he goes from one idea or one passage to the next, the congregation needs to see the connection. It may be quite clear to him, but the hearers, not being able to read his mind, may feel that he has changed the subject with no reason. When a transition is unclear, then the value of what went before it is lost, and what comes after dangles without support in mid-air.

Those who speak as they write may forget that a hearer cannot look back to get the connections. Spoken transitions have to be caught at full speed. A speaker has to assume that some of his audience will not be alert, or that they will momentarily wander off on profitable reflections of their own. They need help to catch up with the preacher. It takes plain transitions to connect an illustration or a quotation with the sermon; transitions are the couplings which keep the train of thought from coming apart.

Transitions are made by connector words: *therefore, however, consequently, besides, moreover, yet.* Transitions can be explained: *having considered, since this is so, we must now.* The outline can be shown by the voice. A pause or a change of tone may mean, "We have finished with that; now hear this. . . ."

It does no good for the preacher to say, "In the third place, . . ." if the congregation is unclear about what the first or second were. With each addition, he may need to recapitulate what came before—" '*The earth is the Lord's.*' We have seen, first, that God as Creator has his purposes and, second, that we as custodians have our duties. Now, third, we can be sure that. . . ." Communication studies have discovered that *redundancy is one of the most important elements in clarity and in learning.* The review of his major points gives the preacher a chance to repeat in the same words the most important things he wants the congregation to remember. Elaborate wording weakens this. These statements should be strong and clear.

There has been some recent prejudice against "linear" sermon construction. McLuhan has taught that modern minds are conditioned less by the linear perceptions of the printed media and more by the all-at-oneness of television. All-at-once styles of preaching have not yet won wide acclaim from congregations. There may be here a confusion of the stages in getting a sermon to the congregation. When the minister is assembling the material it is coming at him from all sides. But when he is delivering the message to the congregation, then he has to use the communication forms that are most appropriate for that situation, and these are still largely linear. Nothing could seem more aimless than the meandering of a bee that is gathering honey. But when she is ready to deliver it, the little insect makes a beeline for the hive and deposits the honey in precise containers. We can hope the preacher's mind and spirit rove freely while the sermon is being assembled, but when he is ready to deliver it, he is in the beeline stage. A vacation is delightfully free from linear living, but to get to the vacation spot requires very orderly planning and progression. The sermon takes us to where we can revel in our faith.

Exceptions to Logical Sequence

The progress of thought should usually be logical, but not always. The build-up may be emotional. Antony's funeral oration is Shakespeare's model of how to incite an audience. It has three things to say: Caesar loved you, his murderers are scoundrels, go and punish them; but it does not finish with them in that order. Instead, it keeps coming back to them, at ascending levels of intensity, until the crowd is in a killing frenzy. A sermon can have that sort of structure. There should be progress in it, so that it moves in a definite direction, and does not just wander around until it collapses—but the progression can be emotional rather than logical. It may keep coming back to the same subject like a refrain, in such a way that the hearers are being increasingly convinced, or stirred into action. This requires highly perceptive and intelligent planning, with each sentence skillfully placed for its effect.

Some excellent sermons have no perceptible divisions or subdivisions at all. Each sentence flows into the next as thought flows, with no breaks. This is the hardest sort of sermon to build because its structure is the opposite of careless. Each part has to be precisely planned for its effect. A spider building a web may appear to be wandering, but there is a necessary reason for each seemingly aimless maneuver. Conrad's novels appear to be drifting from scene to scene with no reason, but a great story is taking shape. The reader is often unaware of a fiction writer's painstakingly worked-out designs. A biographical sermon, a sermon that is seeking to rouse a strong emotional reaction, or a sermon that is intended to be a memorable experience for the listeners may seem to have no outline, but its design will require specially painstaking craftsmanship.

Another obstacle to logical sermon structure may be the Bible. The text can make hard problems for good homiletical design. The thought in the Epistles is often more rhythmic than progressive. In the imposing last verse of the book of Jonah, the prophet is asked whether God should not have pity on a great city full of people, with many thousands of children, "and also much cattle." That would make an impressive three-point climax for anyone who prefers cows to people.

We should hold as nearly as possible to a logical sequence, but human beings are not machines, and human necessities may require the outline to be skewed. Psychological considerations may override the logical. When a preacher has rationally demonstrated that something should be done, he must interrupt his line of thought to stir the emotions that make people want to do it. An abstract sequence has to be broken by something from real life that brings it down to earth. Minds grow weary and attention wanders. When the going has been heavy, something has to be put in for relief.

People listen and understand better when their minds are fresh. They also remember better what is heard then. If a sermon states errors and then answers them, the congregation will be in a better condition to understand and remember the errors than the refutation. By all logic, the most important things a minister has to say come when he has built up to them, but that may be the time when the congregation is least able to be impressed. A minister may be wise to put the great things he believes first, and the problems with them later. A sermon is not a cliff hanger which maintains suspense by keeping people guessing how it is coming out. The enjoyment and understanding of a sermon can be increased if the congregation knows from the beginning what is going to happen. The minister can state the answers before he looks at the questions from all sides. After a clear affirmation, he can go on, "Some might say, . . ." or "In our worst moments we may doubt. . . ." A preacher can put the most important things he has to say in a few strong sentences and use them in the introduction; then the sermon builds up to them.

The responses of the hearers may play havoc with an outline; the chagrined preacher discovers that they have their own priorities. Something his design lifted up for great importance may make no impression, while a dramatic little story he used only to illustrate a minor point may be what everyone remembers. The preacher has to take account of this sort of emphasis. Whatever is most interesting is major, whatever is boring is minor, no matter what the outline shows.

Symmetry

The time and emphasis that are given to a sermon's parts should correspond to their importance. Beauty requires harmonious proportions, and so does sense. A sermon on the Trinity that gave the Persons five, two, and ten minutes would have heretical implications. Egregious disproportion is confusing. The hearers get lost when one main division is given three minutes and another, twelve.

One teacher, two generations ago, used to tell his sermon classes to determine how many pages filled the sermon time. Two of these were subtracted for the introduction and conclusion. The remaining blank pages were to be put in three equal stacks. When the sheets in each stack were filled, that point was finished. Surprisingly luminous thoughts used to flow down such tidy channels, but most modern preachers would find a precise proportioning artificial. Topics that are parallel in outline do not always need equal time. But a reasonable attempt at symmetry is important.

When the sermon outline has been made, the preacher must estimate how much time each part merits, and try to hold to something like those limits. This may save him from the typical preacher fault of using up so much time in the beginning that what comes toward the end is slighted. Many a sermon has the ungainly figure of a humpback whale. Just when the most telling part of the sermon comes, the preacher has to jettison much of his best material and rush for the exit. He does not finish, he just quits.

There should be symmetry, not only in the time that is given to each part, but in the emphasis and highlighting. Important matters should not be duller than the less important. The most determined efforts to make a sermon lively and impressive should be devoted to the parts the preacher most wants the congregation to remember.

Good sermon structure is a secondary virtue. The primary requirements are something important to say and an interesting way of saying it. Good structure does not make good preaching, but poor structure prevents it.

X

Examples of Sermon Structure

A preacher needs a wide variety of sermon styles. Never let the congregation guess what you are going to do. If they know as soon as you get into your topic how you will treat it, there is no novelty and no excitement to keep them listening. Those who anticipate the preacher's methods are inclined to be bored.

A speaker who has the same audience every seven days will have to have many sorts of structures to keep his sermons fresh. What is even more intimidating, the structures have to be his own. No congregation wants a parrot in the pulpit. A sermon is truth transmitted through the personality of the one who gives it. Books offer sermon designs, with helpful illustrations. Bible commentaries suggest outlines. There are even mail-order companies that will deliver a year's supply of sermons. (When someone asked my wife whether I used this service, she answered, "If he does, I wish they wouldn't get the sermons to him so late on Saturday nights!") But a minister who takes the role of preacher has to be the preacher. Even using someone else's outline spoils the creative excitement that is necessary for sermon-making. A preacher needs constantly to study sermons from all sorts of sources, not so that he can copy their ideas, but because they are the best possible stimulation for his own inventiveness. They will set him to speculating about new approaches.

1. *The two-point sermon.* Many sermons fall naturally into two parts. It is the form for contrasts—the material and the spiritual; life and death; truth and error; conservative and liberal; theory and application; denial and affirmation.

Many texts have two parts. Isaiah criticizes those who forsake God's deep well and use shallow cisterns. Psalm 137, from early in the exile, asks hopelessly, "How shall we sing the Lord's song in a foreign land?"; and then Psalm 139, from late in the exile, tells how marvelously they did sing it. Man looks on the outward appearance, but God looks on the heart. Seek—and find.

2. *The three-point sermon.* Much fun is made of the conventional three points, but there are reasons for them. A two-point sermon does not

offer enough chance for movement and variety; four may tax the memory. The treatment of many sorts of subjects seems to work out best in threes— the principle, its application to reality, and what to do about it; the arguments for, the arguments against, and the solution; past, present, and future. Jesus is Prophet, Priest, and King. Salvation includes justification, sanctification, and adoption. Many texts have three parts: "I am the way, and the truth, and the life." "Ask . . . , seek . . . , knock . . ." Three may seem to be mystically ordained, as in the Trinity, and the three dimensions, and the fact that the tripod is the most stable base. Perhaps a better reason is that three is the number of points that can be adequately developed in a sermon of ordinary length.

3. *More than three points.* There are often reasons for four or more divisions. The sower's seed fell on four sorts of ground. The holy city is foursquare. Jesus named six acts of Christian charity. There are seven last words, nine beatitudes, and ten commandments. The more rapid motion through a greater number of points may make a sermon seem livelier. There is a great advantage for a hard-pressed preacher; the more points there are, the easier it is to find a little something to say about each of them. A sermon on the ninefold fruits of the Spirit (Gal. 5:22) is a good one for the Sunday after the annual convention.

4. *The logical construction.* The design in which there is a necessary progression from each point to the next one is much used, and for good reason. This is the way a good mind works; this is the course by which thoughtful people are brought to right conclusions. The progression might be: (1) What is wrong; (2) the damage it does; (3) the remedy; or (1) good; (2) better; (3) best; or (1) could be; (2) should be; (3) must be; (4) now go do it.

A sermon on the denomination's fund for disadvantaged people might have this sequence: (1) The reasons for the fund; (2) its practical philosophy; (3) how the money will be used; (4) why this is essential Christian action; and (5) how to make your contribution.

A special sort of logical construction is the syllogism, with its major and minor premises and conclusion. (Those terms would not be mentioned.) John Baillie's argument for life everlasting takes the form: *Major premise*—a good God will not discard what has value; *minor premise*—human souls have value; *conclusion*—a good God will not discard human souls.

The Hegelian dialectic, as a thinking process, is as useful for Christians as for communists. By setting two opposites, the thesis and antithesis, against each other, it reaches a synthesis. For a sermon this could be: (1) God's will is peace; (2) God's world is full of conflict; (3) be an instrument of God's peace. A sermon on predestination might say: (1) If God's will is sovereign, he decides everything; (2) if God's children are moral beings, they must make decisions; (3) God in his love limits his sovereignty.

The logically progressive structure is often used with a figure of speech: root, trunk, fruit; base camp, climb, summit; planting, cultivating, reaping. A sermon on *Helping People Walk With God* could picture those who pass up the church. The stages might be: (1) CONTACT—getting them to look toward the church; (2) CULTIVATION—bringing them up the front walk till they have looked into the church and its faith; (3) COMMITMENT—bringing them inside the door as members; (4) CONSERVATION—putting arms around the new members and walking up the aisle till they get a good start in their new life.

5. *The psychological construction.* Popular courses on public speech or salesmanship like to recommend outlines that depend entirely on the hearers' reactions. The steps are often colorfully named. Such an outline might be: (1) *Bang!*—get attention; (2) *Bait*—indicate you will talk about what the people want to hear; (3) *Buildup*—explain the matter; (4) *Bonanza*—picture a happy result; (5) *Buckle down*—tell what to do.

Psychological and logical considerations can be combined. For example, you may: (1) Get attention by the way you introduce the sermon theme; (2) relate the theme to the hearers' needs; (3) show how things can work out; (4) tell the difference it will make; and (5) call for a response. A sermon on *hate*, both psychologically and logically constructed, might work out like this: (1) Story of a man who killed his business partner; (2) how enmity poisons our lives; (3) the cure for this that Christianity offers; (4) the joy of freedom from bad relationships; (5) what to do about it today.

6. *Separate units.* There may be a sermon in which the segments are all related to the single topic, but with no buildup from one to the next. An example would be a sermon on the names Jesus gave himself—the Good Shepherd, the Bread of Life, the Vine, the Door, the Light of the World. A sermon on the Women at the Cross, the Great Promises, or Where the Church Is Failing might be of this sort. The disadvantage of this design is that it does not readily give the congregation the feel of motion. It should be cumulative, however. There may be an emotional buildup, or the completing of a picture.

7. *Choices.* A variety of possible views may be presented. "As a Christian confronted by the growing use of drugs in this community, your response may be . . . , or . . . , or . . ." A sermon on duty can weigh the possible actions in a given situation. A sermon on faith can consider different views. Various ways of meeting personal problems can be presented. Often the preacher will tell which choice he thinks best fits the Christian faith. Sometimes he will make the best case he can for different points of view, and leave the decision to the hearers.

8. *Questions.* A series of questions can make an interesting outline. "Do you know why you came here today?" "Are you getting what you want?" "Will it make any difference to you tomorrow?" There can be a sermon on the questions Jesus asked, or the questions that were asked him, or today's five most urgent questions, or the questions about prayer, or what people want to know about the World Council of Churches. This method offers the interest of a dialogue; it must therefore have something more than the minister's asking questions of the congregation, and answering them himself. It can be like an honest dialogue if the preacher quotes conversations he has had, or studies contemporary attitudes or whatever will give him answers from outside himself if he is

asking the questions. He needs questions from outside himself if he undertakes to give the answers. "Question box" sermons can be unusually interesting. There may be an actual box in the church, or questions can be solicited by a mailing.

9. *Polemic.* Today absent opponents do not get the drubbing in the pulpit that used to entertain parishoners who love a one-sided fight, but there is still need for an answer to false views. There are seductive errors, damaging misconceptions, and corrosive cynicisms that must be dealt with. It is often more dramatic and effective to confront untruth by answering its spokesmen than it is to speak in the abstract. Voltaire, Freud, and Marx have played the role of the heavy in many pulpit dramas. Contemporary pagans, popularizers of false philosophies, and exponents of corruptions have to be opposed. The timeless struggle between good and evil is not imaginary. There are alluring sources of intellectual disease, and prominent defenders of ruthless political attitudes; so there will always be occasion for sermons to refute views that are seen to be dangerously misleading.

The old books on homiletics gave major attention to "polemics." They found good texts for it: "Be able to give instruction in sound doctrine and also to confute those who contradict it." (Titus 1:9) "Always be prepared to make a defense to anyone who calls you to account for the hope that is in you." (I Pet. 3:15) "Contend for the faith which was once for all delivered to the saints." (Jude 3) There was good advice on polemical preaching: (1) Give close attention to clear definitions; confusion about terms defeats many arguments; (2) study the rules of logic, which preachers are often accused of ignoring (look up the article on *Fallacies* in an encyclopedia); (3) avoid superlative, extravagant statements; (4) be scrupulously fair, because the opposition does not get to answer; (5) throw the burden of proof on the other side; (6) use testimony; (7) give your best arguments first.

Congregations may enjoy the spectacle of their preacher, with the gleam of battle in his eye, advancing to the fray; their praise may tempt him to be overly addicted to this preaching style. But the polemic preacher risks presenting himself as narrow, disdainful, opinionated, or out of his depth, so let him be aware of the dangers and then, when a strong word is needed, speak out with all his might.

10. *Self-Debate.* There are difficult matters which church people need to consider in the full light of their Christian faith, and their church should be their helper in this. The minister knows he should use his sermons to give all the help he can, but he does not wish to be a partisan advocate for any side. He may be undecided himself, or not have an adequate grasp of the subject, or not want to use his access to the pulpit to get an unfair advantage for his personal opinions. The right way might be to get speakers for the various opinions, but that is not always possible. The minister may therefore undertake to do it all himself. He makes the best case he possibly can for the opposing views, hoping he will at least have moved the hearers ahead in their thinking as Christians.

This is a possible method for sermons on such subjects as drug control, capital punishment, abortion, or censorship. Whenever I have preached on pacifism, I have made the most convincing statement I could for the pacifist position; then I have given the Biblical, logical, and practical reasons against pacifism; then I have offered the help of discussion and reading to those who want it. Does that encourage in the congregation a detached attitude when there should be strong opinions? I think it is more likely to move people from indifference or superficiality into the hard thinking that can bring them to conclusions.

11. *Not this, or this, or this, but this.* The advantage of this structure is that it makes the truth plainer by setting it against various false views. To the question "Who is Jesus?" can be given the answers in the Gospels, which are like some that are given today. He was seen as a political Messiah, as an Old Testament style prophet, as a charasmatic teacher—but the true answer was Peter's "You are the Christ, the Son of the living God." Christian peace can be presented, not as passivity, placidity, nor detachment, but as powerful action with no inner conflict. The best way to deal with such questions as what a Christian is, what heaven is, why church membership is important, or what we owe our country may be to consider first the wrong or partial answers. Then, with the misunderstandings cleared away, the sermon can give the better answer.

Sometimes the right view is given with each false one. A sermon on "What shall I do with Jesus who is called Christ?" (Mt. 27:22) might try the answers: (1) Remain puzzled by him; (2) dislike him; (3) be indifferent to him; (4) admire him, and set over against each of these, "Take him as the Lord and Master of your life."

12. *The reverse sermon.* The preacher may hope to astonish and stimulate the congregation by saying the opposite of what they expect—"Christianity is done for," "Democracy has always failed," "What marriage needs is more hatred and less love." The shock might be in the sermon's title: *The Harm That Good Men Do, The Curse of Being Human, Get Rid of the Church.* Some good things can be said in the course of defending the proposition, which in the end usually turns out to be as harmless as honeydew. This is less a technique than a trick; it may get the preacher credited with being profound and emancipated—"That guy sure makes you think!" There may be a sudden reversal at the conclusion—"Evangelism is out of date, bad manners, impossible for our sort of congregation—now let's get to it!" This method cannot be repeated often, but it has its uses.

13. *Structures for expository sermons.* Most of the structures listed in this chapter can be used with sermons that start either with a text or with a topic. There are special structures that can be used in the exposition of longer passages.

a. One method is to go through the passage just as it comes. This is difficult with passages that change the subject with each verse, but it is ideal for others.

b. When themes weave in and out, it may be well to select and rearrange—"In verse twelve of the next chapter Paul returns to. . . ."

c. Often, without doing too much damage to the facts, an outline can be imposed upon a passage. This will be partly artificial; the Bible authors did not write from outlines. But it can help hearers get hold of what is said.

d. A fanciful title may indicate a fresh approach to a passage: *Your Manufacturer's Instructions* (the Ten Commandments); *"Herr Baedeker Enters Heaven* (Rev. 21); *The Christian's Personality Inventory* (Rom. 12); *The Constitution of the Christian Church* (The Sermon on the Mount, with Article I—Requirements for Membership [Mt. 5:3–12]; Article II—Duties of Members [Mt. 5:13–16]; Article III—Bylaws [Mt. 5:17–48]; Article IV—Ritual [Mt. 6:1–18]; Article V—Finance [Mt. 6:19–34]; etc.).

14. *The figure of speech.* An analogy can carry a whole sermon. This was a method Jesus used—the vine, the sower, the bread of life. The prophets liked to base an extended message on a single figure—the potter, the unfaithful wife, the river of life. It can be a very effective way of making a sermon colorful, clear, unified, and easy to remember. The Bible's images serve well for this—the pillar of salt, the body of Christ, the shepherd. There can be sermons on modern images—*"The Theology of Westerns," "God's Radar," "Guided Missiles and Misguided Men."* Astronomy, physiology, botany, athletics, physics, art, ships, and planes are common sources for stretched-out illustrations. There is danger that playing with the image will be the whole sermon so that it says nothing that is not obvious. The figure is not content, it is a framework for content.

15. *Literature as a base.* A play, story, poem, biography, nonfiction book, or essay may give the background for an entire sermon; but a review or a retelling of the writing is not a sermon. The sermon is the minister's transmitting to the congregation what happened to him when he read the piece. If it suggested to him fresh insights into Christian truth, and if it kept opening up more as his mind returned to it, it is likely to provide a vivid and interesting sermon.

Arthur Miller's play, *Death of a Salesman,* has inspired some good preaching. In Peter DeVries' novel, *The Blood of the Lamb,* the narrator has had a strict Calvinist upbringing. He also has had an erratic life and a bad marriage. His little girl is in the hospital with cancer. She dies on the day he takes her a beautiful cake with her name on it in blue icing. That evening he stumbles from a bar past a church with a stone figure of Christ on the cross. He takes the cake from the box and hurls it squarely into Christ's face, and watches the icing drip down on the sidewalk. A sermon that interacts with the incidents which mark the father's round trip to despair has a chance to say a good deal about the problem of suffering.

Long poems like John Masefield's *The Everlasting Mercy,* and Kipling's

The Explorer can be unfolded to support an entire sermon. A short poem, like Markham's "Outwitted," or Ella Wheeler Wilcox' "One Ship Drives East" can be used repeatedly like a refrain, as its image illustrates each stage of a sermon's progress.

Hymns may be used for sermons in two ways: A story about the author, or about some effect the hymn has had, can be the background for a sermon; also, many hymns are short sermons in poetry, with each verse developing the theme—"Take my life and let it be . . ." and "Jesus calls us . . ." are examples. The congregation sings the hymn, and each verse may be sung or read with the portion of the sermon that is based on it. A bonus with hymn sermons is the increased love of hymns, and a chance to learn new ones.

Biographies provide some of the most inspirational and instructive sermons. Kant believed that morality could best be acquired through biography. The lives of religious persons can teach church history and doctrine; sermons can introduce us to those who will enrich our lives.

When a minister reads a book or an article that rouses him to Hallelujas, he may share the experience with the congregation. The sermon is not what the book or article says, but what it points to. A whole sermon may be based on a brief quotation. There is the magnificent reply of the early Saxon missionary, Brindon, to King Brude of England, who had asked, "What shall I expect to find if I accept your gospel and become Christ's man?" Brindon's answer was, "If you become Christ's man, you will stumble on from wonder unto wonder, and every wonder will be true." There is a sermon on Jesus in Browning's words, "Through such souls alone God, stooping, shows sufficient of His light for us in the dark to rise by, and I rise!"

Sometimes, of course, the sermon will be based on literature in reverse. William Ernest Henley might be reassured to know how many sermons have been preached to deny his "I am the master of my fate: I am the captain of my soul." Reverse use is polemic preaching.

It can be objected that sermons should be based on the Bible. It is true that what people want from the preacher is not reflections on his general reading. The Church's purpose is not to provide classes on great literature. But non-Biblical writings can set the scene for the conveying of Biblical truth. A literary and a Bible reference can be interwoven.

16. *Original fiction.* Not every minister is a Henry Van Dyke, but every minister has one advantage the professional cannot match—he can produce what is planned for his particular congregation and its needs. In a Christmas family service, with little children and grandparents attending, a story may be the best way to reach everyone. If no new story with a worthy Christmas import can be found, the minister's only hope may be to write his own. The best way for him to warm up for this is to read all the Christmas stories he can find. However unsuitable most of them may seem, some place among them his imagination is likely to catch fire. What he writes may be an adaptation of one of them or a combination of several. It is more likely to have no clear resemblance to any of them,

but he could not have produced his if he had not read the others. Congregations have an indulgent attitude to their minister's fiction; they are likely to prefer it to the best that is in books.

Some ministers write sermons in dramatic form—as monologues, dialogues, or with a larger cast. These are presented as the musings of Samson, chained to the mill; what the Prodigal Son's elder brother told a friend; or the trial of Jesus in the setting of a modern courtroom. This can be good Bible teaching, and powerful preaching. The first experiments may have mishaps. A monologue that is addressed to an imaginary hearer may present the unexpected problem of how, before an audience, to talk toward the same empty spot for fifteen minutes. The minister may enlist other actors, or play several parts himself. Some ministers do their dramas to such good effect that they are important events in the church calendar. Some do them in costume, but much more modest attempts can be useful. To write and give a drama is much more difficult than to write and give a story, but it does not have to be masterfully done to be a welcome change in sermon styles.

A sermon may be preached from an imaginary situation. The minister may announce that the officers have decided to close the church and sell the building. Then the sermon can consider getting a group to buy the building to start a new church that can be just what a church ought to be. The preacher may imagine that a newly discovered Dead Sea Scroll proves that Jesus was not crucified, but died of old age, and he may then investigate what we still have left for Christian faith. In the early 1960s Helmut Thielicke in Germany preached on what he would say to young Communists on the day his country is reunited. John Calvin Reid gave a sermon on marriage that the Devil wrote for him. After a friend of mine had a conversation with the man who was robbing his house, I preached a sermon that took the form of a conversation a church member might have had in that situation with a robber who had a sense of humor and a faint interest in religion.

17. *One word.* A sermon can be planned around a single word. "What do you mean when you say 'Amen' at the end of a prayer?" the minister might ask. Then from the Bible, and from what people feel they mean, he can identify such meanings as the assurance of God's power, the acceptance of God's will, the alignment with God's purposes, the adoration of God's holiness. A sermon on *The Deadly Sin of Accidie* could introduce an interesting and useful word, and give help with a common ailment. There are sermons in word origins. To be *dissipated* is to be scattered. The *kind* accept others as their kin. Church traces to *kyros*—power—it is a powerhouse. To *saunter* is the lazy gait of the shiftless vagrants who pretended to be going to the Holy Land. They would knock on the doors of the pious and say, *"à la Sainte Terre,"* looking for handouts. The question, "Are you sauntering through life?" could cut in several ways. The great words of religion are instant sermons—*holy* (whole, healthy), *at-one-ment, redemption, conversion.* Untoward is from the Greek *skolios,* which means curved, not pointing to anything. So an "untoward genera-

tion" (Acts 2:40 KJV) is not aimed toward anything. Where the Beatitude in English says, "Blessed are the meek," the French New Testament says, *"Beureux les debonnaires"*—and who would not rather be debonair?

18. *Meditation.* A "meditation" is based on a Bible passage. It does not expound it, it reflects on it. The manner is quiet, and there is an undercurrent of strong emotion. The preacher gazes out over the city from the Mount of Olives, or he joins the mother of Sisera as she looks through the lattice and wonders, "Why is his chariot so long in coming?", or he recalls scenes in which Jesus acted out a Beatitude. The structure is free. The preacher may retell a Bible incident in a way that gives fresh insights. He may speculate about the hidden dynamics of a conversation. He may reveal the deeper levels of some Christian truth. There are dangers in trying to present new meanings in the Bible. The deep things the preacher discovers may not be there, though he is presenting them as Bible truth. But the Bible's meaning is inexhaustible. A meditation may enrich the congregation with the benefits of the minister's long, hard thought and prayer.

A meditation is a demanding form because it cannot have some of the usual devices for holding interest—humor, practical affairs, vigor, argument. It may readily be dull. That is why it is most often used for briefer talks—as at Communion services or to introduce group prayer. There must be special effort to make it crystal clear. It needs striking phrases to hold attention. Beauty, which is related to spiritual depths, is important in a meditation. The style is sometimes like poetry in prose. The vocabulary and descriptions can become too opulent, but people at church are supposed to see visions and dream dreams. A preacher should not become overattached to the meditation style, but he ought to learn how to use it because he will need it.

19. *Props.* Sermons can center in some object of beauty or special meaning. Stained-glass windows were first intended to teach the Bible, Christian history, and doctrine to congregations that were largely illiterate. Symbolism has the same use. Literate Christians also need visual lessons and the uplift of beauty. Christian symbols or figures that are visible from the pews can be aids to preaching; art objects can be brought for this purpose. Banners may help preach the sermon. Other objects can be used to help convey the message—a globe of the world, a flame, a plumb line (the invisible vertical—Amos 7:7), various forms of the cross with their special meanings, incense, a scroll. A projector may be used to put a picture of whatever object or scene the sermon needs before the congregation. Moving pictures can be shown. Props require meticulous preparation; fumbling and adjusting makes a service seem improvised.

Filmed episodes or recordings from plays have been used to introduce sermons. One minister played lyrics from the Broadway musical, *Man of La Mancha,* at intervals during his sermon. Soloists or the choir can give that sort of help. Portions of historic speeches, messages from church people known to the congregation, recorded replies to questions the minister put to people can be used. The playing of recordings should not be lengthy. If communication in person is made to seem unimportant, people are bound to wonder why they came.

There is a point at which such aids become gimmicks. A sermon is a part of a worship service, and devices that might be useful for a classroom could destroy the sense of the beauty of holiness. If a sermon were intended only for teaching, we could expect to have blackboards and examinations. However, a much wider variety of aids can be reverently and fittingly used than are commonly attempted. The fact that sermons are so much confined to the sound of one voice can be attributed less to reverence and fitness than to lack of creativity. The failure to use new ways to enrich worship and preaching comes partly from unthinking acceptance of tradition and partly from the comfort of familiar ruts. It takes less initiative just to talk. Other appropriate and effective ways of communication are available, and most of us have not made enough use of them.

20. *Innovative forms.* Some of the insistence on new styles of preaching does not recognize that most of them can be used only rarely. One Sunday in our church a man in the balcony called out a criticism of the sermon; then a woman from below stood up to answer him. Soon there was a lively debate, with several other participants. The congregation was shocked at first, and then appreciated the value this had in stirring thoughts and feelings. But the novelty was essential. We could not have tried this again very soon. A young minister told me that he is not much interested in preaching because he believes that something like *Jesus Christ Superstar* is a much better method. It left me wondering how many times a year the average church could present something like *Jesus Christ Superstar*. Dialogue or team sermons have many advantages, but there is a limit to how often they can be used. For one thing, when they are well done they take a great deal more time to prepare than does a one-person sermon. They are usually not well done, but the congregation enjoys variety enough so that it is not too critical of commonplace and disordered thinking. If enough time is given to its preparation, a sermon by two or more ministers can be intellectually and spiritually impressive, but that amount of time is not often available. The other limitation is in the congregation. Interest in some of the novel forms, which is lively at first, may not stay at a high level. For some very small groups a variety of unusual sermon styles may be permanently useful, but the thought that these will become the regular sort of preaching in the typical congregation is probably an illusion.

The rest of the truth, however, is that a much greater variety is possible for the typical congregation than is used. The hard problem for preaching is jaded congregations. That is why the minister must try to be as many different preachers as he can by using a wide variety of sermon structures. He also needs to change the whole method of presentation as often as he can find ways that will really do for the congregation what needs to be done. Experiments risk the possibility that there will be more entertainment than upbuilding. The minister and the less traditional members of the congregation may be so intent on novelty that they do not notice that "the hungry sheep look up and are not fed." But that is not, statistically, the greatest danger. The number of preachers who carry experiment to the point of frivolity is certainly much less than the number of those who plod on and on in the same routines and miss the healthy variety they might have.

Dialogue can be one of the most effective methods of reaching minds and hearts. Congregations like it because it is dramatic. It is more interesting to listen to two speakers than to one. Unwelcome views may get a better hearing in a dialogue. The dialectical method of looking at a subject from various positions before reaching conclusions is the way a good mind operates, which is why some of the greatest teachers have used dialogue. For Socrates, it was the regular method, and it was Plato's literary form. Catechisms give the illusion of two participants. Anselm put one of the theological classics, *Cur Deus Homo,* in dialogue form. Reports of disputations and colloquies enrich the literature of many branches of learning.

Pulpit dialogues can be either tongue in cheek or honest statements of two points of view. In the former, one speaker is often assigned to inform or correct the other. Real dialogue gives a chance to view a subject through two personalities, who may disagree or may merely speak from different perspectives.

Adequate preparation is not easy. The temptation is to present a superficial talk show, with each one improvising from the top of his mind. If the speakers have had unusual experiences or are masters of some branch of knoweldge, the unplanned talk may be worthwhile, but it usually supplies more entertainment than solid substance. The speakers may meet a number of times in advance and develop the lines of thought they intend to follow. At its best, they meet often enough to have the course of the dialogue pretty well worked out.

For a group sermon, all these problems are multiplied; it is much harder to foresee the direction the talk will take. Those with the least to say may monopolize the time. The example of television shows is not very helpful. Television participants are usually from some field in which they are far ahead of the viewing audience in knowledge and experience, so that almost anything they say will be informative. A church service does not take breaks for commercials, which can give the participants a chance to replan. The sermon time may pass before unrehearsed speakers find out how best to participate. A good group sermon has to be almost like a play, with a script.

These difficulties may keep group preaching from being regularly used, but it can occasionally do a great deal of good. To hear young people, church officers, or public school teachers express themselves on important subjects can be a valuable experience, even though what they say is spontaneous. A church service is not the place for just another public forum, but earnest expressions on what is of importance for Christianity can well suit the mood of worship.

Chancel drama can have the inner benefits that Aristotle counted on in his *Poetics*—catharsis, insight, and increased sensitivity. It can "catch the conscience," as Shakespeare intended. Its increasing use is a good sign. There are several traveling companies of semiprofessional players who splendidly demonstrate the value of drama in church services. A play may use the whole sermon time, or a brief episode may introduce the sermon theme or be an illustration. The playlets have a tendency to be ironic—a person falls and lies injured while the uncaring minister goes on preaching about love, or an evangelist pummels someone who will not cooperate in being saved. But they can go deep—two people on a park bench reveal their battered souls and the world's indifference.

In considering innovative sermon structures, the minister has to remember that even people who otherwise are open to what is modern may be unhappy when someone lays rough hands on the church services. They cherish the stained-glass feeling, and the joy of being uplifted by a familiar service they have come to love. In an agitated world full of change and surprise, they want their church to embody dependability. This does not mean that there should not be innovations; it does mean that when something startlingly new is tried, people should be carefully prepared. Those who are regretful should be heard with sympathy. Love and loyalty for what the church service has been are virtues to be prized. This love and loyalty can usually, with tact, be transferred to new ways, if the new ways deserve it.

XI

Introductions and Conclusions

THE INTRODUCTION

There are two elements of structure every sermon has to have—an opening and a closing. These two parts are the most critical. The introduction can have several very important purposes:

1. The opening makes the *first impression*. It can give the preacher a flying start or a handicap. His opening sentences may set listeners for him or against him. They may decide he is someone they like, trust, and want to listen to; or they may develop a bias against anything he says if he is hesitant, colorless, unpleasant, rasping, or unprepared. The preacher's manner is important. He should look happy to be there. If nervousness makes him seem miserable, it will be contagious. He can take command and appear to be about to do something significant. Some preachers, before they start, take a friendly look around the room as though establishing a good connection. Others have a long pause, as though getting ready to plunge into something great. Calculated devices will seem histrionic. The minister must put what he is really feeling and wants the congregation to feel into that first appearance. He should have himself together before he starts. If he fumbles with his notes, uses his handkerchief, takes a drink of water, or misspeaks his first sentences, the congregation may decide to spare him the embarrassment of their attention. The first words should be well in mind and given looking at the congregation, not at the notes, and with just the right effect. Whatever happens to the rest of the sermon, the delivery of the introduction and conclusion must be well prepared. Eye contact is especially important.

The preacher has the hard necessity of making an unused voice sound right on the first word. Plays usually start with a few throwaway lines so that the actors' voices and the hearers' ears can be getting adjusted. When a voice is first raised to the level of public speech it is likely to pipe, squeak, quaver, or sound husky. Singers vocalize to get ready and a minister has to learn how to prepare his voice box. It is easy to become compulsively dependent on lozenges or breathing exercises which do not really make any difference. A little humming and quiet throat-clearing

94

just before standing up may help. At least they make a speaker think about his first sounds. It is important not to be tense. This may be like the advice of the stewardess—if you find that something dreadful has happened to the plane, "breathe normally." It is possible, however, to keep the tension of the moments just before preaching from tightening the vocal organs.

2. The opening has to command *attention*. The congregation may be settling down after the sermon hymn, staring around the room. If a Scripture reading just before the sermon was not interesting, minds may have wandered. People may expect to enjoy the sound of the minister's voice as mood music for daydreaming. The audience is hanging in the balance, poised to be lost. The minister's opening words have to mean, "Wait a minute! Don't touch that dial; this is something you want to hear!"

A minister needs a wide variety of ways of starting sermons. If he has only a few sorts of openings, they lose their force. The possibilities are endless:

The minister may repeat his text and then say something striking about it—"Paul can't be serious! Everyone knows that isn't true."

The first words may startle—"Ours is the most murderous generation this world has ever seen."

People may have to hear what comes next—"The strangest man I ever knew lived in a cave near my home town."

A conversation can be dramatic and revealing—"Reticent people will open up their hearts to strangers. I never learned my seat-mate's name."

The opening may promise desirable information—"If your prayers are disappointing, it may be that you have not learned how to pray."

There may be an aphorism—"If the gates of hell are locked, they are locked on the inside."

A question may be used—"How do you know you are a Christian?"

The start may be provocative—"I am sure you love God, but do you like him?"

A pointed illustration can get attention while it introduces the sermon theme—"The human hand is a marvelous machine."

A poem, especially a picture poem, can be good—"A garden is my soul, which I must tend or slight until I die." (Puzzling poetry does not serve here.)

There may be a prose quotation—"John and Phoebe Brashear were astronomers who worked together for years. On their tomb are carved the words, 'We have loved the stars too fondly to be fearful of the night.' "

The opening may shock—"In the time it took me to read the Gospel lesson about Jesus and the little children, four children starved to death."

Interest in the Bible can be piqued—"What in the world was that mysterious malady Paul had? He gave four clues."

Humor is useful—"On the Sunday of our last Every Member Canvass, I spoke of it as a 'Visitation.' One of our members later told me how Webster's Dictionary defines the word. Here is the definition: 'Visitation—an affliction sent by God.' "

A news event can be effective—"We have all been shocked this week by the riots at the penitentiary."

There may be a hard-hitting statement to the congregation—"A year ago we set some very high goals for the mission of this church. It is time for you to know what has been done."

Arousing curiosity is good—"Hospital chaplains report that there is one chapter in the Bible that patients ask for above all others. Would you expect it to be in the Old Testament or the New?"

A story may serve several purposes—"Two years ago the Boston police reported the conversation between a suicidal man who climbed out on a ledge twelve floors above the street, and the janitor for that floor."

There may be nothing to get attention except hard and serious thinking —"Theology has given three sorts of answers to why Christ had to die."

Heading straight into the Bible is often the best way; a Bible character or story may offer an engaging start. Some ministers read the text and then look up and say it again in a different tone.

Occasionally the best introduction is no introduction. The preacher plunges immediately into the full course of the sermon, just as Cicero started his oration, "How long, O Catiline, will you continue to abuse our patience?"

It is fatal for a preacher to try to clear away some dull preliminaries before he gets into his sermon. By the time he has laid out the road from Jerusalem to Jericho, or reconciled the various renderings of the text, he may not have an audience. The introduction has to deal with what is specific and real. Anything abstruse must come later.

3. The introduction gives the *sermon's theme.* There is often reason for the old jibe, "What did he preach about?" "I don't know; he never said." When the people know the sermon's subject, they have the reason for listening. They may miss the significance of what is said if they have not yet been told what the sermon is getting at. Each listener must see that the sermon is important to him. There may be a sermon that holds interest by keeping the congregation guessing about where the preacher could possibly be going, but this is special. An introduction may, by implication at least, make a contract. It promises the congregation members what they will get if they give their attention. If the sermon then changes the subject or is not equal to the promise, a contract has been broken.

4. An introduction may reveal the *plan* for the sermon, with a preview of the main points. A mystery story gets its interest by not revealing the outcome until the end; a newspaper story gets its interest by revealing the outcome in the lead sentence. Sermons can be of either sort. Usually, when people know in advance what course the sermon will take, it piques their curiosity. It may also help the sermon to sink it; this is the technique of the debater who tells in his first statement what his argument will be. A good preview can entice hearers—"You may think of John Calvin only as a great brain. Today I want to tell something of what an interesting

man he was, and of the heroic life he lived, and of the revolutionary things he taught."

When an introduction is too long it steals time that is needed for the rest of the sermon. Congregations become impatient and wish the preacher would get on with what he is there to do. A long introduction transgresses against symmetry; it has been likened to an oversize porch on a small house.

It is a mistake to begin a sermon with an apology. The reasons for wanting to do this are obvious—too obvious. The minister fears he will not get credit for his real abilities, so he tries to save his reputation by explaining why he is not at his best. The plane was delayed, he lost his notes, he has just recovered from a fever, he was expecting a different sort of audience. By this he is persuading people that they should be disappointed. He does not convince them that he is a great preacher, but only that they should have stayed at home. People do not enjoy making allowances. There is always reason for hope; let the minister's expectation of something good set the mood for himself and for the congregation.

There are some questions about introductions on which writers on preaching give opposite advice; this demonstrates that homiletics cannot be taught by rules. Almost any rule should sometimes be ignored. What is important is that the problem be pointed out. The minister needs to know what the advice is; then, if he thinks he should disregard it, he can sin gladly.

The majority opinion seems to be that the start of a sermon should be calm, deliberate, low-keyed. Too vigorous a beginning has been called as unpleasant as the sudden lurching forward of a bus. Paul Scherer is quite definite: "Never begin with heat or on a high note. You will blow up somewhere in the middle if you do, with the last ten minutes reserved for the falling of pieces over the landscape." (*For We Have This Treasure,* p. 205.) Thus a speaker should reserve the most explosive parts until the hearers begin to tire. It is better to work up to a climax than to work down from one. On the other hand, some able preachers believe that a good deal of force at the beginning will attract attention and give promise of an interesting sermon. A skillful engineer can start a train so quietly that it may roll a considerable way before the passengers know it has started, but that is exactly what a preacher does not want. There is at least agreement that a sermon has to be lively in every part. There is no time for a low place, and especially not at the start. But vitality can be expressed in different ways. A calm tone may be more emphatic than a shout. Quiet earnestness may get attention better than excitement does. Informal intimacy may lay hold of a congregation more powerfully than does oratory. The more peaceful sorts of vitality are better at the start, with the more vehement later, though this depends on the sermon; some introductions have to be fervent.

You can get different opinions on whether or not it is good to offer a prayer just before the sermon starts. An obvious objection is that it is too late. If the minister prepares his sermon carefully, he already knows what he is going to say; the chance for improving the words of his mouth and the meditation of his heart is past. The minister's own plea to God for help could be given before he stands up in the public eye. The prayer seems to be intended to create a mood. Of course, the effect on the hearers is a part of the intention of every public prayer, but it should not be too obviously a technique. On the other hand, it is surely right to invoke God's blessing before so great an enterprise. Perhaps we may say that a prayer before the sermon is right if it asks for God's help, not with what the sermon is, but with what the sermon does. The prayer may seem less like a part of the minister's performance if it comes before the Scripture is read, and so asks God to use for good both the reading and the sermon that will apply it.

Many ministers believe that having the sermon immediately follow a major Bible reading shows that the sermon is an interpretation of the Scripture, and helps the congregation see the connection between them. A pause or a change of tone is needed to mark the place where the Bible stops and the minister begins. The reasons for not having the sermon follow the reading are partly physiological; a hymn gives people a chance to rouse and stir before they settle into the longest item in the service. There are also psychological reasons. The two together extend the attention span—they make the sermon seem longer. If they are separated, the sermon can be shortened by telling part of what needs to be said about the Bible at the time when it is read. Moreover, if a hymn is on the Scripture-sermon theme, it is not necessarily an interruption when it comes between them.

We best learn how to preach by seeing how the masters do it. It would be hard to tear one's mind away from any of the following introductions, but not one of them is a trick. They all honestly prepare for the theme of the sermon and set the tone for it.

Sparhawk Jones, preaching to the students at Princeton University, used surprise. He read his text (II Ki.8:13), "Is thy servant a dog that he should do this?" and looked for a moment at the congregation. Then he said, "Dog or no dog, he did it." (*The Craft of Sermon Construction,* W. E. Sangster, p. 127.) (Anyone who wants to try this should be warned that the text was misinterpreted. The RSV clarifies it: "What is your servant, who is but a dog, that he should do this great thing?")

Ralph Sockman roused curiosity when he started out "To be 'picked on' is a heartbreaking experience for a child on the playground." (*The Higher Happiness,* p. 153.)

Harry Emerson Fosdick tells what prompted his sermon—"This sermon springs from conversations with two young men. In intellect and character they represent the best we have, one a Jew, the other a Christian." (The title—*A Fundamentalist Sermon by a Modernist Preacher*—also gets this sermon off to a flying start.) (*The Power To See It Through,* p. 190.)

Paul Scherer held out the hope of interesting information—"I want to talk to you tonight about the perils of the Christian life. It's something we don't often talk about. We don't like to think about them." (*Great Preaching Today*, Alton M. Motter, ed., p. 189.)

Frederick Speakman started a story that had to be finished: "I had an uncle who could explain everything, at least to his own complete satisfaction." (*Love Is Something You Do*, p. 43.)

James S. Stewart managed to get a provocative question and his sermon's sustaining picture into two brief opening sentences: "How do you regard human life? I suppose the three most frequent descriptions of life, the three most popular pictures, are these—a battle, a voyage, and a march." (*The Gates of New Life*, p. 83.) This shows how a question can be an excellent start. It sets minds to working and draws the preacher and the congregation together.

THE CONCLUSION

A preacher should give his best care to the composition and delivery of his closing passage. There are good reasons why this is so important:

1. The conclusion gives the final chance to *impress the message* on the hearers. It may summarize the outline, or at least say in an emphatic, concise way what the sermon was about. By this, those who did not quite follow the minister's thought, or those who are confused because their minds wandered, have one more chance to understand what has been said. A summary can implant truth by repetition.

2. The close has the best chance to be *remembered*. What the minister most wants the congregation to recall can be said very clearly at the end. Whatever mnemonic devices he has used—an alliterative outline, key words, aphorisms—can be reviewed at the end and anchored in the hearers' minds.

3. The *lasting impression* of the sermon will depend most upon the close. The sermon might have had to say things that were gloomy, alarming, critical, pedantic, or unbelieving, so that people might go out with feelings that are negative or depressed. Whatever mood the preacher wishes to be the final effect can best be imparted at the end. But that mood should never be drooping. Sermons should face reality, but the final reality they face is God.

4. If the sermon looks toward any sort of *definite result,* the conclusion can point people directly toward it. It may call for some action—"You will find cards in the holders," "Tell me or one of the church officers," "Before today ends, sit down and write that letter," "Take a piece of paper and make a list of . . ." The result may be less tangible—"Lift up your hearts, and be glad!", "Seek out some way by which you can . . ." "Resolve to make this summer the best . . ." If a sermon is not just to drift off into the air and disappear, the best place to tie it to something that will make a difference is at the close.

5. The conclusion may bring a sermon to an *impressive climax*. The course of the sermon may have been educational, logical, or analytical,

without much that was stirring. But a good conclusion can lift people to a height of strong feeling about it all. Samuel Goldwyn said his formula for making a good movie was to start with an earthquake and work up to a climax. The conclusion should be brief and pointed. Usually it is separate from the main body of the sermon because it has special purposes. But sometimes the winding up of the last point may be just right for finishing the sermon if that last point was the end product which gathered up what came before.

Some teachers insist that the climax to a sermon should come just before the end, not at the end. After the height of emotion or emphasis, there is a low-keyed sentence or two before the minister is through. James Stewart says, "You will never weaken the force of your final appeal by keeping it restrained. In nine cases out of ten, quiet notes are better than crashing chords." In any case, a sermon should not just run out of what it has to say, and quit, like a caller who suddenly picks up his hat and walks out the door. A peroration is no longer expected, but some of the old-time orators could make it a powerful means for achieving their purposes. Without a peroration, we would never have had Patrick Henry's, "Is life so dear, or peace so sweet, as to be purchased at the price of chains and slavery?" or Daniel Webster's "When my eyes shall be turned to behold, for the last time, the sun in heaven. . . ." A speaker who has for a considerable time been demanding the attention of an audience needs some way of rounding out, of making a graceful exit. An impressive close means that the sermon got some place important.

The conclusion is burdened with two handicaps: The minister prepares it when he is the most tired, and the congregation hears it when they are the most tired. A minister who works straight through the sermon gets to the most important part, the conclusion, when his creative powers are playing out. He also gets there, unless he is a well-disciplined planner, when he sees that the sermon has become too long, which is why conclusions so often seem scanty and weak. Some ministers resist this fate by preparing the conclusion before the rest of the sermon has been finished. This has an additional advantage—with the conclusion finished the minister knows right where he is going as he works. But this can be inhibiting. Even when the outline has been carefully prepared, the sermon is still taking shape during the work on it, so the preacher cannot be sure, until the work is nearly over, just what the conclusion should be. Perhaps the solution is that a good idea for the conclusion should be worked out while the mind is lively, though the actual drafting of it might come last. At the end, when the hearers are most tired, they should get the freshest part of the sermon.

Luther's advice on when to end a sermon is still good: "When you see your hearers most attentive, then conclude." That recalls the rule that the time to break up a party is when it is still going strong. Sometimes a speaker feels a moral obligation to cram in at the end all the other good things he has thought of. I once heard a distressed lecturer say, "Oh, I wish there were more time because, if I did not have to stop, here's what I would have said . . ." and on he went. Every preacher knows that feeling, but when the time to quit has come, then every good idea is the enemy of all the others.

Sometimes, when a conclusion does not turn out well, the speaker plunges on, hoping to improve it. In that emergency, each try usually falls flatter than the one before, and the congregation feels that the preacher is desperately running around the room, looking for an exit. The old advice for a caller who cannot think of any way to leave is "Stand up"; the best course for a minister who is looking for a way to quit is to sit down.

It is a mistake to introduce a new idea into the conclusion. The minister looks over his preparation sheets and sees that other great text he wishes he had used, that sparkling thought for which there never was an opening. So in they go at the conclusion, and hopelessly, because there is no chance to use them properly. A striking statement or an illustration may seem so good that the preacher uses it for his conclusion, though it has only an oblique connection with anything that came before. Thus the arrow wobbles off course just before it hits the target. The parliamentary rule that sets a deadline for new business must apply to sermons.

A preacher should beware of reassuring words like "finally" or "in conclusion." These mean, "I know I'm taxing your endurance, but take hope." When he goes overtime he should not call attention to it; people will not forgive him because he admits it. If he and the congregation are victims of something that has prolonged the service, he may properly say so, but usually it is unwise to make people any more aware of the clock than they already are. Hurried speech or shortening the last hymn advertise a disaster with the timing. The few seconds saved are not worth it.

People need to know when the minister finishes the body of the sermon and starts on the conclusion; otherwise the structure will seem confused. The transition can be marked by a pause, or a change of voice, or by what is said—"Now as you go out into this week ahead . . .", "Thus we have seen that . . .", "So now let us . . .", "This, then, is what Paul says to us . . ."

In the last quarter of the sermon a preacher must be careful to say nothing that suggests he is about to quit when he is not. Several emphatic sentences, a poem, or a powerful illustration may put the congregation in a home-stretch state of mind. Then, when the preacher goes on, they feel betrayed. It is not that they are in the church unwillingly, or want as little sermon as possible, but in any extended performance, when the audience is physically and mentally anticipating a change, it is unpleasant to have it snatched away. When a lovely concert goes beyond the expectations or a baseball game has extra innings, even the devotees feel discomfort in readjusting their timing. That is why one of the most damaging comments on a preacher is, "He passed several good stopping places." People will endure a long sermon better than one that seemed about to end and did not. The minister must examine what he expects to say to be sure that no unintended note of finality is there. There are many old jokes on this subject, and they are all bitter—"An optimist is someone who reaches for his hat when the preacher says, 'And finally, brethren . . .' "

Like an opening prayer, a closing prayer can be good if it is a real prayer; if it is an oratorical device, it should be avoided. It readily deteriorates into an apostrophe, like "Milton! thou shouldst be living at this hour." The closing prayer is often exploited to summarize the sermon, drive home a point, or make a final appeal to the congregation. But at the ending of a sermon the need for God's blessing and help may be so strongly felt that it should be put into a prayer.

The purpose of the sermon determines the form of the conclusion. It may be a plea, exhortation, warning, restatement of a great truth, promise, direction, encouragement, challenge, thanksgiving, praise, or assurance. The conclusion may recapitulate the sermon or exalt the text. The form of the conclusion must be varied and unexpected. Every preacher rightly has some sorts of conclusions he uses more than others, but one that is used too often goes stale.

A quotation may be used if it is vivid and easy to understand. Some have objected that a quotation here amounts to the minister's admitting that, "I do not feel equal to the responsibility of closing this sermon, so I am calling in someone else to do the job." But if such help will occasionally do the best job, it should not be rejected.

A poem can be just the right conclusion, though ministers count on topical anthologies too much for this. The poem may be from the hymn book; the hymn might then be sung.

The closing sentence should be carefully designed. It cannot be subtle; there will be no chance to think about it.

A sermon may properly be closed with "Amen!" when the preacher needs to say "That's right!" or "So be it!" But often the word is nothing but an awkward way of quitting. The preacher is groping, so he uses the *Amen* as verbal punctuation that lets him back off. By this he muffles the effect of his final sentence and retreats with a pious exclamation that is out of place.

The conclusion may be a call for decision—"Isn't this the day to get this settled? Won't you be happier when you do?" or a challenge—"God is saying to you as he said to Moses, 'You have been circling around this mountain long enough; go on!' " There can be an appeal—"May we . . ." or "May God . . ." The ending may be a question—"Are you satisfied right now with where you are?" There may be a resounding final paragraph, with the last words especially impressive, as in the Sermon on the Mount—"And the rain fell, and the floods came, and the winds blew and beat against that house, and it fell; and great was the fall of it."

The conclusion may be an illustration. This can be a picture—"An astronaut, looking back at this spinning ball God made . . ." or an analogy—"When the familiar landmarks are all out of sight, look above you to the stars, and see your path still marked across the sky."

A paired introduction and conclusion can make good structure. To return to the opening illustration, or text, or thought pulls a sermon together and makes it finish what it started out to do. Richard C. Raines ends a sermon, "So I close as I began with the invitation and admonition . . ."(*Great Preaching Today*, Alton M. Motter, ed., p. 178.)

The last words may be deliberately spaced and imposing, or delivered with a headlong burst of vigor. Occasionally the most impressive close is just a sudden stop. With the sermon rushing ahead at full course, the minister abruptly quits and lets surprise add force. Sometimes, after powerful superlatives, the minister makes a very low-keyed understatement and sits down. This indicates the impossibility of saying what should be said. I heard Sir Winston Churchill close his "Iron Curtain" speech with an unforgettable example of dramatic underplaying. He had spoken of what the looming danger demanded of England and America. But if these two nations rise to the challenge, he concluded, "the high roads of the future will be clear, not only for us, but for all; not only for our time, but for the century to come." As he delivered these final words, Mr. Churchill was turning back to his chair. He spoke them over his shoulder, still aimed at the microphones. The attitude was that of tossing off a final remark while leaving. It was many times more impressive than it would have been if he had come straight at us with all his force.

Martin Luther King was a master of introductions and conclusions. There has rarely been as fine a close as the one to his "I have a dream" address in Washington—". . . we will be able to speed up that day when all of God's children, black men and white men, Jews and Gentiles, Protestants and Catholics, will be able to join hands and sing in the words of that old Negro spiritual: 'Free at last! Free at last! Thank God Almighty, we are free at last.' " (*The Days of Martin Luther King, Jr.,* Jim Bishop, p. 328.)

Henry Sloane Coffin closed with a promise—"That is the Easter which may be ours now—a life committed to Christ, and in his comradeship growing fit for the Master's house here and forever." (*God's Turn*, p. 90.)

Frederick Speakman ended a sermon on religious songs with a challenge—"That's our song. That's our Christian song. Maybe you can't sing it, but you can march to it!" (*Love Is Something You Do*, p. 25.)

David MacLennan gave a series of questions: "There is a question before the house—your house, my house. It is this: Where are *you* going from Bethlehem? Do you know where you are going? And whom you will follow, and *Who* is going with you?" (*Joyous Adventure*, p. 70.)

Leslie Weatherhead, in a sermon on the use of Sunday, closed with a story and a striking final sentence. He told of a dying old man who was frightened and sent for him. "When, as tenderly as I could, I tried to talk to him about God and religion and the soul, he said, very bitterly and brokenly, mumbling as he said the words, 'I have led a very busy life. I have never had time for that sort of thing.' *But he had had four thousand Sundays.*" (*When the Lamp Flickers*, p. 115.)

Helmut Thielicke ends with a hard hitting reminder: " 'As you did it unto one of the least of these my brethren, you did it to me.' . . . Our pocketbooks can have more to do with heaven, and also with hell, than our hymnbooks. He who has ears to hear, let him hear!" (*The Waiting Father*, p 103)

XII

The Time for
Sermon Preparation

FINDING TIME

A quaint set of instructions, which a Bishop wrote for his pastors, begins, "When you sit down on Saturday night to prepare your sermon . . ."
That does not seem to work. Dr. Fosdick's rule was to have one hour of
preparation for every minute of preaching. Thus, getting ready for a
twenty-five-minute sermon would take half of a fifty-hour work week.
Finding enough time to give to sermons is a preacher's unremmitting
difficulty, but it cannot be avoided. Those who think they have some
short-cuts are invariably wrong. There are glib preachers who can put on
a facile performance without much preparation, but for the hearers it
becomes like eating cotton candy. When the young poet, Racine, wrote
to a critic for advice, he said, "I ought to tell you that I write with great
facility." The critic answered, "I hope to teach you to write with great
difficulty." A natural gift for unreflected expression is a dangerous one.
A minister who counts on it will always miss doing what he might have
done. Natural fluency has been the ruination of many preachers; they
love to talk and do it easily, charmingly, even brilliantly, so they come
to rely on this instead of on hard work. The result is that their sermons
become flashy and empty. Hard-pressed preachers may fall back on the
hope that it is God who makes any sermon a success. An old German
pastor gave Martin Niemoller his experience with this, "I count on the
Holy Ghost, but the only time he ever spoke to me in the pulpit he said,
'Heinrich, you're lazy.'"

Ministers know how great a sermon ought to be, so they never feel
that they are ready. "Art is long, and Time is fleeting." When a minister
is seen doing furtive scribbling just before he preaches, it does not show
he has procrastinated; it is his last chance—if only the choir will sing a
long anthem!

Because finding time for preparation is so critical for preaching, the
minister needs to put his best intelligence on the way he arranges his
work. No doubt many others—doctors, policemen, authors, musicians—
think they have the most unusual of occupations, but the minister can

show good reasons why his is. For one thing, it is almost impossible for him to have a working schedule. When I moved from a pastorate to teaching, I found this striking difference—a teacher pretty well knows when he starts a day how it will be spent; a pastor never does. The assumption is that a minister is available when anybody needs him; if he is a rigid schedule-keeper with one eye on the clock, he has missed his role. At the meetings of church agencies, I have noticed that it is the busy laymen who usually arrive on time and the ministers who come in late. This may show that businessmen have to learn to keep their appointments and ministers can be easy on themselves, but I think there is another reason. When someone, by telephone or in person, tries to stop a corporation president when he is starting to a meeting, he goes on; a minister does not. Much of a pastor's time is controlled by other people, mostly without prearrangement.

For a year I received morning phone calls from a member of our congregation who was going blind. We usually talked of nothing very serious. She called because she had come to associate the sound of my voice with the church, worship, God, and the great reassurances. When the prospect of the last ray of light flickering out was too grim, she wanted to hear that Sunday-morning sound. I could scarcely have said, "Tell her to leave her number." We had in our congregation a retired lawyer, a man of fine intellect, who greatly loved the church. He was fretting at the lack of an important occupation, and our bylaws needed to be revised, so I persuaded the church officers to ask him to undertake the job. I had assumed it would be done in a reasonably short time, but our consultations about it went on for months. Whenever there was danger that the work would be completed, he would call me to his home and propose a new approach. The reason, of course, was that this task was his tie to life; to finish it would yield ground to death. It must also be admitted, however, that ministers get so used to having their schedules invaded by people's needs that their defenses become porous and they give way to trivialities.

A minister also finds it hard to plan his time because of the limitless variety of things he has to do. A good deal has been written about the "maceration" of the minister by his many functions—pastor, preacher, administrator, educator, counselor. With the confusion of the unpredictable demands, the minister is likely to get to them as they come, without giving them priorities. It is ironic that the highly important duty of preparing to preach is the one he can most readily postpone. No one forces this duty on him until Sunday morning. Let us also recognize that the minister's much-bewailed multiplicity of roles is one of his greatest compensations. His work never lacks variety. Boredom is no problem when you enter a new line of work several times a day.

The minister's working time is crossed up with other people's. Their days off are working days for him. He must do much of his work at night, when people can be available for calls and meetings. His unscheduled hours are the very ones when his mind is at its best for thinking about sermons. People may see no reason why ministers should not be interrupted at those hours. I was the only minister member of a Human Relations Board, whose chairman was a railroad lawyer. People would call me at any time of day with messages for the chairman because "I don't like to interrupt a man when he's at work." Ministers have to become resigned to all the polite people who begin their mid-morning calls with "I hope I didn't get you out of bed."

The minister's working habits are complicated by the fact that he never gets caught up. There is no factory whistle to release him. He can never say, "My day's work is done." He is constantly hounded by the thought of all he is not doing, which any real minister of Christ would surely do. If he has failed to call on someone before an operation, or if he has insulted the congregation and the Lord with a half-ready sermon, it is no help for him to know that he was trapped by circumstances. Guilt for what could not be helped still feels like guilt. It is not what a minister does that wears him out, it is what he does not do. He is engaged in a pursuit in which there is no overtaking.

It can be equally correct to say that a minister works extraordinarily long hours, and that he never works at all. If "work is something you would rather not be doing," then a minister gets paid for not working. His occupation lets him do what he would gladly do on his time off if he had another job. I do not mean that sitting through committee meetings, arranging transportation for the state convention, or exorcising the demons from the mimeograph machine are anybody's favorite occupations, but even these are part of the minister's hobby. Anybody is to be envied who can make a vocation of his avocation. There are onerous requirements, but I believe there is no other occupation in which a worker can spend so large a proportion of his time at tasks which he finds fascinating because they are overwhelmingly important.

A minister's work is never finished, so he always has undone tasks he can use as excuses for shirking what he finds most laborious. Laziness for the minister is not loafing so much as it is doing an easier job when there is a harder one he ought to do. I read church magazines when I should be reading books, and I read books as an escape from writing letters, and I write letters when I ought to work on sermons. I can always persuade myself that these postponements are efficient, because at the moment I do not feel up to the exacting task—I am dull, sluggish, sleepy, my spirit is earth-bound. It has been well said that "the symptoms of laziness and fatigue are practically identical."

I have always liked Dr. Coffin's definition "A minister is an accredited friend at large," but think of the excuses this gives for the easy life. A minister is working when he is just being friendly, so he can diligently loaf at the town hang-outs, and conscientiously go to all the high school games. He needs to share his people's interests, so the great text "I sat where they sat" can sit him in front of the television set. It is hard to fight sloth when it wears the garb of saintliness. It is great good fortune to have a job in which you can know you are working when you are having dinner with people you enjoy, or attending the club for couples of your age, or on a church camping trip. But the lack of any clear distinction between a minister's personal pleasures and his work brings the continual temptation to give the pleasures the priority.

The minister must live with the constant strain of self-direction, and that is the hardest strain of all. He has to propel himself; no one takes from him the burden of decision-making; no supervisor tells him what to do. Hour by hour he must goad himself. But self-direction has its compensations. A minister can often leave his work when others could not; he can take his wife to the airport; when his children are in a school performance, he may be the only father who gets to be there. When he is snug in his study, drinking his second cup of coffee, others may be fightign snow and traffic on the way to work. The fact that he may be digging through a hard book still does not make his task look very grueling.

The minister is inclined to be defensive about this. He knows that when those who were fighting traffic are snug at home, he may be out in the dark and snow with his flashlight, trying to find house numbers. He resents the assumption that ministers are soft. As Cowper put it, "O why are farmers made so coarse, or clergy made so fine? A kick that scarcely would budge a horse may kill a sound divine." It is a tradition the public seems to cherish. The ushers at the Radio City Music Hall were instructed, when the ticket line extended out of doors, to bring inside cripples, pregnant women, and clergymen. It is no wonder ministers are tempted to talk about how hard they work, and even to slip references to their heroic endeavors into sermons.

Ministers' distractions may make them disorderly. They can drift and dawdle and let their studies become lounges. I doubt whether there are many professions in which the average number of working hours is as high as it is in the ministry, but some ministers may keep busy with the undemanding tasks and shirk the hard ones. However, there are many more who have developed remarkably strong wills because they have to be self-directed. The irregularities and interruptions have forced them to be well-disciplined. They know they could take a free ride on the workers of the world, and the thought appalls them. They are driven by their sense of the infinite importance of what they try to do, and by their love for it. They have felt in their souls the truth of Jeremiah's warning, "Cursed is he who does the work of the Lord with slackness." (Jer. 48:10)

A minister who is determined can have fairly regular times for sermon preparation. The congregation can be told why he needs his morning hours for serious study, and it is remarkable how well people will respect that request. His church secretary, if he has one, or his wife can learn to shunt routine demands to other hours. Lyman Beecher left instructions that when he was working on a sermon he was not to be interrupted unless the house caught fire, and then not until the flames had reached the second floor. If a minister has his study at home (which may be unwise if his children are small), he must be away from domestic demands. What man would not want his frantic wife to tell him when the washing machine floods the floor? But in every home such emergencies keep coming. The assumption must be that during his working hours he is just as remote as though he were in a downtown office. If the minister's study is at the church, there must be some way to keep him from being accessible to the person with nothing to do who stops by to keep him company, or the inspector who comes to check the fire extinguishers. The problem may well be, not that people are inconsiderate, but that the minister likes to be interrupted.

A minister needs good rising habits. When he has come home late from a meeting at the church, it is easy for him to feel justified in unwinding with a television show and sleeping an hour longer the next morning. The trouble is that this costs him the best working hour of the day. Frederick W. Robertson, one of the greatest preachers to preachers, said, "Early rising is to commence the day with an act of self-denial which, as it were, gives the mind a tone for the whole day. . . . Late rising is the prelude to a day in which everything seems to go wrong." It is strikingly true that starting late does throw a whole day out of gear. However good his reasons may be, a minister still feels furtive about late rising. He knows the truth of what Governor White of Mississippi told seminary students: "The attitude of many a congregation would improve if its members knew that their minister went to work each morning at the same hour as the average layman." (Commencement Address, Louisville Presbyterian Seminary, 1940, from *The Register*.)

A minister needs a regular schedule for his work. It will often be broken into, but he can probably keep to it more often than not. The hardest work should be assigned to the freshest hours. James Denney used to advise his students to distrust all intellectual work that was done by artificial light. Novels and magazines can be reserved for the duller hours. The stages in the sermon preparation can be given their appointed times—say an hour on Monday for working up the whole conception and purpose, Tuesday for the rough outline, and so on. One advantage of regular routines is that our minds tend to perform when they are expected to, just as the digestive tract gets ready to function at the usual meal times. Regular times end the strain of separate improvised decisions. With a schedule, we can make our habits work for us. One reason we get so tired on the days after moving to a new home is that our automatic actions are broken up. Nothing—the light switch, the silverware —is where we can put our hands on it without thinking. We have to deliberate even about such repeated actions as turning up the heat or looking for the mail. William James said, "The more of the details of our daily life we can hand over to the effortless custody of automatism, the more our higher powers of mind will be set free for their own proper work. There is no more miserable human being than one in whom nothing is habitual but indecision and for whom the lighting of every cigar, the drinking of every cup, the time of rising and going to bed every day, and the beginning of every bit of work, are subjects of express volitional deliberation." (*Psychology: Briefer Course*.)

PUTTING OUR MINDS TO WORK

When we schedule our sermon work by stages, we can have the help of two additional mental powers—the reflective, and the subconscious. An hour of sermon work on Monday and another on Tuesday will usually produce more than will the same two hours on Friday and Saturday. The earlier start lets us have the sermon in our thoughts during all the hours when our minds are not occupied—when we are dressing, traveling, or doing routine tasks. Our minds have to have something to do; if there is nothing else for them, they play word games, run over songs, or create imaginary conversations. If we have become excited about a sermon, we may reflect on it very productively during our free times.

The subconscious mental operation is more mysterious. Everyone has experienced it, and no science can explain it. You may have searched your memory in vain for a name; then, an hour or a day later, it will be delivered you without your having throught about it in the meantime. Something out of sight has been scanning your storage files and has come up with the answer. Astonishing discoveries have come by this process. A scientist who can find no clue to a problem he is pondering is interrupted; when he gets back to the problem the next day or a month later, the solution is there like a flash. It is like the working of a computer, though the print-out is much slower. Novelists, poets, and musicians ascribe some of their best creations to this. There are important limitations to it. It is arbitrary; often the great idea comes and often, just as unpredictably, it does not. The assignment must be definite; the more the minister has thought about a specific sermon problem, the more likely he is to get an answer. If on Monday he has gotten no farther than wishing he had a good vehicle for his next Sunday's sermon, his subconscious mind will probably not take the job. But if on Monday he has agonized over half a dozen formats and discarded them, when he goes back to the problem later in the week, the elusive idea may quickly come. It might never have come on Monday, no matter how long he had worked.

This subliminal sort of mental work goes on better during times of relaxation. If the conscious part of the mind is working hard, it seems also to claim the unconscious part. But during resting, play, sleep, or any activity that does not require much thinking, the subconscious mind is free to get caught up with whatever it has become interested in. This part of the mind, like the lungs or heart, seems not to need sleep.

The thoughts that do not seem to have come from one's own thinking are readily ascribed to some sources outside the self—to a previous incarnation or to God. They cannot invariably be attributed to God, because they are given to sinners as to saints, and for evil ends as well as good. What comes mysteriously is not necessarily God-sent. But believers can regard the subconscious as a channel God can use. Anyone who prays for God's help in solving a problem may not only be assigning that problem to the workings of his subconscious mind but also opening the way for the Holy Spirit's help. The workings of the unconscious mind are unpredictable, but they are unquestionably of great value in sermon-making. It is inefficient not to start the work early enough to take ad-vanage of both the reflective and the subconscious help.

There is another helper that may seem to be at cross-purposes with these—desperation. There is nothing that throws the mind into high gear like the knowledge that Sunday is at hand. Desperation is like a drug on which preachers can become dependent.. They may have found that, however far ahead they start, the earlier time is used for indecisive exploration and unsatisfied looking for material. Not until near the end of the week do plans take shape and definite preparations start. Only when there is no more time for pondering do the critical decisions get made, so why not wait till then to begin? Illogical as this reason may seem, all preachers know its force. Any intellectual work can take forever unless the time is limited. Desperation forces a wayward mind to con-centrate; it forces decisions. Panic can be stimulating. The efficiencies of working under the gun are undeniable.

But there are formidable disadvantages. One of these is the loss of the time for reflection and the subconscious process. Another is the risk. Work that begins on Saturday morning may produce an adequate sermon by midnight if there are no visitors, phone calls, family demands, or church emergencies, or if no time is lost heading up blind alleys that have to be abandoned, if the brain stays lively, or if the hoped-for material looks as good close up as it did in anticipation. There are enough such hazards that the chance of getting by all of them is poor. The midnight deadline will fairly regularly get moved on to 2 A.M. or later. And the part of the sermon that was prepared in those last hours may show that not even desperation can stimulate an exhausted mind. The result is too often a hagggard preacher with a sermon he would never have offered if he did not have to.

The reason sermon work early in the week is inconclusive is that the material and ideas really are not good enough. The minister has such high hopes for his sermon that nothing he can think of seems right. By the end of the week he will use almost anything, because he has to.

Desperation, like other drugs, may require increasing doses. If habit makes a minister comfortable with sermon work that starts on Saturday, he can get to where he does not worry too much if he does not get at it until noon, or if a wedding takes up half the afternoon. It is an exciting way to live, which is a large part of its appeal, but it is not exciting for the congregation.

Mental work does require deadlines. A brain always tries to slide side-ways from its assignments. It is pressure of time that keeps a mind on its job and producing well. It is strange that when you are working on a sermon, it is not until almost time to break off for a meal or an appoint-ment that the ideas begin to flow. A preacher has to set his own deadlines. If he tells his brain on Tuesday, "You have only one hour to produce the sermon outline, and you are going to have to work fast," it will not quite make it, but it will come close. Any self-imposed deadline can be just as stimulating as the one Saturday imposes, if the preacher makes it so.

The source of the problem is simply that the preparation of sermons is the hardest work a preacher has to do. That is why his mind is so ready to drift from it, and why he so easily persuades himself that he should put his other tasks ahead of it, and why the habit of Saturday preparation is so likely. That is why some ministers are able to persuade themselves that preaching is not important; to work with committees, make calls, or attend to community affairs is a welcome relief from the strain of sermon preparation. Sir Joshua Reynolds said, "There is no expedient to which a man will not resort to avoid the real labor of thinking." When you sit down at your desk and confront the necessity of mental labor, every sort of escape occurs to you. You have to get coffee, the ventilation has to be adjusted, the typewriter needs fixing, a phone call must be made. You pick up a book to look up a reference, and find yourself browsing in the unrelated pages. You tackle the text, which somehow suggests a limerick. If you were digging a ditch, you would know when you laid down your pick; if you were delivering parcels, you would turn back from deliberately going up the wrong street. But when you are thinking of how to put your thought into words, there is nothing tangible to hold you to it. There is no work in which the temptation to loaf is more treacherous than in mental effort.

The preacher has a peculiar love-hate relationship with his work. There is nothing his flesh recoils from as from the hours of sermon writing—and there is no other time when he is as happy. As he looks ahead to years and years of sermon deadlines, he feels like Sisyphus; every Monday he has to thrust his aching shoulder against the stone and start rolling it up the hill; and every Sunday it tumbles back down, and the ordeal starts again. During his school years he looks forward to graduating from the dreaded twice-a-year strain of final exams—then in his church he finds he has to face it every seven days. To have to supply that weekly quota of uplift, no matter how downcast and hopeless he may be feeling, and to bring it out of his heart and not just produce it by techniques—that consumes him. There are hard hours when a minister is inclined to apply to himself Sara Teasdale's lines:

> From naked stones of agony
> I will build a house for me; . . .
> And every stone where I have bled
> Will show a sign of dusky red.

But before he dissolves completely in self-pity, he has to acknowledge the sheer joy of sermon-making and the bliss of those Sunday noons when it is all over, and he feels that something good was done. There is drama in the preacher's life—fierce endeavor, mounting intensity, high stakes, crisis. The pain is an exciting pain.

The minister's writing desk is like his pulpit—the dread drains away when the action starts. Usually when we approach any part of the sermon task, we find the time is not right. We do not feel spiritual, we discover we are tired, our thoughts flow as sluggishly as cold molasses, we can't get interested. Surely we can do better sermon writing when we feel creative. Here is laziness, dug in for one more stand. Here also is the evidence that the mind's higher powers have to be warmed up. What writer or artist could turn from balancing his checkbook and immediately start creating?

There are two aids to getting in the right mood for sermon writing. One of them, as has been seen, is habit. It is a mistake to say moods cannot be scheduled, because, to some extent, they can. If you are in the habit of doing sermon work at the same time and place, the carryover from all your past labor propels you into it. The rooster salutes the dawn because the recurrence of the expected time makes him feel like crowing. The usual hour, with the pen and paper in their expected places, helps put the minister in the state of mind for doing what he is used to doing then and there.

The second way to get into the right mood for working is to work. The brain has to be warmed up on the job. There is nothing like touching a piece of paper with a pen for making a reluctant mind surrender. Ralph Sockman said that it is when we start writing that the ideas start. What is written first, before the mind is really ready, may have to be done over, but it gets things going. The heartbeat does not pick up until the exercise has started. The power of the Holy Spirit is not given to those who with folded hands are looking up toward heaven, waiting for a visitation; the power is given to those whose hands have already picked up some task that is too great to be done without the Spirit's help. The minister who waits for the right mood to start his preparation may find that Sunday comes before the mood does.

It can be a great relief to us, who may think we are hopeless dullards, to learn that some of the greatest preachers have suffered from reluctant minds. We can guess how often John Oman has strained to pump from a dry well when he laments that a preacher has to prepare inspiring sermons when he is not inspired. Phillips Brooks' own bad hours must be back of his stern admonition, "The first business of the preacher is to conquer the tyranny of his moods." (*On Preaching*, p. 65.) Paul Scherer is giving us a glimpse into his study when he says, "Just do not quit . . . change your position from desk to the chair . . . walk up and down, but keep at it. . . . There is virtue in laying down the law to these recalcitrant selves inside of ours. If they will not agree to your schedule, you stage a sit-down. You say to them, 'No work, no do anything else. We'll see who's who.' " (*For We Have This Treasure*, pp. 181–82.)

XIII

Working on the Sermon

The right way to prepare to preach cannot be prescribed. Different minds have to work in different ways. I once knew a minister who never wrote a word during his sermon preparation. He worked hard—pacing the floor, looking up references, cudgelling his brain, organizing his material —but it was all done in his head. Few ministers could do it that way. At the other extreme is the minister whose whole purpose in preparation is to produce a literary piece. He may be so intent on the writing that when he reads the sermon to the congregation it will sound as though he is looking for typographical errors.

Henry Ward Beecher in his time was generally regarded as the country's most distinguished pulpit orator. He would have about six possible sermons turning over in his mind each week. On Sunday after breakfast, he would decide which one was most ready and would go to his desk and write out the introduction. He then started writing out a very full outline. As eleven o'clock approached, the outline would become more and more scanty. When the church bell rang he would leap from his chair and run to the church. In the pulpit he would read the introduction, then speak from the notes he had made, and the ending would be entirely extempore. This method would have been impossible if Dr. Beecher had not been a rare genius, whose mind was richly stocked and continually boiling with sermon ideas, and whose personality could have made the multiplication table sound exciting. His printed sermons, which were taken down by stenographers, are not impressive.

Harry Emerson Fosdick wrote out his sermons. He was not dependent upon files because of his phenomenal ability to pick up a book he had read long before and find just what he wanted. With all his rare abilities, he still used twenty hours or more preparing the sermon for each Sunday. In the pulpit he read his sermons. The delivery was not his major asset. The sermon methods of Dr. Beecher and Dr. Fosdick, perhaps the outstanding American preachers of their times, could not have been more different.

Bishop Gerald Kennedy selects a year's sermon subjects in advance. He does not do his desk work on the sermon in long stretches, but puts in briefer periods on the four days before he preaches so that, consciously and unconsciously, his mind can be working between these periods. He takes an hour on Wednesday to make an outline without much detail. In an hour on Thursday he expands this into a much fuller outline. He does no more writing. On Friday, with the outline in hand, he talks through the sermon to himself, out loud. On Saturday and early Sunday morning he does the same. By then he is so familiar with the outline that he does not need it, so he delivers the sermon without notes. Not many could do it that way.

The rest of this chapter does not tell how to write a sermon; no two ministers would do it the same way. It does tell what goes into sermon building.

1. *Picking the theme.* As has been said (Chapter VIII), there are great advantages in selecting a year's sermon topics or texts in advance. The themes for special Sundays, such as Christmas and Easter, may need to be planned two or three years ahead. As the date approaches, the theme designated for that Sunday has to be investigated. It may not seem nearly as important as it did when the year's topics were selected. The outline or the material may not hold much promise. If that is not found out before the sermon information is turned in for the Sunday bulletin, the minister may be in trouble. Much ingenuity has been devised to connect sermons with the announced titles and Bible readings. Ministers who cannot make up their minds in time become adept at finding titles and texts that will suit anything they might want to say, such as "The Things That Matter Most," on Rev. 3:22—"He who has an ear, let him hear."

2. *Stating the purpose.* It is on old rule, and an important one, that a preacher should start by drafting for himself a brief, definite statement of what he intends the sermon to accomplish. This will give the sermon unity and power. (Chapter IX.) John Henry Jowett said, "No sermon is ready for preaching, nor ready for writing out, until we can express its theme in a short, pregnant sentence as clear as crystal. I find the getting of that sentence is the hardest, the most exacting, and the most fruitful labor in my study." (*The Preacher, His Life and Work,* p. 133.)

3. *Bible research.* The Scripture references the preacher has in mind must be studied to find out what they really mean, and how they can be interpreted to the congregation in a vivid way. (Chapter V.) The preacher tries to think of other passages and general teachings in the Bible that might be helpful. He uses commentaries, a Bible dictionary, various versions, related passages, and his own pondering. This is necessary both for enrichment and for avoiding blunders. A minister recently told me how a layman who knows Greek had to set him straight. The sermon had been on John 1:12, "To all who received him, who believed in his name, he gave power to become children of God." It had told how Christ gives the strength and ability to live the full, rich life that God intends for his children. After the church service, the layman pointed out that "power" in the English New Testament often translates the Greek word *dunamis,* which does mean strength or force, but in this verse the Greek word is

exousia, which refers to authority, like the power of attorney. The verse means that Christ offers the rights and privileges that belong to the children of God. There is a great sermon in it, but it is not the sermon that was preached.

Many an intended sermon with an exciting Bible angle is wrecked by such a discovery. Then the preacher struggles with his conscience—"Maybe what I want to say is sort of what the passage means; anyway, the Bible says it in other places. If King James authorized it, isn't that enough?" But virtue amid the ruins has to be its own reward.

4. *Rough outline.* On the basis of the stated purpose, and with some idea of the material he will have, the preacher makes a preliminary outline. This sketches what the development might be. If he keeps a notebook of possible sermons, what has accumulated there may indicate a sermon plan. This first outline may have the Bible basis and tentative ideas for how to get into the sermon and how to end it. Before he settles for just an orderly development through major points, the preacher looks to see whether there might be an original sort of conception that could carry the whole sermon and give it interest and force. (Chapter X.) Perhaps a striking container is all that was in view before the final work started. Fresh and inventive sermon forms are desirable, but they can be seductive; a clever container is no substitute for important content. Especially when a sermon's format is original and entertaining, the question must be asked, "Does anybody need it?"

5. *Accumulating ideas.* Possible ideas for the sermon are jotted down without much order. They come from such sources as the preacher's thinking, his experiences, his recollection of what he has read or heard, his Bible research, his files of sermon material, the sheet from his notebook of possible sermons.

6. *Full outline.* With so many ideas now in view, and with the progress in the conception of the sermon which comes while assembling the ideas, the complete outline can be drafted. The minister scans the disorderly idea sheets and tries to see the structure that will make the best use of the material. The full outline may be quite different from the rough one. The full outline should not be a classified index of the items, but a chart on the sermon's progress. (Chapter IX.) It lists as many main points and subpoints and lesser points as are needed for good planning. There should be wide spaces between its lines so that the ideas from the idea sheets can be transferred to where they belong on the outline. (You can save time but lose clarity by numbering the items on the sheets and transferring only the numbers to the outline.)

7. *Proportioning.* With the possible material now outlined before him, the preacher can estimate whether the whole sermon, or any of its parts, have too little or too much. He can see which parts are likely to lack interest or clarity. He can see where there should be cutting, or strengthening. This cannot be mechanical. Living truth perishes on a Procrustean bed, where it is stretched out or lopped off to fit the space. A perfection of structure that was achieved by counting lines would be deadly. But

some proportions are necessary. For obvious reasons, a sermon cannot be too much longer or too much shorter than is expected. Minor matters should not be given major time just because the preacher happened to come upon a good deal to say about them. Unless he plans ahead, he will be expansive in the early part of the sermon and will have to slight the last part, which is usually the most important. It is in the latter part that the minister gives the final truth, the solutions, and the practical guidance. Unless there is careful proportioning, a sermon on Rom. 5:20 KJV, "Where sin abounded, grace did much more abound," is likely to have sin abounding through three-fourths of the sermon and grace much less abounding because the time ran out.

Proportioning requires heroism. Quiller-Couch's "Murder your darlings" is a stern rule. When we have a sparkling idea which we will enjoy using and which we believe the congregation will appreciate, it takes courage to leave it out of the sermon just because it does not belong there. The ability to omit is one of the most important skills. Preachers can apply to themselves the observation in a *Time* book review: "One of the things that Ernest Hemingway taught a generation of imitators was that the way to write good stories is to leave things out. Not just the bad bits, but good ones, so that what remains bears an extraordinary tension." (May 1, 1972, p. 81.) When one illustration, statement, or quotation makes a matter clear enough, it is always a mistake to use another just because it is so good. *The quality of a sermon is shown by the quality of the discard heap.*

Each part of the sermon should also get its fair share of the preparation time. Many sermons start better than they end. When the minister prepares the first part of his sermon he is a perfectionist—trying, and rejecting, and trying again. This takes so long that the last parts must be dashed off in the little time that is left, and by that time his tired brain is slowing up. So the part that all the rest was working toward, the part that most determines the result, is the weakest. Gaius Glen Atkins advised ministers to spend two-thirds of their preparation time on the last third of their sermons.

8. *Prayer.* The urge to pray is strong in those tense moments just before starting to preach, but the need to pray is even greater when what will be said is being worked out. Turning the thoughts to God elevates the whole conception of what the sermon should be doing. It exposes and removes the longing for praise, the fear of criticism, the temptation to warp the truth, the readiness for shoddy techniques, and all the unworthy impulses that can creep into preaching. Sermon-making requires a stream of decisions about what to say and how to say it; talking with God makes those decisions good ones. A lively sense of God while the sermon is being thought out is likely to be communicated to the congregation.

9. *Composition.* The ways of putting sermons into words differ as widely as do ministers. Some work out the sermons in their heads, with only a loose reference to an outline. Some, with the full outline before them, think through it again and again as they work out what they intend

to say, but they do not write it. Others write out the whole sermon. I think most ministers should write their sermons in full, especially for the first few years. The reasons are:

Writing, reflecting, and writing again provide for the best thinking.

Writing gives a chance for strong and good emotions to develop and get into the sermon.

Writing preserves the best that thought and feeling produce. It does not inhibit inspiration, it keeps it. Much of the best thought that comes during sermon preparation will be lost before the sermon is delivered unless it is preserved in writing.

Writing makes it possible to work out the clearest, most beautiful, most powerful ways of saying things. It is the exercise through which, week by week, you learn to express yourself—that is, to develop style.

The only way to time a whole sermon, or any part of it, is to write it out.

Writing saves you from impulsive utterances you will regret.

If your sermon is written, you do not fear a complete failure. You are not precariously dependent on how you happen to be feeling in the pulpit, where weariness, nervousness, or ill health can keep your mind from working well.

You can rewrite, revise, and cut to improve a written sermon as you cannot one that is only outlined.

With a manuscript before you, you can prepare your delivery more thoroughly than you can if you have nothing to refer to. The more nearly you know what you will say, the better you can prepare to say it.

A written sermon is kept for future use, reference, or rewriting.

A written sermon can be copied. Hearers often want to read a sermon, or to give it to friends. Mimeographed sermons can be taken to the ill, or to others who might be interested. They can be used for study groups. To copy from recordings is cumbersome; what is recorded is not literature. (A friend of mine said his secretary told him, "There's just no place to put in punctuation.")

We must also recognize that there are disadvantages in writing sermons.

Writing is an onerous physical labor which consumes time that could be used to improve the sermon.

Writing and speaking require different styles. (Chapter XIV.) When a sermon has been written, some of the inappropriate written style is bound to come out in the preaching.

A sermon should be a live communication from a person to persons, not the rendition of a piece of literature that was prepared in solitude.

The inspiration that radiates from the people to the preacher and the stimulation that comes from the excitement of preaching are lost when a sermon is finished in advance.

The habit of writing makes speakers dependent on it, so that they are handicapped when they have to make a talk that could not be written in advance.

Too much thinking at the speed of writing makes slow thinkers.

It is almost impossible not to be too conscious of a manuscript. If it is in reach during the delivery, the speaker is sure to look at it when he should be looking at the hearers. Even if he does not have it in sight, he will be reading it from the back of his mind, which makes for remoteness from the congregation.

With the good reasons for writing sermons, and the possible handicaps, we have to find the method that will give us the most advantages with the fewest penalties. One way is to write out the sermon, but not to preach what has been written. The preacher knows what is in the written sermon, just as he knows a story he has read, but he is not at all concerned with the precise wording. He uses the written sermon as a treasury from which he brings what he has ready for the congregation, but he uses the forms of expression that spring to his mind while he is speaking.

Professor Henry H. Mitchell, in his book *Black Preaching* (pp. 198–202), says that a minister should relate to the sermon he has prepared as a "soul" musician relates to the piece of music he is using. "No jazzman elaborates on the theme until he has mastered the theme, the instrument, and the diatonic scale. When he does his thing, creating and playing 'from the bottom of his soul,' he has already practiced the basics for hours. To be sure, he is creating, Black fashion, and he is in dialogue with his audience which is comparable to the Black-preaching dialogue. But the least informed Black jazz buff can feel the difference if the artist has not done his homework. So it is with the Black preacher."

To get free from a manuscript requires courage; a timid speaker may panic at the thought of cutting loose from the safe and sure support of the sermon he has written. He has to trust his culture to save him from sounding illiterate, and his readiness in speech to save him from freezing up. Without daring that trust, he will never discover his real abilities or develop them.

Good writing can be the enemy of good preaching if the author falls too much in love with what he has produced. A minister with literary gifts may labor over every word until the sounds and the meanings within the meanings are exactly right. Then he may not have the fortitude to risk all this loving artistry to the hazards of what he may remember while he is speaking to the congregation. So, relying on his memory or manuscript, he delivers the sermon word for word as it is written. He is not really speaking to the congregation, but to his artist's conscience and to the imaginary editors who may sometime clamor for his manuscripts. The unnatural delivery will leave the people too much lost in their thoughts to know what a gem they are missing. If such a gifted minister will take the chance of speaking freely to the congregation, he can know that all the work he has devoted to the sermon writing will not be wasted. The spoken sermon may be quite different from the written one, but he will speak far better for having written well. Some of his best ideas and phrases will be lost, but they may be more than replaced by those that are inspired by the congregation. He will have the advantages of both arts. He will sacrifice something of content for delivery and something of delivery for content, looking for the point of intersection that represents the greatest total good for the congregation.

Many preachers take into the pulpit a more or less full outline of their manuscript, with quotations that are too long to be memorized written out. Another way is to take the whole manuscript, with key words circled or underlined, perhaps in color. This saves the labor of making a separate outline. The disadvantage is that it puts the whole manuscript in sight, and that is a lure many preachers cannot resist. I have watched many young preachers, starting out determined to be free from their manuscripts, then stealing more and more furtive looks, and finally reading every word. Only if his eyes can resist the magnetism of the written page should a preacher who wishes to seem to be speaking directly to his congregation risk marking his outline on his manuscript. Some good preachers have read their sermons to the congregation. There may be many whose makeup is such that this method is the best for them. But there is no question that most congregations like a preacher to speak directly to them. When church members say, "Our minister doesn't even use a note!" they seem to feel they have a status symbol that is supposed to plunge all others deep in envy.

Whatever method a minister uses, he should periodically try others. Unless he does, he may never find the way that is the best for him. Let the minister who reads his sermons get up the courage some Sunday to go into the pulpit without even a note, and let the extempore preacher surprise his congregation by reading the sermon. Habits soon solidify. A minister may start with a method that is wrong for him and stay with it. For ten years I wrote my sermons in ink because I assumed the typewriter inhibited creative thought. Then one week I typed the sermon, and I have never since written one by hand. To experiment with various methods of sermon preparation and preaching will prevent such slow learning. For our own equipping, we need to develop a variety of ways in which we have some skill.

10. *The Mechanics.* Larger type (pica, at least) and fresh ribbons make an outline or a manuscript easier to scan while preaching. There should be plenty of space for alterations between the lines and in the margins. The minister who learns early to type rapidly and correctly has a most valuable labor-saving skill. Some brains may be able to do their best work by dictating to a machine what a secretary will later type out, but most cannot do this because they have to read, reflect on, and revise what they are writing. Putting words in capitals, underlining, and asymmetrical positions of words on the page are aids to quick scanning.

Some ministers lay out words, phrases, and sentences on the page so that the position represents the thought. They believe this helps their style, makes a page easier to scan, and pictures what the delivery ought to be. It also looks interesting in print. One of Peter Marshall's published sermons has a passage that looks like this:

They stood blinking at flashes of lightning like daggers of fire.
There were eyes watching this Man on the Cross . . .
   shifting doubting eyes
      eyes through which Hell itself was looking
         eyes with gloating in them
            other eyes that looked and never saw.

Lips were moving . . . fierce fastened lips drawn in thin lines of cruelty . . .
open lips that vomited blasphemy like craters of hate.

Faces were looking up at Him . . . white faces
      mad faces, twisted and distorted
     laughing faces . . . convulsed faces . . .
faces jeering and roaring round the foot of the Cross

(Mr. Jones, Meet the Master, p. 91.)

If a minister settles early on the sort of paper he will use for his manuscripts and outlines, he can keep his sermon files uniform. The first decision is whether he will be a turner or a slider. A turner uses a ring notebook and writes on both sides of the sheets. The largest standard size that can be turned without being too visible is the most convenient. This is probably 6 by $9\frac{1}{2}$ inches. Double that space is exposed with each turning. Worship notes for each service and a collection of basic materials, such as invocations, confessions, benedictions, and installations can be carried in the same notebook. A slider can advance his sheets without their being seen and can use larger sheets than can be turned, but the writing can be on only one side. Loose sheets are not as convenient to carry as are notebook pages, and there is danger that a passing breeze will cause a loss of speech. Some of the pulpit reading-stands that architects prescribe are so tiny that large sheets cling to them precariously. A minister does not have to submit to furniture that interferes with preaching; and he cannot keep his mind on his delivery if he is distracted by worry about what is happening to his notes. The modification of pulpit furnishings is not expensive. The stand should be large enough for books and papers; its height should be right for the minister who uses it most, and his eyes should not have to drop too far from looking out at the congregation. Its slant should hold what is read at the right angle, without the danger of having everything slide to the floor. The lights should provide for easy reading and for the illumination of the preacher's face—a speaker's expression is an important part of his delivery. The microphones should be placed where the preacher can forget them and where he can talk to those farthest on the right and left without a loss of volume. A preacher needs a timepiece he can look at without being caught. I have always installed a big clock where I can see it without glancing sideways, and where no one else can see it at all. A shelf or table for more materials should be in reach. Pulpit hangings with intense colors are a visual distraction for the congregation.

Dr. Cleland McAfee recommended a useful method. If your writing is going well and you have to interrupt it, your concentration and excitement may be lost when you return. But if you break off in the middle of a sentence you have not yet thought through, when you return to work on it you will be right back on the track.

11. *Visualizing the people.* A minister does not have to work in solitude when he prepares his sermon; he can be talking directly to people he knows. The excitement and inspiration of the audience can be with him in his study. Sermon preparation should be dialogue. When a minister has in mind particular people for whom that sort of sermon is intended, he can think of them as being right there with him. He says something to them, sees them looking skeptical, and tries again. When a statement is too complicated, it is received with blank expressions and has to be rephrased. Let the preacher think of the various sorts of people he will be seeing in the church—the farmer, widow, waitress, high school student, doctor. What are they getting from the sermon?

The best sermons often continue discussions the preacher has had with members of the congregation. During sermon writing, their part in the discussion has to be imagined, but if a pastor knows his people, what he expects them to say will be in character. That is why preaching away from home often seems so barren to the preacher. When he is in his own pulpit, he feels that he is taking his part in a family discussion; when he is away from home, he feels that he is declaiming to strangers. But even in getting ready for an unknown audience, he has to picture the sort of people he assumes will be there, and he tries to talk with them. Some of the directness and fervor of extemporaneous preaching can be in a written sermon which is in imagination spoken directly to real people. The style can then come very close to what is right for spoken communication. And all those apt things we are never quick enough to think of on the spur of the moment come out so beautifully when we have had time to try them out in imagined conversations. That is why a sermon can often be so much more personal than a conversation. Things a preacher has longed to say, and could not say, to those whose hurts, follies, or need for encouragement are on his heart, he can say to them as he imagines them sitting in his study. Then, on Sunday, he actually says to those people what he believes they most need to hear.

If a minister has worked out his sermon this way, some of the feel of a dialogue will be in it when he preaches. It may appear in what he says: "If you agree with me, we can now go on . . ." "We are now ready to . . ." or "I suspect some of you may be thinking . . ." or "Now that I have said this. . . ." This should not be a habitual mannerism or a rhetorical device. But if a preacher is really thinking in these terms, it is well to show it. If this is honestly done, the people can feel that they and the minister are working their way together through the sermon. Questions may be more than rhetorical. They may show that the minister really is very much concerned about the congregation's thinking. "Can we really believe?" "How would you answer?"—such questions make a sermon seem like like a shared enterprise.

12. *Revision.* Just when the preacher wants to think his work is done, he has to start again. With the whole sermon before him, illogicalities in structure may be apparent. Wordings that are clumsy, complex, dull, and ungrammatical will be discovered. A first draft will always be too wordy; it must be run through the wringer until every dispensable word has been squeezed out. If the meaning would be as clear with any sentence or paragraph removed, it has to go. A lean style keeps hearers listening; wordiness gives gaps through which minds can slip out for their own wandering.

At this stage, the sermon is almost sure to be too long, even after the useless words have been cut out. This is where living flesh must be excised; parts the minister knows will strengthen his sermon have to go, only because there is no time. The minister may wonder desperately whether he can save his treasures by hurrying his delivery, which should never be any slower than it has to be, or by stealing time from other parts of the service for just this Sunday. He has to recognize that there is no hope in this. The easiest way to cut is to remove a whole section, which can be saved for another sermon. If this would be too severe a mutilation, there has to be an item-by-item hunt for what is expendable. Quotations, illustrations, and what was put in for relaxation are examined. When these are removed, the progress of the thought may not be weakened, but what remains may be a sermon that will be logically impeccable but so dry and concentrated that no one will listen to it. A minister who knows how many lines of writing ought to go may have to search back and forth until he has removed them, bit by bit.

13. *Preparation for delivery.* Each preacher has his own peculiar way of getting his sermon in mind, and it is always well for him to keep trying to find a better way. A minister who writes only an outline may go through this several times, thinking out what he will say, and then go through it aloud. If he speaks without notes, he will memorize the outline. A minister may read his sermon silently, and then go through it aloud, first rapidly for content and then experimenting with the delivery of each part. He may try to shake loose from the written words and improvise, glancing only at underlined key words. Some practise the delivery from the pulpit of the empty church, others think the time is better used by practising at home.

With every method there has to be some place for vitalizing. The minister must come to feel what he will be saying; it is not enough for him to have in mind the words he wants to speak, he has to remind himself why they are so important so that his whole heart will be in them. He can deliver his sermon readily, clearly, and with the right inflections and still not deliver himself with it. A minister with great skill in expression will sound theatrical unless he is remembering as he preaches how much it means to him. He has to be excited by the knowledge that what he is saying is really true. This element in sermons used to be called "passion." Today "involvement" describes that electric concern which passes from the speaker to the hearers. Vitalizing gets him in the mood for this as he thinks his way through each part of the sermon until he cares about it. This can be an early stage in the preparation for delivery; getting the sermon in mind is easier after this is done.

This getting excited by the contents in advance may save a minister from a strange pulpit malady. A minister is often baffled by a feeling of unreality while he is preaching. He cannot get going. It is like running in deep hay. He feels like a voice crying in the wilderness. The condition is mysterious; it often comes when both the preacher and the sermon have seemed to be in excellent condition. The more the minister struggles to be free, the worse it gets. I believe this state most often comes from the preacher's having something other than the sermon chiefly on his mind. The words flow out with no interruption, but at the top level of the preacher's attention is irritation at whispering in the choir, worry over a tight throat, a fear of forgetting, or a feeling of disapproval from the congregation. This problem is likely to come at the most momentous occasions because what the preacher is mostly thinking about is the importance of preaching a great sermon. When a minister is not chiefly interested in what he is saying, the sermon becomes a performance. Pretending to be thinking of what is being said is an act, and not a very good one. No amount of pulpit-pounding or histrionics will cure the awful sense of hollowness, because what the struggler is really thinking about is "What's wrong with me?" The only cure is actually to turn the top attention from the distraction to the thoughts that are being expressed. This will be easier if a vital concern for them has been worked up in advance.

XIV

Style

Your style is the way you express yourself, and it is yourself that is being expressed. Schopenhauer said that style "is a safer index to character even than the face." If you are pompous, confused, abrasive, or careless, your style will be too. If you are warm, direct, and gracious, your style will reflect it. The sort of words you like to use, and whether you incline to simple or intricate sentence structure, are clues to your character. There are brash and modest, pugnacious and gentle styles. Flaws in your style may reveal flaws in you; attempts to acquire a better style may help you be a better person.

But beyond the basic requirement of personality there is still the need for craftsmanship. Techniques will not make a preacher, but a preacher will be wasted without them. You cannot learn to preach by memorizing rules any more than you can learn to sing, paint, or write stories that way; but singers, painters, writers, and preachers will flounder until they learn some skills. They will have to be those that suit each one's special makeup. Instruction in the preacher's craft can say no more than "This is what has been learned through the years about what makes sermons most effective—*now do it your own way.*"

There is a vast difference between art and artifice. The use of psychology to move crowds and manipulate emotions is not the preacher's business. But when a minister has something of consuming importance to say, it makes a world of difference whether or not he knows how. The whole effect of a story or joke depends on the teller's skill. In the first form, Keats' poem began, "A thing of beauty is a constant joy." A friend remarked that it did not seem just right. The poet worked it over and over until he came up with, "A thing of beauty is a joy forever." It is hard to say why altering one word changed an ordinary statement into an immortal line. That is style.

Artistic techniques without a strong artistic impulse deteriorate into triviality. This can happen to a preacher who acquires the skills of expression without a message he is burningly eager to express; then for him style becomes stylized. When the arts of preaching become ends in themselves, it can be like the president's oratory, which W. G. McAdoo described as "an army of pompous phrases moving over the landscape in search of an idea."A preacher must never let himself become a technician, but he has to have technique.

There is nothing more disastrous than the attempt to preach a great sermon, as many a preacher has learned to his sorrow when he has put all his skill into an address to some important assembly. It is when he strives for greatness that he falls on his face. We might think that great preaching requires an exalted topic, a mind-staggering conception, and sublime thought. But the best sermons have a limited topic, a crystal-clear conception, and down-to-daily-life thought. A minister's Easter sermon is often his poorest. John Robinson, minister to the Pilgrims, said, "As a woman over-curiously trimmed is to be mistrusted, so is a speech." That is a good warning for Easter Sunday congregations and preachers. Stylishness is the enemy of style.

Paul told the Corinthians he had never tried to be impressive because Christ had sent him to preach the gospel, "not with eloquent wisdom, lest the cross of Christ be emptied of its power. . . . I did not come proclaiming to you the testimony of God in lofty words or wisdom. . . . My speech and my message were not in plausible words of wisdom, but in demonstration of the Spirit and power." (I Cor. 1:17; 2:1,4) A person who is on display before a crowd finds it very hard not to try to give the impression that he is a scholar, or brilliant, or eloquent. That is the preoccupation with skill that blocks the message. James Denney of Scotland put it clearly: "No man can bear witness to Christ and himself at the same time. No man can at once give the impression that he is clever, and that Christ is mighty to save."

The preacher seeks the sermon style that is right, not only for him but also for the congregation. He would not preach the same way to theologians and to Girl Scouts. Styles change. Those that were just right for a former generation might be just wrong for now. We can learn much from the great ministers of the past, but we cannot imitate them.

A minister cannot take over any other preacher's style, but he does use models. He needs to identify those he especially admires and try to learn from them. Saul could not put his armor upon David, but there were doubtless skills in combat he could have taught the shepherd boy. The models of good English prose in the last century were supposed to be writers like Ruskin or De Quincey. There are admirable contemporary examples. News magazines can well be imitated for their clear, interesting, personal style. Some religious journals and authors give instructive samples of the worst prose. Ministers can see in them the faults toward which those who deal with religious subjects are inclined to drift—the unnecessarily specialized vocabulary, the in-group pretensions, the convoluted syntax. There is a danger that the books and magazines preachers need to read to keep up with religious thought will influence their sermon style. When the minister moves from some of the sources of his sermon to the preparation of it, he has to know he is moving out of one world and into another. They have different languages and thought patterns, and there needs to be an antiseptic shield between them.

Good conversation is a better model for the preacher than is platform eloquence. Dr. Broadus made an interesting suggestion that is still good when he said that the conversation "of intelligent women may also furnish admirable and influential examples of clear, sprightly, varied, and every way attractive style." (*The Preparation and Delivery of Sermons*, p. 354.) Thus, women preachers start out way ahead.

The difference between written and spoken styles must be kept in mind. A preacher who patterns his sermons too closely on literature may gain some reputation as a literary preacher, but he will not communicate with the congregation as he should. The difference between the two styles is not as great as might be supposed. Good literature is written to be audible in the mind of the reader—the sounds of the words are heard from the page. Competent authors, and certainly preachers, can write as though they were talking to someone. Many of the essentials of good style are identical for writing or speaking. A course on how to write will have much that preachers need, but the differences are important.

THE DIFFERENCES BETWEEN WRITTEN AND SPOKEN STYLES

1. Writing is for a solitary reader; speaking is for a group.

2. Writing can be intended for just one sort of person; a sermon must be for a variety of ages, interests, and educational levels.

3. The emotional interaction between an author and reader is much weaker than that between a speaker and hearer.

4. A reader can reread when his mind has wandered or he has missed the meaning; a hearer cannot go back to get what is lost.

5. A reader sets his own pace; a hearer has to take the speaker's pace. It is quite easy to comprehend in writing such a sentence as "We must accept God's love in trust, humility, obedience, gratitude, and joy." But if a hearer thinks of the first word, the next four slip by with no attention as his mind jumps on to the next sentence. The one use of such a string of words in preaching is to build up an emotional impression that does not require thought.

6. A reader has punctuation as a clumsy substitute for what a speaker reveals vocally. The voice shows questions, exclamations, completed or uncompleted thought, connection or separation. Punctuation is more definite but less expressive than the vocal indications. A good speaker never needs to say the clumsy "Quote unquote."

7. Structure, with paragraphs and numbered main and subheadings, can be visibly revealed on a page. Orally not much beyond main divisions can be shown.

8. A writer has footnotes, titles, and enumerations which do not interrupt the flow; whatever a speaker conveys must be said.

9. A writer must put into words what a speaker can dramatize without

them—*angrily, hesitantly, sadly.* A gesture, facial expression, pause, or tone can say what a writer may need a sentence to express.

10. Grammar is more important in writing than in speaking. A speaker can have unfinished sentences, lost clauses, dangling participles, and floating pronouns which sound all right because eye and ear communication clarifies them. Newspapers had fun printing exactly what President Eisenhower said in press conferences; it was a grammarian's nightmare in writing, but it sounded all right. (Some egregious blunders, however, are more shocking to hearers than to readers. "He wants you and I," or "Let everyone do their duty," can distract a congregation.)

11. A piece of writing is a physical object, a product that can be fingered, passed around, and evaluated. It is bad for a sermon to be thought of as a production. It is an experience, an interaction between persons. What is left of it is not the thing but the effect.

12. When a manuscript is finished, a writer's task is done. A speaker still has a great deal more hard work to do.

Each of these differences shows why the words that are spoken cannot always be the same as the words that are written. A preacher adjusts to this difference in styles in two ways: First, he writes his sermon in the words he expects to use in speaking to the congregation. Second, when he preaches, he uses loosely what he has written. It supplies what he says, but not the way he says it.

THE QUALITIES OF GOOD STYLE

(1) Simplicity

The form of the sermon should above all else be simple, direct, and vigorous. Those who aspire to more showy qualities must make them secondary goals. The first necessity for a sermon is to be understood, and that is best done in the plainest terms. Simplicity is difficult. The unpracticed writer or unskilled speaker falls naturally into artificial and complex expressions. Reshaping first efforts until they sound unstudied is hard work. Somerset Maugham said, "A good style should show no effort. What is written out should seem a happy accident," then he goes on to tell of the grueling labors good authors endure to make their writing sound spontaneous. (*Summing Up.*) Jimmy Durante described the same process in preparing a television show: "We woik a munt fer eighteen hours a day to make it look unrehoised."

Short sentences with straight-out construction—subject, verb, object— are generally the easiest to understand. Participles and infinitives should be kept to a minimum. The active voice has more vigor than the passive —"Bring the fatted calf and kill it," rather than "Let the fatted calf be brought and killed."

Every word that can be spared should be cut out. Beecher's advice

was, "Don't whip with a switch that has leaves on if you want to tingle."
Sometimes words pile up when a minister keeps trying to improve what is
not well said, and the more he tries the weaker he makes it. Redundancy
comes from the illusion that adding descriptives increases the impression, whereas every unneeded adjective or adverb weakens the word to
which it is attached. A *tall giant* is not as tall as a *giant. Smiling joy*
seems less happy than *joy.* A *secretary* is more clearly a secretary than is
a *ravishing secretary.* We thoughtlessly put in empty phrases because we
are used to hearing them—"as you may or may not know," "if I may
be permitted to add," "the question as to whether," "books of a not
too costly sort."

Words are wasted and statements weakened by too scrupulous qualify-
ing. A sermon is not a legal document. Speakers and hearers can trust
each other's common sense, so every reservation does not have to be
spelled out. Whenever possible, a preacher should omit such limiting
words as *nearly, not entirely, usually, a little bit, it may be, I think, it
seems to me, although, perhaps.* An unrestricted statement may be presumptuous or exaggerated, but qualifiers should be kept to a minimum.
Some modest disclaimers have blatantly immodest intentions: "I may not
be the wisest person in the world, but . . .", "I do not know as much
about the future as God does . . .", "I do not consider myself to be tradi-
tionally pious . . ."

The direct, lean, compact sentence has a force preachers need, though
too much conciseness can be a fault. If tight-packed sentences come too
fast, the listeners do not have time to absorb them. The cure is not to
pad with unnecessary words, but to add words that enlarge the meaning,
though they might have been left out. Repetition can be used to give
people a chance to think. It also can add emphasis—"Rejoice in the Lord
always; again I will say, Rejoice." (Phil. 4:4) A redundancy occasionally
adds something; "My precious, darling grandchild" at least expresses
enthusiasm.

There are also exceptions to the rule that short sentences are best.
Too many of them strung together can have an unpleasant staccato
effect. Beauty, majesty, and feeling sometimes require long sentences
for their full expression. A speaker's intonations may carry a hearer
through a sentence where a reader would get lost. Daniel Webster could
make a long, rolling sentence like a symphony. His speech on the
preservation of the Union ends with a sentence that runs through
thirteen lines, though it still would be easy for the listeners to follow.
Sometimes a longer sentence can carry a thought through to its conclusion better than do shorter ones. Kant, in his *Religion Inside the
Bounds of Pure Reason,* has a sentence that is two pages long. It is like
a beautiful complex equation, which has parentheses inside brackets
inside parentheses. Kant would have been sure his full thought could
not be rounded out in any other way. It makes plausible the old story
of the German who said to his wife during a lecture, "Shall we go now,

or wait for the verb?" The rule that sermon sentences should be short and simple is important, but it can be ignored when the preacher knows why.

(2) Clarity

Obscurity is the deadly enemy of preaching; the greatest possible clarity must be the preacher's goal. Any supposed excellencies that make his meaning more difficult are vices. The purpose of style is to reveal thought, not conceal it. Matthew Arnold decreed, "Have something to say, and say it as clearly as you can. That is the only secret of style." The preacher must ask not only "Will this be understood?" but also "Can this be misunderstood?"

Sermons have to deal with some of the deepest concepts that can engage the human mind—with God, being, soul, goodness, truth, time, eternity. A preacher who was always easy to understand would defraud the congregation. The necessary difficulty of the subject matter makes it especially important to use every possible aid to clarity and to eliminate every avoidable obscurity.

Sources of Unclarity

(a) *Unclear Thinking.* The greatest aid to clarity is clear thinking by the minister. If he slights the rigouous mental exertion of getting his own thoughts in order, what he says will be opaque. Some of the very muddy prose in supposedly profound writing reveals the authors' failure to work out in their own minds what they mean. When a preacher labors over a sentence to make it clear, he is usually figuring out his own understanding of it.

Bad writing reveals bad thinking: "Everybody do their best," "He only died a week ago," "Everyone does not speak German," "Don't be gone longer than you can help," "It's hard to read, much less answer, my mail," "I shouldn't be surprised if it didn't rain," "I like to watch bricklayers, and I have chosen that as my occupation," "There is a chair by the pulpit on which you are to sit," "Lying on the front pew and kicking his legs in the air, the minister saw a baby." A student sermon said, "I praise God for being at Princeton Seminary." For a while there was danger that *hopefully* would come into common use as a mixed-up substitute for *it is to be hoped*. To say, "Hopefully, he won't get drunk" is as illogical as to say "Happily, he searched in vain for his bottle." Clarity is the guide in many grammatical uncertainties. Split an infinitive or close a sentence with a preposition if that makes the meaning clearer. Good thinking, clear statement, and good grammar go together.

(b) *No Paragraphs.* There is an old rule that a preacher should speak in paragraphs because that makes him easier to understand. When he gives a topic sentence and then tells what he has to say about it, the audience can follow him. A good paragraph is an assembled module.

(c) *Lost Emphasis.* Emphasis makes meaning clearer; by showing the relative importance of the ideas, it helps the hearers sort them out. It is shown by tone, pauses, and gestures. In the jealous girl's statement, "I'll never see what makes him love her," the meaning depends entirely on which of the eight words is stressed. In writing, emphasis is shown by the position in the sentence, with the greatest at the close, and the next at the beginning. Displacement from the normal position gives emphasis: "What makes him love her, I'll never see."

(d) *To Absent People.* Clear preaching will be directed to the sort of people who are in the pews. We are often tempted to speak to those who are not there—to our one-time seminary professors, to other ministers, to the writers of religious books and magazines. We spend our time in their mental world; they rouse us to disagreement or agreement; we want to impress them—so on Sunday mornings we have it out with them, with the congregation allowed to listen in.

The mental commerce we fancy we are having with these clever people is actually dull compared with the brilliance that is required to talk understandably with the sort of people who are there. Phillips Brooks said that the greatest compliment to his intellect he ever received came from an eleven-year-old newsboy who attended church every Sunday and listened intently. Dr. Brooks asked a layman to find out from the boy why he came. He explained, "Oh, I like to hear Dr. Brooks. You see, he doesn't know any more than I do."

(e) *To Ourselves.* We preach to ourselves. A minister has his own spiritual and personal problems he is needing to work out. There are subjects that fascinate him. If his special interest is counseling, world peace, philosophy, belles-lettres, he will long to talk about them. His members may not share either his interest or his comprehension.

(f) *Professional Boredom.* Ministers may be obscure because they are bored with the banal. They are professionals, and they may have gotten tired of the simple, moving things that are still fresh for most of the congregation. They may think they have to find novel or subtle forms of expression that will simply puzzle the less blasé.

(g) *False Dignity.* A false idea of the dignity required for godly themes may make sermons difficult. The simple, artless, even breezy directness of clear preaching may seem to the minister unworthy of his lofty task.

Martin Luther made plain what he thought of all this: "I do not aim very high in my pulpit at Wittenberg, as if I were addressing none but scholars and doctors and magistrates, of whom there may be forty in the building, for there are also present two thousand plain folk and lads and lasses, and to them I speak as their need requires. If the others do not like it, the door is open, and they are free to depart."

(h) *Sloth.* Preachers may be obscure because they are lazy. It is hard to work to translate from the expressions that first come to mind to the way they should be put to an audience. So the minister may say what comes natural to him and shirk the difficult next step.

(i) *Pendantry.* A minister may be unable to talk people-talk. A difficult, complex way of speaking may be the only language he knows. He may be incurably pedantic. In that case we can hope he has other qualities that will be useful for his congregation to make up for his preaching failures.

(j) *Ministerial Jargon.* A minister may not understand the difference between his vocabulary and assumptions and those of the people he is talking to. Dr. Falconer, a minister who was in charge of a radio mission to Scotland, told how delighted he was when he thought one of the preachers was making a thrilling talk to lay listeners in their own terms. Dr. Falconer said that the studio engineer was beside him, so, "no doubt with eyes ashine, I turned to my colleague and asked him what he thought of that. He looked at me with puzzled concentration for a moment, and then he answered, 'Honestly, old man, I haven't a clue to what the man was talking about.' " Dr. Falconer comments, "Your good Christian soul, born and brought up in the Church, trained in her ways of thought, expression, and worship, for the life of him cannot understand why the non-church-goer does not receive with a like enthusiasm the traditional preaching of the Word." (*Success and Failure of a Radio Mission,* pp. 18, 25) Many members of the church do not understand what the preacher often assumes is plain and obvious. It has been said that most sermons are like a safety match which can strike fire only when it is rubbed on a surface that has been especially prepared. Many church people may understand the words but still have no mental pigeonholes into which to fit such expressions as *Christ will give you, come to Jesus, consecrated to Him, cast your cares on Him.* Thus they can have no meeting of minds with preachers who use these terms. There may be a crooning value in the good old phrases, but no clear content.

With all this there is no implication that a minister should preach down to people. A good guide is, "Do not count too much on the people's knowledge, or too little on their intelligence." Their technical religious knowledge is different from the minister's, but if he talks to them as to those of inferior mental ability, there is no hope for him. Dr. Brooks said that a minister who does this "grows to despise his own sermons, and the people quickly learn to sympathize with their minister." The preacher whose attitude is, "This is pretty poor stuff, but they love it," has become a panderer. Never in the deepest privacy of his own mind must he ever entertain the thought that he could offer his congregation anything less than his best; he must know that they are worthy of a ten times better sermon than he can ever preach. "Never talk down to your audience; they are not there."

This has been a chapter of reversals. With all that has been said about the supreme importance of clarity, it must be recognized that there are a few reasons why a sermon may not be entirely understood. If a preacher stays within the limits of what he can make plain to people, their understanding will not be stretched. When they are perplexed at first, they may think their way to comprehension. Curiosity can be a stimulus to learning. Moreover, there are some sermons that are not intended to be understood in any common-sense way; their purpose is more like that of poetry; they are to evoke a response, to waken feelings. The appropriate question is not so much "Did you get it?" as "Did it get you?" One more good reason for obscurity—a congregation is diverse. A minister has to mystify some people in order to reach others. Often some look baffled while others are intent. A minister who tried to preach to everyone every Sunday would have to stay within too narrow a rut. One necessity in sermon planning is to make sure that there are not too many Sundays when any sort of worshipper will be left out.

A sermon may be purposely obscure; a minister may be so scornful of the ordinary that he tries to make an art form of being baffling. This may be satisfying for the preacher, but not for the congregation. There is, however, another sort of enigmatic preaching for which there can be reason. It has the charm of the unobvious. The preacher tries to leave room for the play of fancy; he wants to stimulate the hearers' creativity, so he sets them to looking out into unexplored vistas and throws out suggestions they have to follow up themselves. Unexplained allusions can be rewarding and exciting—the problem is that there are many in most congregations who do not go in for this sort of thing. Even those who enjoy it may not get much. A sermon is not for playing hide-and-seek. It might take care of both sorts of needs if the preacher includes clear statements of the important things he wants to say along with the less prosaic ways of saying them.

Almost always, however, clarity is indispensable. A lucid statement is likely to be accepted as true; a confusing one will be doubted. Obscurity sets up an enmity between a speaker and an audience. People will suspect that he is showing off, that he is not interested in them, that he is not their sort of person. Their resentment will defeat what he hopes to do.

(3) Logic

Classical rhetoric assumed that a speaker's most important skill is the ability to think straight. It gave much attention to such topics as fallacies, refutation, relationship, testimony, logical appeal, and the syllogism. A preacher can benefit from a study of these. He cannot well persuade, teach, disprove, or motivate if his thought processes are confused. Often we know better than we practice. When we suspect ourselves of an irrationality, our zeal hurries us along. We fear that if we pause to reflect, it may spoil a good sermon. Our enthusiasms betray us into logical lapses which our audiences detect with condescension or disdain.

Untidy thinking produces messy sermons. Those familiar fallacies the books on logic warn against are pulpit pitfalls. We base sweeping conclusions on insufficient evidence. A few corrupt officials can be proof that the downfall of the country is imminent. We overstate—"If you aren't radiant, you're not a Christian." We shift the meaning of the words we use so that a sermon on Religion that is Pure and Undefiled (Jas.

1:27) ends up dealing with pornography. We beg the question—"You know that you can trust in God because his goodness never fails." Our evidence from nature or archaeology often is convincing only to those who already accept our assumptions—"And pointing to the stars, the great scientist asked his unbelieving colleagues, 'Gentlemen, who made those?' " Assumed answers to prayer often display the after-it-therefore-because-of-it fallacy. We may set up improper either-or propositions; when a preacher thundered, "I would rather run off with my neighbor's wife than be a racist!" someone whispered, "Who wouldn't?" We make faulty generalizations—"This country has grown great and prosperous because men came to North America seeking God, while they came to South America seeking gold." There are non sequiturs—"If you take God as your partner, how can you fail?" (You can't—but you may go broke.) There are false conclusions—"His eye is on the sparrow, and I know he watches me." (His eye was also on the pterodactyl.)

Sermons often have self-contradictory propositions. It is not really logical to entice the congregation with the rewards of selfless living, or to promise that God can make them independent. There is some inconsistency in the familiar prayer of confession which tells God every week that "we have erred and strayed from Thy ways" so "there is no health in us," and then asks him every week to grant "that we may hereafter live a godly, righteous, and sober life."

(4) Interest

James Black of Scotland took a survey of his church members to see what they thought had most to do with making a sermon effective. Unanimously they passed up eloquence, dramatic power, emotion, brilliance, and logic to say that being interesting was the most important. If a sermon is not interesting, people will not listen to it; then no other quality is of any use. We need to remember that it was said of Jesus when he spoke in the temple, "The common people heard him gladly." (Mk. 12:37 KJV) They were not hoping for signs that he was finishing, they were not looking for a door to slip out by—they were enjoying listening to him. Can a minister who is speaking for his Lord be dull? To make Christianity tedious, boring, dreary is indeed a heresy; it is sacrilege; it is a sin against the Holy Spirit. There are ways of making sermons interesting:

What Makes Sermons Interesting

(a) *Reality.* It takes reality to make a sermon interesting. P. T. Forsyth put it plainly: "The cure for dullness in the pulpit is not brilliance but reality." "Reality" means a definite connection with human life; a Biblical sermon that is concerned only with Ezekiel and not with us is lacking in reality. So are sermons about the Bible which never get to our needs. Jesus often quoted Scripture, but we cannot imagine him treating it as literature. Sermons fail to have reality when they answer questions we are not asking, or deal with matters that make no difference to us.

Reality does not require immediate practicality. For a student who is upset by the apparent contradiction between divine sovereignty and moral freedom, a sermon on predestination can be very real. A sermon on the abstract concept of providence can be real to a person who is distraught by the hideous cruelties in an animal world Christians think God made. A sermon is real when it deals with real people, real situations, and real problems.

Hearing a sermon on theology may be like watching a drama played out on a distant stage. The interaction of covenant, sin, atonement, redemption, and salvation may be a spectacle that does not touch real life at any point. Or, if we accept the invitation to have a part in the drama, we can do it by getting up on the stage and, perhaps with deep emotion, taking a role that has no connection with where we spend our days.

Appeals to Christlike living may be empty oratory because they never get to what we ought to do. Sermons on joy, the life of love, discipleship, grace, and trust may have no bearing on what happens when we leave the church. A doctrinal sermon on sin may serve to convince most of the hearers that they are doing as well as could be expected. They never connect what the preacher says with the memories that gall them, their feelings of inadequacy, or the resentments they are cherishing. People who are desperate for some meaning to their lives may hear nothing in church that will give them any satisfying sense of purpose when they go out of their doors on Monday morning.

To be real, a sermon does not have to be folksy, with a string of sentimental stories about the preacher's experiences with people. The intellectual demands are much more rigorous than that. First, the preacher has to think deeply and clearly about the great truths of the Christian faith. Second, he has to translate these thoughts into the vocabulary and concepts of his hearers. Third, and most difficult of all, he has to connect this with the actual situations of the people in the pews. He has to "bring it home" to them.

The assumption that we give reality to sermons by using illustrations may be misleading. The illustrations must be those we can connect with ourselves. Bible illustrations often fail in this. If the minister tells the story of Joseph as an example of God's loving care, it is not likely that the businessman who is facing bankruptcy or the girl whose parents are separating will get much reassurance from it. Illustrations from ancient Rome, the Boxer Rebellion, or arctic exploration are remote from us. We can get more help by hearing about a child's first day at school or a patient's thoughts on the night before an operation, because those are experiences to which we can relate.

(b) *Emotion.* Emotion is important. To give *attention* is to be in *tension*—that is, *stretched.* Unless the preacher can keep up his end of this pull, the attention will draw away from him. Emotion has a pull that will keep a hearer stretched out in spite of his inclination to be relaxed.

The quick and powerful emotions are the easiest to use. Those connected with violence and sex are mainstays of the entertainment industry. Readily interesting emotions are attached to personal interests—greed, pleasure, safety, popularity, success—as advertisers well know. Christianity offers the preacher the emotional pull of love, loyalty, reverence, awe, joy, indignation, sympathy, delight, admiration. Delight in intellectual pursuits is an emotion; it is interesting to observe the passion with which those who wish to be coldly rational will assert their preference for reason and their mistrust of feeling.

A preacher must richly use emotion, both to hold attention to his sermons and to give them power. How unlike Jesus we are in our calm, deliberative preaching. Think of the passion that must have throbbed in his voice when he denounced the Pharisees, wept over the city, shamed those who exploited the poor, glorified the heavenly Father, or implored people to love each other. Think of the burning words of Peter, Stephen, Paul, Savonarola, and Luther, and of all who have preached Christ as he should be preached. James S. Stewart has said, "Let anything in the name of cheap emotionalism be banned; but it is a tragedy to jettison emotion as well. . . . Only Spirit can cast out spirit; and nothing could be more futile or pathetic than the attempt to set a tepid Christianity over against a scorching paganism, a casual take-it-or-leave-it argument for faith against the almost mystic fervor and passion of the false ideologies which bestride the world today." (*The Expository Times,* August, 1952, p. 354.)

The typical trouble in the churches I know best is not empty minds but starved hearts. Ministers hide the emotions they really feel. Even when they care deeply about a subject, they tend to deal with it at arm's length. Our sermons need more warmth in content and delivery. People come together to hear sermons because being with each other and with the preacher opens their hearts to emotions they would miss outside the fellowship. If mental help is all they are given, the advantage of being together is lost. They could as well have stayed at home and gotten their information out of books.

(c) *People.* People are more interesting than things. The most interesting subjects for a hearer are, in this order: himself, his family, someone he knows, someone he does not know, a group he belongs to, a social abstraction. People as individuals are more interesting than are people in the mass. Newspapers do not build big circulations by social or political news, but by telling about persons. A sermon is made more interesting by every personal word—a name, personal pronoun, title, group term. Every sermon should show at an early stage the difference it makes to each hearer and to other persons. Do not use impersonal references if you can mention real people. "It is said . . . "is much less interesting than "The man next door told me . . ."

(d) *Giving Life to Abstractions.* Abstractions make sermons deadly dry, but abstractions are the preacher's business. He has to show the life-and-death difference made by such abstractions as love, sin, grace, and salvation. The solution is to keep abstractions from being bare. They have to be clothed in human flesh.

S. I. Hayakawa has a "ladder" of abstraction. It starts with "Bessie," a real cow. Then up the ladder, toward increasing unreality, come *cow, livestock, farm assets, assets,* and *wealth.* Obviously, Bessie is the most interesting item on this ladder.

A minister may have the mistaken idea that a sermon is the marshalling and deployment of generalities. For the preacher it can be exciting to trace the difference between repentance and remorse, or to demolish false views of personality. This offers a sort of action—the clash of concepts and working out of puzzles. A sermon can be a mere word game, a maneuvering of ideas which makes no contact with real living. Some sermons never mention any actual person or situation. A Biblical sermon may get no closer to where we live than Palestine, and two thousand years ago. The whole thing is played out in a never-never land where no one is living.

The difference between the wrong and right way to get at a sermon starts with the first stages of the preparation. Suppose the sermon subject is forgiveness. One minister might begin by looking up all the Bible references. He will then go on to examine the place of forgiveness in theology, and he will consider the intellectual problems it presents. Getting really excited, he will plan to unfold to the probably uncaring congregation the seeming antithesis between forgiveness and justice. Then, with joy, he will show how these are reconciled in the covenant relationship. This is supposed to hit us hard because we see now that the divine forgiveness is the model for our relation to our fellow men. The sermon closes with an appeal to everybody to be more forgiving.

Real preaching requires a completely different start. The minister should begin by wondering what forgiveness means to him. He thinks of the people he resents, and recalls how often he stares unseeing at a book because the memory of an old quarrel crossed his mind. He thinks of the things he is so ashamed of that they make him cringe. He thinks of the people he knows who are torn up by grudges—the man who goes to a bar because he dislikes going home, the couple who came to him for counseling because they cannot forgive each other, the business man who broods over his partner's unfairness, the office that is ravaged by grievances. He guesses that there is not a person in the congregation who is not sometimes tasting the bitter aloes of old wrongs. With any heart at all, the minister will be so in sympathy with his suffering people he could not possibly preach one of those ten-feet-off-the-ground, concept-juggling sermons. He will go to the Bible to find out why it talks so often about enemies; he will get to the covenant, and rejoice in the glorious assurance that God in Christ forgives us. Whether his sermon starts with the Bible or with the problems, he will see the great truths in terms of the people who are on his mind, not in terms of the abstractions he has been shuffling. The preacher will never come to forgiveness by getting such concepts as reconciliation and acceptance lined up in neat and empty patterns until he comes to it through such concepts as son-in-law, roommate, foreman. A sermon is never a circle around an idea, it is an ellipse around two foci—one is a Christian truth, the other is an actual human situation. (Chapter XVI.) The abstraction and the reality are the two necessary elements in every sermon. We do not treat subjects, we treat people by using subjects.

We also escape the deadening effect of our necessary dealing with abstractions by putting them in real terms. Jesus did not say, "Solitude in prayer is necessary," he said, "Go into your rooms and shut the door"; he did not say, "Enmity is irreconcilable with worship," he said, "Leave your gift there before the altar and go; first be reconciled to your brother"; he did not say, "Cultivate consistency," he said, "If your right eye cause you to sin, pluck it out." The incarnation was necessary because the concepts about God had to be dramatized on our stage. Human hearts cannot be satisfied with abstractions. If nothing better is offered they will worship a sacred rock or a clumsily carved piece of wood. Jesus made God real to us by letting us see him in action on our scene. That is just what preachers have to do with the great Christian truths like hope, power, guidance, and redemption. They have to clothe these with actuality.

If the minister talks only in abstractions, the people will try to understand them by thinking of pictures, and their pictures may not be good ones. C. S. Lewis wrote, "A girl I know was brought up by 'higher thinking' parents to regard God as perfect 'substance.' In later life she realized that this had actually led her to think of Him as something like a vast tapioca pudding. (To make matters worse, she disliked tapioca.)" (*Miracles*, p. 90.) If the minister refuses to describe the heavenly love in terms of a person who loves, the people will have to think of it as like electromagnetism—which is a picture from a lower level.

(e) *Making the Familiar Interesting.* The minister has to make what is familiar interesting. All the most important Christian truths were given by Jesus and his apostles many years ago; the high points in the Bible are well known to most churchgoers. They will not be on edge to find out how Judas died, or whether Paul prefers law or faith.

A minister may assume that his task is to proclaim the gospel, but it cannot be that simple. He has to proclaim the gospel to those who have not heard it, and to explain it to those who have. All but a few people in most congregations already know the basic Christian message. The gospel is the good news, but *old news* is a self-contradiction. A sermon should start with where the congregation already is and go on from there. The most frequent reason that is given for not attending church is, "I just don't get anything." People do not come to hear what they already know.

We might like to hope that there is a mysterious qualiy in sacred things that keeps them from ever getting tiresome. Ministers sometimes seem to believe that a miracle suspends the ordinary laws of tedium in church. Unhappily, it does not work that way. When a minister starts his sermon by telling in his own words exactly what the Scripture reading has just said, the congregation will be bored. We do not want to hear again that Joseph's brothers sold him into Egypt. When we are told that the human heart cannot be satisfied with materialism, or are assured in detail that prayer makes a difference, our prayer will be, "Lord, how long?" That is what Paul Tournier called using a battering ram on an open door.

Saying obvious things in obvious ways can have some of the blessings of a holy rite. A preacher may accept this as his proper function, but he can hope to do much more than that. If he uses his Christmas sermon to inform the congregation that a king named Herod did not want a Messiah to be born in Bethlehem because Herod was a wicked man, not many will be listening. But how many fresh and exciting things are said about the Christmas story every year! It is an inexhaustible source of interest and delight because it has inexhaustible connections. Every possible human problem is related to it, and the Christmas light shines into every nook and cranny of the soul. A minister has boundless resources for keeping familiar Christian truths and Bible sayings interesting because they have boundless implications. Consider, for example, these resources:

How the Familiar Is Made Significant

A sermon can increase the *intensity of our feeling* about something we know quite well. (Chapter III.) Andrew Wyeth can paint a picture of a well known old barn that no one has paid much attention to for years— and can reveal in it what was never seen before. There is no use informing the congregation that Jesus washed the disciple's feet as an example of humility—unless the story is told in a way that will make people feel the humility as they never have before.

Pounding on hearts with something people already know may *break down resistance to* it (Chapter III.); it may bring them to a stronger commitment to beliefs they have long accepted without being much affected.

There can be *new angles* on old truths. Someone who has long cherished a belief in the Holy Spirit may still get a fresh insight from being told that in the Holy Spirit we have the Motherhood of God. No church member in a long lifetime could begin to get all the needed slants on the sacraments, prayer, Christian duty, or the resurrection.

Countless *fresh applications* of Christianity are needed with every development in human life. People who are drowsing through a sermon on the Ten Commandments may sit bolt upright when they are told that they are breaking several of them through the stocks and bonds they own.

A good sermon *makes us participants*. You may be bored by a familiar play, but if it is recast with you as a performer, you will become intensely interested. Preaching can give us a role in some of the most familiar dramas of the Christian faith.

The familiar is needed to *keep us from forgetting*. Moses commanded the Israelites to go over the same old words every day, "Lest you forget the Lord." Youthful idealism fades; high resolves are forgotten; hearts grow cold. Charles Laughton said that when a play has run so long that the actors are becoming stale, he has them assemble in a dressing room and read their lines as they did the first time, to recapture the excitement they felt then. There are sermons whose chief purpose is to restore to sparkling freshness what has faded for us. Great truths that seem banal must be made exciting.

What we have heard most is likely to be the most important. It is the well-traveled roads that lead to the most desired destinations. Henry van Dyke said, "It is by forgetting platitudes that men and nations are ruined." It is a wonderful thing to be a preacher of the saving platitudes. Those who dismiss as trite what they have heard before may miss the point.

Old truths need *fresh wording* to make them interesting. Preachers have to become adept at original wording and unconventional expressions to keep people listening. Truisms which are put in novel ways can be saved from tedium.

(f) *Change of Pace.*   It takes a change of pace to maintain interest. Not even Paul Revere could have waked up the same people by saying the same thing every seven days. J. S. Kennard, from the last century, puts it vividly: "Attention is held by frequent transitions from the didactic to the pictorial, from affirmation to interrogation, from description to dialogue, now a quotation and now an anecdote, now a verse of poetry and now a flash of humor, sometimes a deliberate pause, especially after a passionate passage, and a new commencement in a different key, the quiet conversational manner following a fiery declamation. . . . Attention cannot be gained by hammering the Bible, nor screaming at the people. Often a whisper or an emphatic pause is very effective." (*Psychic Power in Preaching,* p. 63.) There is some possibility that Dr. Kennard's hearers would be whirling, but many of the old-time preachers were masters of contrast. They had to be, with their long sermons. Their skills are even more important in our time, with the limited attention span many people have for serious discourse.

A change of pace gives people a chance to use a new set of muscles and shift the load. A dramatic illustration or something that is funny gives a pause for relaxation, and the congregation is refreshed. A composer wrote a beautiful piece for the coronet, but it was never used because he forgot to put in any place for the player to inhale. By a shift of moods, the monotony is broken up. Charles H. Spurgeon's advice to his students is still good: "Keep on, on, on, on, on, with commonplace matter and a monotonous tone, and you are rocking the cradle, and deeper slumbers will result; give the cradle a jerk, and sleep will flee." (*Lectures to My Students,* Series I, p. 224.)

It is also important to have a change of pace from one sermon to the next. Do not let people be able to expect what you will do. Give a factual sermon one Sunday and a fanciful one the next. Have four points, and then no points. When people are expecting a summation, suddenly quit.

(g) *Sermon Titles.*   Sermon titles may rouse interest. If people see the title in the bulletin early in the service, they may be looking forward to the sermon. A title can also help people understand what the sermon is trying to do. A title can be published in advance or posted outdoors where people can read it before they come into the church.

Harry Emerson Fosdick was a master of appealing sermon titles. Some of them were: *Living Under Tension, The Secret of Victorious Living, The Power to See It Through, On Being Fit to Live With, The Wrong Way to Build a Church, Christ and the Inferiority Complex, A Little Morality Is a Dangerous Thing, On Being Strongly Tempted To Be Christian, A Great Time To Be Alive.*

The best source of interesting titles is interesting ideas for sermons. A minister who cannot think of a good title may have to wonder whether his sermon is commonplace. A title is usually better if it offers something people want. *Strength For Tomorrow* would be a better title than *The Cruse That Was Never Empty; What Paul Can Tell You About Disappointments* is better than *Why Paul Went To Macedonia.* Sometimes, however, a title is fraudulent advertising. During a fevered Kentucky political campaign, I announced a sermon on *The Real Election Issues.* I was embarrassed when the church was crowded with outsiders who were expecting something sensational, and what I had for them was a sermon on the Ten Commandments.

Humorous sermon titles can be useful, but there are risks. Such a title is likely to be a pun, and a pun has to be sudden; when it is looked at long, it fades. The week the story of Cain and Abel was used for class preaching, we had sermons on "Raising Cain," and "Are You Abel?" When a somewhat mature committee submitted to our denomination a report on human sexuality, it was unfavorably reviewed in a sermon entitled, *Love and the Sexegenarians.*

(h) *Dubious Devices.*   Along with proper ways of making sermons interesting, some dubious devices must be mentioned:

Emotion can be exploited. Cheap sentimentality, and the emotions roused by scandal, crime, anger, fear, and longing, are easy sources of quick interest. Attention will be caught by the sound of such words as *sheriff, sex, mugging, communism, president, adultery, success.* All of those may need to be mentioned in church, but there must be a better reason than the desire to titillate.

The use of fear and longing tests the preacher's conscience. The Bible abounds in threats and promises. Any preaching on evil or good has to imply both dangers and rewards. Christianity holds out the wonderful blessings Christ offers, and raises the dreadful possibility of missing them. I once heard a distinguished preacher say, "I would rather scare them into heaven than see them go to hell unafraid." But we can be sure that exploiting terror or greed simply to rouse interest will be wrong.

The pulpit sensationalist can hold an avid interest. He will also cheapen the gospel and earn Milton's condemnation of preachers whose—

". . . lean and flashy songs
Grate on their scrannel pipes of wretched straw;
The hungry sheep look up, and are not fed,
But, swoln with wind and the rank mist they draw,
Rot inwardly, and foul contagion spread."

Exaggeration makes sermons interesting. All the great orators count on superlatives. Think of Churchill's "This is England's finest hour," and "Never have so many owed so much to so few." It would be hard to prove that those assertions were true, but he needed them. Preachers use superlatives: "It was the hardest decision Lincoln ever faced"; "Not in this century has there been so important an assembly as this one"; "The generation gap has never been as wide as it is now." Each of those statements may be dubious, but superlatives are what make speeches strong. Are they honest? James Black advises, "Do not be afraid of exaggeration." (*The Mystery Of Preaching,* p. 86) Almost any straight statement would not be strictly true without some reservation, but every reservation weakens. It could be argued that an exaggeration is a rhetorical convention audiences will understand as part of the game. And, if something might be true, why not say it? No one can prove it is not true that "John Calvin was the finest gentleman of the Reformation," or that "Western civilization was saved at the Eisenhower's humble home in Kansas." The speaker usually believes his superlatives until the speech is over. Here again, the burden is thrown on the preacher's conscience. We can, at least, be sure that when exaggeration verges on deception it must be avoided.

The use of the *phony shocker* was mentioned. (Chapter X—the reverse sermon) "Christianity owes its existence to the lack of a lunatic asylum in first-century Jerusalem"; "Morality is the great affliction of mankind." This usually turns into something bland, but it does serve to stir up interest, at least among the gullible.

Another useful but reprehensible trick is to give *startling information* no one else has. The preacher lets it be known that he has it from reliable but confidential sources that the Japanese emperor has for seven years been secretly a Presbyterian, or the lost ending of The Acts is hidden in the Vatican, or the leading candidate for the presidency is a practicing polygamist, or the Pentagon has a secret device for paralyzing by television, or Stalin expired singing, "Just As I Am." Stories not much more credible than these are a common resource of preachers of a certain sort. They probably do not invent them, but if they hear such a tale, and it seems to be useful, they do not risk spoiling it by checking. It is a safe rule that anything so astonishing that is not in general knowledge in a country with a free press is probably not true.

(5) Beauty

Beauty is a reminder of God. Sermons need beauty, both in what they say and in how they say it. Beauty in sermons does not usually come from adornment. It can be found in clarity, in the apt word and moving thought. The experience of the aesthetic in a sermon can open the way to what is good and right. Beauty is a delight that should be one of the sources of the joy of worship.

A preacher has to pay attention to the rhythm of his sentences and to the tone fall, not just for the pleasure they can give, but for their effect. In this he has to trust his ear; no rules or counting syllables can help. William Strunk, in *The Elements of Style,* shows how the sound of Thomas Paine's sentence, "These are the times that try men's souls," makes it strong. Just why is hard to see, but when the sounds are changed, the sentence dies—for example, "Times like these try men's souls," "These are trying times for men's souls," "Soulwise, these are trying times." Mr. Strunk points out that when Lincoln began his Gettysburg Address, "Fourscore and seven years ago," he risked transgressing against brevity, common sense, and ordinary usage because the sound of those opening words was so important. The natural "eighty-seven years ago" would not do.

There are a few guides; we are told to avoid a repetition of words or sounds, especially hissing sounds. A strong sentence should not end with a succession of weak words or unaccented syllables, like *generosity.* But mostly preachers learn by getting the feel for good effects from those who can create them. The Bible in the older versions and Shakespeare can be absorbed into our inner rhythms. Compare Shakespeare's "Cowards die many times before their death" with the way a public speaker would be likely to put it, "Before they reach the end of their lives, cowards have many experiences of dying." "Had I but served my God with half the zeal I served my king," might have been expected to be "With half the zeal with which I served my king," which would have ruined it.

Robert Louis Stevenson can show us how to tune our hearing to the beat of words. When he was dangerously ill he prayed: "Give us courage, and gaiety, and the quiet mind. Spare to us our friends, soften to us our enemies. Bless us, if it may be, in all our innocent endeavours. If it may not, give us strength to encounter that which is to come, that we may be brave in peril, constant in tribulation, temperate in wrath, and in all changes of fortune and down to the gates of death, loyal and loving to one another." His prayer for the night sounds like a lullaby—". . . bring us to our resting beds weary and content and undishonoured, and grant us in the end the gift of sleep." *(Vailima Prayers.)*

Someone who has a good sense for sound can have the sounds and rhythms help the sermon—the up-beat, down-dropping, rough, irregular, melodious. I doubt whether anyone says, "Here we need some dismal *d*'s," or "some sibilants would help," or "let's give this sentence a lilt," or, "make this paragraph end like the slamming of an iron door." But when a minister is sensitive to effects like these, they come out to match the way he feels, without being devised. Primitive orators do it well entirely by instinct.

Antithesis is a device the Bible often uses, and so can speakers: "The sabbath was made for man, not man for the sabbath," "Ask not what your country can do for you—ask what you can do for your country."

Everybody makes fun of alliteration, and everybody uses it. Its sound can be pleasing, though when it is carried a fraction too far, it becomes ridiculous. Good writers utilize it, and even flaunt it in their titles—*Love's Labour's Lost, Beside the Bonnie Brier Bush,*" "*Song for Saint Cecelia's Day,*" "*Devils, Drugs and Doctors.*" *Time* magazine describes a revolutionary band as under a "fog of fatigue, fear, and frustration." But it is foolish to let alliteration be a reason for using words that are not quite the best. It is even more foolish to let a sermon's contents be influenced by the desire to have the key words for the main points start with the same letter. Alliteration is used judiciously by literary professionals, and too much by semi-pros, which should be a warning for preachers.

The ugly is admissible in the pulpit when the message requires it. Sermons have to deal with the unsavory. The church forces its members to look squarely at the most repellent realities so they may recognize what Christians have to do, but anything that is unnecessarily offensive damages a sermon. If a minister is describing advertising methods, another product will serve him better than a deodorant. A uselessly detailed description of something repulsive will make people remember the sermon with a lingering impression of disgust.

Beauty is not as prized an attribute of public speech as it once was. Majesty, elegance, and embellishment are not in vogue. The most sought-after qualities now are functional. But beauty does not go out of date; Shakespeare, roses, sunsets, and Phidias are timeless. The more beauty a sermon has, the better it will communicate God's love and loveliness.

(6) Right Mood

The mood should match the sermon. The mood is established by the preacher's manner, by what he says, the words he chooses, and the shape of his sentences. A sermon on courage must not seem uncertain; one on beauty cannot be unpleasant; one on hope should not feel depressing. I heard this year a sermon on Phil. 4:4, "Rejoice in the Lord always" in which the preacher began by reviewing all of the dreadful things in the world that make joy difficult. He then proved to us from the Bible that it is the Christian's duty to be joyful. He complained that even among Christians he finds little gladness, and offered some unhappy examples. He denounced us for not being as joyful as we ought to be, and sent us back into the dreadful world with a stern admonition to lift up our hearts.

Every minister has a prevailing pulpit mood that reveals both what he is and what he would like to be. It may be chirpy optimism, majestic sweetness, kindly scholarship, or boyish unconventionality. We all are like the entertainer who can play any piece as a waltz. We need to develop a wider range of moods that will help propel our sermons toward their goals. With the many sorts of themes a balanced preaching program needs, we cannot do our best with one or two manners. The material, the way it is expressed, and the way it is delivered must be harmonized to increase the effect of a sermon, or a paragraph.

(7) Right Length

The length of a sermon is critical. If it is too short, the preacher has squandered his chance; if it is too long, it destroys the good that might have been done because the hearers have been benumbed and prejudiced against anything the preacher says.

There is no natural limit for a sermon. Even in our hurried time, a skilled lecturer can have an audience hoping after an hour that he will continue. Our forefathers expected three-hour sermons; they were "irksome only to the ungodly," and a minister was disciplined for sloth if he did not preach that long.

The proper length for a sermon depends largely on the expectations. A congregation's receptive machinery is timed to operate within the limits it is used to. In the circles with which I am most familiar, a fifteen-minute sermon seems miniature, twenty minutes is short, twenty-five minutes is usual, and thirty minutes is long. Occasionally a minister will win favorable comment by announcing that he never intends to preach more than fifteen minutes, but there can always be someone who can outbid him for popularity by cutting it to ten. A minister is unwise to have most of his sermons so precisely timed that, if one of them ever goes somewhat over or under that time, people will feel a contract has been broken. They must understand that preaching cannot be so standardized. A radio preacher in St. Louis, who thought he had just gone off the air, startled his unseen congregation by following the benediction with, "Oh boy, right on the nose!" Sermons cannot be right on the nose. There are practical limitations, however. If a church service ends too soon, parents may disturb the church school; if it goes on too long, church school children may be creating a disturbance outside the doors and dinners may be getting overcooked.

The dislike of long sermons does not show that people are averse to preaching; it does show that serious exercise is work. Paying attention is a strain. Voltaire said, "I find all books too long." Reading a book or listening to a sermon is never the line of least resistance. Ministers need not be too intimidated if they get the impression that many people would prefer mini-sermons from mini-preachers. When we read a newspaper, we drift toward the comics, not toward the editorials. Besides, there is something to what a minister told a parishioner who hinted that the forty-five-minute sermon had been a little too long; the minister said, "Young man, you're a very small jug, and very soon filled."

A sermon seems so long to the hearers and so short to the preacher! On any important subject he has so much to say and so little time in which to say it. If he believes that the Holy Spirit has something to do with what he wants to say, then to leave out any of its seems like a sin against the Holy Spirit—and also feels like it. He knows his purpose is important.

P_T. Forsyth protested, "Brevity may be the soul of wit, but the preacher is not a wit." *(Positive Preaching and the Modern Mind.)* But the minister has to recognize that he could never within one sermon say what should be said. He can never finish, but he can always quit. Out of all the things he has in mind to say, he gives a fragment and puts the rest where he can find it for some later sermon. In an old movie, Edna May Oliver is knitting something that stretches across the floor and out into the hall. She explains, "It started out to be a scarf, but it got away from me." Many an eager preacher has that feeling. He knows he ought to quit, but he cannot bear to deprive the people of the rest he wants to say. If some brilliant inspirations that came to him while preaching have stretched out a sermon that was planned for reasonable limits, the preacher's desperation may be pitiable. Shall he simply sit down and omit the conclusion and all that the sermon was getting to, leaving just a mutilated stump? Only a preacher who has suffered through this crisis will know how difficult it is. But the emergency tends to become a weekly one. Without stern self-discipline, a preacher lives between irritated congregations and sermons that scramble to inadequate conclusions.

Unforeseen use of time in other parts of the service may upset the sermon plans. An anthem may turn out to be a good start on a cantata, a baptism or installation may take longer than had been anticipated. The minister may stubbornly refuse to let his sermon be deformed, and risk having it poorly received. He may plunge wildly ahead, even though talking too fast saves little time and sadly diminishes the effect; or he may try to drop out sentences and phrases, which cannot usually help much. His best hope is to make a quick decision to drop out a sizable section and to preach the rest of the sermon as it was planned. A sentence or two may bridge over enough to save the sequence of the thought.

The hard questions of sermon length are made easier when we think of a sermon not as a literary production but as an experience for the congregation. What is inadequate as the treatment of a topic may still be a great event.

XV

Words

Words connect human beings with one another. Words are the containers that carry what is in one mind and heart to another. There are other semaphores that people use to communicate with each other—gestures, facial expressions, deeds—but none of them can transmit the wide range of thought and feeling that can be conveyed by words. It is words that break into our solitary confinement and save us from sterile isolation.

Communication is basic for the Christian faith. God's children can be joined to each other in love and fellowship because spirit communicates with spirit. The *Koinoneia,* the Communion of Saints, the Sacrament of Communion require a sharing in Christ which is made possible by words, and which goes beyond where words leave off. God communicates with us by his words and by his Word.

Words are the most powerful physical objects on earth. Whether in the material form of sound waves or of ink, they have a collective force that exceeds that of anything else man can lay hold of—explosives, rockets, chemicals, or nuclear devices. They are the greatest healers in the world; 2500 years ago Aeschylus declared, "Words are the physicians of a mind diseased." Words can make whole nations sick, as Nazi Germany has demonstrated. The wounds from words are the most damaging injuries most people ever suffer. Human destiny is shaped by words. Joseph Conrad was thinking of words as physical objects when he said that nothing humanly great "has ever come from reflection. On the other hand you cannot fail to see the power of mere words; such words as Glory, for instance, or Pity. . . . These two by their sound alone have set whole nations in motion."

Ministers, who deal with words, can use them for God's glory and for human good. They have to learn to become proficient with this signaling device.

WORDS HAVE CHARACTER

Ministers have to get a feel for words, because words are more than containers for meanings. The study of semantics has shown that it is not just what words say that is important, but what they are. Communications theory, with its study of symbols, reveals the great complexity of what happens between people who are using words. In the "word experience" there is a dimension of depth which far exceeds what we ordinarily understand as apperception.

Words have their own character, which is not always connected with their meanings. A publication of the Marsteller Company identifies tall and skinny words like *lily* and *intellect; fat* words—*bomb* and *slobber;* feminine—*slipper, peek;* masculine—*oak, steak;* muscular—*earth, cask;* fast—*rocket, piccolo;* slow—*cow, damp;* young—*surprise, tickle;* old— *lavender, velvet; Cleveland* is beige, *Asheville* is green. The right choice of words requires a sense of their distinctive quality.

Words, quite apart from what they signify, can be beautiful or ugly. In a survey, poets were asked to identify the ten loveliest English words. They chose *violet, lullaby, golden, murmuring, wearily, lovely, tranquilly, fluting, hush, melody.* Tennyson believed his most beautiful line was, "The mellow ouzel fluting in the elm." No one could make sounds like *klunk* or *zowie* stand for something lovely. Poets are sounding what they mean, as much as saying it, when they tell of the fog coming in "on little cat feet," and "the tintinnabulation of the bells," and "the cool kindliness of sheets," and "horse chestnuts, glossy-new," and "the graveness of iron."

A man is known by the word company he keeps. The words he uses reveal the sort of words that keep running through his thoughts. They show his taste. A speaker is colored by the tint of his words; when a man is associated with words like *darlingest* or *teenie-weenie,* he will be thought of as effeminate. People's pet words like *fabulous, so what, guts, screwball, naturally,* are clues to attitudes. Our feeling for people depends on whether their words are inclined to growl, croon, lift us up, or push us down. Some good people have an unfortunate predilection for ugly expressions like *nitty-gritty, lunkhead, put your money where your mouth is, it irks me.* A person who is unusually addicted to malodorous words probably has a malodorous mind.

The effect of a sermon depends partly on the coloration of the words it uses. They help create the mood. People chuckle at the story of the palpitating woman who thanked the preacher for "that blessed word, 'Mesopotamia,'" but that word did what words are supposed to do.

SPEAKING THE RIGHT LANGUAGE

James Denney, the Scottish scholar, says, "The Christian preacher is apt to underestimate the capacity of a congregation to understand his thought, and overestimate their capacity to undersand his language." A preacher may have no idea how different his vocabulary and thought forms are from those of the congregation. When I tried to help our Session Clerk word a motion, he objected, "I can't say it that way; that's preacher talk." I thought I was using simple, basic English. Part of the problem of "preacher talk" is not words but mental processes. Bookish and common-sense minds use different logic. Connections that seem obvious to one will seem unrelated to the other. Priorities are different.

The difference in words is a large problem. This has three forms: First, ministers use common words in special ways; this is likely to be irritating. Such words are *involvement, relevant, posture, image, role, encounter, confrontation, wholeness, stance.* I copied from a church bulletin a reference to "costly caring with a gutsy, cutting edge." Second, ministers use nonreligious words few people understand. A book review in what is supposed to be a popular religious journal had: *maieutic efficacy, laicized self-awareness, paratactic condition, paradigmatic event,* and *febrile epiphenomenon.* Third, ministers use religious terms which are neither understood nor appreciated by a good many people: *covenant, blood, redemption, incarnation, reconciliation, led, mighty acts, consecrated, Kingdom.* Ministers may get, from words rich in Scripture and tradition, an aesthetic delight which they expect the worshippers to share—and indeed, some people who have little understanding of such expressions may get an emotional pleasure from their sounds. Paul's warning is needed: "I would rather speak five intelligible words, for the benefit of others, . . . than thousands of words in the language of ecstasy." (I Cor 14:19 NEB)

There will be many in most congregations who have little knowledge either of doctrine or of the Bible. The common Christian words can scarcely be understood by those who know little of the temple sacrifices, Hebrew history, or Pauline conceptions. If the minister uses the words that seem most natural to him, he will be speaking in an unknown tongue. Halford Luccock said that when we preach in a way that does not communicate, we excommunicate.

W. E. Sangster told of hearing a woman in an air-raid shelter witnessing to a vagabond whom the emergency had thrown in her way. She told him of the Yea and Amen to God's promises, of the new dispensation, of the mighty outpouring of the Spirit, and cautioned him that all man's righteousness is filthy rags. When the all-clear sounded, she promised she would intercede for him at the throne of grace; the bewildered man found his tongue enough to answer, "Okey dokey."

We have to learn to put the timeless faith in vivid modern terms. Sometimes the demand for relevant and contemporary language makes preachers think they have to use brand-new words, like the latest slang of the business community, or such youthful terms as *vibes, zonked, plastic, rap, kinky,* or space-age neologisms—*countdown, blastoff, all systems are go.* But finding new words is far less important than finding new expressiveness in ordinary words. We must develop an ability to stretch out the old one-word shorthand symbols of the Church into phrases that say in simple English what the old Latinisms mean. Thus the term would not be *converted,* but *turned around;* not *sanctification,* but *being like Jesus;* not *servanthood,* but *living for others.*

A difficulty with trying to speak the language of present-day Americans is that present-day Americans speak so many languages. There are half-a-dozen languages in any congregation. Take the verse in the King James Version—"If the trumpet give an uncertain sound, who shall prepare himself for the battle?" In the terminology of the Men's Council this would be "Unless the trumpet lays it right square on the line, who will do a bang-up job?" For the Christian Education Commission: "Unless the trumpet has the dimension of urgency, who will activate his objectives in the area of group antagonisms?" For the Youth Fellowship: "Unless the trumpet tells it like it is, who will be turned on to the hassle?" For the preacher: "Without a clarion challenge to conquest, who shall fling his heedless heart headlong into the hostilities?" A minister has no hope of becoming proficient in all the modern languages, but he can use the clear and simple English everybody understands.

In one of his letters, C. S. Lewis insisted that, just as ordination exams used to require condidates for the ministry to demonstrate proficiency in Latin, they should now require the translation of a passage from some theological work into ordinary English. Those who failed this would not be ordained. "It is absolutely disgraceful that we expect missionaries to the Bantus to learn Bantu but never ask whether our missionaries to the Americans or English can speak American or English. Any fool can write *learned* language. The vernacular is the real test. If you can't turn your faith into it, then either you don't understand it or you don't believe it."

An Anglican rector became very discouraged over the effect of his preaching in a small English parish. He increased his study and worked harder on his sermons, and still the pews were largely empty. A new idea struck him; he began to frequent the village marketplace and list the words he heard the people there use in their ordinary conversations. When he had a vocabulary of a few hundred words that were in universal use, he began to translate his sermons, after he had prepared them, into that vernacular, never using a word that was not on the list. As Bishop Stephen Neill told the story, the church was soon overflowing and loudspeakers had to be set up in the yard to care for the crowds who came to hear "the parson who talked sense in the pulpit."

Jargon is a problem in every field of interest, including religion. Jargon is specialized language, used unnecessarily. With all the ridicule of their esoteric terms, specialists need them to make distinctions that cannot be made in ordinary speech; they use them as quick expressions for what would otherwise have to be laboriously written out. Imagine the wordiness of a television manual that could not use terms like *raster* or *resolution*. The problem comes with all the nonexperts who pick up the pretentious words, not because they need to be that precise, but because they are intoxicated with them or wish to appear learned. Ministers may need the technical expressions for their own thinking, but for most of their church work they do not really need the difference between *hermeneutics* and *interpretation, Angst* and *anxiety, hubris* and *pride, eschaton* and *end of the world, Christocentric* and *centered in Christ, Lukan* and *in*

Luke. The preacher who uses the specialized word has to have some reason other than the desire to impart information. The very ugliness of some technical terms, swollen out of shape by prefixes and suffixes, gives them a perverse fascination.

This abuse of language gives occasion for healthy ridicule. Professor Fay rewrote the Gettysburg address as a jargon expert would have given it: "Eight and seven-tenths decades ago the pioneer workers in this continental area implemented a new group based on an ideology of free boundaries and initial conditions of equality. We are now actively engaged in an over-all evaluation of conflicting factors. . . ." (Prof. Richard D. Fay of M.I.T. in *The Christian Century,* July 25, 1951.) But reality outdoes invention. The following passage, dealing with a revolution in Latin America, came to me through the mail from a church agency: "In a situation where revolution is a human imperative, a theology which has been freed from ideological overhang and to which the utopic dimension has been restored will be in effect revolutionary, as the Gospel itself is revolutionary. A Christian praxis that effectively demythologizes the major institutions of society instead of sacralizing them frees men for revolutionary action." We cannot object to the existence of such terms. People accept as necessary the new and difficult words imposed on them by medicine, politics, sociology, and economics. Religion is one of the intellectually demanding fields and its extraordinarily profound thought cannot be put in easy terms. But it is the needless obfuscation that is bad.

Doctors who are unnecessarily mystifying are suspected of being quacks; so are ministers. Ministers ought to have some knowledge in a wide variety of learned areas. Most of us cannot really become competent in many of them, so we are constantly tempted to give the appearance of knowing difficult things by using difficut words. We snatch technical expressions from the physical and social sciences, and even in theology and philosophy we may toss out terms from higher levels than we have reached. The avid use of an abstruse vocabulary may betray insecurity.

Ordinary words may be turned into cant; religious writers and speakers create a sacerdotal language by giving words a special meaning. Preachers may then use these words until they weary their congregations. Anyone who has been much around a church has observed the careers of such words as *lifestyle, awareness, affirm, authentic, presence, alienation.* They once had a fresh significance, but with overuse they now are sing-song. The English also have this problem. Mervyn Stockwood, Bishop of Southwark, wrote, "I am no longer allowed to talk to my clergy. Instead I have a dialogue with them. If the talk lasts longer than an hour, the dialogue is 'in-depth.' If I question the avant-guard opinion of a junior curate I do so because I am vulnerable and feel threatened. . . . Should an argument develop between us, it either leads to an exposure situation or a 'crunch.' . . . If I am lucky enough to preach a sermon to confirmation candidates that makes sense, I am told that it is meaningful and has improved the episcopal image. I like to think that I am reasonably tolerant in my religious views but now I have to

be open-ended. Well, sir, having indicated my area of concern and involvement, I must now start to phase out this letter to you; otherwise
my ideas will begin to jell and form a bottleneck. Of course your younger
readers will say that I am insecure and afraid of not being accepted. I
am, sir, if you will allow me to spell it out, Yours meaningfully, . . ."
(Letter in *The Times,* London, August 7, 1968)

Not only authors and preachers, but also church officials, with their
combination of bureaucratese and religiously elitist speech, help make
church communication difficult. A publication of the United Presbyterian
overseas agency listed the major languages, beginning with those that
are easiest for a missionary to learn. It ended, "475 Riverside Drive [the
church headquarters] is one of the world's more difficult language areas."

Pretentiously opaque expressions and current academic clichés can save
preachers from having to think out just what they mean, as they would
have to do to express themselves in ordinary terms. The hearers can enjoy
that same release from mental labor. A minister who thinks in obscure
terminology may be cut off from communicating not only with less pedantic people but also with himself.

But true and necessary though all this is, we have to recognize that unusual words do have their uses. A good resounding mouthful like *an-
fractuous* conveys more than does *irregular. Carapace* may mean no more
than *shell,* but it says more. Unusual words may be beautiful, a *velleity*
has charm a *notion* lacks; *moidores* clink in the mind more musically than
do *dimes.* The rarer word may have a touch of humor; *wampum* is funnier
than *currency. Tergiversation* describes the act; and *lubricious* pictures
the condition. It is harder to disobey a *ukase* than a *command.*

"Royal thoughts need royal clothes." Words are costumes, and there is
sometimes value in dressing up. Majestic sentiments are not conveyed in
baby-talk. A lofty passage may be an aesthetic satisfaction for the speaker
and the hearers; an orotund expression may be just what is needed. Life
is three-dimensional, and the demand for plain, common-sense vocabulary
may reflect the indifference of a materialistic age to depth and height.

An unfamiliar word may be interesting and instructive. To explain
the *perspicuity* of the Scriptures, or *Donatism,* or *phototropism* may
enlarge the congregation's thinking, not only with a new word but with
a new insight.

Tastes cannot be disputed, and even bureaucratic terminology must
satisfy an aesthetic need in the bureaucrat. Someone must love words
like *maximize, incremental, infrastructure.* Perhaps the in-group terminology of special fields satisfies a cultic sense; when a minister uses an
exotic word in church, the congregation may have the pleasurable feeling
of being admitted to something special.

Unusual words can have great force. Things said simply may be unim-
pressive. To protest, "But that is different" seems weak, while to say,
"The diversity of the situations suggests that it is hazardous to attempt
to subsume them under identical frames of reference," at least keeps the
question open. In the field of mental health, the scientific-sounding ter-

minology is part of the therapy. There is no use paying someone who uses words you understand. Mystique is important.

We need to reexamine the idea that Christianity should be discussed only in terms that are suitable for everyday concerns. Every human interest has its special words. New horizons are opened up to people by giving them terms they have not been using. A general ignorance of the Bible fixes where we have to start, but not our boundary. When we help people understand unfamiliar Bible phrases, we help them understand new Bible thoughts; luminous new expressions from the Bible can shed light into corners that have been dark. Jesus said, "My words will not pass away." (Mk. 13:31) The things he talked about are permanent. A knowledge of what he meant by *sin, save, love, lost, forgive* is desperately needed by a generation to which those words, in the sense in which he used them, are unintelligible. Those words should be opened up, not given up. When we abandon a distinctive religious vocabulary, we perpetuate the very ignorance we deplore. A generation that talks readily of *ecosystems* and *superego* should not find it too hard to understand *repentance*. The real problem has never been the words. "The unspiritual man does not receive the gifts of the Spirit of God, for they are folly to him, and he is not able to understand them because they are spiritually discerned." (I Cor. 2:14) Sometimes the old words may be the very tools we need to open up what to the natural man at first seems to make no sense at all.

The conclusion to all this is that we ministers must be as plain as we can possibly be, we must try our utmost to use the language of the people we are talking to, we must constantly resist our inclination to cant and jargon; but when uncommon words will accomplish the most, then we will use them.

WORDS TO FAVOR

The nouns and verbs carry the load; adjectives and adverbs prop them up when they need it. William L. Shirer said of Winston Churchill, "His nouns are pictures and his verbs work." Try to use nouns and verbs that are so strong they will not need support—not a *violent, gusty wind,* but a *tempest;* not he *walked aimlessly,* but he *sauntered.* Where it matters, never use an empty word when you can find a loaded one—not a *bad man,* but a *crook, scamp, wastrel, libertine;* not a *bad woman,* but a *minx, hussy, baggage, harridan;* not he *went,* but he *dashed, slouched, charged, loitered;* not he *thought,* but he *pondered, mused, puzzled, reflected;* not he *looked,* but he *peered, scanned, ogled, pored.*

Use specific words. Jesus never said *providentially,* but *your heavenly Father will;* he did not speak of *humanity,* but of *your brothers.* Do not say *tree* when you know it is an *oak,* or *weapon* when you can say *revolver.* "He ran a good race" says less than "He won by a yard." Herbert Spencer, with these two sentences, showed how much stronger the specific can be:

"In proportion as the manners, customs, and amusements of a nation are cruel and barbarous, the regulations of their penal code will be severe." Now the definite—"In proportion as men delight in battles, bull-fights, and combats of gladiators, they will punish by hanging, burning, and the rack."

A good motto for any public speaker is this:

> I shoot the hippopotamous with bullets made of platinum,
> Because, if I use leaden ones, his hide is sure to flatten 'em.

Use words that hit hard—brisk, stinging words. Words that refer to sight, hearing, smell, taste, touch, and movement are forcible.

Pick the short word, unless a longer one is clearly better. Rudolph Flesch in *The Art of Plain Talk* asserts that the readability of words can be measured by counting their affixes (prefixes, suffixes, and inflectional endings—*disapproving* has three). He believes that if there are fifty-four or more affixes per one hundred words, the reading will be very difficult; with twenty-two, it will be very easy. In the King James Version the average is about twenty. Short words make speech clear and vigorous. You can see this in the Revised Standard Version. Matthew 11:28–30 ("Come unto me . . .") has fifty-eight syllables in its fifty words. Revelations 3:20 ("Behold I stand . . .") has thirty-five syllables in thirty-two words. It would be humiliating for some of us to compare our sermons with really vivid and descriptive writing. Only about five percent of the words in the poetry of the scholarly Pope and Tennyson have more than two syllables. With the colorful Swinburne, it is scarcely two percent.

Anglo-Saxon supplies the common, household words. They are more readily understood than are words derived from Latin and are likely to be more forceful and specific. Indeed, the common reason for preferring Latin derivatives to Anglo-Saxon is the desire to sound less pungent and more elegant—compare *gut* with *intestine, louse* with *parasite, belly* with *abdomen.*

"Say 'you' twenty times, where you say 'I' once" is common advice. It is true that the most interesting subject for every hearer is himself, but whenever the speaker needs to say *I* let him say it straight out, without such fussy evasions as, "Some have suggested," or, "We might say." A plain, "I know" or "I saw" is a direct communication from a real person to real people, which is what a sermon is supposed to be. Say *we* whenever it allies the preacher with the congregation, but never as an insipid way to avoid being direct—not "We must recognize that God wants us to care about our neighbors" but "You know God wants you to care about your neighbors."

Avoid the obvious word in favor of the unexpected one. If the sentence is important, back off from the first words that come into your mind and try some less automatic ones. It is expected when you say "devout Christian," "fit of anger," "exciting game," "dear old grandmother," so think up something better. When you discover a memorable phrase, you can wonder what it evolved from. A sentence like "Life is supposed to be great" may have gone through several stages before it became, "Life is not a shabby thing we are to grovel through." Perhaps "You knew he was a good man when you saw him walk past" had to make many trips through the author's mind before it became "When he walked, his left foot said 'Amen' and his right foot said 'Hallelujah.' "

Whoever gave the rule, "Use words on the edges of their meanings," was illustrating it; you can scarcely say that a meaning has an edge. To say "The Holy Spirit is the present tense of God" uses the prosaic "present tense" out at the end of its meaning and makes it interesting. "Outside the shower stall grumbling about his riparian rights," or "I went to the marriage license office and picked up my declaration of dependence" stretch the meaning of words as far as they can go.

There is no such thing as a synonym. Every word has its distinctive shade of meaning, and a preacher often has to search long for the word that is just right. One word that is precisely in tune can transform a leaden sentence into one that rings like a bell. Mark Twain said, "The difference between the right word and the almost right word is the difference between lightning and the lightning bug." Felicitous words are so important that a preacher is likely to spend a good deal of time looking for them. A thesaurus is one of the most needed books. It often gives you just the word you want, and, just as often, thumbing through the index and definitions stimulates your brain and it comes up with the word before the book does. The wealth of near-synonyms is subdivided by their slightly different connotations. My word-finder under *brave* has twenty-three words grouped with *bold,* another twenty-one with *courageous,* and eight more with *adventurous.* If you want to call someone just the right sort of fool, this book offers you 114 possibilities, subdivided under *idiot, oaf, clod, dunce,* and *dotard.* It gives you over a hundred ways to be happy; just reading them picks you up—or, as the books says, *cheers, enlivens, elates, exhilarates, gladdens, animates, rejoices, delights, transports, ravishes,* and *enraptures* you.

Onomatopoeia is an important help for speakers. When the sound of the word supports the meaning, the preacher gets double service from it. Words like *clatter, slither, babble, oleaginous, click,* and *hush* speak two ways. Words whose sound is harsh, incisive, soothing, and trumpet-like reinforce the meaning. For some reason the *d* sound suggests depression. Think of all the dark, dreary, dismal words that begin with *d,* the *dis-* and *de-* words that are so discouraging and despairing, and the other deadly, dull, and doleful ones. Genesis starts with a good example of onomatopoeia in the Hebrew word, *tohuwabohu,* which means, "without form and void." That is the sort of word we look for.

When you come upon a word you specially like, or one you have not been getting enough use of, make at least a mental note of it. Keep it as a special pet until you know it will stay with you. Also, identify the words you do not like or have been using too much, and resolve to fence them out.

SEXIST TERMINOLOGY

There is reason for the growing discontent with the use of male terms to include both sexes. We might hope that this usage is just a convention that is needed because there are no genderless singular pronouns, so one of the genders had to be chosen. *Man,* in early English, simply meant *human,* so its inclusive use just retains the prior meaning. But the present practice is not that innocent. Assigning to women words that ordinarily are considered masculine gives women a *mutatis mutandis* place, and makes masculinity seem the normal and preferred condition. As I wrote this book, it would have been impossibly cumbersome to use for every reference to preachers either genderless or both male and female terms. But the way it had to be done unquestionably puts an aura of masculinity over the preacher concept. I could put male references with my male pronouns, but not female references. I could say, "The minister can be thinking of his sermon while he is mowing the lawn"; I could not say, "The minister can be thinking of his sermon while he is sitting under the hair dryer." I could refer to his cutaway coat, but not to his long dress.

Attempts by preachers to avoid using male terms for both sexes produce some agonizingly distorted prose. Singular pronouns, *he or she,* have gender; the plural, *they,* does not; so there is a tendency to throw everything into the plural. Preachers use *they* as though they cannot count high enough to know the difference between singular and plural— "Let each one do their duty." It would be no worse to say "An alert preacher will be on their toes." Terms with no gender get piled up— "Let each one do that one's part," or "A person has to do what a person's conscience says a person ought to do."

Even if that sort of wording were endurable, it would be too laborious for ordinary use. Academics may struggle with it, but busy workers, children at play, or anyone with very much to do will not take the time. The centuries of development of the English language cannot be reversed by fiat. There is not much chance of a general acceptance of bisexual words, such as *shehe* or *hiser.* It would be a great deal better if our language did not use male terms for both sexes, but it does, and preachers who try to avoid this cannot be consistent or gramatical. And after all, it is men who are most disparaged by the assumption that the male gender is as close as you can get to no gender at all.

Quotations make problems. One of my students quoted Paul as saying, "If a man or woman is in Christ he or she becomes a new person altogether." (II Cor. 5:17) Whatever Paul said, he did not say that, and neither did J. B. Phillips, whose translation was being used. Paul's copyright has expired, and he cannot defend himself against misquotations, but J. B. Phillips' copyright is still in force and he would not approve this distortion of his text. There is the same problem with quotations from hymns, creeds, and literature. Not all hymns can take the time to be as inclusive as "A noble army, men and boys, the matron and the maid," and few are as frank as "Though every prospect pleases, and only man is vile." Some quotations make difficulties for us, but it is quite clear that it is not right to quote an author as saying what he or she did not say.

The first thing preachers must do is to criticize their own thinking to try to get rid of sexist assumptions. Second, they must constantly be on guard against any avoidable terminology that implies a male priority. Third, when good grammar or good prose gives no escape, the sexless male terms should be used in a context that makes it clear that no primacy is implied.

WORDS TO AVOID

Pare out all words that add little or nothing—"face up to" (why *up to?*); "He was called to a rural church situation" (why *situation?*); "He devoted the duration of his life to research" (why *the duration of?*); "a member of the student body" (why not just *a student?*). There are useless combinations of words that keep springing up in our sentences like weeds—"as to," "along the line of," "because of the fact that," "with a view to."

Leave out *that, which,* and *who* whenever the meaning is as clear without them—"he said that he was going," "the way that I do things," "he deserves the approval which he gets," "the man whom I admire." The word is needed in "I ordered that he be sent," "the flea that infected the rat," "his departure, which I regret."

Whenever possible, avoid the empty words *some* and *thing.* Too much preaching ends up somewhere over the rainbow—"and in conclusion, I urge you to do something." Somehow, sometime we have to get specific, so why not now? *Thing* can often be replaced by a word that says something. If "It is a hard thing" means "It is a hard *fate—choice—situation,*" why not say so? Or why not just "It is hard"?

Avoid worn-out, obvious words. There are tired pairs which try for emphasis by redundancy—*well and good, sick and tired, one and only, each and every, carefully and prayerfully, loud and clear.* Every year has its pop superlative—*fantastic, beautiful, fabulous.*

A cliché is a reflex-action plagiarism; it is an expression that has been used so much it has gone stale. A speech by a cliché-lover started, "I am tickled to death to have this once in a lifetime opportunity to say a few well-chosen words on a subject that warms the cockles of my heart. I may say without fear of successful contradiction that there is nothing on God's green earth that is nobler than a tried and true cliché." But even though these ready-made phrases are derided as signs of no orginality or taste, they have uses for a preacher who knows what he is doing. Some of them are expressive and evoke the right emotional response. They must be inspected, but good usage does not always rule them out.

Many words, which serve the learned pose, become popular because they are so conveniently imprecise. On a single page an eminent theologian uses *dimension* in five quite different senses. *Perspective* offers the same advantage. *Existential* can respectably mean *real, experiential, present, nihilistic,* or *Kierkegaardian. Lifestyle* means *personality, taste, way of doing things,* or *philosophy of life.* It is a great advantage to have a word that displays you as an intellectual and lets you be a sloppy thinker. Some of the display words are almost always used incorrectly. *Parameter,* which has become fashionable, is a complex mathematical expression; most of those who use it seem to confuse it with *perimeter. Paradigm* says nothing that *model* or *pattern* could not say better.

Self-deprecating expressions sound insincere—"I may be wrong," "If I may suggest," "As one humble observer," "What I am trying to say is . . ." They are not necessary; no one thinks you are omniscient.

Words that claim everything are not needed to add strength—*absolutely, totally, unquestionably.* They dare the listeners to think of exceptions, so they do.

Liberals often add to their difficulties by using the very words that are most offensive to the common-sense, basic-English sort of people. The semitechnical words picked up from the social sciences seem to label the impractical theorist, the shallow activist, the intellectual snob with no understanding of life's realities. Liberal vocabularies are long on argumentative irritants and short on emotional appeal. A "disadvantaged female in a culturally deprived milieu" seems less pitiful than a "poor woman in a slum."

Words can be too obnoxiously Christian. Some ministers use *share* as a synonym for *tell*—"Let me share with you . . ." You expect them to say, "Would you share with me what time it is?" Words like *meaningfully* or *fulfillingly* are more sweet than satisfying.

Unpleasant words should be avoided unless the preacher is speaking of something he wants disliked. Such additions as *anti-, dis-, ambi-, -ary, -ation,* and *-ness* tend to make words ugly. Some words are disagreeable—*prissy, smirk.* Nouns and adjectives tortured into verbs are repugnant—to *pastor* a church, to *dean* the conference, to *fellowship* around the coffee table, to *finalize* the data. E. B. White's classic comment on this was, "We would as lief Simonize our grandmother as personalize our writing."

Positive words usually tell more than do negative—compare *tardy* with *not punctual, dull* with *not interesting, fickle* with *inconstant, waste of time* with *useless, away* with *nonresident.*

There are some doubtful matters. Slang is useful in sermons to say what cannot be said as well in any other way. Expressions like *cool it, hang loose, ripoff, lay it on him, up tight,* and *put-down* are beautifully descriptive. Other slang does not have any useful connotation—*bugs me, his bag, bummer.* Slang serves when a speaker wants to suggest breeziness and informality—it gives relief from heaviness. Slang can be interesting and amusing. It can catch attention. It can give the feel of a situation in which slang would be the normal speech. Slang is used to get rapport. Ministers talk to high school assemblies in what they imagine is teenage style and to penitentiaries in street argot. This often works; the high school students may be delighted, but it is still condescending, and when it misfires it is a disaster. It sounds like affectation when a preacher tries to use the dialect of the youth culture, black militants, or the drug environment. The pulpit needs common speech, but the language of a special group is not common speech. Slang can show disrespect for the occasion or the audience—a confusion of chatter with important discourse. The Korean language has five levels—the speaker's level and two degrees above and below it. The language used depends on the dignity of the person addressed or the situation. English is not that rigid, but the speech level does indicate an attitude. Slang may come from a lazy habit of not thinking beyond the first terms that come to mind. It can suggest careless, superficial thinking. Often, ministers do not have the feel for it. When Mark Twain's wife tried to shame him by repeating his profanity, he said, "You have the words, my dear, but not the music." Slang may sound forced and ingratiating. When it is dropped into a sermon with no apparent reason, it may seem like a too-jocular poke in the ribs.

Folk sayings are useful when they are picturesque: *can of worms, throw the book at him, out on a limb, holding the bag.* But there is no good reason for using them when their meaning is not apparent: *get on the stick, the whole ball of wax, beating his time.*

The use of earthy words is puzzling; the refinement that forbids the strong old Anglo-Saxon terms but permits their Latinized equivalents seems hypocritical. A mature preacher likes to assume that he and his hearers are above childishness and overdelicacy. Should not the pulpit set an example of innocence, and not of an unwholesome aversion from reality? Everywhere else there is much more use of words that used to be ruled out, so why should the pulpit not be free from artificial Victorian conventions? Clement of Alexandria said, "We need not be ashamed to call by their proper names things which God was not ashamed to create."

But there are problems. One is that a line has to be drawn somewhere, so we cannot be free of conventions. Even the most sophisticated will be startled by hearing in public unusually candid references to sex or to what Paul called "our unpresentable parts." (I Cor. 12:23) Many people in any congregation are not emancipated at all, and do not want to be. The minister may not be one of them, but it is their church too, and things that will damage the service for them should not be introduced without a necessary reason.

It is safer to use synonyms for double entendres, which may come out with indecorous connotations. A good workman will not risk creating effects he did not intend. The congregation may enjoy the slip, but they will be distracted, and they may feel that the preacher is not as bright as he should be. A playwright who was lecturing at Duke University began: "Today I stand before you with a plain, unvarnished tale." He was surprised when some of the students smiled, so he quickly added, ". . . to tell." Then the assembly exploded.

The preacher who calls God Jehovah is indicating scholarly discrimination; if he pronounces it, *Yahweh,* or even more, *Y'h'v'h,* he implies fluency in Hebrew as well. Because no one knows how the word should be pronounced, playing around with guesses at it is clearly pedantic; and because the Hebrews in Bible times said *Lord (adonai)* or *God (elohim)* when they read the *Jehovah* word aloud, we need not hesitate to do the same. The *Jehovah* is not a part of our mother tongue; it does not help the mood of worship. In sermons it indicates that God is a foreigner.

In the choice between old and modern English word forms, the Church is in an awkward stage. Preachers used to get the feel for the old style from the *King James Version*. The *Revised Standard Version* and the *New English Bible* use mostly modern English except in direct address to God, when they use both *you* and *Thou*. Both have Jesus address God as *Thou* in John 17, where the *Today's English Version* has him say *you*. The loss of practice in the old style results in some peculiar wording in the pulpit—"hadest," or "you art." In pastoral prayers, God, in the same sentence, may be addressed as *you* and *Thou*, which cannot fail to be distracting to those who are being led in prayer. Bible quotations in sermons have the same strange inconsistency.

Perhaps, in a few years, more agreement about the forms to use in prayer will emerge. Only recently has the older practice not been taken for granted. There are good reasons for both ways. In any case, ministers will need proficiency in both of them. Sermons have to quote from the literature of devotion; traditional prayers and liturgies will be used. Any literate person should know the old style. It is an easy dialect to learn, and an enriching one.

The Bible is a good example of the level of speech to use in sermons. For many years it was assumed that the New Testament reverently used a special form of Greek, which was unlike that of the Greek classics. Then Adolph Deissman discovered fragile papyri sheets in the dry sands of Egypt, with our first examples of ordinary writing—the letters of a schoolboy to his family, merchants' notations. Scholars were astonished to find that they were written in the Greek of the New Testament, which showed that New Testament Greek differed from classical Greek not because it was so lofty, but because it was so common. It was not "Holy Ghost Greek"; its words spoke to the minds and souls of simple people. The good news of the Carpenter, which God intended for everyone, was put in everyday language. That is why the Apostles could so readily transmit it to the masses and the learned. As Luther said, "Speak to the cook and you'll hit the king." That is the language the Church most needs today. But it will not be an ordinary language. Christ does do something wonderful for our vocabularies. As Paul explained it, "He has enriched your whole lives, from the words on your lips, to the understanding in your hearts." (I Cor. 1:5 Phillips)

XVI

The Use of the Bible

A preacher is a professional plagiarist. Those who come to hear him assume that the best of what he gives is not his own. A minister can preach only because he has been preached to from the Bible.

WHEN IS A SERMON BIBLICAL?

Bible quotations do not make a sermon Biblical; if they did, much of the worst political demagoguery would qualify as preaching. Many "Bible preachers" who scorn "pulpit essays" and "sermons from the morning paper" manage to find that God's word says just what they believe about political and social matters. Their forefingers can scarcely drop on the Bible without hitting a warning against Communism or the follies of the government. On the other hand, a sermon that never mentions the Bible until it is well underway may be soundly Biblical if its conclusions are based on Scripture. A sermon is Biblical:

1. When it presents a major Bible theme and attitudes.
2. When it is related to the Bible's central message of salvation through Jesus Christ.
3. When it explicitly refers to what the Bible says. This may raise questions. Could not a sermon on the Apostles' Creed be Biblical, without any direct references to Scripture? I think not. Creeds, pronouncements, hymns, and other Christian literature are, at their best, reflections on the Bible. Preaching needs to be more than a reflection on a reflection.
4. When it is an ellipse around the two foci of the Bible and a present need. A lecture about the Bible is not a Biblical sermon. Biblical preaching must continue the redemptive act as the ancient word is made effective in the present situation. The timeless and the timely are the twin foci for all Biblical preaching. A Scottish professor used to tell his classes, "Every sermon should begin in Jerusalem and end in Aberdeen, or begin in Aberdeen and end in Jerusalem." Either can be Biblical.

A topical sermon, one that begins in Aberdeen, has great advantages. It has a ready-made interest. People listen more attentively when they see how the sermon applies to them. They understand the Scripture reference better after they know its connection with their lives. But if we have only topical sermons, we never get outside the circle of our interests. The Bible is not a manual in which to look up answers to our questions; it is intended to force God's questions on us and to give us answers we may not want. Our guide here is that faithful rule for preachers: "Don't do anything always." Many a time the topical approach will be the best, but it should not become a rut.

AN EXTENDED OR A BRIEF BIBLE BASIS?

Preaching can use either an extended Bible passage or a brief text. The use of extended passages has been a favorite method of some of the greatest preachers. There are good reasons for it:

1. It teaches the Bible as it could never be learned through scattered fragments. Congregations that are used to this sort of preaching are likely to know the Bible unusually well.

2. We will never come to understand the great passages, or the great personages, through one verse at a time. Nothing in the prophecy of Joel can be understood without looking at all three chapters. The effect of the 103rd Psalm accumulates—no fragment can convey it. The Beatitudes are not epigrams; it takes all of them to give each one its meaning.

3. The big picture often must be seen. The urgently needed (and neglected) message of the Revelation is in the whole book, not in single verses. It is all the story of Job, not any portion of it, that has the meaning. A major Bible book can be satisfactorily treated in a single sermon, and it often must be, because the same congregation will never return.

4. A message from a big section of the Bible will often be more persuasive than one drawn from a single text; a single text may seem to be less Bible and more preacher. A wider basis in Scripture may get something accepted that would otherwise be resisted as too critical, radical, or pious. The story of Jonah seems to have been designed to get those who were fiercely bigoted to accept the idea that God is the Father of all humanity. This method is still a good one for dealing with social issues.

5. The Bible is not a book to be read so much as a territory to be lived in so that we come to feel at home. It is a place where we encounter God and where we move around until we begin to pick up the attitudes. Broadly based Biblical preaching gives the feel of dwelling in the Bible.

6. Preaching on extended passages offers a chance for imaginative description, character delineation, and dramatic structure. The skills for this have to be developed, and they usually can be.

7. It is easier to find interesting things to say about fifty verses than about one, an advantage that has been noted by rushed or slothful

preachers. This is why many churchgoers have a prejudice against this sort of preaching—they expect it to be shallow. But it does not have to be, and at its best it can be exciting for the preacher and the congregation.

8. A wider passage is not as subject to distortion as is a single verse.

9. This sort of preaching can start some life-long love affairs with portions of the Bible. A person who had never thought of the Epistle to the Philippians as a whole might, by a sermon, be introduced to its graceful, joyful charm and become entranced with it. With a whole book to count on, a preacher can fling out treasures with both hands.

The use of an extended passage also has some hazards:

1. It can be rambling. The Bible was not written to provide outlines for sermons and the sequence of ideas in a passage may offer no recognizable line of thought. Some preachers pretend to see an outline when none is there. It is better to regroup the verses to give some sort of order. It is hard to hold attention when a sermon wanders. A prophet or an epistle can make us feel like the disappointed purchaser of a dictionary who said, "It's a hard book to get interested in because it changes the subject so often."

2. A passage may have so many good teachings that the sermon has too many goals. The impact is scattered and nothing solid is accomplished.

3. The treatment of a whole section tends to waste time on irrelevant details—on Hebrew marriage customs or Palestinian topography. It may say too much about the past and too little about the present.

Preaching from a single text has special advantages:

1. A vivid text can be exciting; it sets bells to ringing.

2. A good text will be remembered, which will help the sermon and its message to be remembered. A text lodged in the memory is like a stake to which a great deal can be tied.

3. Preaching on the great texts stores them like treasures in people's hearts. When they are known "by heart" they are there when they are needed. If the preacher quotes the text repeatedly, it will be recalled.

4. A single text streamlines a sermon toward a definite accomplishment.

5. A text can give the sermon's structure. A verse like Rev. 3:20 has an obvious outline: "Behold, I stand at the door and knock; if anyone hears my voice and opens the door, I will come in to him and eat with him, and he with me."

6. A text can open up illimitable truth. A text could be only a picture which decorates a wall, but a good text rightly used can be a window through a wall which opens up on boundless vistas.

THE ABUSE OF THE BIBLE

The use of words from the Bible does not make a sermon Biblical. Unless the Bible is allowed to say what it means, playing with its words can do great harm. The idea that anything from the Bible will be a source of blessing is superstitious—it is not unlike sewing Bible verses in children's clothes to ward off harm. A minister can exercise ingenuity and some humor devising trick, whimsical, or punning texts. A sermon on encounter groups took the text, "Comfort me with apples, for I am sick of love." This can be fun, but there is no real connection with the Bible.

A scoffer has said that the Bible is like a neutral country in time of war—available to serve both sides. That has too often been true. Unless we scrupulously let the Bible say only what it is intended to say, it can support almost anything. It is because the Bible has so much power that it is subject to so much abuse. Paul warned of this: "We use no hocus-pocus, no clever tricks, no dishonest manipulation of the word of God." (II Cor. 4:2 Phillips) A preacher needs to identify some of the common ways of misusing the Bible because, with the best of intentions, he is likely to fall into them.

1. *Proof-texting out of context.* Using Bible fragments out of their settings in a misleading way can dishonestly exploit the Scriptures. When two experienced proof-texters confront each other, it is like two gunslingers shooting it out in the middle of Main Street. They whip out their pocket Testaments and fire verses or, if they are really fast, just the numbers: "Have you never heard of Acts 4:12?" ("There is no other name under heaven given among men by which we must be saved.") "Of course, but how about II Peter 3:9?" (The Lord is "not wishing that any should perish.")

This sort of thing demonstrates that the Bible was never intended to be used in snippets. This can be shown by the verbal contradictions in the Bible. For example: God said, "Man shall not see me and live" (Ex. 33:20) but "Blessed are the pure in heart, for they shall see God." (Mt. 5:8); "Let your light so shine before men . . ." (Mt. 5:16) but "Beware of practicing your piety before men" (Mt. 6:1); "Work out your own salvation," (Phil. 2:12) but "By grace you have been saved . . . not because of works" (Eph. 2:8, 9). The proof-texts about war have divided the Church. Jesus said, "I have not come to bring peace, but a sword" (Mt. 10:34), so violence can be right; but "All who take the sword will perish by the sword" (Mt. 26:52), so Christians must be pacifists; but "Let him who has no sword sell his mantle and buy one" (Lk. 22:36), so it is the Christian's duty to bear arms.

The Bible is not a *Poor Richard's Almanac,* with each verse a maxim, standing by itself. A verse can be understood only in connection with what has just been said and what comes next. When we use a text to support a sermon, or throw one in to prove a point, we have to be sure it is in harmony with the whole sweep of Scripture, and not just an incomplete fragment. Sects have been based on Bible quotations torn from their context. All sorts of strange religious aberrations can come from this. The first use of chloroform in childbirth was widely denounced as unscriptural because the Bible says, "In pain you shall bring forth children." Fortunately, Dr. Simpson, a pioneer in anesthesia, knew the Bible. Did not God, he asked, cause a deep sleep to fall on Adam when he removed Adam's rib in order to make Eve? God's obstetrical example seemed to answer the objections.

Of course there are many great Bible texts that can be used by themselves. John 3:16 is rightly called the Gospel in miniature. The three words "God is love" compress volumes of theology. We do not have to study the context in order to understand rightly verses like "In everything God works for good with those who love him," "It is more blessed to give than to receive," "You shall love your neighbor as yourself," "Though our outer nature is wasting away, our inner nature is being renewed every day," "If anyone is in Christ, he is a new creation," "Freely you received, freely give," and "Rejoice in the Lord always." The riches of the Christian faith are put within reach through such verses.

2. *Pretexting.* A sermon may appear to be from the Bible because it has a Bible setting, though the passage says nothing that the sermon says. I still remember a sermon I heard years ago on Acts 27:29, "Fearing that we might run on the rocks, they let out four anchors from the stern." The sermon title was *Four Anchors.* There was an unforgettable description of Paul's ordeal in the storm, and of how the ship was saved from running wild and smashing on the rocks by those four anchors. The preacher told how every life needs anchors, and the four he recommended were family, friends, work, and church. It was strong preaching, but the text gave the message no more Bible support than if it had come from *Moby Dick.* Of course it could be a Biblical sermon if the need for anchors and the importance of family, friends, work, and church were supported by other references to Scripture. It is probably allowable to use the Bible to supply a good preaching device like that one. But we must beware of pretending that what we say is therefore from the Bible.

A similar use could be made of a later incident in that same chapter, using Acts 27:44 (KJV). When the ship foundered, people leaped into the sea and got to land, "some on boards, and some on broken pieces of the ship." So many a person is saved by the broken pieces he has left—broken health, broken faith, a broken career. There is a great deal of Bible truth in that, but none of it is from the text. The problem with pretexting is that it lets the preacher present his personal philosophy as though it is the word of God. He himself may not know that he is doing it.

3. *Text stretching.* We are supposed to use exegesis, which means getting out of a text the meanings that are there; we are not supposed to use eisegesis, which means putting into a text meanings that are not there. I recently heard a splendid sermon on suicide, on the text Acts 16:28, "Do not harm yourself, for we all here." The minister pointed out that a person on the verge of suicide often feels utterly forsaken and alone. He needs to recollect how many still are with him—friends, family, real Christians everywhere—"we are all here." This could properly be a text on how things may not be as bad as they seem; the despairing jailor needed to know that his prisoners had not escaped. But he was not really being reminded of good company.

A German author tells of hearing a sermon on the benefits of early rising, with the text "Mary Magdalene came to the tomb early." The Prodigal Son's destitution has been used to teach the importance of using money wisely. By enough stretching, the text "Simon's mother-in-law lay sick with a fever" could be used for a sermon on in-law relationships, health care, or the fevers of life. Preachers and paleontologists practice the same art. By chains of implication, a scientist can find enough indications in a five-inch fossil to reconstruct a dinosaur. Some texts and sermons are related in that way, though not always with such rigorous logic.

The emotional power of Bible words tempts us to exploit them to give force to what we say. Many sermons on redemption through Christ have been preached on Job 19:25, "I know that my Redeemer lives." In spite of Handel's *Messiah,* that is not what Job means. He is sure an advocate will be found to defend him of the charge that he must be a dreadful sinner. He is expressing his belief in the ultimate decency of things, but not with any clear reference to Christ. What the 23rd Psalm says about "the valley of the shadow of death" is often used for sermons on dying, and improperly. Gen. 31:49 is used for an affectionate "Mizpah Benediction" on those who separate. What Laban is really saying is, "The Lord keep an eye on both of us because we can't trust each other." The danger of distorting the Bible forces us to investigate with great care to see whether our texts mean what we hope they do. Often the sad reward for such conscientiousness is to have our best plans spoiled.

4. *Text twisting.* It is usually unsafe to preach from inferences. What the Bible may seem to imply is not a clear enough guide. A parable teaches only its main lesson. The parable of the rich man and Lazarus cannot be used to show the conditions of the life to come, any more than the parable of the unjust judge can be used to show that God's morals are poor. (Lk. 16:19–30 and 18:1–7) The parable of the sheep and the goats does not prove that there will literally be a Judgement Day. (Mt. 25:31–46) Jesus' saying, "If a man does not abide in me, he is cast forth as a branch, and withers; and the branches are gathered, thrown into the fire and burned" does not authorize the Inquisition. (Jn. 15:6) Paul's use of military metaphors (Eph. 6:10–17) does not show scriptural approval of militarism, though it does show that Paul did not shrink from warlike terminology. Good hermeneutics requires us to determine what a Bible passage was intended to say to those who heard it first. When we make a deduction which points to something else, we are twisting the text too far.

5. *Text desertion.* A text is often used like the first-stage rocket on a space vehicle. It gets the sermon into orbit and then is jettisoned. If there are other texts on board that can be fired later, the sermon may get to some sort of goal. Otherwise it may be doomed to roam in empty space.

Text desertion is fraudulent advertising. The congregation is asked to give its attention with the implication that the text will be used, then the preacher breaks the contract and gives the consumers something other than was promised.

6. *Uninspired sources.* There is much in the Bible that is not at all the word of God. It has the sayings of cynics, doubters, atheists, and scoundrels of all sorts. With relentless honesty, the Bible puts all the reasons for unbelief in billboard type. We may be tempted to be unhappy, but the Bible shrieks despair. We may be inclined to doubt, but the Bible moans, "Curse God, and die!" The jaded wise man of Ecclesiastes sets up worldly fallacies so faith can have a shooting gallery. There is always danger that we will quote some sub-Christian passage as God's word to the congregation. Abraham, Isaac, and Jacob cannot be assumed to speak heavenly wisdom, and the friends of Job are not supposed to be inspired. Neither is Job himself, in much that he says, but in how many funeral services have hearts been crushed by Job's dreadful words, "Man, that is born of a woman, hath but a short time to live, and is full of misery." These are quoted in the Book of Common Prayer as though they were holy writ, whereas they are what Job said in the depths from which God rescued him.

7. *Allegorizing.* There are allegories and symbols in the Bible. Leaven, fire, water, blood, and serpents are expressly intended to be signs. But when we go beyond what the Bible identifies as symbols and invent our own, then we are forcing meanings on the Bible that never were intended. The passion for allegorizing almost ruined the preaching and writing about the Bible in the early Church; almost anything could be understood to have an apparent meaning, beneath which was a symbolic meaning, with mysterious meanings at several levels below that. The simplest Old Testament stories were given recondite significance. The Song of Solomon was supposed to be about Christ and his Church.

A preacher with a good imagination can ornament his sermons with symbols the Bible does not authorize. When he does, he is making the Bible say what is not intended. Ecumenical enthusiasts interpret Christ's seamless robe as his intention for an undivided church. The fragrance of the ointment in the alabaster box is seen as Christian prayers, whose sweet aroma wafts to heaven. The Wise Men bring to the infant Jesus the homage of Asia, Africa, and Europe. There is no limit to how misleading this can be.

8. *Embellishment.* The Bible writing gets great force by leaving out details. The stories in the Gospel of Luke are considered to be among the most perfect ever written, partly because they have no elaboration. How much more we would have told (and do tell) about the Prodigal Son, the Good Samaritan, and the travellers to Emmaus. The Bible's spareness leaves wide room for preachers' imaginations, and they richly use it. Some of the inventions have been accepted as Scripture; the Bible never says that there were three Wise Men, or that Jesus fell under the weight of his cross, or that the Simon who carried it was black.

When a preacher says "must have," it is a warning that he is about to force his fancy on the Scripture. "David must have been . . ." means that David is about to be assigned some imagined motive or quality that serves the sermon's purpose. The next time it may turn out that he "must have been" something quite different to suit another sermon. One Holy

Week Judas may be presented as a disappointed idealist; the next year he may be an avaricious crook; another time he may be an impatient activist trying to hurry Jesus. It has suited so many sermons to describe Mary Magdalene as a prostitute that it is commonly assumed that she was, though the Bible never says so. A minister may be allowed some dramatic license in describing action, or in character development, but he must never use what he has added to support what he wants to teach. If he does, he is telling a congregation that his notions are the word of God.

By these abuses a preacher tries to make it appear that his views are from the Bible; he thus presents himself as God. This sacrilege can be disastrous. The Bible is too powerful in its effect on human life for us to dare claim its authority for human fallibility. Many a Christian has been influenced by a distorted conception a minister said was in the Bible. Jeremiah lashed out at this: "Do not listen to the words of the prophets who prophesy to you, filling you with vain hopes: they speak visions of their own minds, not from the mouth of the Lord." "Behold, I am against the prophets, says the Lord, who use their tongues and say, 'Says the Lord.' " (Jer. 23:16, 31)

Preachers who dress up their prejudices as inspired wisdom have done dreadful damage to persons and to society. The unspeakable evil of human slavery was made acceptable to Christians, in complete disregard of Jesus, by the abuse of Scripture. For example, the curse on Ham was supposed to be blackness, and his descendents were supposed to have populated Africa, neither of which has the slightest connection with what the Bible says. I have in my file a sermon preached by a college president in 1954 to show that segregation is required by the Bible. It would be hard to find more ingenious examples of how the Bible can be abused. "You shall not make marriages with them" (Deut. 7:3) *(proof-texting);* "You shall not wear a mingled stuff, wool and linen together" (Deut. 22:11) *(pretexting).* Jesus said, "Go nowhere among the Gentiles, . . . but go rather to the lost sheep of the house of Israel" (Mt. 10:5–6) *(text stretching).* "Paul recognized the master-slave relationship" *(text twisting).* "The children of Ham . . . occupied the continent of Africa" *(embellishment).* This soars to its climax in a lofty allegory, "Round the throne was a rainbow" (Rev. 4:3—"a fitting symbol of the spectrum of the redeemed humanity made up of the peoples of every nation, kindred, race and language . . . yet each preserving its own distinctive genius and virtues."

PRELIMINARY BIBLE STUDY

A minister is taking an awesome risk when he ventures to tell a congregation what the Bible says. If he is mistaken, he is implanting a falsehood with all the authority of holy Scripture. It is easy to be mistaken. In Second Peter is the candid warning that the letters of "our beloved brother Paul" are not easy. "There are some things in them hard to understand, which the ignorant and unstable twist to their own destruction, as they do the other scriptures." (II Pet. 3:16) We are "ignorant" when we skip the study we need to do to understand a text; we are "unstable" if we lightly assume that it says what we want it to say; "destruction" is not too strong a word for the damage done by twisting Scripture.

We must study the Scripture we use in sermons to find out what it really means. For a considerable while I assembled material for a sermon on Ecclesiastes 10:2 (KJV)—"A wise man's heart is at his right hand; but a fool's heart is at his left." I interpreted this to mean that most people's hearts are at the left, so most people are foolish; therefore we need not be intimidated by majorities; truth is not established by counting noses. Unfortunately for me, when I was getting ready to preach the sermon I found out I had been mistaken. The text means that a fool does things left-handedly; he is clumsy, as with the French word *gauche*.

Many a great sermon on abstinence has been preached on Colossians 2:21: "Do not handle, Do not taste, Do not touch." But when the text is rightly understood, it backfires. The sentence starts in verse 20, "Why do you submit to regulations, [such as] 'Do not handle, Do not taste, Do not touch'?" The Bible has verses to be used against drinking, but this is not one of them. Proverbs 8:17 (KJV)—"Those that seek me early shall find me"—is used for sermons to young people. It really refers to those who get up early in the morning. (It might indeed be a good text for youth.)

A translation is never perfect, so it takes word study to uncover the riches of a text. In the story of Jesus' conversation with the woman of Samaria, in the King James Version he and she both speak of a "well." But in the Greek, she calls it a *phrear*, which means "cistern," and Jesus calls it a *pege*, which means "fountain." She is thinking of stale drainage water and he of a pure spring. When Paul says, "Bear one another's burdens," and then almost immediately, "Every man shall bear his own burden," (Gal. 6:2, 5 KJV) it sounds as though he does not know his own mind. But the contradiction is removed when we find out that the Greek has two different words for "burden." Paul is saying that Christians should give and receive help, but not be parasites. The unpleasant suggestion in the text "Blessed are the meek," (Mt. 5:5) is removed when we look up *praus*.

We need study to help us understand ways of expression that are unfamiliar to us. When Jesus advised people to pluck out their eyes or to hate their fathers and mothers, he was using a style of hyperbole that was peculiar to his time. Apocalyptic writing, in the Bible and in secular examples, has its own conventions. We need to study these in order to understand the apocalyptic literature in Daniel or the Revelation.

We need Bible study in order to locate the various passages that can help us interpret a text. The Bible is its own commentary. A sermon on prayer may have as its primary text Luke 18:1 "They ought always to pray and not lose heart." Immediately we see that we need to know more of what the Bible means by "pray," so in the concordance we look through the verses with the words "pray" or "prayer." These help us understand what Jesus is talking about, and give us insights that need to be included in the sermon. From our own recollection and from books on prayer we might find other Bible passages we need.

We have to study to discover ways the text can be applied. A sermon on Job may need to compare Job with some modern views of human destiny—with Camus, Marcuse, and Solzhenitsyn, B. F. Skinner, and with MacLeish's drama, *J. B.* Some of the recent books on Job will give that information. A minister who is preaching on a parable will do well to refer to some of the books of sermons on the parables to discover important applications which would not have occurred to him.

Many texts cannot be understood apart from the circumstances in which they appeared. Most become far livelier when the occasion for them is known. A preacher needs to find the answers to the five WH's: WHO? WHOM? WHEN? WHERE? WHY? (a) WHO? asks about the life situation and personality of a person who said it, or of the author of the book in which it is found. (b) WHOM? investigates the persons addressed to discover their needs, prejudices, and problems. (c) WHEN? looks into the historical situation and the course of events that led up to it. (d) WHERE? studies the church, community, or country to which the text was addressed in order to see how it applies to similar conditions now. (e) WHY? asks the reason for what the text says. Why did the author say it?

One hazard of this sort of Bible study is that the minister gets too interested in it. With all the work on the sermon still to be done, he goes off on fascinating by-paths that are not needed for his present purpose. It sometimes takes discipline, when necessary questions have been answered, to get back to the hard work of sermon preparation.

Necessary as Bible study is, it must not stifle the preacher's originality. Commentaries answer questions about sermons that are being prepared; they rarely by themselves supply good sermons. It is not enough for a preacher to offer his congregation the results of his scholarship. A rehash of what the most approved commentators have to say about a text is not a sermon. Preaching is "truth through personality," and when study has revealed the truth about a text, it still needs fresh, original transmission. As Pastor John Robinson told the Pilgrims as they set sail on the first stage of their voyage to New England, "There is yet more truth to break forth out of God's Holy Word." Looking up what others have found in a text will not take care of its inexhaustible possibilities for the present preacher and congregation.

A preacher who has done a great deal of interesting work in getting ready for a sermon is tempted to tell the congregation all about it. But much that a speaker needs is not necessary for the hearers. Some idea of where the Galatians lived is useful for the minister as he tries to get the feel of the Epistle to them. But there is a very limited number of church members who want to go through scholarly arguments over the north or south Galatia theories. The congregation wants the meal—they do not want to watch it being cooked.

A minister may exhibit his scholarship in a way that implies that only those who have done all the reading he has done can expect to understand the Bible. The belief in "the intelligibility of the Scriptures" is essential. The most untutored reader, who comes to the Bible through faith in Christ, can find the saving truth. Preachers who explain how mistaken everyone will be who does not approach a text through Hebrew, or form criticism, may build the impression that it is useless for the layman to try to read the Bible. I remember a sermon on the Good Samaritan which told us that the best *Formgeschichte* scholarship had found that the parable did not belong with the question about "Who is my neighbor?" It had been lifted from another location in the Gospel, where the Samaritan represented Jesus, with his unaccountable grace. It was an interesting speculation, which the preacher presented as fact. Our conclusion would have had to be that all Christians across the centuries have misunderstood a story that seemed so simple, so no one can assume that he understands anything about the Bible. That, of course, is nonsense. The marvel of the Bible is that its essential teachings are understandable for children and inexhaustible for pundits. Those who publish books have to offer what other books do not have. This may lead the Bible commentators to say what no one else has ever said because it is unlikely. A preacher cannot present as truth everything he gets from able scholars.

THE TOOLS

A minister needs good tools for his Bible study. (See those listed in the Appendix.) He may be less put off by their expense when he recognizes how much of his help for the congregation depends on them. Their original cost can be seen against a lifetime's usefulness.

The most useful single book is likely to be a one-volume Bible commentary. This will be used more often than a set of commentaries, just as a desk dictionary is used more than the unabridged. With a thousand or so pages, such a book can comment on most of the chapters in the Bible and on the important verses. It will tell about the authors, recipients, circumstances, and summarized contents of the Bible books, and will have articles on such matters as the Pentatuch, the Pastoral Epistles, Prophecy, the Messianic Hope, and the Parables.

The next most convenient volume may be a Bible dictionary. This explains the Bible's contents, not by verses, but by subjects. Bible characters, places, books, and topics are listed alphabetically.

More adequate commentaries require a good many books to deal with the whole Bible. These are needed to explain the meanings, the applications, and the WHO? WHOM? WHEN? WHERE? WHY?. They may even offer illustrations and sermon outlines, through this is not their most important use. A complete set, from Genesis to Revelation, is uniform and convenient. The disadvantage is that, with the various authors, some of the volumes will be inferior. A better set of commentaries can be selected one at a time. Most ministers will need the advice of those who know the literature. A Bible scholar whose tastes are congenial can help. Some theological seminaries offer their students lists of suggested commentaries. It is well to try out a commentary to see whether it meets your sort of needs. A commentary someone praises highly may seem to you to answer every sort of question except those you want to ask.

You need more than commentaries. Wordbooks, which go beyond the scope of Bible dictionaries, are important. So are redactional studies of Bible books, or sections, which do not give verse-by-verse comments but look at the writers' purposes and views. Books on the lives of Bible persons, including Jesus, and on such topics as the parables, miracles, Palestine, or Holy Week can open up exciting insights you will be eager to bring to the congregation.

The dogmatic teaching of the church is intended to save ministers from eccentric interpretations of the Bible. Systematic theology tries to summarize by topics what the Bible says. A preacher needs to be acquainted with the doctrines of the past, and with the currently accepted teachings of his church, if there are any. In most denominations a preacher does not have to be bound by church doctrine, but he should know when he departs from it, and he should usually tell his congregation when he departs. A minister whose interpretation of some part of the Bible differs from that of most Christians, should offer it to the congregation only after much thought and prayer. He has a heavy majority against him. He should beware of the seduction of the role of brave and brilliant heretic. On the other hand, we should remember Dr. Fosdick's warning that sheltering the Bible under dogma is like putting a roof over a sundial.

A preacher needs at his elbow a complete and scholarly concordance for each translation he uses often, and a harmony of the Gospels. If he is able to use them, he needs Greek and Hebrew Bibles and dictionaries. A parallel or interlinear Greek-and-English Testament saves a great deal of dictionary thumbing. Those who do not know the Bible languages can do a good deal of research into the meanings of Greek and Hebrew words through a concordance that gives them with the English.

A shortcut to Bible scholarship is offered through the various translations; when you see how the translators have interpreted a text, you have a good basis for your own interpretation. This is fastest with a book that puts the translations in adjacent columns. I suppose for most churches the nearest to approved translations we now have are the Revised Standard, the King James, and the New English Bibles. Almost in this company are Today's English Version, the Jerusalem Bible, and J. B. Phillips' paraphrases. Somewhat older, but still important, are the translations by Knox, Moffatt, Goodspeed, and Weymouth, and the Old Testament translation edited by J. M. Powis Smith. There are other useful ones. In all of these, one can quickly see what competent scholars think the Bible means. When the scholars disagree, the preacher has to do his own study to determine which seems right. It is a little devious for him to shop around to find a version that says what he wants to say, but if he can persuade himself that the wording he wants is also right, he can use it with good conscience. He must beware of making too much of a striking phrase unless what it seems to say in English is the intention of the original language. Novel translations tempt preachers to pretend that accidents of wording are Holy Writ.

Through most of Christian history, there has been a succession of official Bibles that were the only ones to be used at their time and place. A minister who used any other wording in the pulpit would have to explain why he was doing something so irregular. We are now in the unprecedented situation of being able to use several different versions with equal propriety. It is probably well to have one that is expected, and to identify others that are used. Some ministers are finding the new freedom so heady that they are mixing versions, or creating their own. This is highly dubious. Most of us are not good enough scholars to be trusted to do our own translating. Church members know this, and when they catch us making up the Bible it encourages a flippant attitude to Scripture. It is one more form of passing off our own notions as the Word of God.

One advantage of different versions is the fresh interest they create. Those who are so used to the old words that they find it hard to listen to them may sit upright when they hear something in a surprising new way. The familiar version has Peter say to Simon the Sorcerer, "Your silver perish with you!" (Acts 8:20) In Today's English Version he says, "May you and your money go to hell!" When we look it up in the Greek, we find that is exactly what he said.

New versions can also show us the right way out of old difficulties. Christians for generations have been shocked and puzzled by Matthew 5:48, "You, therefore, must be perfect, as your heavenly Father is perfect." That was a key verse for Perfectionism, which holds that true Christians never sin. The Greek word for "perfect" is *teleios,* related to "teleology," which means "all the way to the end," "complete." In preaching on this text I found that the New English Bible in its first edition took a try at this difficult verse and made it, "You must therefore be all goodness, just as your heavenly Father is all good." That was not satisfying, so the second edition nine years later says, "There must be no limit to your goodness, as your heavenly Father's goodness knows no bounds." So we are not to aim at less than our best, we are not purposely to compromise. There, at last, seems to be a translation that is closer to the Greek and can apply to us.

THE PREACHER'S BIBLE KNOWLEDGE

Books will never take the place of the preacher's own knowledge of the Bible. His most used concordance must be in his head. There is no other source from which he can locate the parts of the Bible a sermon needs. Suppose he wants to find the Bible's teaching about grace, or crippling anxieties, or whether Christians can participate in revolutions. There is no topical listing of texts that will give him enough help. He finally has to depend on his own recollection of what is in the Bible.

Lack of first-hand acquaintance makes the Bible harder to accept. The Bible on the shelf is a far more difficult book than is the Bible in use. Those who have come to love the Bible will live with its perplexities and cherish its beauties; those who come to it cold will miss its beauties and see mostly its perplexities. Dr. Julius Moldenhawer, late in life, told the Union Seminary graduating class that many of the problems in the Bible that had once so bothered him had "gone to that very quiet limbo where they snuggle down for a long slumber side by side with that ancient puzzle propounded for the confusion of the pious: Where did Cain get his wife? . . . The Scriptures give us so strong and steady a sense of the presence of God, so warm an assurance of his help and comfort, so clean-cut a revelation of his justice, his power and his love that anything which interferes with this, in its great purpose of showing us the face of the Almighty, is either absorbed or thrust aside." This does not mean blind faith, it simply means that, when we know for ourselves what the Bible really is, the problems can be lived with. One of the characters of Charles Schulz, "Peanuts" says, "I think I've made one of the first steps toward unveiling the mysteries of the Old Testament. I'm starting to read it."

The young pastor who is in charge of youth work for the Egyptian Evangelical Church told me how shocked he was when he led a work camp that included young people sent by an American church. He said, "All my young people have read the Bible through, most of them several times; those American students had never looked at it." It is quite possible for those American students to follow their church interest into a seminary, and pass courses in exegesis, theology, and the prophets, still without reading much of the Bible. They can go on through years of their ministeries, preaching on one verse a Sunday, and remain largely ignorant of what is in the Bible. But their preaching will be hack work, a weekly job to be done, without any chance of giving to their congregations a real sense of what the Bible is about.

There are reasons why Bible reading is so readily postponed by ministers and laymen. The Bible is for Christians the most urgent and least pressing book. It does not have to be read right away, as do magazines and newspapers. It does not have to be read to keep up with what others are reading and talking about. Bible reading can always be postponed for the first free moment, a moment that for most people never comes. Curiosity does not goad us. We already know that the Hebrews will make it to the Promised Land, and we are familiar with Paul's preference for love. Deuteronomy is magnificent, but our minds wander. The story line in Jeremiah is hard to trace.

His people's needs make a minister long to know the Bible better. Wars and rumors of wars bring a frantic need for some glimpse of what this world is coming to which we never get from the world. People are lost until they can find out who they are, where they are going, and what life is all about. When ministers see all the desperately groping people who have lost their hope and lost their way, they rush to their Bibles to find the saving truths that they can offer. A pastor knows his people's needs; he knows he has a chance on Sundays to help fill these needs, and he dare not come with empty hands.

A minister should read the Bible fast, to get a quick reminder of what is in it. He also should read slowly, pondering what strikes him, marking the pages, looking up answers to what puzzles him. There is little good in grimly laboring through the least interesting portions. This has all the religious benefit of a devotee's prostrating himself all the way along the road from Allahabad to Benares. The best study pursues some lively interest. Why do Old Testament professors, according to a recent poll, list Jeremiah as their favorite Old Testament book? Is there a sermon series for next Lent in Colossians?

Dr. Jowett said it is a good thing for a preacher "to be always engaged in the comprehensive study of some one book in the Bible." (*The Preacher*, p. 119.) Teaching a class or offering a course on some part of the Bible may require special study; this may make a cherished addition to the parts of the Bible the minister specially knows and loves. A minister preaches his way into a growing knowledge of the Bible. One sure advantage of Biblical preaching is the benefit to the preacher. A minister cannot help looking for material for sermons whenever he reads the Bible, but if he reads it only to get sermon help, he will never have the help he needs.

The Scripture we have memorized supplies the words we need when we prepare our sermons and make our pulpit prayers. It is easy to commit to memory the passages we use most often for church services, sacraments, and funerals. Our whole thinking and living is colored by the Bible passages we can recall. Deuteronomy looks to that ideal of having the words of God "kept in your heart; you shall repeat them to your sons, and speak of them indoors and out of doors, when you lie down and when you rise." (Deut. 6:6–7 NEB) That is a good way to live.

XVII

The Sources of Sermon Material

Where does a minister get what he puts in sermons? As he looks forward to preaching every Sunday for years on end, he might despair of ever finding enough to say.

THE PREACHER'S FILES

A preacher's filing system is the key to his whole store of sermon material. All the wealth he has gained from experience and reading will be of no benefit to his congregation unless he can find what he wants when he needs it. What comes from sources outside himself and his own recorded ideas go into the file.

If a filing system is too complete and complicated it can be an aggravating waste of time—it may take longer to file the notations from a book than it took to read it. On the other hand, if a file is too simple, its owner will waste time trying to get from it what he needs. If everything relating to the church is filed under CHURCH, a minister will have hundreds of items to sift through. CHURCH needs subdivisions like Attendance, Building, Definition, Failures, Fellowship. There could be too many cross-references, but if there are too few, a minister can spend an hour looking in vain through all the references to MARRIAGE for something he has filed under FAMILY.

A great deal of hard thought and investigation should be put on the starting of a filing system. There are systems available for sale to ministers. All I can say is that I prefer my own, which could be expected. The method must fit each user's special mentality and methods, but a great deal can be learned from finding how others do it. A poor way of filing will be a sad burden for a preacher, but after a while changing to a better way will be arduous, if not impossible.

For many ministers the basic unit is a *card file*. Under topics from Abortion to Zeal it lists what the minister may want for sermons. Items that are short enough to go on the card are written in full, or cut out and pasted there, with a reference to their source. A notation describes whatever is too long to be written on the card, and tells where to find it. It is well to write in enough to show why the item is important. Something we put in the file may be like a stone which looks so bright and interesting when we pick it up on the seashore and so drab the next day.

When there are several references from the same book, it is burdensome to write out the title and the author's name with each one. W. E. Sangster advises listing in a notebook and numbering each book that is read, if there are to be references to it. Then only the number need be copied in the file. I write on the file card the author's last name but abbreviate the book title, so Kepler CTAJ refers to Thomas S. Kepler's *Contemporary Thinking About Jesus*.

The decision on the right-size cards is important. Standard sizes are 3 × 5, 4 × 6, and 5 × 8. With smaller cards, less blank space will be wasted on unfilled cards. Larger cards are easier to type on, and larger clippings can be pasted on them.

Bible references are filed under the subjects, so the cards become a topical concordance. Many ministers also keep a file of sermon texts, noting possible uses of each text and entering the date of any sermon that used it.

When any item from the card file is used, the date should be written on the card; it should also be put on the margin in a book that is quoted. This saves the preacher from using favorite items too often, and helps him find sermons he has preached on the various subjects.

A set of numbers or symbols for quickly indicating quality is useful. Such marks beside a poem, quotation, responsive reading, or any other item show at a glance how it is rated, from useless to superb.

A *folder file* takes pamphlets, sheets from magazines, and typed pages. Its items are cross-listed in the card file.

A *future sermon notebook* has separate sheets for each sermon a minister is accumulating. There may be up to a hundred of these. Whenever a good thought for one of them comes to him, he writes it in. Periodically he leafs through the pages, writing down ideas for contents or structure that come to him. Sometimes a page that seemed exciting when it was started will remain too long with no development, so it has to be culled. This notebook will be a prime source when a schedule for future preaching is being laid out. When there is a subject a minister thinks should be preached on because it has been neglected or is urgent, he may study the cards on this subject from his file until a good conception for a sermon comes to him. This will start a new page in his sermon notebook. There may be eight or ten notebook sermons the minister is actively turning over in his mind.

Ministers may record and *file their sermons* by texts, subjects, or dates. One who tends to remember sermons by dates and pastorates will file them chronologically, though the whole record must be scanned to find texts and subjects. When a sermon is preached, it is recorded in a purchased "Pastor's Record," or in any blank journal, with the date, title, text, and subject or subjects. A three-digit grade can show the preacher's evaluation of the congregation's response, the material, and the overall conception.

A 111 sermon would be a masterpiece; 999 would show an utter failure. Manuscripts on typewriter-size paper can be kept in a file box or drawer. Those on notepaper can be kept on shelves in cheap ring binders.

The building and keeping up of sermon material files that are of increasing value is hard work—but it has to be done. Each minister must devise the system that best suits his mentality. Some keep their accumulating sermon material in notebooks, which to me would seem cumbersome and inflexible. A minister accepts the filing task because he is appalled by the thought of all the splendid material for sermons that has passed through his mind and been lost forever because he made no record of it. In *Through the Looking Glass,* the King gasps, "The horror of that moment I shall never, *never* forget," to which the Queen answers, "You will though, if you don't make a memorandum of it."

THE PREACHER'S OWN MIND

Most of what a preacher says comes out of his own mind while he is working on his sermon. As far as he knows this is his own creation, though complete originality is probably very rare. All of his past reading and conversations, what he learned in school, the events he has lived through, the prayers, hymns, and sermons he has heard, and his dreams and new hopes are the seedbed from which his newest ideas flower. Even the ideas he has from others are in a special sense his own because what he has stored up and how he reacted to it depend on his peculiar being and affections. An interesting mind is one that has been richly stocked. Some of what a minister puts in his sermons may, indeed, be original with him. Every teacher of religion "who has been trained for the kingdom of heaven is like a householder who brings out of his treasure what is new and what is old." (Mt. 13:52)

The minister's own thinking, inspired by the Bible and the Holy Spirit, is the chief source of what goes into his sermons, but if it were the only source his preaching would be constricted and repetitious. The gospel is too great for one small mind to be its channel. The preacher needs to bring his congregation what has come from many hearts and minds. He has the whole wide world to draw from.

A minister who is caught up in his preaching task will have sermon ideas coming to him when he is not working on a sermon. When he is mowing the grass, driving on the highway, or trying to get to sleep, something that would be useful in a sermon may occur. He must record it at once on any sort of paper he can lay his hand to. The dreadful story of the way Coleridge lost the rest of his poem, *Kubla Khan,* should impel him. The poet woke from a dream with the whole poem so clearly in mind that he was writing it at top speed until he was interrupted by "a man from Porlock." When the visitor left, no more of the poem could be recalled. So the minister pulls off the road, turns on the night light, or gets to the lobby in the movie house so that he can write down what has come to him before it disappears. He not only records the original idea but keeps on writing as long as the afflatus lasts. The flash of insight may have to do with the next Sunday's sermon, or it may be just a luminous fragment for some unknown time, but it comes to his mind when it is running free, not when it is harnessed to the job at the desk.

READING

A preacher must read a great deal. Anyone who gives much mentally and spiritually must get much, and reading is the best channel from the hearts and minds of other. This does not mean that a preacher must be of the bookish type. There is danger, indeed, that too much absorption in books will produce pedants who are ill at ease with people. A man's common sense and humanity may become sicklied o'er with the pale cast of bookishness. The wonderful thing about the ministry is that it can use people of all sorts of temperaments. There are competent preachers whose intellectual level is about that of the popular magazines. Their sermons are more like the Epistle of James than the Epistle to the Romans. They cannot work up much interest in linguistic analysis or modern poetry, but they may do more for a congregation than do those who become experts in these fields. But even the practical, human-interest types still have to read. A preacher's mind is on display with every word he utters, and a flabby, unexercised mind is a repellent spectacle. A preacher does not have to be a scholar, but he has to be someone to whom the hearers do not condescend, whose mental workings will be respectable, who has an interesting mind, whose range of information will not make the knowledgeable members of the congregation feel patronizing. Someone who does not keep stimulated by current reading will be seen as an anachronism, still displaying as his newest ideas what people were talking about ten years ago.

The most concentrated sermon source is other sermons. A preacher needs to know what other preachers are saying not because he intends to appropriate it, but because that is the best concentration of just what he needs to think about. The greatest benefit a preacher gets from reading sermons is the way they set his own wheels to turning. What he gets may not seem to have any similarity to what started it. The most important reason for ministers to read sermons is that they are human beings who need good preaching, and they rarely get a chance to hear it.

Getting sermons from sermons has the great danger of enlarging that unreal world which only preachers inhabit. We tend to get our observations, opinions, and alarms from other religious professionals instead of from real life. People recognize the desk-generated concepts which preachers pass around among themselves. But if our primary source of sermons is our knowledge of what goes on, then other ministers can make us more perceptive. They can give us a larger view than we get in our own parishes, and deeper insights than we can come to by ourselves.

Just as painters learn to paint by going through phases in which they try to learn from one master after another, so preachers learn to preach by discovering someone whom they especially admire and by deliberately trying to use his style and type of thinking. It is not a slavish imitation, it is a way of learning. For a while there may be one person whose books you are reading and whose methods you are adopting; two or three years later there may be another. A minister also needs others than preachers as models for his style.

George Buttrick once said that he always reads newspapers standing up because his legs get tired. There is value in a quick look at the headlines, and a scanning of the columnists and editorials, but the slavish reading of a newspaper consumes time with no adequate return. News, which a news magazine can give in one story, has to be repetitiously started over and renewed day by day in a newspaper. Readers are attracted from column to column by what is undeniably interesting but of no new significance. Murders, holdups, scandals, and fires become redundant; reading of more of them ceases to add to one's understanding of the human scene.

Magazines are a better source of knowledge than are daily papers, but anything of lasting value in them is hard to preserve. They keep us up with what is being done and thought better than books can. But when one looks at the bulk of a year's stacked-up magazines, the question is bound to occur "Would not the reading of that same amount of printing in good books have had more lasting value?"

Treatises on homiletics commonly list the basic books every preacher ought to know. Here are some of those most frequently recommended: Plutarch—*Lives;* Augustine—*Confessions;* Dante—*Divine Comedy;* a Kempis—*Imitation of Christ;* Shakespeare—many plays and sonnets; Bunyan —*Pilgrim's Progress;* Luther—*Freedom of the Christian Man;* Baxter—*Reformed Pastor;* Woolman—*Journal;* Law—*Serious Call;* Pascal—*Thoughts;* John Wesley—*Journal;* Milton—*Paradise Lost;* Von Hugel —*Letters;* W. P. Livingstone—*Mary Slessor.* Anyone will be shocked by the omission of his favorites from this sort of selection. A preacher does well to keep such lists in mind, and to check through them as guides to his study; but no one needs to feel illiterate if he has not mastered all those classics. There are well-read preachers for whom reading clear through *Paradise Lost* would have the same religious value as a barefoot pilgrimage to Mount Sinai.

It is also recommended that ministers keep up their studies in these fields: Bible, Bible interpretation, theology, philosophy, church administration, ecumenics, pastoral care, worship, homiletics, psychology, art, mental therapy, history, the sciences, sociology, politics, the contemporary scene, drama, fiction, and poetry. To put down so many branches of knowledge seems comic until we check and discover that there is not one of which a minister can afford to remain ignorant. If a minister enjoys reading, it looks as though he is in the right profession. But suppose a taste for printer's ink had no part in the motives that called him to the ministry? And suppose he is discovering that all the essentials of his work, including sermon preparation, conspire to make him a functional illterate?

There are meliorations. A preacher's education before he was ordained has probably given him a basis in most of those studies. He does not have to attack all of them at once; bit by bit, across the years, his mental furnishing can become impressive. Summer is a time many ministers count on to catch up on their reading. In my latter pastorates I worked out a compromise with conscience; I never preached an old sermon from September to June, or a new one in the summer. Partly that was a solution to the preacher's dilemma of not wanting to preach the most needed sermons to summer half-congregations, and not wanting to preach a second-rate sermon any time. This, and the slower pace of church organizations in the summer months, gave time for reading.

Some congregations now provide an annual study leave for their ministers. Such a leave may sometimes be most profitably used not for enrolling in a course, but for holing up somewhere with a stack of books.

A minister should force his way through difficult books to keep his brain in trim and to gain understandings that are more than superficial. But he must beware of the compulsiveness that forces him to finish any book he starts, even though it is of little profit. He should not keep digging without much sign of pay dirt. He can do most of his reading in the fields in which he is most interested. If that were his only rule, he would be confined to pleasant ruts, so there must be some duty reading; but we learn most from the books we enjoy. A minister needs hobbies in his reading—subjects in which he enjoys becoming especially well informed. It is, of course, an advantage if his hobbies can also be useful in his work, but a minister needs to read for his own good and growth, not just for sermon help. He will also need reading for pure pleasure; a bow that is never unstrung loses its spring. In the more difficult fields it is better to read the popularizers than the sources, unless one is a scholar. You can learn a great deal more about what Kant taught by reading his interpreters than by reading Kant, unless you are a professional philosopher. Great thinkers often are poor communicators. A minister's knowledge of the sciences, including the mental and social sciences, can be better gained from good writers who are amateur scientists than from good scientists who are amateur writers.

In general, it is better not to read new books until time has had a chance to distinguish those of lasting value from those that are temporary fads or the triumphs of publishers' promotion. This will keep you in a shadow when your friends are displaying their up-to-date attainments, but it is usually impossible to know whether a book is really worth reading for two, or three, or ten years. There are exceptions. The whole value of some important books is their immediacy. To delay reading a book like *Future Shock, The Greening of America,* or *The Autobiography of Malcolm X* until time proved its importance would be a mistake.

A book that is used soon is remembered; what is not used is lost. It multiplies the benefit of reading to have a purpose in view. If a book on church administration is read just before it is used as the basis for a planning conference, it will do the minister a great deal more good than if it is read for its interest and then put aside. If a book is used in a sermon, a class, or conversation, it is much more likely to be remembered.

If a minister keeps at hand a list of books he wants to read, his priorities can be intelligent. Too many of our selections are accidental; we read the books we get as gifts, the ones we pick up as bargains, or those someone happens to mention. The list of books to read may include some we have been wanting to get to for years, some from recent reviews, some from fields where we feel deficient, some we hope will serve an immediate purpose. A book we thought at first we had to read may come to look decreasingly important, and drop off the list. Such an informal list may be the closest we can come to a long-range reading plan.

There is great advantage in owning any book you expect to use again. Libraries are of great help, but you cannot mark up a library book, and it will not be at hand when, all at once, you need it. It is worth six dollars to save the values of a book it took sixty dollars worth of time to read. How much is it worth to have material for a sermon, or even to have one good sermon illustration? A minister can buy a great many books without having to spend as much for his equipment as a physician or mechanic does. Expensive reference books should be tried out before they are purchased; a commentary, dictionary, or encyclopedia that is just right for someone else may be just wrong for you. Work with such books at the library until you know whether or not they have what you need.

It is useful for a preacher to make notations and comments in the margins as he reads—his recorded disagreements may be the best help for his sermons. Notations that will go into the sermon material file can be written inside the back cover. This provides a helpful list of the high points in the book, and it will show you on moving day whether to discard or keep a book.

Never lend a book that you expect to use again! This is not a crabbed rule—it is an absolute essential. A workman cannot afford to scatter his tools. It is dreadful to have a sermon blasted because, when you reached for the book that had something essential in it, the book was not there. It is hard not to lend because you want your friends to know your friends, and when you are enthusiastic about a book you are eager to share it. People often need your books to work out a worship service, a lesson, a talk, or for their own help. One solution is to have the book put in the church library; another is to use some of your church contribution to buy books for lending. Many otherwise good people are neglectful about returning books they borrow, so a minister who lends his books will soon have a mutilated library. The members of his family have to understand that his library is out of bounds for scattering around the house or around the neighborhood. Sermons are so important that in order to save them, we will be forgiven for transgressing the injunction, "Do not refuse him who would borrow from you."

THE PREACHER'S OWN EXPERIENCES

The preacher's own experiences can supply much of his most effective material. He needs to be an avid observer of the human scene, noting conversations and incidents that will demonstrate Christian truth. A traffic accident, a child's distress, what a delivery man told him, a big moment on a camping trip, a crisis in the school board, the happy resolution of some family's crisis—through these, abstractions are brought down to earth. The truly moving is the commonplace. Ministers are inclined to fill their sermons with quotations from famous people and with scenes from the turning points of history. But the words of the man who was fixing the refrigerator will be more convincing for the congregation than a saying of Napoleon; something that happened in the community will get to people better than will something that determined the outcome of the battle of Marathon. Truth is stronger than fiction, and an event the minister observed will be more moving than an event from a novel.

Just as an eager preacher will do all his reading with an eye out for anything that might add strength to a sermon, so will he go through life making notes of anything he hears or sees that might have a useful message. Some of my minister friends carry small notebooks for such records, as well as for jotting down what comes to them while reading, thinking, or attending meetings. A trip with a devoted note-taker is almost as bad as a trip with a camera enthusiast. Years ago I traveled through Switzerland with a young minister who constantly held up our party while he scribbled. When we complained, he would answer, "I don't think the Lord gave me this trip for my own benefit." We were tempted to answer, "Nor for ours," but he became one of this country's most admired preachers. My pocket space is too limited for notebooks, but I am grateful to the bank for all its blank checks I have taken from my wallet for hasty notes. Things we are sure at the instant are so important we could not forget them often slip away. The reason for note-taking and files is in the proverb, "The slothful man roasteth not that which he took in hunting." (Prov. 12:27 KJV)

There are cautions a minister must have in mind in talking about his experience. Let us consider the pros and cons. The reason for using the first person is that it adds reality and interest. "Someone said . . ." is less impressive than "The man at the filling station told me . . ."; "I read in last week's paper . . ." is weaker than "When I saw that truck bearing down on me . . ."; "There was . . ." is a poorer introduction than "In my home town . . ." We are more interested in people we know than in strangers. Eyewitness testimony is more convincing than hearsay. Comedians know a story will seem funnier if they claim it happened to them or to someone else who is present, even though everyone knows it never did. A minister need not apologize for using the first person; it is the only person he has. An apology implies it is bad manners for him to tell what he heard, saw, did, or thinks—and it usually is not.

With all the prejudice against "the vertical pronoun," it is the necessary first half of personal communication. Some ministers are too shy about using such expressions as "I believe . . ." or "I have seen . . ." It can be presumptuous—"I want you to remember this, and never forget who told you . . ."—but ordinarily an "I" statement simply locates the thought process in that room instead of out in an anonymous somewhere. "There is reason to believe" or "It might be concluded" are lifeless; "I think" or "I am sure" have a human source. Similarly, the "you" pronoun attaches what is happening to the hearers instead of to nobody in particular. Expressions like, "Haven't you often noticed . . . ?" or "That is why you . . ." make the congregation the actors in the sermon-drama which otherwise would be played on a distant stage with a faceless cast. The desiccated pronoun "one" or unspecific nouns like "people" leave a sermon in mid-air. Think of what it would do to the Sermon on the Mount to change every "you" to "one"—"Why does one see the speck that is in one's brother's eye, but not notice the log that is in one's own eye?" Of course Jesus could speak with authority as we cannot, but "you" constructions are not usually autocratic or judgmental. When they would be, a "we" can usually avoid the bony forefinger—"We lavish our affection on ourselves." "We" saves the minister from talking down and makes him one with the congregation.

The knowledge that a minister is a real person with their sort of problems can increase his ability to help the people of the church, in sermons or in private. His willingness to reveal himself as less than perfect gives a sense of openness and trust. On that sad Sunday when Father Damien for the first time commenced a sermon, "Fellow lepers . . ." he had a new power. When we go to a doctor, we are not particularly interested in hearing about his aches and pains, and there is not much value in hearing about a minister's troubles unless he has something more to tell. But when he shows the way out of doubt, fear, and discouragement, it is important to know that he is not the butterfly who "preaches contentment to the toad." A minister's hardest experiences can be redeemed by the good they bring to others. Dr. Arthur John Gossip's famous sermon, "But When Life Tumbles In, What Then?" was the first sermon he preached to his congregation after his wife's bewilderingly sudden death. Printed as a pamphlet, it has helped countless Christians through their grief.

So there are important reasons for a minister to use the first person in his preaching, but there are also important limitations on it. The preacher's telling of his own experiences cannot be repeated as often as can other cherished material. A congregation gets caught up on hearing about its minister's conversion. In some congregations the minister's favorite autobiographical pieces give occasion for some gentle ridicule. Church members, whose minister has visited the Holy Land, may become more familiar with what he saw and felt than they want to be.

When a minister talks about himself, the temptation to self-glorification is almost irresistible. A person who is on exhibit every seven days readily becomes an exhibitionist. His *ecce homo* becomes introverted. It is natural for him to select and improve the incidents that will present him in the best light. His half of the conversations he reports will be so wise, the kindly things he does for those in trouble will be so noble, that he will appear twice as big as life. His pulpit gives him a chance to gratify the natural human desire to appeal for sympathy, to drop in references to how hard he works, to shyly draw aside the curtain of his reticence to reveal trials bravely borne. Name-dropping can slip in— "When I was called to the capital to meet with the governor . . ." (the Governor welcomed the state clergy convention); "As a leading business-man in this city said to me . . ." (why should not the boy who served his sandwich be so designated?) The revealing references can come so slyly: "On my way to address the bar association . . . ," "At six o'clock Monday morning in my study . . . ," "Among the two hundred names on my daily prayer list . . . ," "As I lay sleepless, sick at heart over the famine victims . . ."

The disclaimers by which self-advertisers try to cover the offense usually aggravate it—"I say in all humility," "I just happened to be lucky." When I was in college a minister was brought to the campus whose addresses were largely accounts of his honors and achievements. After each such revelation he would declare, "I say it not boastfully, but to the glory of God." He at least supplied the students with an expression whose humorous uses took many forms.

One of the several bad effects of a self-glorifying minister can be a preacher-centered church. Many people want a great-hearted, great-souled hero figure who will illustrate their religion, and a preacher may succeed in giving them what they want. A church's admiration of its minister can be a source of strength, but such a minister should not be the one who uses his chances to show off in public to make himself the object of idolatry.

The minister has to know in his own heart whether his motive is God's glory or his own, and he can easily deceive himself. Perhaps the test can be like the old question about whether some Sunday activity breaks the Sabbath—if you do not enjoy it, it's all right. If a preacher enjoys telling something about himself, if he relishes preparing for it and putting on the effective touches, then he had better leave it out. Whatever is in bad taste will leave a bad taste.

THE PREACHER'S OLD SERMONS

Another source of sermon material is the minister's old sermons. These can become addictive. That is not usually the problem in a first parish but after that, the possibility of using an old sermon in an emergency can make emergencies the normal state; each week produces a better excuse than the one before. Father Valentine, in *The Art of Preaching*, says with some sarcasm that with ingenuity a preacher can even repeat sermons in the same parish. He need only start out, "My dear Brethren. If you remember, three weeks ago today I spoke to you about the holy sacrifice of the Mass. Today I want to renew that plea and to say again . . ." He adds, "Having gotten off to such a flying start, how can you fail?" The only way to break the addiction and to end the weekly moral struggle is to impose on oneself the unbreakable rule, "Not one more old sermon, no matter what."

But old sermons can be a source of new ones. Often, when you finish a sermon, you know that a great deal more could have been done with it. It is well then to write across the back of the last page your thoughts about how it might be improved. What you get from this will not be a modification but a new building, constructed out of the ruins of an old one. In your sermon notebook you may have a list of old sermons which you would like to try again. Ministers who have been in a series of churches are likely to have some sermons that have been preached in a different edition in each church. These are likely, at last, to become their best ones.

Old sermons can be mined for good bits. Usually your old sermon looks to you like a last year's bird nest, but you may find some parts that deserve a better use. A sermon, like any other work of creative art, may have to be put away and tried again to become right. A sermon part that has been reworded and reaimed may increase in value in another sermon.

THE THEATER

The theater, with its exposure of the whole human drama, is a natural source for sermons. Shakespeare has been the preachers' constant help, and modern plays can reveal our present state. A minister who picks his plays wisely can learn a great deal that will make him a more understanding preacher; he may also get material he can use for sermons. It is not necessary to go to theaters to enjoy good drama; many of the best plays are on records that can be taken from the local library. The scenes you construct in your imagination as you listen to the plays are often better than the ones the theaters provide.

Movies can have a good deal for sermons. Their disadvantage is that it is difficult to get movie scripts for quoting, while the best stage plays are available.

There is every reason to expect television to be a good source for sermons, but it rarely is. There are some superb programs on television— documentaries, new dramas, old movies—but in general, sitting in front of a television set is a slow way of getting much for sermons. Perhaps commercials break up the mood, perhaps low expectations are a handicap. It may be that my generation was not trained to get what television has, but in several years of hearing student sermons, I have noticed that, while there is a great deal of reference to stage plays and movies, there is almost never anything from television.

THE CONGREGATION

The congregation is a source for sermon material. Conversations, sermon seminars, question boxes, and all the interplay of the church life provide a great deal that a preacher needs. (Chapter XXVIII)

PLAGIARISM

Plagiarism, which literally means "kidnaping," is the theft of other people's brainchildren. It is an insidious sin because it is not easy to identify. Very little that any of us says or writes is really original; we have been using others' thoughts and words ever since we learned to talk. Goethe, who seems preeminently the creative genius, admitted, "Very little of me would be left if I could say what I owe to my predecessors and contemporaries." Twenty-one centuries ago Terence declared, "Nothing is said nowadays that has not been said before," and it was Emerson's opinion that all literature since Plato is quotation.

Using other people's ideas in general is no sin; it is the specific use of the products of other minds that is wrong. It has always been a temptation for preachers. Jeremiah hears God sternly condemn the prophets "who steal my words from one another for their own use" (Jer. 23:30 NEB); this sin is still associated with the ministry. Pascal said with sarcasm that when preachers use the editorial *we* it is literally true. Plagiarism is larceny. Publishers have no illusions about it; they know that when someone takes material from their books without acknowledgement or compensation, he has stolen money from them. Plagiarism is lying. A minister who preaches as his own what he has taken from someone else is trying to deceive the congregation. In presenting himself as abler than he is, he is falsifying. Whatever excuses he may give himself, he outrages the ordinary person's sense of right and wrong. There are scandals over this. The president of a church college was ruined when an address he made to an educational association was found to be someone else's. When a flamboyant preacher's sermons were shown to have been stolen, it did not save him when he explained that he thought they were his own; his memory was so phenomenal, he said, that a sermon he had read would come out of his unconscious recollection with every comma and syllable intact!

The line between right and wrong is sometimes hard to locate because it is all right to use some sorts of material that we get from other people.

1. There is an anonymous mass of ideas from the common warehouse of humanity. There are stories, proverbs, humor, felicitous expressions, folk wisdom which no one would ever think you were claiming as your own.

2. There is more specific material which so many have used it has passed into the public domain. If a preacher were to try to acknowledge the source of such ideas, he would have to say something like, "By

Wesley, out of Jowett, by way of Weatherhead." There are some sermons almost everyone has used—for example, *When Angels Depart,* on how to keep the glory from departing, from Luke 2:15, "When the angels went away from them into heaven"; and *Half-Baked Religion,* from Hosea 7:8, "Ephraim is a cake not turned." A preacher does not have to admit the source of Fosdick's illustration of the farmer who thought he was driving up-hill because the back wheels were off, or of Coffin's story about the man who discovered gold in California and died in poverty.

You may use a ringing phrase like "Steer your ship with hope ahead and fear astern" without adding "as Thomas Jefferson said." Indeed, the occasional use of a quoted good expression is a first step toward learning to create your own—"The faith of the Galilean is too great for our small hearts," "Will the fire that burns in the Bible blaze upon our modern hearths?" "When he walked through the room, it was as if suddenly you heard pipes playing." These are borderline cases. You cannot use as your own something that is very striking and original, but if it is just apt, it can be taken.

3. Whatever is definitely someone else's mental product has to be acknowledged. This includes ingenious outlines and vehicles as well as quotations. If an outline is fairly obvious, it can be taken; but if it is distinctive, it cannot be offered as one's own. Any quotation longer than a sentence belongs to its originator.

There is an old saying that what is improved in passage is not stolen. Minor improvements do not change the ownership, but if the coins have been melted down and reminted, you can call the coinage yours. Charles Lamb said he had milked three hundred cows for something he had written, but the butter was his.

The best test, in all cases of uncertainty, is to ask, "Would I be embarrassed if I got caught?" If you were to look at the back pew and see there the author of what you are using, would you feel guilty? If some literate church member were to say at the door, "I know where you got that," would you be disconcerted?

Plagiarism is a character-killing vice, because it grows. The more we steal, the more we are inclined to steal. It is self-defeating because the more we depend on others, the less able we are to borrow wisely. The quality of a preacher's mind is shown by what he wants to take. The less he is a hard-working and creative thinker, the less he will have the good taste to borrow well. A second-rate mind will pick up second-rate material.

One has to be more meticulous in giving the sources in writing than in speaking. What is merely spoken does not depreciate the value of others' publications, or cast doubt on their originality, as does something that is put in print. What is written can have quotation marks and footnotes which do not interrupt the flow of thought as does the continual interjection of authors' names in speaking. The frequent mention of distinguished names can sound like a display of scholarship. Indeed, a minister who wishes to feel innocent might tell himself, "I'm not a plagiarist, I'm just not a name-dropper." Professor H. H. Farmer's advice is " 'As has been said,' or 'as someone has said' is sufficient. The introduction of a proper name, especially if it is a well-known one, tends to divert the mind of the hearer not only from the content of what is being said, but also for the moment from the living person saying it." (*The Servant of the Word*, p. 63.) The use of quoted material may be shown by a change in the manner of speaking. The indecorous finger wiggling gesture can always be avoided.

It is easy to find excuses for stealing. There is truth in the adage "All work and no plagiarism makes Jack a dull preacher." A minister may convince himself that what he is doing is in the best interest of the congregation. If he has had a hard week, using others' ideas may seem the only way to give the congregation the sermon it needs. Moreover, people are not as interested in what they know is second-hand, so it would be poor technique to spoil the effect of what might be a very useful sermon. A minister might plead that plagiarism is evidence of the great Christian virtue of humility. To all of this James Russell Lowell has the final word in his protest against plagiarism:

> In vain we call old notions fudge,
>   and bend our conscience to our dealing;
> The Ten Commandments will not budge,
>   and stealing will continue stealing.

There is nothing wrong with preaching another minister's whole sermon when you say you are doing it. The organist does not compose his own pieces, and a preacher may come upon a sermon so great that he is eager for his people to have it. He may know that any changes he could make would be damaging, so he uses it exactly as it was written and lets the congregation know who occupied the pulpit. I must acknowledge that my attempts in this have not been very successful. The sermons were far better than the church was used to, but no one seemed to be much impressed. No doubt the delivery was inadequate, but I suspect that people prefer an ordinary sermon that is intended for them to an extraordinary sermon that was written for some other congregation. " 'Tis a poor thing, but mine own," may be their feeling.

XVIII

Quotations, Poetry, and Illustrations

This will be a chapter of pros and cons because each of these special sorts of sermon material has great advantages and great abuses. There are so many separate things to say that they are put in numbered lists to make them clearer and more concise.

QUOTATIONS

There are good reasons for using quotations in sermons:

1. A quotation can bring beauty, force, excitement, or memorable wording into a sermon in a way the preacher could not match. It may be so nearly perfect that any change or adaptation would be a desecration.
2. Quotations bring the support of respected authorities. They assemble witnesses to testify to what the sermon says.
3. A quotation can offer a tactful way of saying what the preacher prefers not to say by himself. With something that is controversial, or charged with emotion, or that might seem authoritarian or bad manners, it is often wise to use the statement of someone else.
4. Quotations can be educational as they inform the congregation about important people or sayings.
5. A quotation can enliven a sermon with a welcome change of pace.
6. The Bible's words are often just what we need. We struggle to find the right expression for our thought, while a pungent quotation from the Bible would say it perfectly.
7. Quotations can add color and drama. A quotation from Shakespeare, someone's dying words, a statement from a crisis point in history may be moving.

There are cautions that need to be remembered:

1. Too many quotations spoil a sermon. Phillips Brooks said, "Constant quotations in sermons are, I think a sign of crudeness." There is a "scissors and paste" style of sermon which is largely made up of items the preacher

has gleaned from his reading. It is not what congregations most need or want. Too much quoting may reveal a lack of trust in one's own ability.

2. Quotations are often treated as though they were proof; testimony is not proof.

3. The many possible associations with a quotation or its author may divert the listeners' attention to what is irrelevant.

4. A minister who quotes may seem to be showing off his learning.

5. With all the good reasons for quoting the Bible, we must still resist a tendency to keep throwing in odds and ends of Scripture when our own words would serve better. A minister may have a sentimental feeling for a verse that has no emotional interest for most of the congregation. There is justified dislike of the intemperate scripturizing that interlards speech with bits from the Bible.

6. People lose esteem for a preacher who misquotes familiar words, just as they discount one who does not check his facts. It is taken as a sign of careless work and superficial thinking.

POETRY

Longfellow wrote:

> God sent his singers upon earth
> With songs of sadness and of mirth
> That they might touch the hearts of men,
> And bring them back to heaven again.

This is a function poets share with preachers. In many ways their aims are similar. Both try to inspire, to plumb the human heart. Both try to bring beauty, to stir love, indignation, horror, pity, ecstasy, to reveal the riches which the material world can neither give nor take away. Madame de Staël said, "Poetry is the natural language of all worship." Poetry and worship both look to what is of ultimate worth. Sermons need poetry because poets often say the things sermons need to say far better than the preachers can.

Good poetry, like hymns, can be used repeatedly, as prose cannot. The old favorites do not lose their usefulness; they become old favorites because their truth and beauty are always needed. Ministers, as professionals, can get tired of hymns and poems that are still fresh and welcome for the congregation. The best-loved poems can awaken old devotions and renew ardors that have cooled. Ministers need to become familiar with the classic and contemporary poets that other preachers find most useful.

A church service is not a class in literature or esthetics. The poetry that is used there should be judged only by how well it serves the intended purpose. This, unhappily, rules out much of the finest modern poetry because it is too cerebral or comes at too deep an emotional level to have much effect when it is first heard. Poetry which hearers have to sit and think about must be sadly put aside. The preacher may love it and long to transmit what it means to him, but if it is too subtle to be caught at the speed of preaching, he will have to find some other way to share it.

Ministers are sometimes charged with being too tolerant of doggerel. It is easy to grasp at top speed, but it may be painful for the sensitive. The tool has to be suited to the task, and if a poem of less than classic quality will do what needs to be done for most of those in a particular congregation, it can be used. Bad poetry is bad, not because it is simple or unsophisticated, but because it is lazy. The author did not do enough work to get it past the slovenly stage. Words that may be passable with music may be infantile without it. There need be no artificial criteria. If James Whitcomb Riley does what is needed, he is as respectable as Shakespeare, but there is no place for trash in a worship service. It is painful for discriminating people and makes them feel that they are not where they belong. Simple verses will sound less jingly if the delivery emphasizes the meaning, and not the rhyme and rhythm. One great advantage of poetry in sermons is that it can lodge truths in the hearers' memories that would soon be forgotten if they were put in prose. Poetry with rhyme and meter does this better.

Poetry is usually not as easy to understand as is prose, and the listeners get more from it when they are told in advance what to listen for. It is better to do this in the course of the sermon, not as a separate introduction to a poem—"This same mistrust of barriers is what Robert Frost has in mind in his picture of two neighbors building a wall," or "George Santayana also believes that we find our surest guide, as Columbus did, by faith's vision." Only the part that is necessary for the purpose should be quoted. The preacher can explain what leads up to the lines he is using rather than quote the preceding ones. It is better to tell what Thomas Gray was doing in the churchyard than to recite all the early stanzas of his "Elegy."

A poem can give relief when a sermon is getting heavy. It can bring color, human interest, or an emotional high point. Poems are often used for conclusions and, less often, for introductions. This is good only when it is not habitual.

One of life's great delights is to read all you can of a poet who, you have discovered, is especially for you. There are collections of poetry for preachers. Many of these are rubbish, but a few are selected with judgment and taste. A good collection with a topical index is valuable. General anthologies are more likely to put you in touch with the best poets of the past and present. References to useful poems can be transferred to the sermon material file.

An obvious place to locate poetry is the topical index to the hymnal. This can sometimes serve, but the requirements for a good poem and a good hymn are not the same. W. E. Sangster reports that his hymnal, with a thousand hymns, has only seventeen authors with any reputation as poets. Some of the finest poets put all their skill and talent into trying to get into the hymnal and never made it, but the words to some of the best-loved hymns are embarrassing as poetry.

ILLUSTRATIONS

It is illustrations that make speech effective. The commonest illustrations are single words—*sweetheart, highbrow, grasp, electrify.* Some scholars insist that every word originated in an illustration. Languages develop terms that may seem intangible, but it is the picture words that have the power. Sermons need more such words—not *new,* but *green* or *raw;* not *old,* but *hoary* or *tottering;* not *sad,* but *heavy-hearted;* not *glad,* but *soaring.* Words that seem abstract are often forgotten pictures. The very word *illustrate,* meaning "to cast light on," is an illustration; a *scruple* is a bit of gravel in your shoe you can't ignore; *cowardice* is a dog's drooping tail; to *inculcate* is to stamp with the heel; a *husband* is the band that holds the house together; a *curriculum* is a race course; a *disaster* is star-crossed.

Metaphors and similes are quick illustrations. Jesus was a master of all sorts of illustrations. He used quick ones—"You are the light of the world"; and longer ones—"Why do you see the speck that is in your brother's eye . . . ?"; and extended ones—"There was a man who had two sons . . ." There are 65 metaphors in the Sermon on the Mount, and 164 of them in the first three gospels. The most spiritual message ever given was conveyed in a wealth of material terms.

An illustration can be as short as the word "hot" or as long as Bunyan's *Pilgrim's Progress.* Aesop and Dante taught wholly by illustrations, and all teachers of morals and religion must rely on them. Virtues and spiritual states must be presented in terms of tangible realities. The tendency to think and speak wholly in abstractions is not a sign of intellectual advancement, but of having lost contact with actuality.

Some of the reasons illustrations are indispensable for sermons are these—and the list could go on and on:

1. Tangible representations and analogies help the congregation understand. "A picture is worth a thousand words," and it is often the illustration that makes the listeners see what the minister is trying to say.

2. Illustrations make a sermon interesting. An Arab proverb says, "He is the best speaker who can turn ears into eyes." A sermon without illustrations is like a television program with the picture tube turned off. An illustration is the oasis that turns a dry and featureless stretch of sermonizing into scenery.

3. Illustrations put abstractions in terms that can be grasped. There is no such thing as brotherhood, there are only people in brotherly relationships; there is no such thing as beauty, but there are things that are beautiful; duty is no reality apart from the actions it requires. We may concede, with some of the medieval schoolmen, that universals have an objective reality in the mind of God, but in the minds of the Sunday

morning congregation they do not, unless they are revealed in specific instances. The manipulation of abstractions can be very satisfying for the preacher because he already knows what he is talking about; he may be aware of an actuality behind the generalities he juggles, but the congregation will not be unless he shows it to them.

4. Illustrations can make the preacher's reasoning understandable. For example, he may, to his own satisfaction, have demonstrated on theological grounds that the chief social and political questions are primarily religious questions, but many will not follow his thinking at all until he illustrates it with a specific question—government measures to restrict population growth, perhaps, or industrial pollution as a sin against the world's Creator. A good illustration can do more than can air-tight logic to help people share the minister's conclusions. It is wrong to offer an illustration as proof; logically, it never is. But it can make the truth believable.

5. Illustrations serve as demonstrations; they are the laboratory part of preaching. When a minister is preaching on such subjects as prayer, family life, evangelism, or courage, his true stories show people how to try what he recommends.

6. Repetition is necessary for teaching. What a sermon says in a flat statement can be said again by an illustration.

7. Illustrations keep a sermon from being forgotten. They are remembered best, so they are like pegs anchored in the memory. What is tied to them will not drift away. Thoughts that are well illustrated will be kept.

8. An illustration can break down resistance. An unwelcome duty, a hard truth, an attitude that prejudice wants to reject may be accepted if an illustration makes a strong appeal.

9. An illustration can give the inspiration of a good example or the warning of a bad example. It can use heroes as they should be used.

10. The emotions can be powerfully moved by illustration. No minister of Jesus Christ could ever preach without emotion. The choice is never between emotion and no emotion, but between the right emotions and the wrong ones. The wrong emotions are not expelled by reasoning so much as by the right emotions. The preacher uses illustrations to help people feel as Christians ought to feel. There are cheap emotions that are disconnected from any action, like a motor that is racing with the clutch let out. Preaching should both stir the Christlike emotions and put them into Christlike action. Illustrations serve both these purposes. The preacher is a teacher of right living, but if right living came from religious knowledge, the theological scholars would be the greatest saints. In too many well-worked-out, reasonable sermons, the preacher is like a blacksmith who is pounding on cold iron. If a church wants to bring human beings more into the pattern of Christ, it will have to raise their emotional temperature until they can be shaped. The warmth kindled by illustrations can soften hard hearts and make rigid natures pliable.

11. A good story allows vicarious participation. The hearers, by imagination, become participants in the drama with which the sermon deals.

It takes skills to use illustrations well, and there are hazards. Here are some of those skills and hazards:

Sermon illustrations should be as brief as they can be without sacrificing their effect. The art of story-telling has no place in the pulpit beyond where it serves the sermon's purpose. Details that are not needed for the story can bring a character to life or make a scene real, but this must be weighed against the time that will be lost from other parts of the sermon.

Multiple illustrations should not be used for the same purpose. A fisherman will not increase his catch by tying several kinds of bait to the same hook. Ministers are tempted to add illustrations, either because they love them so much they cannot bear to leave them out or because they feel that no one of the illustrations seems quite right. Several partly appropriate illustrations cannot do the work of a single good one.

Do not use an illustration that does not really elucidate your meaning just because it is interesting, entertaining, or decorative.

Beware of illustrations that sound good but cannot bear reflection. To say that we come to God at last as rivers find their way into the sea is proper only for a pantheist.

It is usually a mistake to devise a sermon to be a setting for an appealing illustration, or for several of them. If the sermon is in mind first, illustrations can be chosen to move it toward its goal. If the illustration is in mind first, the goal and the development of the sermon must be adapted to it.

A minister is fortunate if he can find an illustration that is strong enough to support his whole sermon. The sustaining illustration may be a story, poem, or metaphor. It may be a Bible figure such as blood, leprosy, or fire. (Chapter X) Dr. Fosdick's fine sermon, *Every Man a Gambler,* refers to gambling in almost every paragraph.

The mood of the illustration should fit the dignity of the subject. To use the domestic habits of the beetle as an example for Christian marriage, or to call the Trinity a troika, would seem inappropriate. I remember a sermon in which a little girl's impatience to finish her piano practice illustrated the world's longing for the Lord's return.

The point of an illustration must be made crystal clear. Some minds do not make connections readily. Those whose attention has been wandering until an illustration caught their interest may have to be told again what the sermon is getting at. The surest way to apply an illustration is to tell in advance what it is supposed to show, or to attach a moral to the end—"and so we see . . . ." Hearers, however, consider either of these an affront to their intelligence. They are flattered, and admire the artistry, if the application is left entirely to them. To do this, and still make the point plain, requires subtlety. Strong statements of the truth that is meant can be made just before or after the illustration, or both. It helps if some of the words that are used in the illustration are picked up in these statements. There is danger not only that people will fail to see the intended meaning but that instead they will see a meaning that is not intended. A romantic description of the Crusades to illustrate heroic Christian action may persuade someone that the Moslems have no right to be in the Holy Land.

Use dialogue and direct quotation, instead of reporting in your own words what was said. Direct quotation is dramatic, indirect is dead.

Beware of hobbies. Some preachers seem to get most of their illustrations from ancient Greece, athletics, or Scottish life. Do not hold to the stock stypes—football player, prom queen, rising young executive.

Illustrations that require a great deal of explaining waste valuable sermon time and their application may be lost in all the detail. By the time you have explained to the congregation what a laser beam is, or why Washington had to cross the Delaware, the point may be forgotten. Illustrations should be brought in as fast and incidentally as possible, not with a big buildup. An illustration is only a tool for a purpose, not something to be featured for itself. Do not use an illustration to illustrate an illustration—grace is like an electric relay which you can understand if you think of a man controlling the floodgates in a dam. If the first illustration is not clear by itself, it cannot be saved.

Do not present fiction as fact. It should be made clear whether a story is true or not. Ministers excuse the pretense that something really happened as a harmless way of adding interest, just as comedians make themselves the butts of their stories. The difference is that the comedians do not expect to be believed, while the ministers are hoping to deceive. A preacher who is caught being loose with the facts will be trusted in nothing. Congregations will begin to guess that no minister could possibly have as many conversations or experiences that are useful for sermons as their minister claims to have. When a minister tells something that actually happened to another minister, he is strongly tempted to present it as having happened to him. It is remarkable how preachers' children all over the country say the same bright things the same year. More than once I have heard ministers assign themselves flattering roles in stories I knew were old ones. It does not make for respect. Samuel Butler complained of "the irritating habit of theologians and preachers of telling little lies in the interest of great truth."

Ministers have to beware of telling what sounds improbable even when it is true—a punishment for their bad reputation. If what you tell sounds unlikely, you should give some corroboration.

The accuracy of illustrations must be checked. If, in telling of the martyrdoms in the fight against yellow fever, you refer to the anopheles mosquito, you will be identified as unreliable by all who know that the anopheles transmits malaria.

Avoid the incredible illustration. There are some pulpit favorites that exceed all possibility, like the story of the man who put his last dime on the counter and then saw that it said "In God we Trust."

Some of the familiar heroes of the pulpit anecdotes we may begin to feel we have met too often. There is the restrained fellow who always says things "quietly." "And looking the burly foreman squarely in the eye, he told him quietly, 'Yes, I have read the building code, but have you read the gospel?' " If he has anything to say, why doesn't he say it straight out and get off this creepy quietness? There are the strange creatures that never were on land or sea—"After my sermon at the college, a lovely coed told me at the coke bar, 'Daddy-O, you walked all over my needs this morning. You really bugged me.' Slangy? Yes—but sincere." (Which is probably more than can be said of her creator.) "And leaping to his feet, with the light of workmanly pride shining from his face, the stonemason cried, 'I, Sir, I am helping Sir Christopher Wren build a cathedral!' " He should have been helping David Garrick put on plays.

One has to admit that a certain fatuousness sometimes appears in sermon illustrations. Only the preacher could take them seriously. When the mountain missionary asked the urchin if he knew who God is, the little fellow answered in all innocence, "Is he that man whose other name is 'Damn?' " Or there is the little drummer boy who was ordered by Napoleon to beat the retreat. With a defiant smile on his blood-flecked lips the little lad replied, "Sire, I cannot beat a retreat, I can only beat a charge!" The minister I heard use this ended it, "To which the shamed Napoleon answered, 'Beat it, boy, beat it!' " (and none too soon). The minister's children are often made to share in this. Their infant voices still proclaim exactly what their father needs for Sunday morning.

It is easy to be tactless in sermon illustrations. To criticize Christmas cards with doggies on them may embarrass all those who have just sent that kind. To illustrate stewardship by telling what a blow it is not to be offered a second cup of coffee may offend the minister's recent hostesses. To speak of the abuses of the medical, legal, or military professions as though they are typical, or to imply that divorce is the result of a bad example in the preceding generation, may seem unfair. To quote the man who said, "I found out after I got married that I had only been half-alive before," may be just what the married need to hear, but it may not be a kind thing to say to the unmarried.

Illustrations which serve to show off the minister at his best should be avoided, even when they are true. As has been said, first-person illustrations are the most effective, but there is a built-in danger. When the preacher appears in a sermon illustration, he is likely to be an example of virtue and spirituality, because that is what sermons are about. It is almost inevitable that he will present that part of an experience which shows him as wise, kind, humorous, and heroic. It is an advantage most people do not have.

A preacher must be scrupulously careful to keep his illustrations from betraying confidences. His best illustrations come, of course, from the lives of people in the church, in former churches, or in the community. But to expose in public what he knows about people can be an unpardonable breach of trust. If he assumes that the people will not mind because the incident is harmless or flattering, he may be very wrong. If he feels sure that the people could not possibly be identified, he still may create mistrust. If a conversation or a counseling experience is reported in the pulpit, people will become uneasy about telling the minister anything they do not want revealed. If what is told might have happened to someone in the congregation, the hearers will be trying to guess who it was. Ministers' families can be resentful at being exposed in public, or others may be resentful in their behalf.

Some ministers believe it is ethical to change meaningless details in order to conceal the identity of those who are mentioned. It would be wrong, of course, to change anything that would add weight to the story or alter the evidence. But to call a carpenter a plumber, or to say that something that took place in New York happened in New Jersey may seem a harmless way of protecting people from being recognized. A minister who wants to quote his wife may refer to her as, "A saintly Christian woman whom I know." It will probably be true, but the intention will be to deceive. Perhaps the test in these matters can be, "Would I be ashamed to have people know I'd done it?"

Every illustration has a part that does not apply, and that part can be the preacher's undoing. When a minister said that the Church is like the tree from which Zacchaeus saw the Lord, someone asked, "Is that why the Lord told him to get out of it?" Military metaphors can imply a trust in militancy the minister does not intend. The use of the Reformation heroes as examples must not encourage people to accept their intolerance. A story that condemns sinful gaiety might also suggest that Christians should be staid.

Some of the good old faithful sermon illustrations have worn out their usefulness. Ministers, as church professionals, may think an illustration is hackneyed when it is still fresh and useful for people in the pews, but there are some stories that anyone who has heard many public speeches would like to see retired. When Halford Luccock, as "Simeon Stylites," had a weekly letter in the *Christian Century,* he asked readers for their nominations for the illustrations most entitled to a rest. Those sent in most frequently were these, and in this order:

That is how the dawn comes up in the Pyrenees!"
"He's not heavy; he's my brother."
Gabriel: "What if your disciples do not tell?" Jesus: "I have no other plan."
Doctor: "Go see the clown, Grimaldi." Patient: "Sir, I am that unhappy man."
"I'm tired doing nothing. Send me to Hell." "Where do you think you are?"
The story of the Great Stone Face.
The body reduced to its chemical constituents is worth 98¢.

"Your vision of GPC did not mean 'Go preach Christ,' but 'Go plant corn.' "
"You should have seen this garden when only the Lord was working in it."
The jigsaw puzzle with a face on the other side.

Illustrations that depend on special personal characteristics must usually be avoided. An obvious example of this is the ethnic story. Jokes
about black, foreign, Indian, or mountaineer groups must be entirely
ruled out, even when they are intended to be affectionate. Ethnic wisdom
is a little less dangerous, but it also may be offensive. This is a loss
because folk sayings often have just the sort of insights sermons need.
Preachers who have a genuine gift for dialect are deprived by this re-
striction; their skill can be a real and valuable art, but at present it must
pretty well be put aside. There was a time when such dialects as Scotch
and Italian could be used in stories, but in the present state of society
about the only ethnic groups that can safely be portrayed in pulpit
illustrations are Sumerians and Hittites.

Illustrations that have to do with physical or personality traits may
hurt those in the congregation who have those traits—or hurt their families. There is a hard line here for the preacher to find. If he talks about
suicidal tendencies in the presence of those in whose families there has
been a suicide, or if he talks about compulsive eating in the presence of
the obese, he may cause pain. If he tries to settle these matters by avoiding all such references, he loses the chance to deal with real problems
in a definite way. In meeting this dilemma, the minister must be willing
to be endlessly careful. After that, his guides will be his sensitivity and
his longing to give help.

Preachers must beware of illustrations that are so diverting that the
hearers will spend most of the rest of the sermon time thinking about
them. After any especially interesting illustrations, there needs to be a
something to win back the attention—a pause, perhaps, or some very
arresting statements.

Where does the minister find all the illustrations he needs for so
many sermons on so many different themes?

1. The best of all sources is the Bible. The Bible and sermons have
the same subjects, and the Bible is richly stocked with illustrations. It
has the Old Testament's stories and lives, the gorgeous imagery of the
Psalms, the powerful figures of speech used by the prophets, Jesus' similes
and parables, the events in the gospels, and the multimedia splendors of
the apocalyptic visions. All these are spread out by topics for the
preacher's use. Taking illustrations from the Bible has the advantage of
building up the congregation's Bible knowledge. It is more important
for church people to become familiar with the Bible than with Greek
mythology or contemporary fiction. Bible illustrations keep sermons in
touch with revealed truth.

2. There are encyclopedias of pulpit illustrations, arranged by the
topics sermons are supposed to need. If the editor has good taste and
understanding, such a collection might be of some use, but for a dis-

criminating preacher, its illustrations never seem quite right; they fit someone else's sort of mind. They can be tied onto the sermon, but they never seem to take root there. There is a mustiness about them; they have the smell of archives. A collection of selections from good literature, arranged by topics, can be helpful for sermons; such a collection is intended to be read through, not to be a source of separate items.

3. The best collection of illustrations a minister can have will be in his file. As time goes on, they accumulate from many sources—from his experiences, and those he hears about, and from his reading. The need for illustrations is one more reason why a minister has to read more than religious literature, which is largely abstract. The vivid, pictorial, dramatic illustrations he needs come from newspapers, magazines, fiction, plays, biography, science, and history.

4. The sermons of good preachers are an unfailing source of illustrations. If they are original, credit should be given to their authors, but many of the best ones are in the common store that preachers pass around.

5. A minister will count most of all on the illustrations that come up out of his own mind while he is working on a sermon. He finds them in his memory or he creates them. A knack for seeing analogies or thinking up parables can be developed.

Immanuel Kant sent the manuscript of his *Critique of Pure Reason* to a philosopher friend for an appraisal. The work is 800 pages long in print and wholly without concrete examples. The friend returned the manuscript half read, saying he feared he would go crazy if he tried to finish it. He asked plaintively why there were no illustrations. Kant replied that putting in illustrations would have made his book too long. Let preachers who begrudge giving up their time for quotations, poetry, or illustrations be warned. If congregations are to hear and understand what is said, pure reasoning is not enough.

XIX

Humor

It is easy to show on pragmatic grounds that there should be humor in preaching; its important uses cannot be questioned. But how can we make a place for humor on religious grounds when there is so little humor in the Bible, which is supposed to be the sermon's source and standard? There is almost every other sort of literature in the Bible—fiction, drama, history, poetry, statutes, letters, and much more, but scarcely a line of humorous writing. There are flashes of irony that are first cousin to humor; like Job's sarcasm with his friends, "No doubt you are the people, and wisdom will die with you." Paul says mockingly to his critics, "Accept me as a fool . . . for you gladly bear with fools, being wise yourselves!" The Old Testament's few references to laughter have mostly to do with derision or incredulity. The New Testament in one instance refers to laughter as mockery and twice mentions it as the opposite of weeping—beyond that it never refers to laughter or even to smiling. It is no wonder that some of our ancestors interpreted Christianity in pretty solemn terms. They knew Christian joy, but they did not consider joy a laughing matter. The Bible refers to gladness, and to being merry, but this has not been supposed to describe the preacher's demeanor in the pulpit. Luther frequently brought humor into his sermons, but in that he departed from what was generally approved.

It is significant that the clearest examples of humor in the Bible are in the words of Jesus. Some of what has been written about the humor of Jesus strains too hard; it tries to show that every difficult statement he made can be interpreted as a joke. But there is no doubt that Jesus intended some of his sayings to be funny. His droll exaggerations and delightful incongruities reveal his enjoyment of the ridiculous. Some of his sayings cannot be understood without the laughter that went around. With what relish of the absurd he pictured those meticulous ones who gag on a gnat but gulp down a camel with no difficulty. He made fun of the man with the log in his eye who was all in a stew over getting a speck of dust out of his brother's eye. Jesus seemed to take the sting from a rebuke by humor. He described the pompous rich who bustle up to the gate of the kingdom as like a camel, with his supercilious expression and preposterous hump, trying to force his way through a needle's eye. There seems to be a gentle raillery in the way Jesus gave nicknames. James and John kept exploding, so he called them "Sons of Thunder." There was both banter and affectionate confidence in it when he named unstable Simon "Rocky" (*Peter*). It was in Jesus that humor most broke into the Bible. It is such an exception to the gravity of all the rest of the Bible, and of his mission, that it is no wonder this has been neglected. Pictures rarely show Jesus smiling, but he must have smiled. Children do not like somber people, but the disciples had trouble keeping them from Jesus' arms.

There are sorts of humor we cannot associate with Jesus. When we laugh at the ridiculous it is often a mockery of someone's peculiarity in conduct or appearance. To be roaring with laughter can suggest a sort of weakness—people break up because they are overcome, something inside them lets go, which can be a good relief, but it is still a loss of control. Some of our humor is laughter at ourselves; by it we come to terms with our inadequacies. Some laughter is a sort of nervous spasm; compulsive wise-cracking may no more be humor than a facial tic is a smile. Humor is a healthy acceptance of reality, with all its absurdities; hilarity can be a flight from it. None of these lower sorts of humor fits our understanding of Jesus; with him humor was joy, gladness, and delight. It was an aspect of his love.

After the Gospels there are few touches of humor in the rest of the New Testament. But where would there be a place for it? There is affectionate good humor in the Epistles, but no occasion for jesting. We cannot expect any gay grace notes when the apocalyptic trumpets sound; we would not want graffiti to be scribbled on the jasper walls. There is no occasion for humor in writing that is preoccupied with something else. Senator Albert Beveridge pointed out that there is no humor in the greatest speeches. Patrick Henry, Daniel Webster, and Martin Luther King did not take time for it in their most important addresses. Abraham Lincoln was a gifted wit, and there is much that is ludicrous in many of his speeches, but there is no hint of it in his Second Inaugural, nor in his Gettysburg address. There is no joking in the Constitution of the United States, but there was Homeric jesting at the Constitutional Convention. Only men of a humorous mind could have framed so balanced and tolerant a political system, or could have secured its adoption against the narrow prejudices of the colonies. The writings of the Bible could not have come from dry and mirthless minds. The humane tolerance of the prophets, the delight of the Psalms, the exultation of the apocalyptic writings reveal authors who could laugh and the inspiration of a Holy Spirit whose gift is joy.

No one understands humor. A scholarly study of comedy concludes, "We do not really know what laughter is or what causes it." An analytical treatise on humor is like a speech on good manners—the choice of the subject shows the author's lack of it. Investigations of the anatomy of humor turn out to be mostly anatomy and not much humor. The funny has been explained as the shock of contrast, like the big man in a baby costume; or the flight from fear, as with jokes over death; or pleasure at superiority, laughing at a clown; or a defiance of convention, the dirty joke; or a play on words, the masseuse who rubs people the wrong way; or surprise, "These are the conclusions on which I base my facts." Such attempts do not really offer an explanation. Humor is like beauty. A contemporary philosopher declares that aesthetics is the least satisfying branch of philosophy. No one knows what beauty is—we can only accept it as the gift of God. Humor is also God's mysterious blessing.

If you make an address on the causes of war, write a hymn, or bring the assurance of God's eternal love at a funeral, there may indeed be no place for humor. But a Sunday-morning church service is a different sort of occasion. It is a family gathering. People come there to experience Christianity, not just to learn about it. The preacher's purpose is not merely to issue solemn pronouncements of eternal truth; he is a person in the midst of persons, and part of his purpose is to facilitate their interaction with him and with each other. By this they gain more of the truth that is apprehended only through Christian fellowship. The preacher's model is more the Sermon on the Mount than the deliverances from Sinai or Patmos. In a church service, including the sermon part of it, learning and experience go together. The congregation comes to hear what God has done for them through Jesus Christ, and to feel it, in their heightened sense of joy, love, and beauty. The sermon should use whatever can raise the people's consciousness of God's great gifts. When Jesus promised, "Your hearts will rejoice, and no one will take your joy from you," he meant more than just a grave smile.

THE USES OF HUMOR IN SERMONS

There are many ways in which humor helps Christian preaching achieve its purposes:

1. Sermons need humor in order to reveal truth. Nothing save God and mathematics is ever one hundred percent. In all reality there are contrasts and comical inconsistencies. Much error and delusion comes from being able to see only one side of a subject, to appreciate only one aspect of the truth. We believe in moral and theological absolutes, but we also have to believe that our human apprehension of them is always incomplete. The humbugging quality of many philosophies can best be exposed by humor. Laughter is the best possible unveiler of the make-believe fantasies to which people can become devoted.

2. We need humor in church to save us from fanaticism. Religion is dangerous for those who have no sense of humor. It is strong stuff; it calls for complete devotion. The objects of Christian faith are of ultimate worth; apart from them nothing else can be important. Whatever is not of Christ is demonic and destructive. These truths head us straight into a deadly intolerance and fanaticism except for two saving qualities—a sense of humor and love. Humor makes us recognize how ridiculously in-

complete is our grasp of what we now see in a mirror dimly, and know in part. Love keeps us from rejecting and despising.

The sickness of the Church as it sank into the dark ages of intolerance and persecution can be seen in a decree of the Second Council of Carthage: "If any clerk or monk utters jocular words causing laughter, let him be excommunicated." We can see the spiritual perversion caused by repressing the sense of the comic in the fate of Perez, the prime minister of Spain. When Perez quarreled with the king he was thrown into a dungeon. There he was heard to shout in a rage, "If it is God the Father who has allowed the king to behave so towards me, I'll pull God the Father's nose." The Inquisition was not amused. It tried Perez for heresy. The verdict says, "This proposition is blasphemous, scandalous, offensive to pious ears, and savoring of the heresy of the Vadois, who affirmed that God was corporeal." So Perez was burned at the stake. Only so literal and humorless a mentality could have committed the horrors of the Inquisition. The Puritans were in many ways among the most admirable of men, but if they had laughed more they would have come closer to true sainthood and avoided the defects history cannot forget. A deadly serious minister can produce the certainty of being on God's side that makes for fanaticism in a congregation. The pulpit must keep people aware of the nonsensicality of their self-righteousness.

3. Humor in preaching helps keep people aware of the incongruity of their pretensions. Our fancies about ourselves are usually in comic contrast to reality, and a sense of humor lets us see this. Our readiness to strut breaks up when we see how ill it becomes our figures. The tendency to agonize, to turn our situations too throbbingly into melodrama, collapses into farce when we glance in the mirror. Good preaching holds up the mirror to human frailties and gives us an amused look at ourselves. A man who was receiving an honorary degree expanded visibly as he heard the citation read. With the usual ingenuity it said such things as "distinguished humanitarian, renowned scholar, accomplished in many fields." When he returned to his seat, his wife whispered, "Whom were they talking about? I wish I'd met him before I married you." That sort of needle for our inflated self-images is what the church must offer as it helps us see ourselves.

4. The ability to see the absurd as comic is the cure for melancholy. Existentialist philosophy makes much of the absurdity of life, but it surrenders to it. The essential absurdity of our state must be faced. We all will more than we can do, and long for more than we can get. The inadequacy of our time on earth is ridiculous. The aspirations of mankind head into blank walls. Love points us straight toward sorrow. Our freedom is a hard load to bear. The pessimistic philosopher sees nothing funny in these absurdities. Neither did Job in Chapters One through Thirty-seven. But in Chapter Thirty-eight Job began to see that there was more to be said. It is the something more which enables the Christian to laugh about what is ridiculous. This sort of laughter is a source of truth.

I was called to help arrange the affairs of a young intern who had killed himself. On the table by his bed was a copy of A. E. Housman's poems. Many young people have passed through a Housman phase when the sour Cambridge Latinist caught their fancy. He writes of life's futility. A typical poem begins:

> Shot? so quick, so clean an ending?
>   Oh that was right, lad, that was brave:
> Yours was not an ill for mending,
>   'Twas best to take it to the grave.
>
> Oh you had forethought, you could reason,
>   And saw your road and where it led,
> And early wise and brave in season
>   Put the pistol to your head.

There is no way to argue with that pretensiously gloomy pose, but humor can bring us back to reality. Hugh Kingsmill demonstrated that with his polished parody of Housman:

> What, still alive at twenty-two,
>   A clean, upstanding chap like you?
> Sure, if your throat is hard to slit,
>   Slit your girl's and swing for it.
>
> Like enough you won't be glad,
>   When they come to hang you, lad.
> But bacon's not the only thing
>   That's cured by hanging from a string.

Humor is the clue to a truth that rises above our melancholy and puts it in perspective. We laugh when we find that gloom is not our dead-end street. This is a discovery that is achingly needed now. A good many modern minds are stuck in the despondent rut. If they are offered a choice of a happy or a grim possibility, they assume the worst one. Maybe ocean pollution is so damaging to the plankton that there will be no oxygen for anyone to breathe by 1999—no one can say for sure, so those who incline toward despair are confident of extinction. The nuclear bomb and the population bomb could blast all human hopes—so there are many who drag on from day to day under the assumption that the doom is sure. Those with this built-in slant toward the dark side are pretty solemn. They do not do much joking. Their laughter is strained and their smiles are confined. Humor died in them before hope did. The Church's ministry to them must restore their sense of humor: the deep wellsprings of merriment must be opened up.

5. We need humor in sermons because a church service ought to be therapeutic. Dr. James J. Walsh of Fordham University said, "Few people

realize that health actually varies according to the amount of laughter. People who laugh actually live longer than those who do not laugh." (*Recreation,* Helen Christine Bennett.) The wise man of the Proverbs said that a long while ago: "A cheerful heart is a good medicine, but a downcast spirit dries up the bones." (Prov. 17:22) A cheerful heart relaxes the tensions that fray our nerves and shatter our health. Dr. William Osler of Johns Hopkins deliberately used laughter as a medicine. With his top hat and frock coat he would go into a sick child's room on his hands and knees. He wanted the little patient to laugh. He said, "Hilarity and good humor . . . help enormously both in the study and in the practice of medicine. It is an unpardonable mistake to go about among patients with a long face."

So it is a mistake for a preacher to subject the congregation to a long face. There are times of great solemnity in a church; there must be sermons that will not make anybody happy. Duty, repentence, and caring about those who suffer must be earnestly presented. But if the prevailing mood of the sermons is somber, it is a denial of the Holy Spirit and a travesty on Christianity. A sour minister is a heretic of the worst sort. "These things have I spoken to you, that my joy may be in you, and that your joy may be full," was Jesus' promise. The prodigal's Father in the parable represents God the Father when he says, "Let us make merry." That is still his invitation. When we come to church there is much for us to make merry about. *Sursum corda*—"Lift up your hearts!"—is the ancient invitation. So the minister does not have to be too embarrassed if something he says makes people laugh right out in church. Many of them have situations that are grindingly hard. They much need the medicine that comes from deep faith and high spirits. Many people do not have much to laugh about. Caught in the daily routine, living from one worry to the next, they may come to church all tense and overwrought. If they can find there a chance to smile, to enjoy the comic side of life, it may be the refreshment they need most. President Lincoln opened the cabinet meeting at which he presented the Emancipation Proclamation by reading a droll chapter from Artemus Ward. When some of the tense Secretaries looked shocked at such levity, the president exclaimed, "Gentlemen, why don't you laugh? With the fearful strain that is upon me night and day, if I did not laugh, I should die; and you need this medicine as much as I do." It was because Lincoln could laugh that he could think of his enemies "with malice toward none; with charity for all." It was men like those rigid Secretaries who led the country into the vindictive follies of the Reconstruction period.

6. When their church helps people learn to laugh, it gives them a way of dealing with afflictions. The triumphant gaity of the Christian spirit is amazing. One of our church members made her tin ear trumpet the symbol of her merriment. This victorious spirit can jest even at the approach of death. When Sir Thomas More, the ardent churchman, mounted the scaffold, he told the executioner, "See me safe up; for my coming down I can shift for myself." One of the older women in our church, clear through her

final illness, made my calls on her times for joking. On one visit she told me, "Don't let them put me in a shroud. When the last trumpet calls me to stand up, I don't want to be all out behind." When the beloved professor of theology at an eastern seminary was on his deathbed, someone asked, "Is he gone yet?" Someone else felt his feet and answered, "No, his feet are still warm; you can't die when your feet are warm." The old man stirred faintly and whispered, "Joan of Arc did." Those were his last words.

This gift of humor can soften the worst vicissitudes. The Norwegian poet, Bjørnson, said the event in his life he remembered with most pleasure was the time when a mob of pseudo-patriots stormed his house. They were angered by remarks he had made in the parliament which they considered disloyal. When they had broken the windows, they marched off down the street singing the Norwegian national anthem. Bjørnson said he sat amid the broken glass and roared with laughter, because he had written the anthem they were singing so self-righteously.

7. We need humor in church because it is a delight we are to enjoy with gratitude as God's good gift. We introduce humor into sermons because this is the sort of joy God wants people to have. Seven of the Psalms summon the temple worshippers to "make a joyful noise unto the Lord." Another Psalm has them say, "Then was our mouth filled with laughter, and our tongue with shouts of joy." The ability to laugh is a special quality of the human spirit. Babies reveal it early, but animals never do. If we do not use it and develop it, we cancel our Creator's plan. It has to bubble up from deep within, as the product of a spiritual quality. Real laughter cannot be produced by using the right muscles, and real humor is not shown by memorizing the right jokes.

8. Sermons can use humor to unify a congregation. Good preaching requires a sense of community. That is why it is so hard to preach to people who are scattered sparsely over a big room. Hearers must be interacting with each other if they are to react rightly with what is being said. There must also be a sense of being drawn together between the preacher and the people in the pews. When a congregation joins in singing, it gives a sense of fellowship. In the same way, laughter joins the members of an audience with each other, and with the speaker. People discover that their minister is a human being when they share his humor; it makes him someone who is closer to them than a pulpit oracle. Robert Louis Stevenson noted that you can read Kant just as well by yourself, but you have to share a joke. When you listen to a newscast on television, there is no great desire to have anybody with you; but when a comedy comes on, you will run all over the house to find somebody with whom you can enjoy it.

9. Sermons need humor to relax the strain of listening. Few minds are capable of following all through a serious sermon without wandering. The subject may be interesting, and the preacher clear and forceful, but listening is work. Periodically mental powers demand a chance to take a breather before they go back to the effort of attention. If the preacher

gives his listeners places to rest and relax, then he and they can come back together, and they will not lose essential parts by taking their own breaks.

Able preachers are skillful at planning these excursions. I once heard Archbishop Fulton J. Sheen give an hour-long historical address. He regularly provided humorous intervals, without quite breaking the thread of his discourse. He reached into his pocket for a sheet from which to read a quotation. The first sheet he produced was the airlines timetable, which he threw on the desk with mock embarrassment; the next paper was a letter, about which he made a funny comment. When he finally fished out the paper he was looking for, the hearers had had several laughs, and they were still listening for his quotation. Experienced preachers can estimate where a congregation will need a change of pace.

10. Humor can help people accept what might be hard to take. My predecessor was quoted as having told some restless boys and girls in the balcony not to wake up their parents, who were sleeping in the pews below. When a minister feels he must express disapproval of something in the church or the community, when he has to rebuke or criticize, humor can keep it from seeming too abrasive. A minister who was disappointed when his officers declined to have Fair Housing Acceptance Cards made available did not issue a denunciation; he simply told the congregation that they could drop in at the Catholic church to get their cards, and everybody laughed.

INAPPROPRIATE HUMOR

There are many sorts of humor that are not appropriate in sermons. In all truth, most of them are not appropriate anywhere. This includes ethnic jokes and those based on such personal qualities as speech defects or being fat, thin, bald, bearded, old, or unmarried. People with no sense of humor count on such subjects to be funny. Malicious or scornful humor must be avoided, though its objects be unpopular. Comic phrases get tedious; after a hundred repetitions it no longer seems funny to call the young people "guys and gals," or the wastebasket the "round file," or Northerners "damn Yankees," or Southern Baptists the "south-of-God Baptists." Most jokes require surprise, so they soon wear out. In the United Presbyterian Church there is every year a standard story that is told in meetings throughout the Church. Its useful life is about twelve months, but there are many ministers who count on these stories to last for a decade. Sermons require a good quality of humor; jesting that may be funny among friends can sound silly in the pulpit. Limericks, which can be jewels of wit and sense, have to be introduced into a sermon with some care if they are not to seem too foolishly jocose. There is a compulsive sort of jesting that is more a nervous mannerism than real wit. A good pun is an art form, and much of the best humor depends on word plays; but the habit of putting an obvious twist on words soon ceases to be funny. Wise-cracking can become an affliction. Hectic facetiousness is not real humor. Ecclesiastes 7:6 describes it perfectly: "As the crackling of thorns under a pot, so is the laughter of the fools." Lines from William Cowper bear on this:

> He that negotiates between God and man,
> As God's ambassador, the great concerns
> Of judgment and of mercy, should beware
> Of lightness in his speech.

To the extent that Cowper meant that preachers must be stiff and solemn, he can be disregarded; but triviality is not compatible with the preacher's task.

The pulpit has no place for humor that has any suggestion of bad taste in such matters as sex, sacrilege, or what is disgusting or ugly. A good rule is, "When in doubt, leave it out." This may bother a minister who does not want Christianity to be associated with artificial propriety, but his own taste is no basis for making rulings on what is artificial. He does not serve best as an example of emancipation from prudery. With its great democracy, the church should be a good home for the matter-of-fact and for those with a strong sense of propriety. Humor that might be unobjectionable for certain homogeneous church groups could be out of place in a congregation, with its wide variety of ages and traditions. The minister must temper the wind to the shorn lamb. It is bad technique to put anything in a sermon that will needlessly interfere with the accomplishment of its purpose. Those who are offended will probably lose the good a sermon might have done them. With all the conscientious reasons why a minister must risk disapproval, he is foolish to add unnecessary ones. The extra spice of unconventionality is not needed for real humor. Ever since the first Christians impressed the Romans by their "purity of manners," Christians have been farther on the side of decency than conventional etiquette requires.

Ministers are church professionals, and they can get so used to handling sacred things that they treat them with familiarity. Some ministerial humor is painful for members of the church. Ministers' feelings about what is holy may be so intense that they release the tension by jokes. A friend said he shocked the church custodian by saying, as he took off his pulpit robe, "Well, check off another one." It is possible for ministers to forget that their jesting about the sacraments, the Bible, church services, prayer, and their own calling may be profanation.

Phillips Brooks was emphatic about this: "There is another creature who ought to share with the clerical prig the contempt of Christian people. I mean the clerical jester in all the varieties of his unpleasant existence. He appears in and out of the pulpit. He lays his hands on the most sacred things, and leaves defilement upon all he touches. He is full of Bible jokes. He talks about the Church's sacred symbols in the language of stale jests that have come down from generations of feeble clerical jesters before him. . . . There are passages in the Bible which are soiled forever by the touches which the hands of ministers who delight in cheap and easy jokes have left upon them. . . . Refrain from all joking about congregations, flocks, parish visits, sermons, the mishaps of the pulpit, or the makeshifts of the study. Such joking is always bad, and almost always stupid. . . . This is the reason why so many people shrink, I believe, from personally knowing the preachers to whom they listen with respect and gratitude. They fear what so often they find." (*On Preaching,* p. 55–56)

It should be noted that the only times we are tempted to introduce humor that is inappropriate is when it is really funny. The old rule "You may say it if the wit exceeds the vulgarity" does not apply in church. It is when the wit is excellent that we have to be most careful.

One other sort of humor that is inappropriate in church is the excessive. We are likely to introduce too much of it because the congregation enjoys it, and so does the preacher. Humor in a sermon is never an end in itself; it is a tool in the service of some purpose.

HOW HUMOR IS USED

The poorest form of pulpit humor is the anecdote. The packaged funny story is the tool of the comedian, and the preacher is not a comedian. Entertainment that is appropriate for a lecture or a banquet talk would seem condescending in a sermon, a concession to a retarded congregation. There are ready-made jokes that are so appropriate that they serve well, but they should not be featured as special items. "It seems there were . . ." or "Which reminds me of . . ." are not introductions that fit well in sermons.

When something amusing is to be related, it should not be brought in as a joke, but as a sermon illustration that happens to be funny. An after-dinner speaker can drop in humor that has only a pretended connection with the purpose of his talk—a preacher cannot. Humor in sermons has to stay within the main channel of the thought. If it makes no real contribution to clarifying or applying what the sermon is trying to convey, it has to be left out. If the sermon is on church union, one of the old stories about "A Baptist, a Methodist, and an Episcopalian went to heaven . . ." would probably have no place. But the story about the professor who roared, "Of course I'm an atheist, but thank God, I'm a Presbyterian atheist!" might help the sermon make a point. To refer to the girl who prayed, "Dear Lord, I ask for nothing for myself, but please give my mother a handsome son-in-law," says something important about prayer.

Sermon humor is best brought in *en passant*. There is no introduction, no detour for it, it is simply a whimsical twist or a facetious comment in the full course of the sermon's progress. Dr. Fosdick, preaching about false humility, said that when a Christian prays, "Oh, to be nothing, nothing!" the prayer is often granted. Dr. Buttrick, speaking of flattery, told of the person at the church door who assured him, "Every sermon you give is better than the next one." Flashes of humor like these add insight, keep a sermon lively, and make people listen for fear of missing something.

Quick light touches brighten services. There may be fancy: "For our Lenten fast this year we might give up watermelon," or a swift contrast with serious matters: "I hope that our church will catch on fire—though ministers have been jailed for being too devoted to that hope." A preacher may make fun of himself: "A minister is a hero twice—when he comes to his church, and when he leaves it." He may make fun of the congregation: "That would be wonderful—if we could just believe that someone here would try it!" The joke may have a point: "The trustees could save a lot of money by printing half bulletins for those who come in late." Such touches can make a preacher seem closer to the congregation, but they have two dangers. The first is that the minister will seem not to be taking the church service as seriously as the congregation does. The second is that the light touch will not sound as light as the preacher had intended. Unless we have thought out exactly how our manner and tone will give the effect we want, the unforeseen weight of the pulpit may make it all seem very ponderous. Then our light touch may have all the grace of a hippopotamous ballet; our humor will be labored and our teasing sound sarcastic.

SOURCES OF HUMOR

Almost everyone thinks he has a fine sense of humor, but there are some whose ideas of what is funny do not meet with general acceptance. This may come from inattention. Those whose interests are serious may have given so little thought to what most people find amusing that they have developed little comprehension of it. There are many sorts of humor, and a person who does not understand some kinds may be very successful with others. We have to find where our knack lies.

When a minister suspects he does not do well with humor, there are several possibilities. Perhaps he is trying to imitate other people's wit and is missing his own style. Perhaps his way of saying what is really funny makes it dull. One reason for this is timidity. What is amusing has to be given with a confident air of "Here is something we are going to enjoy." Half-hearted humor is impossible. A person who fears that his attempt to be amusing will not be good may spoil the whole effect by uncertainty. Some skill is necessary. Poor inflection, bad timing, or throwing away the most important words may kill it. One of the most deadly hazards is a sour face in the congregation. In mid-course of what the minister hopes will be amusing, he sees someone staring at him with an expression he can only interpret as disapproval and disdain; so he wilts and finishes so dispiritedly that no one smiles. It may help to survive that laser beam to know that it probably has no connection with anything that is being said. If, in spite of all his experimenting and studying what others do, a mnister is still unhappy with his attempts at humor, he may have to decide that his resources for it are meager. But this does not have to be too discouraging. No preacher has all the gifts, and this is by no means the essential one.

A minister's best source of humor for his sermons is his own creativeness. As he works on his sermons, amusing items and whimsical turns of expression come to him. He finds in his memory funny experiences and droll phrases that apply to the sermon. But, as with illustrations, he needs more than will come out of his own mind during sermon preparation. Here his file of sermon material should be his help. He needs to be putting constantly into the file, under the appropriate topics, amusing items he can use when those topics come up in sermons. These come from all the familiar sermon sources—from thoughts of his own he has recorded, from his reading, conversations, and events in his life, from the lectures and sermons of others. He will also need a special section in his file for funny stories. These will not be of much use for sermons, but they can save him on those occasions when people expect five minutes of entertainment as advance payment for listening to a speech.

The sermons offer the minister his best chance to lift the spirits of the congregation. There is often a serious intensity in church affairs that comes too close to grimness. We do confront grave problems, in the church and in the world. God has given us a sobering answerability, but that is not all he has given. He has given us the deep reasons for gladness and delight. The clearer we are about the Christian faith, the more lighthearted we will be. The little brothers of Saint Francis were so happy in their discipleship that the people all through the countryside came to call them the *joculatores Domini,* the "joyful ones of the Lord." When our preaching is what it ought to be, the members of the congregation will become the *joculatores Domini*—the Lord's joyful ones.

XX

Controversial Preaching

Controversial preaching is preaching that will meet substantial disagreement. It cannot be avoided. Christianity collides head-on with what
people want to think; it is not a common-sense religion. The gospel has
to arrive as bad news before it can be the Good News. Who wants to
hear that he is a sinner, that the arduously acquired assets on which he
counts are rubbish, that he should love his enemies, and that the might
that produces favorable body counts is a vain thing for safety? "The unspiritual man does not receive the gifts of the Spirit of God, for they are
folly to him, and he is not able to understand them." (I Cor. 2:14) Jesus
is by no means the joy of every man's desiring. Whether the opposition
be called human nature or Satan, any attempt to proclaim and apply the
teachings of Christ is sure to meet with resistance. He warned of this: "If
the world hates you, know that it has hated me before it hated you. If you
were of the world, the world would love its own." (Jn. 15:18–19) "Do you
think that I have come to give peace on Earth? No, I tell you, but rather
division." (Lk. 12:51)

The prophets insist that speaking for God is bound to be controversial.
Isaiah says that people "say to the seers, 'See not'; and to the prophets,
'Prophesy not to us what is right; speak to us smooth things, prophesy
illusions.' " (Is. 30:10) Amos complains, "You made the Nazarites drink
wine, and commanded the prophets, saying, 'You shall not prophesy.' "
(Am. 2:12) Ahab called Elijah "Troubler of Israel"—a good name for a
preacher. (I Ki. 18:17)

It is when matters of faith and conduct are made specific that they
become controversial. It is safe to generalize, but when the preaching gets
into the realities of daily life, the opposition starts. Someone put it well:
"They did not crucify Jesus because he said, 'Consider the lilies of the
field, how they grow,' but because he said, 'Consider the thieves in the
temple, how they steal.' "

Difficult decisions for the preacher are often raised by public issues.
The political party to which many of the members belong has been caught
in a scandal. The city council is considering a measure to loosen the

restrictions on liquor licenses. A low-cost housing proposal is being hotly debated. A bill that would allow off-track betting is before the legislature. Charges of brutality are being made against the police force. A senator has accused the president of exceeding his authority in the use of the armed forces. The town is in turmoil because a football star is threatened with expulsion for cheating. Shall the minister mention these issues, knowing that he is called to deal with real life, or shall he see his function as upholding the great Christian ideals, and let the congregation make the applications? Perhaps the only solution must be pragmatic. The minister decides in each case which way in the long run will do the most good. On many occasions a courageous sermon has given needed moral guidance. There have also been times when a minister excitedly rushed into an issue when he should have been more sensitive.

A wide range of subjects may be controversial, and they change. In the early centuries, doctrinal arguments were bitter. Wild monks from the desert, who were rioting through the streets, influenced some of the Church's statements on the person of Christ. The theological and military struggles at the Reformation centered in the doctrines of the reformers. The duties of Christian subjects to their rulers and the relation of Church and State were hotly contested issues. In America in the last century the struggles were over baptism, free will, Unitarianism, slavery, evolution, and conversion versus nurture. In this century there have been controversies over science and religion, fundamentalism and modernism, war, race, Communism, law enforcement, and the distribution of wealth. Preaching on personal morality—drinking, gambling, sex, Sabbath observance, drugs—has stirred bitter contention.

Religious differences are explosive because they trigger the most powerful emotions. Those on the other side are seen as enemies of God and corruptors of immortal souls. Members fall out over the painting of a church because it has to do not just with decoration, but with desecration. Changes in the order of worship are tearfully resented because they disturb life's holiest experiences.

Whenever Christians try hardest to be true to the faith, the disputes are hardest. Zeal makes the zealot whose personal relationships get strained. The times of great belief are the times of great contention. From a genteel point of view, ardent believers often seem overly abrasive. Martin Luther complained, "What would I not give to get away from a cantankerous congregation and look into the friendly eyes of animals!" John Calvin seems a trifle provocative when in a sermon he called the city fathers of Geneva, "A council of the Devil."

There is a possibility of self-delusion in stressing this tradition of controversy in the Bible and in church history. A minister may come to feel that if he is not in trouble with his congregation he must be unfaithful; Jesus was crucified, so his minister must be. This is a confusion of roles. The minister is not the Messiah, who dies as the Redeemer for the sins of the world. Neither is he an Old Testament prophet, confronting heathen wickedness. The minister is the pastor of a fellowship of Christians who may be closer to Christ than he is. The logic, "Christ failed, so I must fail," forgets that Christ made his cross the source and symbol of the Church's success—"by this sign conquer." Our situation is not that of the stalwarts of the Reformation. There may be a romantic craving for heroism. A minister's life becomes more interesting and dramatic when there are complaints about his theology or his patriotism. Conflict can become addictive. A minister's machismo may make him seek controversy.

Controversial preaching will be only a fraction of a rightly proportioned preaching program. People need to be told what God has done for them through Jesus Christ, to be prepared for the crises of sickness and death, to be helped with family problems and spiritual growth, to have opened up the sources of joy, love, and strength. Many of the riches of the Bible can be offered without raising divisive questions.

We must face the fact, however, that for most of us the danger is not that we will seek controversy, but that we will run away from it. It is exceedingly painful for normal ministers. When they preach on the promises of God, they can go to the door, anticipating beaming, happy faces and expressions of heartfelt gratitude. When they preach on God's radical demands they can expect troubled looks and averted eyes. The people who are offended are not the minister's enemies, they are his flock. He knows that when he alienates someone, that person in the future may need a pastor's friendship and comfort, and will have no one to turn to. Jesus warned that in these matters, "A man's foes will be those of his own household." It is often those we like and admire most we get crossed up with. A minister rarely has the joy of a simple conflict of the good against the bad. It is often those to whom he feels closest in some ways he has to oppose in others. When Jesus said he would "set a man against his father, and a daughter against her mother," he was surely speaking of a congregation. A minister cannot fail to be troubled and worried when he knows that what he says will make some good people unhappy with him and with the church.

SKILLS

When a minister is sure that some unwelcome truth or moral stand needs to be spoken for, his great concern then must be to accomplish the most good with the least damage. There are some matters of skill that need to be considered to get the best reception and to avoid unnecessary offense:

1. A minister should try to avoid controversial matters until he has been in a church long enough for the members to have confidence in him. He may not be able to pick his time if some crisis comes up in which he has to take a stand, but otherwise he should postpone the divisive subjects until people have had time to find out that he is devout, sane, and sincere. There is no reason to expect people to let their opinions be flouted by a stranger. A minister who has been in people's homes,

helped them in their troubles, and been accepted as a friend can question their prejudices and get a thoughtful hearing. Controversy can be endured by those who know and respect each other.

2. It should be as much as possible a Bible-hearer confrontation, and not a preacher-hearer confrontation. The unwelcome teaching should come as timeless truth, not as personal opinion. First we help people see what the Bible says, then we point out the application.

3. The preacher can quote those whom the congregation respects to present what may be hard to take. Heroes or recognized authorities are useful witnesses. The minister does not have to stand alone.

4. The unwelcome part can be sandwiched between what is welcome. What people may not like can be carried by what they do like. The sequence might be: (a) Jesus loves little children; (b) our refusal to let the neighborhood children use our church playground is a disgrace; (c) How wonderfully we provide for children in our church school.

5. Affirmation is usually more convincing than argument. To set up the opposition view and try to demolish it may rally the hearers to its defense. A clear, enthusiastic statement of what the minister believes is more likely to win assent.

6. On difficult subjects a preacher must be especially careful of his manner. Nature presents a hazard here. When a preacher knows people may not like what he says, he is tense and unhappy. At the very time he most needs to seem appealing and relaxed, he is in an unattractive state. When he wants to sound deeply in earnest, his nervousness will make him sound overintense and hammering. The truth every demagogue knows instinctively is that the most important part in persuading people is to make them like the speaker. Politicians try hard to appear pious, warm-hearted, generous. Convention orators present themselves as humorous, brave, forthright, vibrant with the noblest emotions. A preacher does not have to imitate the demagogue, but he does have to recognize that if his manner makes people dislike him, they will not accept what he says, and if they are attracted to him, he has a long start toward winning their agreement.

When ministers preach on social questions they have a tendency to sound opinionated, denunciatory, sarcastic, contentious. They would get much farther toward their goals if they would come across as loving, humble, reasonable, and pleasant.

Provocative words should be banished. *Frankly* means "This is going to be unpleasant, but you deserve it. I am brave and candid and I am going to let you have it right between the eyes." I can think of no occasion, public or private, when the word *frankly* is of any use. Words that suggest combat rouse people the wrong way—*fight, challenge, hypocrite, lie, demand, confront.* The minister's manner should suggest persuasion, not attack.

The preacher has to prepare himself before he enters the pulpit. He must be spiritually ready. The more he dreads the sermon, the more good-humored and happy he must appear to be. Indignation may be called for, but contempt is not. The minister can pray himself into a state of being loving, persuasive, and sympathetic.

7. On rare occasions anger may be shown, but never temper. Anger is a highly contagious emotion, and it rouses anger in the hearers, which intensifies the opposition and makes it more unreasonable. We do not persuade people by fighting with them, but by talking with them. A tug of war makes the opposition dig in more deeply. We get people to our position by trying to understand theirs: "I know how you feel . . . I can see why you say that . . . You have good reason . . . BUT STILL . . ." Anger in the pulpit suggests bad sportsmanship. The minister is safe, but the object of his anger—the governor, the polluters, the chairman of the stewardship committee—has no chance to respond. There are some subjects on which indignation may reach the point of honest anger, but it should not become a pulpit habit.

Bad temper never has any place. It always indicates a loss of control. It brands the preacher as someone with an ugly disposition, weak and petty. A preacher's loss of temper is shown by the shrill edge to his voice, by his trembling or striking the pulpit, by the tension in his face.

Anger can be just as damaging in all a minister's church relationships. There is nothing except scandal that will so readily destroy a ministry as will a bad temper. It is a special trap because a preacher is so often on edge, under a taut sense of public responsibility, and exposed to people who are annoying. There will be someone who regularly grabs him as he is hurrying into the church service, officers who misrepresent and reject what is dear to his heart, a colleague who torpedoes his favorite plan, a wedding photographer who snaps pictures when he has been told strictly not to, and an organist who changes the hymns he has selected. To show temper at such times is surely natural, but it is just as surely a mistake. (I may add gratuitously that a minister who shows irritation with his wife before church people loses standing with them, and especially with the wives.)

Showing anger is not necessarily a matter of honesty, but of a bad habit pattern. We do what we are used to doing. A graduate of Michigan State University told me that in his engineering class three students asked the same foolish question. Then a fourth student put up his hand and asked, "Professor, how is it, when you have been asked the same dumb question three times, you don't act irritated?" The teacher hesitated and then said, "That is an important question, so I will tell you. Twenty years ago, my wife had a serious heart attack. The doctor told me she might survive, but with a husband who had as bad a temper as mine, she didn't have much chance. I knew what I had to do, and we've had twenty wonderful years together."

I have found that some of the students in my classes disagree with me on this subject. They believe that to suppress anger is unhealthful and dishonest. To show anger with a person is a sign of openness and trust, and makes possible a constructive resolution to the conflict, which can put the relationship on a higher level. But my experience is that I have never shown heat or irritation in church, in the pulpit or out of it, when I was not sorry afterward. People may forgive it, but to forgive is not to forget; the damage to the relationship remains. I know that repression can build up pressure—"there is no one as dangerous as an enraged Quaker"—but the anger can be displaced by a better emotion, such as sympathy or concern. Exploding does not clear the air; it poisons it. There are other emotions we cannot express—boredom, contempt, dislike, amusement. People like to consider their bad temper the mark of a strong and free personality, but what it really reveals is their immaturity.

Titus 1:7–8 has a clue. A bishop must not be "quick tempered," but rather, "self-controlled." For him to show slow anger might be right. Jesus had anger, but it was not sudden. He saw the abuses in the temple many times before he let his wrath be shown. Quick anger may be not candor but untruth; it misrepresents who we really are or what we really want to say.

8. Have a cold manner with hot subjects, and a hot manner with cold subjects. In preaching on foreordination, the minister may need an emotionally charged vocabulary and a vehement delivery. In preaching on crime control, let his style be matter of fact and his delivery soothing. If the subject itself supplies too much heat, add no more. We have to heat cold iron in order to shape it, but if it is already hot we should not liquify it.

9. The preacher's attitude must show that he recognizes he is talking with Christians who are trying as hard as he is to know the mind of Christ. It is easy for him to imply that what he is giving is "the Christian view" versus "the way you think," that he is a prophet handing down the truth. His manner may be that of one who is entitled to speak the last word because he has been specially schooled, reads the books, and has been commissioned to give religious and moral guidance. His superior attitude to dissent may reveal his consciousness of higher rank. His whole bearing may imply that he is on the side of the angels, over against those who have been corrupted by this world. It must be maddening for lay Christians to hear their dearly held convictions slighted by someone who feels he has an access to heaven that is denied to ordinary mortals.

He so obviously does not have it. Everyone except the preacher will know that some who disagree with him are, by every apparent standard, better Christians than he is. These may be very able ministers or splendid lay Christians. It will seem obvious to some that the minister is not thinking clearly. When he speaks patronizingly of those who expect every bright cloud to burst open and reveal the Lord's return, they will remember defensively that the Bible repeatedly speaks of that return. Political conservatives will have no respect for the thought processes of a preacher who thinks that this "nation under God" should grant any moral standing to nations grounded on atheism. When the minister delivers his opinions with the air of Elijah giving God's word to the

Baal worshippers, the silent people in the pews are likely to be reacting
with resentment—"He's never had to meet a payroll," "He's not had a
normal man's place in the world since he left college."

When he preaches on controversial subjects the only attitude the
minister can take, with any hope of realism or success, is that of a seeker
among others who are as well-qualified as he is. This does not mean
that he has to be tentative or self-depreciating; his manner does not
have to be, "I am probably wrong, but I would like to suggest . . ." He
can be clear and positive in his affirmations, and still avoid any air of
superiority, arrogance, or talking down.

A minister who recognizes how his views and his preaching have
changed across the years will know how wrong he can be. When he finds
that earnest, faithful church members disagree with him, he has to do
some troubled soul-searching. But when he has pondered and prayed
and gotten all the light he can from those whose views are different, and
he still can see no other way, then he firmly declares what he believes to
be God's truth. When John Greenleaf Whittier was unable to accept
the stern theology of his New England neighbors, he put his dissent in
a poem which began:

> O Friends! with whom my feet have trod
> The quiet aisles of prayer,
> Glad witness to your zeal for God
> And love of man I bear.
> I trace your lines of argument;
> Your logic linked and strong
> I weigh as one who dreads dissent,
> And fears a doubt as wrong.

Then Whittier went on to a ringing and beautiful statement of his
belief. That approach is a good one for a preacher.

10. A minister has to recognize reasons why his opinions may be
warped. There is an array of personal inadequacies that are revealed by
a tendency to disagree, to condemn, to find fault. Insecurity may hide
behind an air of superior wisdom and virtue. A minister's lack of spiritual life or religious convictions may impel him into external reform
as the only aspect of Christianity he can appreciate. He may be irritated
by those aspects of religion in which he feels deficient. Or, just the opposite, his selfish resistance to Christian social attitudes may drive him into
an intolerant zeal for what he describes as the deep foundations of the
Christian life.

A minister gives himself away when he shows that he enjoys denouncing. If he exaggerates the evils, or if his criticism is repetitious, he reveals
something in himself makes him enjoy berating. Ministers who specialize
in condemning the ministry or the church may betray a vocational
malaise or a craving for the pose of fearless honesty. The church must
always be its own severest critic, and the minister must be the spokesman

for its confession of its guilt, but there is a sort of self-criticism that becomes an orgy. We see it in the minister who declares flatly that the church is wholly captive to a corrupt society, that it is racist, joyless, deaf to the gospel, a pillar of the status quo, the institution that, more than all others, represses youth, exploits women, and supports war. This may reveal a troubled heart, but its effect will not be good for the church, or for anyone.

The exaggerated denunciations preachers rely on can make a congregation complacent. When they hear that, according to one popular pulpit listing, of every hundred members of the church today, twenty-five never read the Bible, seventy never give to missions, seventy-five do no church work, and ninety have no family worship, their natural conclusion is that they are doing pretty well. When a preacher demands, "Do you know any church leader who cares as much for his principles as he does for his prestige?" most members know so many that they dismiss all criticisms as a pulpit convention that no one needs to listen to.

We are tempted to scold when we feel personally put down. When our proposals are rejected, we feel rejected. We may have publicly advocated a project which the officers will not accept. Perhaps few bothered to attend a program we have labored over. Our sharp admonitions may come more from our humiliation than from our zeal for righteousness.

Ministers are professionally inclined to view with alarm. When someone asked Wendell Willkie about a statement he had made which seemed to disagree with what he had professed when he was running for the presidency, he laughed and said, "Oh, that was just campaign oratory." Immediately pulpits all over the country exploded with sermons about this political cynicism. Ministers were quoted in the press as seeing here frightening evidence of the corruption of character. Anyone who was not so avid in decrying sin would have recognized that Mr. Willkie was simply making a wise-crack, with no moral significance of any sort. At the start of World War II, the song "Praise the Lord and pass the ammunition" had a brief popularity. This was seized on by preachers to show that the country was again forcing Jesus to present arms. While there was abundant reason to fear that this was happening, the song had no bearing on it. All it really demonstrated was that when words with a tricky lilt are joined to a catchy tune, they will be sung.

Bankers, doctors, lawyers have a characteristic professional bias, and so do ministers; there is a party line which ministers are under pressure to follow. It may appear quite unorthodox to outsiders, but it is very conforming within the group. It comes from a minister's denomination and the wing of that denomination with which he is identified, and from where he went to school, and from those whose approval he most craves. A minister's attitude in controversial questions may be more determined by social pressures than he recognizes.

Raymond B. Fosdick, in his biography of John D. Rockefeller, Jr., tells how Mr. Rockefeller suffered from preachers whose reaction to his name was almost a reflex. His teaching a Bible class was assumed to show that he had seized a platform for a capitalist theology. In a speech at Brown University on "Christianity in Business," he said that "business needs the virtues which Christianity encourages." That innocent-sounding proposition was the occasion for many sermons on the prostitution of the gospel for gain. A bishop in a prominent New York pulpit said of an illustration in that speech, "A young scion of wealth and greed, possessed of more dollars than ideas, recently used the figure of the pruning of a rosebush . . . A rose by any other name will smell as sweet, but the odor of that rose to me smacks strongly of crude petroleum." Mr. Rockefeller decided to expand his family's religious contributions beyond the Baptist denomination, so when an appeal was received from the Congregational Board of Foreign Missions, he induced his father to respond with a large gift. A leading Congregational minister got headlines with a bitter attack on Mr. Rockefeller and on his motives. He assumed that an unsolicited gift of "tainted money" had been forced on the church as a bribe. Though he later apologized for his misunderstanding, other preachers took up the cry. We preachers need to recognize how our assumptions bias our opinions.

11. A "self-debate" sermon (see Chapter X) can be useful with controversial subjects. When the preacher makes the best case he can for both sides, he is helping people think in the way intelligent thought operates; it reaches conclusions by considering the arguments for and against. This could, however, encourage indecision or suggest that the minister is unwilling to take a stand. (A man said he was looking for a one-armed preacher who would not keep saying, "but on the other hand . . .") But such preaching can be positive if it strongly presents all points of view. It meets the objection that preaching gives an unfair advantage to one side. There are times when the best way to stand upright is to carry water on both shoulders.

REASSURANCES

The minister who dreads the Sundays when he has to say what some people will not like has some reassurances:

1. He has been called to speak plainly for what he believes. John Knox gave Mary, Queen of Scots, a memorable definition of the preacher's responsibility. She had accused him of exceeding the proper function of the pulpit. He replied, "Ye said, What ado had I to speak of your marriage? What was I, that I should mell with such matters? I answered that, as touching nature, I was a worm of this earth. . . ; but as touching the office wherein it had pleased God to place me, I was a watchman, both over the realm and over the Kirk of God gathered with the same. For that reason I was bound in conscience to blow the trumpet publicly, oft as ever I saw any upfall, any appearing danger, either to the one or to the other."

Most church people recognize that their minister is assigned "to blow the trumpet publicly," to declare the truth as he sees it, to admonish, to instruct. He does this not because he is always right or has a special source of heavenly wisdom, but because it needs to be done and the task has been given to him. Most members also recognize that if the pulpit's necessary function is to be performed, the preacher must be free. That does not mean he is allowed to use his access to the attention of a congregation to do anything he pleases; it does mean that what he says is not subject to censorship. No one can insist that his minister agree with him. People have to assume that their preacher will often say what they do not believe, and they esteem him for it.

2. Church people are professed Christians, and it is remarkable how patient with disagreement they can be. In any crowd of several hundred there will be one or two who are emotionally unstable. They may stalk muttering out the center aisle, or write the preacher unpleasant letters. The others recognize their affliction and make allowances for it. Normal church members keep their disagreement within the bounds of good manners and of love. One persistent item of folklore has it that preachers are under constant financial threat—"We're not paying you to be subversive." Ministers have received such threats, but they are rare. The people who are most generous in their giving are likely to be the most generous in their attitudes. I have had long talks with people who were unhappy about my views, but they have never suggested that they were not getting what they were paying for. The picture of the prominent member who tries to browbeat the minister is largely fictitious. What the minister gets is not bad manners, it is something worse—it is sorrow. People mourn at him. They tell him how they respect him, and love the church, and how it hurts them when the Lord is not honored, or righteousness maintained, or freedom defended. This is not easy for the minister, but it stays within a Christian setting.

3. A church grows during its crises. We do not seek controversy because it can be beneficial, any more than we seek sorrow for that reason, but if a church can hold together in love it does its best learning during disagreements. During World War II, when our congregation was threatened with upset over a proposal to bring an interned American of Japanese descent to our staff, a brother minister advised me that "the peace of the church is a precious pearl that should not be endangered." He was wrong. We did make the addition, and it was a great success, and from it we developed far more as Christians than we could have in placidity. My friend's choice of a metaphor was mistaken; in the parable, the pearl of great price is not peace, it is salvation.

In times of crisis a minister needs to think hard and plan carefully for the creative use of conflict. He needs to read some of the excellent newer studies on this. And he has to be the sort of person who will not be shattered or made intolerant by opposition.

4. It is reassuring for a minister to know that time is on his side. On most social matters in which ministers have given leadership during my lifetime, they have turned out to be right. My first experience with controversy was in my first pastorate. College students were allowed to

bring into the church petitions against the selling of scrap iron to Japan, because it was being used to bomb Chinese cities. Some people were indignant at protest against government policy in the church. The protest did not seem so visionary, however, when the scrap iron was dropped on Americans at Pearl Harbor. Across the years there have been such issues as the steel strike, the traffic in munitions, child labor, Sacco and Vanzetti, the internment of Japanese-Americans, prison reform, the hopeless poor, the policy of official lying, conscientious objection to military service, political witch hunts, integration, freedom marches, Martin Luther King, the admission of Red China to the family of nations. On each of these, ministers have taken widely criticized positions which by now are pretty generally seen as right. There have been embarrassing exceptions; some declarations of synods and assemblies seem unwise in retrospect. But in general, time has dealt kindly with the preachers.

In theological matters, the record is harder to assess. Perhaps because they must always find some novelty by which they can interest their congregations in an old and familiar subject, preachers have a penchant for temporary excitements in theology. This year's far-out shocker, which has many angry and excited, will shortly be off the scene. God-Is-Dead soon died. But if we count by generations, not by years and decades, the preachers' leadership in theology deserves a good report. Even by decades the parish ministers, seen apart from the trend-setters, have done well.

There is a cherished picture of the minister as an unworldly person with one foot in heaven who is sheltered from reality. His contribution is to hold up beautiful ideals, which sensible people will know are entirely impractical. At a board meeting, where I was urging action on a racial matter, an officer, who was opposing my whole program, said, "We like to have our minister feel that way . . ." I was grateful for the genuine kindliness of that, but I could not miss the implication. A minister is to be a dear, gentle visionary, an ornament every church should have. The fine, Christian gentleman who said that is out in the world in the sense that every day he drives to and from his office through a psychological tunnel from which he sees little. The typical minister has learned from personal experiences with slums, city commissions, conferences, and strife situations, from books, lectures, and conversations with a wide variety of people. When a minister preaches on drinking some irritated person in the pews may grumble, "What does that good man know about it? I've never seen him in a bar." To that the minister might reply, "Has a wife called you at midnight because her hard-drinking husband has his head in the gas oven? How many funerals have you conducted for high school students who have been killed because the driver had been drinking? How many people have come to talk with you about their drinking problem, and how much have you learned about it in marriage counseling?" Ministers by profession are, or could be, more realistic about community relations, the corruptions of society, bad government, drinking, drugs, and sex problems than are the members of any other profession, including lawyers and policemen. In other words, when a minister preaches on these questions he can know that he has some special insights. But lay Christians also have special insights. The full truth is that ministers and lay church members greatly need each other's points of view. The Christian judge, the businessman, school principal, and doctor have perceptions the minister ought to have, and lacks.

The Church is disabled by having its clergy and laity living too much in different worlds. If one identical twin goes to a theological seminary and the other to a law school, they will soon become quite different in their abilities and attitudes. Their reading, meetings, conversations, and daydreaming will be in different realms. The danger is that they will become such different human beings that they cannot communicate. Ministers tend to think of their opinionated members as sadly limited by their daily ruts and out of touch with reality; and the members tend to think of ministers as impractical theorists whose common sense and religious sense have been obscured by bookish nonsense. Surveys have shown that the average layman and minister have widely diverging views on many controversial questions. The problem is not that they are born different, or that one is more practical or more Christian than the other, but that they travel on diverging paths.

The Church must do much more to try to bring its members and ministers into the same Christian world. They need to be reading more of the same literature, and hearing more of the same speeches, and talking about them. A well-promoted church library can help with this, and so can book clubs, discussion groups, classes, and conferences. Sermons can start a useful process, but they only begin the discussion. The initiative must be with the preacher as he tries to open more ways by which he and the church members can share their thinking outside the church services. The members need to recognize that the minister's special opportunities for Christian learning and study of human problems entitle him to a hearing; and he must recognize how much he needs their knowledge and experience; he must seek every way to learn from them.

The sort of controversial preaching the Church does not need is the counterfeit. A minister can get a reputation for courageous preaching by boldly denouncing the sins of those who are not there. This is the fearlessness that is shown by taking a forthright stand on the abuses of the unions in a wealthy suburb, or honestly facing the duplicity of the government before student radicals, or not flinching from exposing heresy in preaching to fundamentalists. To be a nonconformist among nonconformists is the safest sort of daring. One of life's greatest pleasures is the thrill of being reckless when there is no chance of getting hurt. Real preaching must be willing to risk the disapproval of the sort of people who are listening.

It is foolish to toss in controversial matters that are not needed for a sermon's major purpose. To say, "I used to think that a Christian is someone who goes to church, salutes the flag, and thinks this is a Christian country," might be right in a sermon on secular religion, but it might wreck a sermon on how faith grows. A preacher has to deal with explosive questions when they can be well-considered, but to make shocking statements in passing is inept. An offhand criticism of Paul or of the pope invites people to go mentally chasing after quibbles when they should be listening to the sermon. A fleeting remark about a touchy issue may be all that the congregation will recall, because it usurped their memories. Sometimes a preacher may get at something difficult by small references, scattered through a number of sermons; but that is done by plan.

Most preaching does not have to stir dissent, but on occasion the minister must be willing to say what many will not want to hear. Without courage and independence he cannot be a preacher. "The bland leading the bland" is a sad description of the church. A preacher can come to fit into his church so well that he agrees with everyone. He blends into the prevailing point of view so thoroughly that he becomes like those souls Dante described as not good enough for heaven, bad enough for hell, or promising enough for purgatory.

In every congregation, times will come when a minister who hoped he could be a priest finds that God has drafted him to be a prophet. At those times let him be as loving and tactful as he possibly can be; let him give careful thought and prayer to what he says; but when he feels he ought to take a stand that to many will be unwelcome, let him not waver or back away from it. Rowland Hill gave the right word on this a century and a half ago, "Rash preaching disgusts; timid preaching leaves poor souls fast asleep; bold preaching is the only preaching that is owned of God."

XXI

Preaching on
the Great Beliefs

There have to be sermons on doctrine because people so achingly need it. The word "doctrine" may have no charm for them, but they deeply long for answers to such questions as: Is love real? Is there any hope? What decency can there be in a world with so much evil?

A congregation that has not had sermons on the great beliefs will be poorly prepared for other sermons. Exhortations on morality that are not backed up by a deep faith will not lay hold on consciences. Good advice about mental health that does not give the shaken soul a solid mooring will have small benefit.

OBJECTIONS TO THEOLOGY

There is some prejudice against theology. It has been considered dry and sometimes, even in sermons, it is. A magazine observes, "Theology is jawbreakingly abstract. And its mood is widely felt to be about as bracing as an unaired vestry." It can be a game of high-level abstractions which make no contact with real life, though the players may get passionately absorbed. It can be a substitute for religion, with its adherents sure that they are Christians because they have the concepts lined up properly. But real Christian theology can never be remote or dry. It tells about the greatest of all romances, the story of the love of God for human beings, a love which enables them to love God and each other. Dorothy Sayers, commenting on the criticism that doctrine is dull, says, "The fact is the precise opposite. It is the neglect of dogma that makes for dullness. The Christian faith is the most exciting drama that has ever staggered the imagination of man—and dogma *is* the drama." (*Creed Or Chaos.*)

It has been objected that what people look for in church is help with their pressing problems, not discourse on remote theological topics. The theologian is presumed to be like Hegel, of whom it was said that if you asked him the way to the post office, he would give you a map of the world. It is true that if a pilot is driving his car to a strange airport, his airline's worldwide flight map will not be much help. But when his plane gets up, he had better have something better than the city map. There is no reason to trust a preacher's advice with daily problems unless he can locate them within a larger plan.

Why are doctrinal structures needed for those who love Jesus Christ? Kierkegaard, with his distaste for generalities, said, "It is as if Christ were a professor, and as if the Apostles had formed a little scientific society." What makes a Christian is not dogmatics but the simple acceptance of Jesus Christ as Lord and Savior. But those words are dogmatics. If you know what you mean by *accept, Jesus, Christ, Lord, Savior,* you are deep in theology.

I attended a revival in New York where the preacher called for "the Jesus Cheer"—"Give me a J" "Jay!" "Give me an E," "Eeee!" When we had finished, I wondered what would have happened if someone had raised his hand and asked, "Tell me, Sir, what do you mean by J-E-S-U-S?" I have a feeling that the preacher would have answered, "Our friend here doesn't get it yet, so twice as loud this time. Give me a J!" What does J-e-s-u-s spell? When you answer that, you are in Christology. Faith in Jesus is as available for the plodding as for the brilliant, but even the plodders have to know what they mean by the words they use and the thoughts they think. Theology is simply the dictionary that defines the words we use when we talk about religion. Without definitions we cannot talk or understand. Doctrinal preaching gives definitions so people can know what they believe. Some theologians are obscure, but the real purpose of theology is to make Christian belief understandable. Dismissing theology does not put Christianity closer to the common man, but farther from him. Some of the new intellectualisms in the Church that decry theology would put Christianity clear beyond the reach of anyone who cannot work his way through Heidegger.

Sometimes it is insisted that what matters is not what a person believes, but how he acts. The practical answer to this, of course, is that what he believes is shown by how he acts. When your beloved daughter falls in love, what you have to care about is not the young man's family or his income, but his creed—not what he thinks he believes, but what he really believes. A miscreant (from *credere*) has a wrong belief. The preacher has small hope of persuading people to do right things until they believe right things.

Beliefs that seem to make no difference can turn out to be matters of life and death. Why should anyone in 320 A.D. have cared whether Arius believed that Jesus was unbegotten-begotten, or just begotten-begotten? But the whole history of Europe and America would be vastly different if Arius had won the argument. As Carlyle said, "If Arianism had won, Christianity would have dwindled into a legend." Christology is just as critical for a person. What you believe about who Christ is will determine how you live and who you are.

The tolerant may like to say, "I don't care about a man's creed so long as he believes in God." But what is meant by G-o-d, if anything? The Scythians thought of God as infinite ferocity, and worshipped him with pyramids of heaped-up heads. Your doctrine of God determines your whole philosophy of life.

Does it matter what you believe about such incomprehensibles as life after death? History shows that when people have little sense of a life beyond, they are inclined to play fast and loose with this one. Societies that are unaffected by this faith tend to cruelty and oppression; transient creatures get less respect than do immortal souls. Preaching is immeasurably important when it helps people know what is meant by God, Jesus Christ, Holy Spirit, life everlasting, personality, sin, hope, love, Bible, prayer, church, freedom and the other great words of our faith.

THE NEED FOR DOCTRINE

Preaching on the great beliefs is needed to summarize the Bible. The Bible is not arranged topically, and when people want its guidance on any subject, they cannot trust their memories. Doctrinal preaching tries to bring together the whole Bible teaching on specific themes. By this it builds bridges from the Bible to our pressing needs.

People desperately need answers to some basic questions. The question of *identity* haunts us from the day we first become conscious of ourselves. It faces us when we stand before our mirrors and wonder what is back of those balls of tissue that are staring out at us. We have to know who we are, and why we are here, and what meaning our existence has.

There is the question of *purpose*. A college dean says that a chief source of upset among his students is the "vocational crisis." What should they be doing? Why do anything? There has to be some reason for what we do. Without at least provisional answers, we would lie on our beds, sunk in apathy. But provisional answers may be far from satisfying. We wonder whether anybody really needs us, and whether our ceasing to exist would leave a vacancy. An adequate answer to such questions cannot be improvised; it demands a faith. Our faith determines which way we turn when we step out the door. Wherever we go, we are on a religious pilgrimage.

We are baffled by the question of *relationships*. In our loneliness we reach out towards others, and wonder how to make connections. If we dislike ourselves, perhaps with reason, we do not see how anyone could accept us.

The question of *meaning* confronts us. Does anything make sense? Is existence indifferent to all that human beings care about? The unceasing injustice and suffering suggest that the only wisdom is despair. We have to come to terms with the fact that we are dying fast. What is far worse, all those we love are dying too, and every day we face the possibility that dreadful things may happen to them. Most of us have had heartbreaks, and we know we will have more of them. If we have any tenderness, we cannot read a newspaper without suffering. So people come to the church, and look at the preacher, and each one is thinking, "Is there something he can tell me?" There had better be.

Doctrinal preaching is needed because the world is lurching through horrors toward even ghastlier disasters. We literally believe that Jesus is the Son of God, and his way is the way life must be lived. Christianity's doctrine of man, its anthropology, is the source of its teachings about how human beings can live together, in personal contacts and in the mass. Politics depends upon theology; every bad political system is based on bad dogma. The battle for the future will be a contest of theologies. The preacher must first point to Christ as Lord and King, and then show the practical applications of that belief. He makes it clear that wars, corrupt governments, slave-labor camps, segregated unions, and bumbling courts are condemned in eternity. Doctrinal preaching can make social indignation not just a fleeting human sentiment, but an undying fire that is kindled from the flame of God's eternal love.

People need a vertebrate religion that will give them solid support and hold their lives together. A chaos of loose opinions and sentiments will not do. A movie starlet who was asked about her religious views answered, "I just believe in everything a little bit." Christianity is not assembled out of odds and ends. It is monotheistic, which means that everything is ordered around the God whom Christ revealed. It is reasonable, which means it cannot tolerate inner contradictions. Reason is a God-given power; its demand for consistency in our faith cannot be ignored.

There is some questioning of the possibility or need of a "systematic" theology. It is pointed out that our experience of religion does not fit into orderly, rational patterns. Jesus gives us, not a structure of doctrine, but a new life. The salvation history is a happening, not a philosophy. This is a needed protest against a religion that is all bones and no flesh. Theology has sometimes been a bare skeleton. There has to be soft and tender tissue. But there is a danger in the opposite one-sided emphasis; a mass of gelatinous flesh is pitiful. A congregation needs to be offered an orderly structure of belief within which rapt experiences, moral principles, and articles of faith can be related to each other and to God's eternal plan. People want a faith that can satisfy both minds and hearts; they want to relate to something firm. A wholly sentimental Christianity will not do. Isaiah said, "Look unto the rock whence ye are hewn," not "Look unto the jelly whence ye are spooned."

There has to be preaching of strong Christian doctrines to save people from the shabby doctrines that are darkening men's minds—superstitions of the marketplace and laboratory, of the night club and the munitions plant. Those who scorn Christian doctrine may be hooked by the most absurd beliefs. I have a page from the Nazi newspaper, *Das Schwarze Corps,* which I picked up in Berlin in 1937. It derides the notion of a divine Jesus and all the mystical excrescences of Christianity. Such foolishness was not for the super-brains of super-men—so they filled their empty souls with wild Nordic myths, and ended in the worship of depravity. They were too enlightened to take God for their Führer, so they took a Führer for their god.

The educated irreligious have their special superstitions, pseudo-scientific fads that are embraced as revelation by those who would never be caught dead going into a church, or would only be caught dead going there. George Bernard Shaw, in the preface to *Saint Joan,* wrote, "I affirm that the 19th century, and still more the 20th, can knock the 15th into a cocked hat in point of susceptibility to marvels and miracles and saints and prophets and magicians and monsters and fairy tales of all kinds." There is plenty of evidence for that around any university.

Everyone has to live by faith; the question is what sort of faith it will be:

1. We may have a steadfast faith, or one that fluctuates with every passing mood. We need a faith on which we can thread our days, which will hold home, work, and play together.
2. Our faith may be brave or timid. Jesus dared people to believe in a God so great that the galaxies and electrons are his creation, and every tiny child is held within his love and care. The intellectually timorous shrink from this.
3. Faith may be noble or mean. There are stomach gods, political idolatries, and cash-value creeds.
4. Faith can be true or false. A true faith will line us up with reality; a false faith will cross us up with it. Judas for a while seemed to have more faith than Peter did, but he guessed wrong. By faith the Hebrews got through the Red Sea, and by faith the Egyptians who pursued them got drowned.

People who worry about narrow dogmatism may miss the point. Faith can be liberating or restricting. The church preaches the great beliefs to save people from the confining ones. As Jesus explained it, "You will know the truth, and the truth will make you free." (Jn. 8:32)

WHAT DOCTRINAL PREACHING CAN DO

It takes more than sermons to impart belief. Christian truth is experienced in worship, felt in Christian fellowship, demonstrated by service in Christ's name. The gospel is not imprisoned within words, but it depends on words to gain access to men's minds.

The distinction of doctrinal preaching from other kinds is a matter of degree. Every sermon, whatever its subject, must make some reference to doctrine. That is what makes a sermon different from a speech. And every exposition of doctrine must be linked with daily life it if is not to be left drifting in mid-air.

Doctrinal preaching can use almost any of the suggested sorts of sermon structure. (Chapter X) In the conventional style, the preacher announced the doctrine he was treating, explained what the Bible says about it, traced it in the writings of the Church fathers and the Reformation, gave the best of modern thought about it, and implored the congregation to live by it. This classroom method should not be disparaged; used by a master teacher, it can be exciting and satisfying. Some preachers present conflicting beliefs and keep the congregation in suspense until the right side wins. That can be an interesting way of dealing with modern false philosophies. A doctrinal sermon often starts with a question someone has asked. If the question came out of a pressing personal need, it can give the sermon an appealing setting. The occasion for the sermon may be a current happening, as it was when Jesus answered those who wanted to know whether the slaughtered Galileans were punished for their sins. The preacher may start by showing people that they have a burning interest they did not know they had. He makes them see why the Holy Spirit is so important for them, or he links predestination with sociology, or he tells why the marriage service starts with an assertion of God's providence, or he shows how the issues raised by the women's liberation movement relate to the doctrine of creation.

Negative doctrinal preaching cannot be avoided. The presentation of truth often requires at least a sideways look at error. The contrast often makes the truth more distinct. A preacher who paid no attention to materialism, Caesarism, sensualism, and nihilism in our world would be strangely detached from reality. With debasing philosophies and pretentious humbug getting so much attention, the minister of Christ must be prepared to expose falsehood and illusion. To become prepared for that will be one of his major tasks. In general, however, we persuade people more by what we are for than by what we are against. Scorn and sarcasm are not persuasive, and the preacher does not help his case by speaking condescendingly of distinguished scientists and philosophers. A good cause is not helped by bad manners. Lambasting pet bugbears can be overdone. The pleasure of hewing Agag in pieces before the Lord may be habit-forming.

The puzzles come when the divergent views are institutionalized. We could probably, with good conscience, criticize a witchcraft coven, a church of Satan, or an astrological society, but should we point out the errors of such groups as the Black Muslim, Bahai, Jehovah's Witness, Mormon, Unity, Christian Science, Unitarian, Catholic, Friends, Presbyterian, Methodist? Our forefathers had fewer uncertainties about this. The sheep were entrusted to the pastor to protect, and he defended them gladly against the Biblical and sacramental enormities of neighboring churches. In Kentucky, in the middle of the last century, Alexander Campbell and Nathan Rice engaged in a public disputation over baptism that continued for eighteen days. We do less of that, partly because we are more brotherly and partly because we do not care as much. The things we want to dispute about are not denominational.

But when members of our churches become enchanted by religious groups which we are bound to see as misrepresentations of Christianity, we may wonder whether we have done our duty. This is likely to happen to people who are going through some unusual distress or crisis. If they had been shown the irrationalities earlier, when they were emotionally able to consider them, they might not have been so susceptible. But it must be recognized that few members leave our churches to go into cults and sects compared to the great number who leave to go into nothing. It is our dread, not of false religion, but of no religion that most impels our preaching upon doctrine.

Always, when we preach on the great beliefs, we are hoping to persuade the unconvinced that they are true. It is not often that we can do this by argument. There are no "proofs" of Christianity. A scientist is said to have had only two of his four children baptized, and kept the other two for controls. But if religion could be demonstrated by that sort of test, it would not be religion. God is not going to tie us up in logic and drag us to him. He wants us to be free to reject him if we choose. Love cannot be coerced.

But there are uses for logical reasoning in sermons on belief. If any belief is accepted, then reason can be used to deduce others from it. Immanuel Kant started with his certainty that there is a moral law and derived other doctrines from that. For example, he said that the moral law commands us to do more than we can do within our life on earth; a moral law that could not be obeyed would be immoral; therefore there must be a chance beyond this life. If people believe that there is a God who cares, or that Jesus is not just dead and gone, or that love is real, or that goodness has a more than utilitarian value, then the preacher can build on from these to other truths.

Reason can be used to show that faith is possible. There are many who assume that a literal acceptance of the Christian faith is no longer conceivable for a person who is intelligent and well-informed. Christian thought agrees that no one can be asked to believe anything that is contrary to what he knows, or that has contradictions in itself. An old way of putting this is that we can be asked to believe that the whale swallowed Jonah, which is improbable, but not that Jonah swallowed the whale, which is impossible. Sermons can often use reason to open the way for faith by showing that, by all logic and observation, the belief is possible.

Reason can offer approaches to belief. These are not proofs, but they can bring a seeker right up to that last step before acceptance. There are approaches through human goodness that is so far beyond what materialism could expect; from the sense of beauty; from the reach toward God; from gratitude; from design in nature; from what makes life good or ruins it—the stars in their courses still fight against Sisera; from love —certainty does not start with "I" but with "we"; from that communion of minds which joins us to others in a mentality we share but do not own. From such reasoning we have inducements for faith; it cannot be forced, but it is not blind.

But, after all, reason is only man's next-to-the-highest faculty. There is a higher one to which the preacher must appeal. This higher faculty is akin to intuition; it is related to the witness of the Holy Spirit. It is something deep in souls that responds to truth as it does not to error. It is like falling in love. This is the recognition the preacher tries to win. He speaks to souls, not just to minds. He pleads with consciences. He tries to reach the deep longings of the human heart for love and goodness, and for God.

Beyond this there is an even greater assent for which the preacher pleads. Faith is not merely giving your agreement, it is giving yourself. You may believe that every word of your church's creed is true, and still be a heathen; "the demons believe—and shudder." The final step in accepting a doctrine is to have it dominate your life. Every doctrinal sermon must imply an altar call. The congregation must know that what the preacher means is, "Don't you believe this? And won't you enter into the new sort of life this opens up to you?"

EVANGELISTIC PREACHING

Any preacher who proclaims Christian truth so convincingly that someone says, "This is for me," is an evangelist. You may be far from a Billy Graham or a Dwight L. Moody; you may have no soul-winning techniques; you may never move your hearers to tears—but if you are eager to share the life-saving beliefs, then you are the evangelism type.

Anything as great as evangelism is subject to confusion. It is said that evangelism has to start by converting the church members and the ministers—and that is true. But the methods and psychology for doing that are so different from those that are needed to reach outside that there had better be a different name—renewal, perhaps, or revival. Besides, a church does not become more spiritual by being turned in upon itself. It is said that the real evangelism does not take place inside the church at all, but out in the world, where Christians are proclaiming Christ by their lives. But it really takes both kinds of witness. Words explain the gospel, and lives exhibit it.

The effrontery of regarding all those on a church roll as Christians, and all of those outside the Church as non-Christians, is obvious. But the Church is on earth as God's intended agency for evangelism. If you did not believe that bringing people into your church would help them to know Christ, then your church would be a fraud that could have no claim on any Christian's time, including yours. A religion based on love cannot be rightly known apart from some recognized fellowship of those who share it. So the preacher longs to have his sermons open up the wonders of the Christian life to those who are not a part of any company of believers. He hopes to help those who are outside to find the blessings God can give them through the Church.

The best occasion for evangelism is not a church service, it is a private conversation, but each can help the other. A sermon can tell more about Christian truth and life than can be readily told in private talk. A sermon can make a more extended appeal for faith. Talk about what Christ can do for life has its best setting in the surroundings of the daily life, but a worshipping congregation also offers some powerful advantages. Cold hearts are warmed by the glow that is kindled in a praying, singing fellowship; there the reality of Christian love and the presence of the Holy Spirit may be strongly felt. Faith, which in solitude may have seemed eccentric and unconvincing, in such a company may seem natural and right and greatly to be desired.

Personal evangelism and preaching evangelism have to help each other. Those who have been talking to their friends about the Christian faith can bring them to the church where the sermon can say important things that could not be put in conversations. When a minister knows that his appeals from the pulpit are too impersonal, then he tries to arrange for callers who can discuss the great issues face to face. The lay members are always the Church's chief evangelists, but the preacher backs them up.

Evangelistic preaching requires a partnership between the pulpit and the pews. The minister can bring the message, but only the church members can bring the hearers. The members have the contacts outside the church; they can say, "Let me stop by for you"; they can tell how helpful the preacher is. This partnership is made definite when certain Sundays are designated for evangelism—perhaps the first Sunday of each month, or four successive Sundays. On those Sundays the members can bring their friends with the knowledge that there will be a specially clear appeal for faith and a way to respond to it. On those Sundays the preacher can know that the members are making a special effort to bring those who are not in any church. The worship on those days will be planned to appeal to those who are not used to it.

There are advantages in special evening services, perhaps through a week. They can attract some who will not come to ordinary services. The church members can work specially hard to bring the hearers. There can be unusually attractive features. The effect of the sermons can build up from one evening to the next. Special services may combine the revival of church members with the appeal to those who profess no faith. A guest preacher may be used.

Evangelistic sermons use a wide variety of styles—logical, dramatic, expository. They usually combine a strong statement of belief with a vivid description of what that can mean for daily life. Their wording should be for those to whom church terminology is strange. They should be lively and personal, with impressive illustrations. Evangelistic preaching is discredited by cheap sentiment, but the appeal should be to both hearts and minds; what Christ means to life cannot be told without emotion. It is too bad that many a minister feels unfitted for evangelism because he is not the sort that loves to tell about his mother's funeral. It is reassuring to know that very effective evangelistic preachers have been as intellectual as Helmut Thielicke and as calmly matter-of-fact as Bryan Green. They may be traditional or modern, sensational or reserved. Their only common qualities seem to be an overpowering sense of the importance of the Christian faith and a love of people.

Your best subjects for evangelistic sermons will be whatever are for you the most important Christian truths. You preach about what you have found to be the most deeply felt and widespread human problems.

Some appeals are dubiously Christian. The use of fear has been hotly debated. Many preachers, who would never dream of frightening their congregations with divine judgment, frighten them instead with personality disorders and nuclear destruction. Preaching cannot ignore the dreadful results of Godlessness or the blessings of the Christian faith. Social pressure can be applied improperly—stressing family tradition or certified respectability. Superstition (pulling God down to man's purposes instead of lifting man up to God's) can creep in if the difference between a covenant and a deal is not made clear.

Evangelistic preaching is intended to bring people to new faith and new purposes; these are far more likely to be permanent if they are expressed. The effect of the finest sermon can fade unless it is fixed by something definite. Those who have always been running away from God by saying, "Not yet," need to be brought to a time to decide. Jesus Christ cannot be taken for granted. Those who have come to faith in him need to know that they have come.

A decision following a sermon may be expressed in many ways—in silent prayer in the church or at home; by repeating after the minister, phrase by phrase, a statement or a prayer; by speaking to the minister after church; by coming to a consultation room; by signing a card; by raising a hand; by standing; by coming forward to take the preacher's hand. The decision time cannot be brief; people need a chance to reflect on something so important. After the invitation has been given, there may be a time for quiet meditation. No form of decision is adequate. It is a symbol, it marks a turning point. It must be made adequate by what happens next.

Shortcuts in evangelism never work; there can be no quick and easy ways. The most important part of evangelism comes after the decision has been made. The person who has turned toward Christ now needs to be helped to walk toward him. That help can be given by preparatory classes, by talks with the minister, by reading, by all the ways for helping seekers get a sound start in the Christian life and in the Church.

The health curve of the Church across the centuries can be traced by the evangelistic fervor in the pulpits. In times of decline, the sermons were intended only for the edifying of church members. Whenever a springtime of the spirit has come surging through the Church, sermons have resounded with the pleas to find the glorious new life that God is offering through Jesus Christ.

THE PREACHER'S OWN THEOLOGY

A preacher has to have a theology. Training schools for ministers once took as their first responsibility the imparting of a sound body of doctrine—three years of Systematic Theology were the usual requirement. The students may not have accepted all of it, but it gave them a comprehensive background against which a theological position could be worked out. The situation in the seminaries is different today. Most of them offer excellent courses in theology, but these can be avoided. Mini-theologies offer many fragmentary views. Only the classical theologies and the surviving cover-to-cover Barthians can claim comprehensiveness. Fashionable new theologies rise and wane at two- or three-year intervals. An eminent theologian has declared, "Theology today is in a shambles—that's the long and the short of it."

A preacher who is lost in that confusion is in trouble. A preacher has to have a theology because his people have to have a theology, and he is supposed to help them with it. They need an articulate body of beliefs to save their thinking, and therefore their living, from scattering into a random jumble of loose parts. The congregation needs a theologian in the pulpit to help them understand the Bible. They seek, as Emil Brunner put it, "an interpreter to translate the great, difficult, strange words of the Bible into the familiar language of daily life." With all that is being written to show that words are insubstantial symbols, we still need them. You have to have a word to have a "word event." Theology (from *theos,* "God," and *legein,* "to talk") is, in simple terms, "God-talk," and God-talk is the preacher's business. The preacher has to be a theologian, and it makes a world of difference whether his theology is Biblical or arbitrary, consistent or disheveled, well-worked-out or lazy, respectable or nondescript.

The preacher's theology cannot be laid before him ready-made.

The first step in coming to a theology is to amass the raw materials. These come from a knowledge of the Bible and of the world, and from inner experience. All your life, God has been giving you the raw materials for theology. They may come to you while you are praying or picketing, in laughter or in tears. Kant said his came from awe at the starry heavens over him and the moral law within him. We get the raw materials when we turn our minds loose for reasoning that is uninhibited by old assumptions, and when we let our emotions have room in which to operate. We get them from the company of those for whom Christianity seems real.

Another necessity for building a body of beliefs is the study of theology. Some of the newer theologians deny that theology can be an object for study—you do not learn it, you "do" it. (Though when Faust chose "In the beginning was the deed" instead of "In the beginning was the Word," he gave the Devil access to his room.) Thus, theology is not a subject but a continuation of God's redeeming act; it is a process; it requires being engaged. You do not master theology, it grows on you. However this may be, there is still a wealth of theological thinking a preacher needs to know about. A twentieth-century theologian no more has to start with nothing than does a twentieth-century chemist. We must think through the systems of the past that are our birthright in the Church, and build our convictions on them by acceptance, revision, or rejection. We must beware of the intellectual's trap of wandering so much in the foggy areas that we lose contact with the central certainties.

You have to learn to think theologically. You need to be able to carry abstractions without spilling them. You must exercise your intellect until it can do the hardest theological task of all, which is the translation of difficult doctrines into clear and living language. When you can manage that, intelligent hearers will bless you, and those who are struggling for faith will look to you for help.

You preach yourself into theology. There will probably be no other preacher you often get to hear. This does not mean that you use your pulpit to work out your own problems, but when you know that your people are hungry for more truth, you struggle for all you can tell them and by that you tell yourself. Never preach more than you believe; the punishment may be that you end up believing it. But preach all the doctrine you possibly can, and ponder, and push for more.

In building a theology, take all the help you can get from a theological school, as a regular or special student. But if you missed the chance for that, the same books are still available for you. However, they get their start, ministers in the long run have to work out their own system of belief.

When Thomas Aquinas had almost reached the end of the monumental *Summa* of theology that was his life's work, he hung up his inkhorn and pen and refused to go back to the task again. The only explanation he ever gave was, "What I have seen so transcends what I have written that I will write no more." The theology was a ladder on which he had mounted to the vision of God's glory, but the theology was nothing in the light of the real splendor. That is what we hope will happen to the congregation when we preach on the great beliefs. We are not trying to present a system of doctrine as Christianity, nor to make the church members connoisseurs of dogma. But we do hope we can help people use the truths that are put in words to rise to a living experience with God of which words could never tell.

XXII

Preaching
on
Individual Morality

Chief Justice Earl Warren, in an address at the Jewish Theological Seminary in New York, declared that lawyers give only very marginal help in questions of right and wrong. They can deal only with the small minority of moral matters on which some governing body has passed a law. Ethical decisions are largely in the far wider area in which everyone has to decide for himself. But most people are quite unsure about ethical decisions. Therefore, he said, "there is an urgent need in our troubled times for the development of the profession of the counselor in ethics." Just as lawyers are employed to tell people what is legal, professionally trained counselors in ethics, employed by institutions or in private practice, could give advice on what is ethical. Judge Warren recognized that "this role properly belongs to ministers of religion and is one of their gravest responsibilities."

Guidance in personal morality has long been thought of as a chief purpose of preaching. The New Testament epistles, which are models for the content of sermons, have abundant examples of this. About a third of the Epistle to the Ephesians, a fourth of Colossians, and almost all of James is devoted to warning against specific vices and exhortation to specific virtues.

Christianity is not a rule-book religion. The Pharisees hoped to have a code so comprehensive it would tell them what was right in every possible situation. They used their thumbs to go through scrolls to find their moral guidance. Jesus wants us to use not our thumbs, but our hearts as we search the Scriptures to find God's will. It is our love of God and of each other, and our devotion to the highest, that will tell us what to do. Moses gave the law carved in tables of stone; Jesus dramatized it. He lived on earth the example of what goodness should be. He guides us less as a law-giver than as a companion. It is the sense of his presence that makes us know what we should do. The Sermon on the Mount is not a rule book, it is a picture book in which he shows what it looks like to be his disciple.

The first responsibility of the preacher, therefore, is not to offer specific rules, but to offer those supreme devotions that are our guides. When William Penn became a Quaker, he asked the Quaker leader whether he could continue to wear his sword. The leader, refusing to hand down a rule, replied, "Wear it so long as thou canst," so Penn discarded it. Jesus was not that indefinite. He gave the great standards for morality and he refused to derive from these a set of rules, but he did not refuse to give illustrations or to point to definite transgressions of the moral standards. He was quite specific in his condemnation of the way the Pharisees arranged their tithes, and of the money-changing in the temple, and of the street-corner prayers the hypocrites so loved. He told Peter, "Put up your sword," not, "Wear it so long as thou canst."

The saying from Augustine, "Love God and do as you please," has often been misunderstood. The great bishop did not mean "If you love God, that is all that matters—you are free of all restraints"; he meant that the love of God will put you under compulsions that would make any set of rules look easy. The Christian faith is totalitarian; it takes over everything a Christian does. "If a man is in Christ he becomes a new person altogether." (II Cor. 5:17 Phillips) His rebirth transforms how he acts in every area of life—how he spends his money and his time, how he relates to his children and his employees; everything is different. During a revival a businessman was approached about joining the church. He answered, "I can't do it. I have a competitor in this city and I have figured out a way to put him out of business. I don't think I could do that if I were a Christian." His caller told him, "You don't understand; that's business. We don't get into a man's private affairs. I'm talking about your relationship to Christ." That is how a congregation could understand Christianity if sermons never talked about Christian goodness in specific terms. The preacher does not legislate—"You can charge six percent interest but not ten," or "When you sell your old car, you can regroove the tires, but not set back the speedometer"— but he must, like Jesus, apply the great beliefs to real situations.

Some of the notorious Christians of the past, with their sweatshops and corrupt political machines, were probably not hypocrites at all. They sat all their lives under preaching that never got near such subjects. They were living by all the truth their churches let them have. A modern minister who says, "I'm no moralist. I preach the lifestyle that comes from love, openness, and celebration" is not enough different from the one who says, "I have nothing to do with a man's business; I'm called to save souls."

When all we preach is generalities, we can count on unanimous approval and very small effect. Platitudes can be poisonous. People listen, agree, and tell themselves they are practicing the principles because they approve of them. The New Testament epistles go into such exact detail about morality because the first Christians needed to know how their love of Christ should affect their daily living. So do we. We need preachers who will help us see in specific terms what a Christian is.

THE AUTHORITY

The minister's primary authority as he preaches about morality is the great foundation truths of Christianity. Dostoevski said, "If there is no God, then everything is allowed." The Greek philosophers argued over the origin of morality. Is it a tribal instinct or enlightened selfishness? The argument is still going on, but for Christians it is settled. The difference between right and wrong has an eternal source. The voice of conscience is not a man talking to himself; its bidding comes from outside him. Our little watches are regulated by sun time. "If there is no God, then everything is allowed," but if there is a God, then some things are not allowed. This external source of right and wrong is identified as a spiritual being who can best be described as Jesus described God. What Jesus was in time, God is in eternity. God can therefore be understood as holy, righteous, caring. Jesus described God as a Father, whose children are infinitely precious in his sight. They are related to each other as brothers and sisters. So love, mercy, justice, and truth have a supernal validity. First you love the Lord your God, and then you love your neighbor as yourself. The minister, therefore, upholds these moral guides before the congregation as a part of his witness to Christ; he can preach from them with complete assurance.

Those are the eternal principles, but how are they to be applied? For his guide in this the Christian has the Bible. Much of it is taken up with the application of the certain morality of God to our uncertain scene. Hebrew history demonstrates that the ways that bring blessing to a nation and the ways that bring disaster cannot be transgressed because they are founded in eternity. The Bible biographies show that what makes or breaks a person has not changed since David's heart was broken for his sin, or since faithless Peter went weeping out into the night.

The Bible does not leave morality in wide, vaulting abstractions. In page after page, right and wrong are demonstrated in down-to-earth detail. Let us see an example of this in what the Bible has to say about business practices—and the example could as well have been taken from other areas of human life, from family relationships, politics, or sex.

The Mosaic law gives a good deal of attention to the application of justice and mercy to the treatment of employees: "You shall not oppress a hired servant who is poor and needy . . . you shall give him his hire on the day he earns it, before the sun goes down (for he is poor, and sets his heart upon it)." (Deut. 24:14–15) Employees are not to be forced to work on their weekly day of rest. There were remarkably considerate provisions: "When a man is newly married, he shall not go out with the army or be charged with any business; he shall be free at home for one year, to be happy with his wife." (Deut. 24:5) Slaves, who were more like indentured servants, were to be released at the end of six years. If a bad-tempered employer strikes a slave so as to knock out a tooth or an eye, the slave shall immediately be set free. "You shall not give up to his master a slave who has escaped . . . he shall dwell with you . . . you shall not oppress him." (Deut. 23:15–16) Grievances are to be considered: "If I have rejected the cause of my manservant or my maidservant, when they brought a complaint against me; what then shall I do when God rises up? When he makes inquiry, what shall I answer him?" (Job 31:13–14)

That last, from Job, illustrates the whole source of Biblical morality. It is derived from eternal principles. That can be seen in the New Testament. On this same subject Paul writes, "Masters, treat your slaves justly and fairly, knowing that you also have a Master in heaven." (Col. 4:1) This illustrates also the application of the eternal within the limitations of the possible. Paul was not accepting slavery, but he dealt with it as a present fact. He put under the institution the dynamite that finally destroyed it when he said, "Forbear threatening [your slaves], knowing that he who is both their Master and yours is in heaven, and that there is no partiality with him." (Eph. 6:9) James warns, "The wages of the laborers who mowed your fields, which you kept back by fraud, cry out; and the cries of the harvesters have reached the ears of the Lord of hosts." (Jas. 5:4) This applied both ways; workers were given the same holy reason for diligence, "rendering service with a good will as to the Lord and not to men." ((Eph. 6:7)

There was that same infinite reason for ordinary honesty: "A just balance and scales are the Lord's; all the weights in the bag are his work." (Prov. 16:11) In Leviticus there is a detailed condemnation of stinginess, stealing, deceit, exploitation, slow payment, unjust judgment, partiality to the rich, and slander; through this comes again and again the resounding reason—"I am the Lord!" (Lev. 19:9–15) That passage could be quoted word for word to support the Better Business Bureau, or Truth-in-Advertising legislation.

Money matters are regulated on the same basis: "anyone sins and commits a breach of faith against the Lord by deceiving his neighbor in a matter of deposit or security." (Lev. 6:2) "If you lend money to any of my people with you who is poor, you shall not be to him as a creditor, and you shall not exact interest from him. If ever you take your neighbor's garment in a pledge, you shall restore it to him before the sun goes down; for that is his only covering . . . And if he cries to me, I will hear, for I am compassionate." (Ex. 22:25–27)

From this, and a great deal more the Bible says about business and economics, we can see how the morality of daily life is traced back to the primary principles of faith. The way these principles apply changes with the situations. No one believes, from these rules for early Israel, that it is now wrong to charge interest or to sell a farm. But what these laws were designed to achieve—justice, mercy, honesty—is just as necessary today as it was then, and as it will be a thousand years from now— because the source is from outside our changes.

Moreover, these applications from the Bible are perpetually valuable as demonstrations of what the timeless moral principles mean. Most of us do not need to be told not to take a millstone as a pledge, and so deprive a miller of his livelihood, or to leave grain in the fields for the poor, but we know exactly what these laws are getting at, and they hit us hard. The Bible's illustrations never go out of date. You will never preach to anyone who will have a legal right to demand an opponent's tooth, or who can be forced to carry a Roman soldier's pack for a mile, but great sermons can always be preached from those situations.

A great deal the Bible has to say about goodness can be preached to our congregations exactly as it is written. Read that marvelous description of the good man, which is Job's closing speech to his accusing friends, and ask yourself how many words you would change: "If I have walked with falsehood, and my foot has hastened to deceit. . . . If my heart has been enticed to a woman, and I have lain in wait at my neighbor's door. . . . If I have withheld anything the poor desired, or have caused the eyes of the widow to fail, or have eaten my morsel alone, and the fatherless has not eaten of it. . . . If I have made gold my trust. . . . If I have rejoiced at the ruin of him that hated me . . ." (Job 31) The Sermon on the Mount, with all its specific detail, does not need amendment. Paul winds up his letter to the Ephesians by talking about falsehood, anger, stealing, work, alms, bitterness, wrath, clamor, slander, malice, kindness, forgiveness, love, lust, covetousness, filthiness, silly talk, impurity, idolatry, drunkenness, worship, thanks, and the behavior of wives, husbands, children, parents, masters, and servants. As we read this we are not inclined to say, "How quaint," but "There's a man who gets around."

The preacher also has the authority of the centuries of Christian experience. A community of people who are under the same moral compulsions have been trying to find how to live by them for two thousand years. They have made some blunders. In the early centuries the Church mixed Christianity with Greek thought, which regarded the flesh as the enemy of the soul, and its morality became ascetic. Christians have tried out moral positions on war, race, and the discipline of children that now seem wrong, even for their time. By discovering the ways of living that fit Christ's purposes, and the ways that are against them, the Church has through the years been learning a great deal that ministers use in their preaching.

Consider, for example, the talk about the "sex revolution." It is not really a revolution, it is a reversion to a morality that has come up repeatedly in the long history of the Church. Its rationalizations were much the same in Restoration England. The only real sex revolution was a revelation. It came into the world with Christianity. It opened up a vital and beautiful new style of life that was in contrast with the world's attitudes then, as it has been ever since. All true romance is derived from it. The choice for it and against it is just what it has always been.

In every age and land, the Church has been in danger of being captured by its culture. Each generation's modernity presents a new situation which is supposed to make the understood Christian morality out of date. The preacher must talk of goodness in a way that will make sense in the new situation of computers, space travel, the pill, the new biology, and the mental sciences, but he does not need to be intimidated by them. Primitive people keep trying to adapt Christianity to their tribal practices, and so do jet-age people.

The recognition that the great moral purposes derived from Christ apply differently in different situations is not a new thought. To pick up the ball and run with it is a virtue in football and a vice in basketball, but there is nothing antinomian in that. When Martha wanted the same rule for her and Mary, Jesus' answer was situational—the same purpose of serving him took different expressions because the sisters were different.

But it would be a great mistake to conclude from this that there are no firm guides. The world is a laboratory in which the results of various sorts of conduct have been pretty well explored. The ways that enhance love and the ways that defeat it do not change overnight. Arsenic is just as poisonous now as it was in the Middle Ages, and so is malice. "A horse is a vain thing for safety," and so is a bomber. Modern technology has filled homes with remarkable appliances, but the essentials for good families are about what they have always been. There are techniques for Christian living. There are ways that make existence cramped and barren, and there are ways that lead into the glorious living Christ makes possible. We do not have to improvise morality. "Old-fashioned" and "conventional" are terms all preachers dread, but often the correct term is "well-tested" or "found out to be right."

It would be intolerable for the preacher, on the basis of his own tastes and cultural assumptions, to stand in the pulpit and tell people how to have good marriages, or how to run their businesses. It is not intolerable for him to tell a congregation about the eternal principles of the Christian faith, or about how Christians through the years have found that those principles apply in real situations.

HOW DEFINITE?

Sermons on morality in general are inoffensive; reference to particular sins and sinners is another matter. When David took Uriah's wife and had him killed, the prophet, Nathan, stalked into the court. First he told David a pathetic story about a poor man with only one little ewe lamb, and a rich man who stole the lamb. David's anger blazed, and he decreed, "The man who did this ought to die." Then Nathan told him straight out, "You are the man." David in agonized remorse admitted, "I have sinned against the Lord." What Nathan did is the function of the Church. It is in the world to point to what is right and to condemn the wrong. Nathan's method of rousing strong agreement with the principle before pointing to the specific sin is a good one for preachers.

The Church in the past has taken this responsibility seriously. The early Presbyterian Church in Geneva kept a critical eye on the business practices of its members. Usurers and monopolists were punished. Cloth merchants whose stock was an inch too narrow were reprimanded. The Puritan who owned the only cow on board the Mayflower sold milk at the inflated price of two pence a quart. This wicked monopolist was forced to sit as the visual aid for a sermon on extortion.

The Church today does not often condemn particular sinners; it does have to condemn particular sins. It does not officially reprove wrong-doers, as was done fairly often in most Protestant churches before this century, but it must be definite enough to bring them to reprove themselves. People who come to church thinking well of themselves should often hear sermons that will send them home feeling guilty and unworthy, thinking less of themselves but more of Christ. Preaching on the great moral concepts is needed; but it is when sermons refer to real living that they do the most good and are hardest to take. A sermon on honesty may do more good if something is said about expense accounts, or Christmas presents for business purposes, or the use of the company car. The minister may talk about snobbishness and have everyone approving; but if he mentions the high school sororities, there may be discontent. When the minister preached on drinking and gambling, the elderly parishoner was delighted; but when he mentioned dipping snuff she grumbled, "Now he's quit preaching and gone to meddling!"

Preachers are often charged with giving too little help with real moral problems because they do not understand them: no one sees himself in the illustrations. Our flat solutions may not fit the contours of reality.

A contractor says, "The only way I can get the permits I have to have is by paying graft. If I go out of business, the faithful employees who depend on me will be thrown out of work." In impoverished states, most elections and all the primaries depend on the votes that can be purchased. Should honest men in these states allow votes to be purchased on their behalf, knowing that otherwise all offices will be held by crooks? A magazine quotes a businessman as saying, "I have plenty of ethical problems in my work, but the last place I would look for help is my church." I have gained insights from conferences in which our church members, meeting in vocational groups, discussed the ethical dilemmas that are faced in their sort of work.

It is interesting that law and medical schools offer important courses on the ethics of those professions, while the subject is little mentioned in ministerial training. If the assumption is that ministers have no ethical problems, it is a mistake. They have hard moral puzzles in such matters as taking members from other churches, plagiarism, salaries, honoraria, expense accounts, discounts, taxes, family duty, confidentiality, outside work. A rigorous study of those questions, from the point of view of Christian idealism, would be a good start on the subject of vocational morality.

In a strange way, we have reversed our ancestors. In their churches they were definite about personal morality but vague about social morality. We are inclined to be definite about social morality but vague about personal morality. The seventeenth-century Presbyterian confessional documents say much about personal behavior—cursing, mocking, courtesy, temperance, quarreling, modest apparel, wanton looks, lascivious songs, false measures, usury, vexatious lawsuits, talebearing, reviling. There is almost no mention of such things as war, race, slavery, poverty, government. The Presbyterian Confession of 1967 has splendid, clear statements on war, race, and poverty; a statement on the relationship of men and women had to be brought in by a revision; beyond that, there is little that is definite about personal behavior. The sociological reasons for the shift in emphasis are not hard to see: shame over past neglect of social morality, a reaction against past strictness in personal morality, concern for the current social emergencies, the present permissiveness.

Preachers cannot be controlled by church fashions. Just as the great battles against slavery were led by Christian ministers and laymen from Churches that had deplorably little to say about it, so ministers today, seeing their people's great need for help in personal morality, will give it.

CHARACTER

The church is a builder of character. To have character means to be a real person, to be genuine. Character requires a constancy that holds a life together and saves it from being just a loose collection of inconsistencies. Christian character gets its stability from Jesus Christ. It has integrity because it is integrated around him. That gives a personality the sort of solidity that Jesus said is like being "founded on the rock"; it will not be blown sideways by a storm. The New Testament repeatedly shows that a Christian is one who is "steadfast, immovable," "strong in the Lord," authentic.

The Church is in the world to build that sort of character, and preaching is one of the chief means it uses. It tries to reach those whose lives have no organizing center, or the wrong center, or conflicting centers, so that they may be integrated around Jesus Christ.

Loyalty to Christ is the source of the firm principles that keep a character from collapsing under pressure. From this loyalty come the ideals that hold a personality from going to pieces under stress. The Bible devotes a great deal of attention to establishing those principles and ideals, and so must the preacher. People come to their churches to be nerved and steadied. Life can be harsh; it takes courage to remain steadfast through the daily grind. People listen to the minister, hoping to have their principles renewed, to be shown again the beauty of their purposes, to be told what Christ expects of them. They come to confirm again the decisions they can hold to when the times get bad.

Christian character is prescribed by devotion to Jesus Christ. What we get from him is not just vague generalities but a very definite model of what a Christian looks like and does. "Jesus Christ is the same yesterday and today and forever" (Heb. 13:8); and the sort of life to which he calls his followers does not change across the years. The New Testament gives numerous lists of Christian qualities, as in the Beatitudes (Mt. 5:3–11), in the ninefold fruits of the spirit (Gal. 5:22–23), and the "whatevers" (Philip 4:8). Those definite traits of the Christian character are urgent themes for sermons. The Church reveals the beauty of such virtues as honesty, purity, compassion, courage, usefulness, and reverence. It helps its members live by them at home, at work, as citizens.

AFFIRMATIVE MORALITY

There has been enough narrow legalism in the Church to make ministers uneasy. They shrink from the stereotype of the denouncer who is bent on spoiling life for the high-spirited. Ogden Nash in "Ha! Original Sin!" hears the preacher saying, "Vanity, vanity, all is vanity that's any fun at all for humanity." But a minister cannot escape having a certain amount of intolerance, just as a crossing watchman does. Anyone with any sympathy who sees around him the broken hearts, broken homes, and broken lives will have some things he is very definitely against.

In its source, the Christian morality is not negative at all. It springs from a vision of how glorious life can be. The Ten Commandments are negative in form, but each one of them is really saying, "Thou shalt have the great blessings God intends for you." Each of the commandments forbids what would narrow life. All the "Don'ts" in the Christian ethic mean "Thou shalt not make a bad bargain." To live a life shabbily when it has such boundless possibilities is what Christ forbids. Laurence Housman gave a valid summary of Christian morals when he said, "A saint is one who makes goodness attractive."

The Christian life is not one of renunciation, but of openings. The entrance to it is so definite that it is indeed a straight and narrow way; it does require the forsaking of the world, the flesh, and the devil in the prayer book sense, but only because they reduce the range. The narrow way is a mountain pass that leads into a wide valley. Christian morality releases us from cautious, crabbed ways and sets us free to live life to the full. The whole purpose of morality is to make life rich and joyful for us and others. Robert Louis Stevenson gave the rule: "If your morals make you dreary, depend upon it, they are wrong." Christ does not subdue the high-spirited and restive; he releases them into the wonder and the beauty of the life whose fulfillment will be "the glorious liberty of the children of God."

XXIII

Preaching
on
Social Morality

A minister I know told his congregation that when he preached in another church, he saw, carved into the pulpit, the plea of the seeking Greeks: "Sir, we would see Jesus." But, he said, by the time a preacher sees those words, it is too late. His sermon is already prepared. Not long after, my friend received from his young couples' club a supply of the sort of paper he uses for his sermons. Across the top of every sheet, printed in red, was that entreaty "We would see Jesus." That is indeed the deepest need of all who come to church. How, then, is there any place for all the social matters preachers talk about? There are sermons on international affairs, ecology, business, labor, war, penitentiaries, revolution, economics, drug abuse, alcohol regulation, lotteries, education, race, elections, health, poverty, crime, deprived nations, the judicial system, migrant workers, population control, housing. Ministers are called and trained to preach Christ, not to preach their opinions on all these public issues. To get some balance on this question we need to look, first, at the reasons against preaching on social subjects and second, at the reasons for it.

REASONS AGAINST PREACHING ON SOCIAL MORALITY

1. The term "social gospel" has no meaning because the gospel is for persons, not for institutions. How can a corporation be converted? How can a government agency look to Jesus Christ as Lord? The Church's task is not to change social entities, but to change human beings, who will then influence their institutions. A judge brings Christ into his courtroom not because his church tells him how to be a judge, but because it tells him to know Christ, and Christ tells him how to be a Christian judge.

2. People come to church to make contact with God, to get their spiritual batteries recharged, so they can go out and live like Christians in the difficult issues they must face. A church is like an aircraft carrier

that is far away from where the action is; but its planes come back to it to be refueled and rearmed for the fray.

3. Preachers are not trained to be experts on every sort of social matter, and their judgments are often incompetent and uninformed. A minister making pronouncements on business matters before a congregation that has people from banks, stores, and industries is a ridiculous figure. Church conventions bring good people from around the country who sit in hotel rooms and eagerly draft resolutions on world affairs, public health, and other highly technical subjects to which they had given little thought before they left home. Those to whom the resolutions are directed recognize what they are and pay small heed to them.

4. Preaching on social issues diverts the Church from its God-given task, which is the increase of faith in Christ. This faith is the world's only hope. People who talk of "Christian principles" or "Christian action" often forget that the word "Christian" is an adjective that gets all its meaning from the noun "Christ." Without him the word grows feeble. There will be no lasting regard for Christ's principles without a regard for Christ, as Lord and Master. Devotion to Christian action will play out when the difficulties come unless it is maintained by devotion to Christ. If the Church would give itself to evangelism, and not to social programs which are not its business, it would do a great deal more for human welfare.

5. Ministers and laymen concentrate on social sympathies when that is all the Christianity they have left. When they have gone spiritually dead, when intellectually they are unable to believe in Christ as Lord, when words like *God, prayer,* and *heaven* have lost all meaning for them, then they satisfy their religious needs by devotion to the cause of the distressed. The violence of their intolerance of "conventional piety," or "middle-class values" often betrays their feelings of inadequacy. (Chapter XX)

6. There is no basis for social preaching in the Bible. Jesus, in the presence of slavery, child labor, imperialistic oppression, and militarism, never referred to them. He was not indifferent to them, but he came to reveal the eternal truths by which alone evils can be overcome. That is what his church is to do. We will not deactivate the nuclear bomb by Church pronouncements on world order. There will be no racial harmony without a change in those vicious pack impulses that always make unredeemed human beings such problems for each other. If hearts are not changed, improved environments will do no good.

7. Social activism is contrary to the traditions of our Church. You find no support for it in Calvin's *Institutes* or in Luther's writings. Luther refused to support the revolt of the oppressed peasants. There is nothing about social morality in the great Reformation creeds.

To many fine church members such arguments will seem so conclusive that only the willfully froward would try to get around them. But there are other Christians, just as good, who will give them no more than an indulgent smile as they go on with the social action they are sure is their Lord's will. Looking out from the pulpit at both sorts of members is the preacher, trying to be helpful to both, and finding it perplexing. Most people in a congregation could not be labeled; they are open-minded. But everyone seems to have at least a slight leaning toward one side or the other. The two different sorts of people often find it difficult to understand each other, but they can love each other, and the Church greatly needs them both.

REASONS FOR PREACHING ON SOCIAL MORALITY

When a minister preaches on social morality, he needs to be able to explain to himself and others why he does it.

1. The reasons for such sermons are sharply plain in the Bible. The Old Testament is full of condemnation of social evil and demands for social righteousness. The laws of Moses are very detailed in their provision for mercy and justice in employment, courts, business, welfare, and land management. Above the door of the Bank of England in London is carved the verse "The earth is the Lord's and the fullness thereof." (Ps. 24:1) That is the clue to the whole economic system of the Old Testament. "The land shall not be sold in perpetuity, for the land is mine; for you are strangers and sojourners with me." (Lev. 25:23) There could be no permanent transfer of title; no one but God could be a great landowner. The Bible regards kings as God's men, who were called to account for their taxes, wars, foreign policies, and welfare programs. In a democracy, where we are citizen-kings, this applies to us. The prophets, in passage after passage, are deep in social matters—taxation, judicial practices, international relations, political corruption, labor legislation, the hoarding of capital. Anyone who finds no basis for social preaching in the Bible must have thrown the Old Testament away.

The New Testament is less explicit about social responsibility than is the Old because there was no social responsibility in New Testament times. Under the iron domination of Rome and its corrupt deputies in Palestine, there was no way to participate in public affairs; there was nothing to be said about the responsibilities of citizens because there were no responsible citizens. Even so, we find in the Epistles a great deal that we have to apply to our corporate affairs. They teach that all men are brothers, that the ties of faith eliminate the barriers of race, sex, and class, that the body is sacred, that war comes from sin, that employer and employee are to treat each other justly and lovingly, that temptation is not to be thrown in people's way.

Jesus did not make pronouncements on the specific problems of one time and place. As the incarnation of the eternal God, he gave the basis for all social regulations for every corner of the earth until the end of time. He set a little child in the midst of his hearers and told how that child was infinitely precious to God. Because of that, Christians ever since have fought for laws to protect children. Jesus never criticized the bloody gladiatorial games, but it was out of loyalty to him that a monk leaped over the rail into the arena of the Roman Colosseum. The monk was torn to pieces by the wild beasts, as he expected, but his protest helped to end the brutal spectacles. Jesus taught that God is a Father who loves all mankind and provides the good things of earth for all his children to enjoy. In his sight the humblest and farthest away are of infinite value. Jesus taught that a loving God intends his children to live joyfully and abundantly, growing in their knowledge of God and their caring for each other. Whatever helps mankind in this is good, and whatever interferes with it is evil. He said that it is the Christian's duty to relieve suffering, heal the sick, help the poor, and secure justice for the oppressed. He warned that to break God's laws brings disaster to a soul or to a nation. An adult class member asked, "Why are we talking about housing in our class? Jesus never talked about housing." The teacher answered pointedly, "Here's something: 'Hypocrites! for you devour widows' houses, and for a pretence you make long prayers.'"

Jesus claimed the sovereignty in all the world's affairs. When he rode into the city on his way to the cross, he was not only claiming a spiritual kingdom, he was revealing himself as the King of kings. He demonstrated this the next day in the symbolic act of casting out the defilers of the temple. In this, he was not condemning just private sinners; he was setting himself against a social system. The authorities recognized that they had to eliminate Jesus to protect their institutions. Whenever we pray "Thy kingdom come, Thy will be done on earth," we are not looking to some future time. We are acknowledging that his will is to be done in the city hall, in the bank, and in the university. He is not the Lord just of churches and homes, he is Lord of all. A book-binder, who was replacing the worn cover on a Testament, could not find room to spell out "The New Testament," so he abbreviated it to "T.N.T." The explosive power of the gospel has toppled thrones and blasted governments. It has burst open the doors to enlightenment, health, and dignity for multitudes.

2. Christ's Church has across the years labored to make a better society. Its preachers have been leaders in this. The fact that Jesus attacked social evils at the deepest level has not restricted his ministers to that. They are not the successors of the Messiah, but of the Apostles. The Apostles and those who have come after them have applied the timeless principles of Christ directly to the social situations of their times. In the Roman Empire, the little band, small at first but powerful in its devotion to its Lord, stopped the worst abuses of slavery, secured the prohibition of the murder of unwanted infants, ended the brutal shows. Gibbon told what the Church did for the next era: "The barbarian invaders conquered every factor of Roman civilization save one—that factor conquered the barbarians." The Church tempered the ferocity of the Dark Ages by the ideals of chivalry; it softened the asperities of feudalism; it reformed the grimness of the Industrial Revolution; it has forced men to hear, in questions of war and exploitation, the point of view of Christ.

The early Reformation was the low point in the Church's historic concern with social sins. There were reasons for that. Before then, the Church not only had an interest in public affairs, it demanded the right to dictate them. When Pope Gregory the Great forced King Henry to kneel before him, barefoot and in sackcloth in the snow, to receive his crown, the Pope was claiming the supreme power in temporal affairs. It was this claim that made Luther and Calvin lean so far backward that they almost renounced any concern at all for public matters. This explains why the creeds from this period dealt with morality almost wholly in terms of private conduct. That is why there are so many Protestants today who are puzzled about why the Church pays any attention to social evils.

Actually, what some of the Reformers slighted in their teaching they more than made up for in their conduct. As the pastor of the church, John Calvin was almost the dictator of the morality of business and government in Geneva. Queen Mary bitterly protested the strong part John Knox took in the affairs of the realm.

The development of a more recent Calvinist shows how the inherited overbalance can be overcome. President Woodrow Wilson came from conservative Presbyterian origins, with a distaste for organized social action by the Church. Earlier he had said, "Christianity must be fundamentally and forever individualistic," and the minister should "preach Christianity to men, not to society." But by 1909, when Woodrow Wilson had matured in the church and in public life, he reversed this. He said, "Christianity came into the world to save the world as well as to save individual men"; "Christianity was just as much intended to save society as to save the individual."

3. All the most important social and political questions are religious questions, and therefore the business of the Church. When laws on abortion are debated, a legislator needs medical, psychological, and sociological information. But essentially the question is a religious one, and he needs a church's help. Capital punishment is a religious question; the records of the social effects need to be considered, but the right and wrong of the taking of a life must be settled on religious grounds and it is a problem for the Church. So is the problem, which is raised by every war, of when it is right to kill another human being; the facts of international politics, trade, and security have to be considered. But the final decision about the terms on which it is right to kill a man, or a woman, or a child, depends on one's conception of God and human life. The question goes to the very essence of the Christian faith.

All of our social arrangements express our theology. Our views on racial questions have to consider sociology, economics, and politics, but essentially they will depend on our deepest convictions about the nature and origin of the human family. Housing restrictions institutionalize a doctrine of man. When I came into a Western airport, I found the ticket counters surrounded by a picket line, and I learned that local agencies of my denomination had helped organize it. The pickets were there because a big airport public works project was getting started, and the construction unions were almost totally closed to any but white workers. It would have been easy to protest, "What business is this of the Church? This is labor relations; this is politics." But when you deny a man a chance to earn the living he could earn for himself and those he loves because of the color of his skin, you are expressing a pagan view of the natural order that is very different from that of Christian theology. Because of the Doctrine of Divine Purpose, a church has to be concerned with the structures of society. A city is a factory for producing people, and the Church must care greatly whether or not this factory is tooled and equipped to produce the sort of people God intends.

4. To divide life into religious and secular compartments is the ideal strategem for forcing Christ out of his world. It means that Christians can fight Satan in one person at a time, but when he escapes behind the fence into the public realm, he may ravage undisturbed. When the devil is corrupting corporations or despoiling men by millions through government action, he is out of bounds and the Church cannot touch him. It is strange that Communists, Nazis, and a certain sort of Christian churchmen have been leading exponents of the view that preachers must deal only with "religious" matters. Churches in Eastern Europe are allowed to operate as long as they stay out of government affairs. Reichminister Goebbels told the churches that getting souls to heaven was their business; worldly affairs were the business of the state. But the Christian faith is not a special slant on certain subjects, it is a special slant on all subjects. Christ makes a difference in every part of life. If he is not Lord of all, he is Lord of nothing.

5. Sin is both individual and cooperative. Dishonesty is evil, whether it is committed by one person alone, by two in partnership, by a thousand through their corporation, or by a hundred million through their country. You may be personally pure and innocent and still foul with the guilt of the groups to which you belong, if you have not set yourself against them. Shared sin may be treacherously elusive. A man who is ethical in his own business may not recognize the guilt which he bears from owning stock in a company whose practices are bad. A nation's sin is shared by every citizen who has consented to it or kept silent. We are like cells, with both an individual existence and an existence in the body of which we are a part. Our Christian faith applies to both aspects of our life, and so does the preaching of the gospel.

Whatever you make of the idea of original sin for individuals, you cannot doubt it for groups. We are born into the sins of our society. Original social sin is passed down from one generation to the next through corrupted social patterns. We take over ready-made the wrong attitudes of our parents, our social class, our church, and our country. Everyone, in this sense, is born in sin. The traditional dogma has held that Christ could set men free from the taint of original sin. Faith in him can save us from our inherited social sins when we are transformed by our devotion to him. This is part of the salvation the preacher has to offer.

6. Christianity is not attentive to the bee and indifferent to the hive. It is a curious inversion of sense to say that the Church is to care about only one person at a time, and to leave concern for large numbers of people to the government. Each person in the mass is infinitely precious to God, and if the Church cares about each of them it must care infinitely about the mass arrangements which control their lives.

Sermons should be concerned, not just with the misery of individuals, but with its causes. It is foolish to concentrate on running an ambulance service to the foot of a cliff when an enlightened Christian conscience would put a guard rail at the top. We need to maintain rescue missions, but we also need to correct those social conditions that multiply broken lives. We need to care for those in prison, but we also need to clean up the conditions that breed crime. It is our duty to give relief for war victims, but it is a greater duty to use any influence that can decrease the possibility of war. It is not enough to treat those ill of malaria, we must also clean up the swamps from which malaria is spread. It is good to preach virtue, but it is also good to preach against the political corruption and unwholesome influences from which vice spreads.

If the Good Samaritan had found dozens of victims of robbers on every trip he took, he would scarcely have contented himself with taking care of one of them. He would have demanded government protection for that stretch of road, or organized a drive to expel the robbers, or launched a campaign to build hostels along the way.

7. The Church cheats its members if it gives them only a partial view of Christian responsibility. It is possible for a person to be a "Bible-believing, born-again, spirit-filled Christian" on one side only—"Ephraim is a cake not turned." There can be people who are wonderful Christians in all their personal affairs and complete heathens in their social attitudes and business policies. It is a state for which their churches bear a heavy blame.

As children, we first learn about Christianity in purely personal terms. We are taught to love Jesus, to say our prayers, to be kind and truthful, and to mind our parents. We hear little or nothing in these early years about being Christian citizens or feeling guilty because of slums. So if our Christian indoctrination finishes in the early teens, we may never be told why the Church is interested in penal institutions or unemployment. Then later, if some church tries to put such matters before us, we will wonder why it has forsaken its religious function. Churches must labor to introduce both children and adults to the part of Christianity they are most likely to miss.

All our lives we are inclined to slight this part. We love most to think about what Jesus offers us—abundant life, joy, peace, the sense of God's presence. It would be good to hear sermons every Sunday on the promises, because they are true. We may not love as much to think about the demands Jesus lays on our consciences. Trying to bring a kinder social order may cost us evenings at home, money, and the privileged status we enjoy. We are constantly inclined to do our growing in that part of

Christianity we most like to think about. Ministers have to preach on Christian social concerns in order to resist the tendency of every Christian to drift away from them.

8. The citizens of a democracy are in charge of the morals of their government. They elect their government, and by their conversations, political activities, and any offices they hold, they share in determining what it does. They are entitled to their church's help as they try to know the will of Christ in the vastly puzzling and important matters they must decide. The Church cannot give them their conclusions, but it can give them light from the Bible and from the best Christian minds of all ages. It can give them the company of earnest Christian friends, who will share their search for what is right.

9. The preacher helps his congregation with the personal social decisions they must make. A union member, a member of a school board, or a corporation officer does not expect his church to solve his problems, but he should expect to get from his church something that will help him solve them, and something closer to the situation than vague abstractions. If the church is too timid in dealing with the religious questions raised by a war, it leaves its members troubled and confused because we all are participants. Its young men should not have to face what may be the hardest religious decision of their lives with no help from the place to which they look for religious guidance. Christian young men may have to go through the struggle of conscience by themselves. If they try to discuss their thinking with their families, their friends, or their draft boards, they may be no more understood than if they talked Swahili, if the churches have given people no basis for understanding. The Church has the records of the best thinking on this subject by Christians of the past and of our time, but it has tended to put these on a back shelf where they will raise no questions, rather than to make them available to those who need them.

10. Preachers are not experts on most public questions, but they have had special training and special study in the understanding of the Bible and of Christian thought. This is what they have to contribute in matters of social morality and this, for Christians, is important. A preacher who would say, "I assure you, on the basis of my investigation, that the policies of the Department of the Interior are impractical" would misunderstand his role. But a preacher who says, "The policies of the Department of the Interior raise some serious questions for those who believe in a just and compassionate God" is doing what preachers are supposed to do.

SOCIAL ACTION

Churches must be instruments for social change because an institution has to be confronted by an institution. If a doctor thinks a government policy is bad for the nation's health, he does not content himself with urging his views in private; he tries to get the medical association to act. If someone becomes alarmed over the danger to the redwood trees, there is not much he can do by talking about it or writing letters; he tries to get some organization to take up the cause, or he forms a "Save the Redwoods" association. If an individual Christian is worried about what is happening in the country, he looks for a Spiritual Public Health Association or a Save the People Society; in other words, he looks for a church. He needs an organization to make his efforts effective.

As World War I came on, Henry Ford decided to devote some of his vast resources to preventing it. He fitted out a Peace Ship, which was to visit the European countries and persuade them not to fight. A magazine cartoon showed what happened. An awful juggernaut of war was grinding ahead, crushing bodies beneath its tracks; hitched against it at the back was a comic little Model-T Ford, with Henry at the wheel, trying to pull the monster to a stop. Not even the world's first billionaire, as an individual, could do much with governments. If Christians are to have much effect on government, or business, or on any of the structures that dominate our lives, they have to join with those who share their views, and the Church is their normal association.

The pulpit is responsible not only for helping the members of the congregation to come at social problems from a Christian point of view but also for making the Church as an organization an agency for social healing. Preaching can summon the Church to its social tasks.

1. The Church's first task is simply to put more people into society through whom Christ can minister. Evangelism is social action. The reason there is not more justice, honesty, and mercy in the world today is that there are not enough people in the world who deeply believe in justice, honesty, and mercy. Our whole hope, as we face a threatening future, is not in better social structures, but in better people. The finest government would collapse if its people were incorrigibly wicked. Any chance for a free, just, and stable society depends on the very sort of character that Jesus Christ imparts.

Christ is still physically present on the earth, not through the body by which he ministered in Palestine, but through the bodies of his followers. "Now you are Christ's body, and each of you a limb or organ of it." (I Cor. 12:27 NEB) The Church wants to have Christ physically present on as many scenes as possible—in banks, homes, and stores, writing editorials, working on committees, turning voting levers. Numbers are important because Christ ministers through his followers, and that healing, loving, change making ministry is needed above all. It is possible for people to be brought to the formulas of faith with no sense of social responsibility, but no one can truly become a follower of Jesus Christ without becoming a saving factor in society.

2. The Church as an organization gets into social action by serving as a training school for Christian citizens. In this the preaching has a major part. Church members can be helped to make their Christian faith decisive in their political opinions and in their choices on election day. They can be shown that political party activity may be a Christian vocation.

3. The Church is a social agency. Public agencies have taken over many services that were once largely cared for by the churches, but not all of them. Many congregations have their own programs for helping the poor, the aged, the ill, the victims of drugs and alcohol, the illiterate. They work in housing, health, and recreation.

4. Raising money is a form of social action. The church collects the funds that provide for homes, hospitals, community centers, denominational social action agencies, assistance to the victims of injustice.

5. Preaching can be direct social action; many important social reforms have started in the pulpits. Ministers have pointed to shameful conditions in penitentiaries, schools, mental hospitals, and courts. God still calls his preachers to sound the trumpet when they see a wrong.

6. Others than preachers may sound the warning call. Declarations by church groups are an important way for an institution to confront an institution. If we believe in freedom, we cannot deny the right of a Bible class or a national assembly to state its views. If it is a church group, some matter of Christian faith and righteousness should be at issue. The statement should tell who has made it, and claim no more. There should be a practical chance for the statement to do some good, and there should be reason to think that the opinions of those who made it are worth hearing. When these conditions are met, declarations by church bodies can be impressive testimony.

Sometimes the Church is forced to speak by those who claim divine sanction for their policies. Christian ministers in South Africa declared in an open letter to the country: "As long as attempts are made to justify a policy of apartheid by an appeal to God's word, . . . as long as it is alleged that application of this policy conforms to norms of Christian ethics, we will persist in denying its validity."

7. A church by its own life can demonstrate the social ideals it proclaims. When it shows how people of different temperaments, races, and backgrounds can be a loving fellowship, it is giving the world a pattern for peace. The way it treats custodians and secretaries, and all its business dealings, can reveal a just economy. The way it divides its money between itself and all the great needs outside itself can illustrate what it teaches about a fair division of the earth's resources.

The minister who longs to take up the cause of the hungry, the defrauded, and the oppressed has an incomparable chance. He is called to make known the way out of our morass that Christ revealed. Sermons can show people what they have to do to decrease the massive wrongs and to increase the sort of life a loving God wants his children to enjoy together. If your indignation and compassion impel you into social activism, be thankful God has let you be a preacher.

XXIV

Preaching
on
Personal Problems

Jesus came to earth to enable human beings to live in love with God, with each other, and with themselves. He came to open up beautiful, rich possibilities of living that had been unglimpsed before. Jesus saw man's frustration and lovelessness, his enmity, worry and feverish materialism. He saw people who were disappointed in themselves, harried by memories they could not change, ashamed of habits they could not break. He saw minds that were battlefields of clashing impulses and crossed-up emotions. He saw people who were lost, with the terrible lostness of those who have lost their enthusiasm, and lost their purpose in living, and lost their sense of God, and lost their way.

To such a humanity Jesus came with the promise "I came that they may have life, and have it abundantly." He offered to deliver people from sad, distraught, colorless existence and to set them free within the inexhaustible delights of the Kingdom of God. This is the good news preachers are ordained to preach; this is the Kingdom into which they are to bring their congregations. This Kingdom is a new state of minds and hearts. It is the new world of those who have accepted the truth that there is a God of love who knows and cares. Our continuing text must be, "Let this mind be in you, which was also in Christ Jesus." (Phil. 2:5 KJV)

This new mentality and new existence is what the messengers of Christ proclaimed as they spread across the earth. They believed that Jesus died to open up new life for men, and that he rose from death as evidence of the victory he gives over the worst the world can do to them. Paul could list calamities that were very actual for him—tribulation, persecution, jailings, beatings, hunger, toil—and testify from his own experience, "In all these things we are more than conquerors through him who loved us." He gave an assurance that Christians in all ages since have treasured because it is so gloriously true: "I can do all things in him who strengthens me." His whole bearing to life makes his troubles count for nothing in the light of his great happiness. That is the message we have for the people in the pews, and we try to show how it works out for the mechanic or the parent, at a funeral or dinner party, on the way to an operation or to an employment interview.

We can trace the progress of that message across the centuries by vignettes which reveal what was happening to countless millions. The worst martyrdom the Romans had for Christians was not death in the arena but labor in the mines. Under the scourge they rowed the galleys to Africa and trekked through scorching mountains to the Numidian mines. There their chains were shortened so they could never stand upright. Brands were burned into their foreheads. An eye might be gouged out to discourage thought of escape. Each was given a lamp and a hammer and whipped underground, never to see daylight again. Their keepers lashed and killed for sport. The lucky died of fever, but many lived on and on. Louis Bertrand, in *Sanguis Martyrum,* describes the messages they wrote with charcoal on the rocks—many of them prayers. One word appears again and again, scrawled in long black lines, "like a flight of swallows chasing one another toward the light"; the word is *vita, vita, vita.* These Christians were expressing their unconquerable faith in life, as they had found it in Jesus Christ.

In the third century, Cyprian, who was later martyred, describes in a letter how peaceful the world appears from his garden, but how dreadful it would look if one could see the robbers, pirates, wars, riots, murders, misery, despair. "It is a bad world, Donatus, an incredibly bad world. But I have discovered in the midst of it a quiet and holy people who have learned a great secret. They have found a joy that is a thousand times better than any pleasure of our sinful life. They are despised and persecuted, but they care not. They are masters of their souls. They have overcome the world. These people, Donatus, are the Christians—and I am one of them." Clement of Alexandria put it all in a lovely tribute to Jesus: "He has turned all our sunsets into sunrise."

This ability to transform the world by the special Christian slant did not play out with the early enthusiasm of the Church. Horace Bushnell in the last century wrote, "I have learned more experimental religion since my little boy died than in all my life before that happened. God is more real to me because of that sorrow." When Robert Louis Stevenson was dying of tuberculosis in Samoa, he received a note from a clergyman asking if he would like a minister to talk to him "as to one in danger of dying." Stevenson declined, but he said he would be glad to have the minister talk to him "as to one in danger of living." Kaj Munk, a Danish pastor who was executed by the Nazis, said in his last moments, "So mighty is the Almighty that he takes the curse in his hand and presses it, till drops of blessing stream from it. This is the very fact that creates hope."

During the Korean War, Pastor Im Han Sang was jailed and tortured by the Communists, but he refused to compromise his loyalty to Christ. When the Reds fled before the American advance, Im joyfully left the jail and started home to his family. He was picked up by American soldiers who thought the ragged, wild-looking minister was an enemy fugitive, and imprisoned him. In his bitterness he asked, "How can God permit this? Does he care? What possible good can there be from this?"

Then he thought of the verse, "What I am doing you do not know now, but afterward you will understand." He devoted himself to a ministry to his fellow prisoners, with comfort, prayer, and Bible study. Harold Voelkel, who reported it, described the great good this did in the prison and the hospital, and the many lives that were changed.

D. T. Niles told of a disaster to a village in India. Violent rains had melted most of the huts, and the whole village was a horrible expanse of muck. The pastor, who had come to comfort, wondered what to say. It seemed a mockery to tell the miserable people that God still cared for them. He went hesitantly to an old woman, who was huddled with her family by the ruin of their home, and said, "Amma! You all seem to be in much trouble here." "Yes, yes," she answered, "and but for Jesu Swammy [the Lord Jesus], we should not be able to bear it." (*That They May Have Life*, p. 65.)

THE PROBLEMS

The knowledge of what the Christian faith has done to transform harsh realities, to heal sick souls, to bring strength, peace, and joy, supports the preacher. Two things are necessary for him: a sympathetic sense of his people's needs and a lively perception of what the gospel can do for them. A minister was quoted as saying that he does not do much preaching on personal problems because he is not interested in spooning soothing syrup into neurotics. In a church I know well, here are some of the people he could expect to see. There is a young woman who left her baby in the bathtub while she answered the phone; the baby turned on the hot water and died two days later from being scalded. In the choir is the couple whose sixteen-year-old son is a blind mongoloid who has been in an expensive institution since early childhood. In the church is a woman who said, speaking of her husband, "We've been disenchanted with each other for years." There is the football coach who has been told that his contract will not be renewed, and the older couple who have been forced by poor health and poor finances to live with their unwilling son and his wife, and the young man who impresses each new boss with his attractive qualities and is always out of work within a year. We could go on and find problems like those in almost every pew. The preacher knows that he has been entrusted with what those people are needing above all. He can help the weak and unstable hold together; he can offer help to those caught in terrific stresses and adversities.

Many of the problems with which the minister can help have to do with bad relationships: (1) There are bad relationships with others— enmity, anger, resentment, failure to forgive, obsessive prejudices, aggression, resentment of authority, shyness. (2) There are bad relationships with oneself—guilt, shame, inferiority, self-rejection, pessimism, self-punishment, lack of confidence. (3) There are bad relationships with the world—fear, despair, unrealistic hopes, dread of impersonal structures. (4) There are bad relationships with God—doubt, disbelief, dislike, fear, estrangement, no feeling. For these the minister has to offer the Gospels' teachings about reconciliation. The word "reconciliation" may have been used so much in the last decade or so that it has been worn as smooth as a faceless old coin; but the word contains the most practical necessities for daily living—forgiveness, love, trust, and repentance.

Not all the personal problems are those of weakness or disaster. Perhaps the most common problem of all is simply that of missing how great life might be. We grind along from day to day, working, eating, and sleeping, but only half alive. We do not love enough, or feel, or care, or enjoy ourselves enough. We are getting ready for an epitaph like "Born a human being, died a wholesale grocer." In total contrast is the wind-up of Habakkuk's prophesy. He has been looking at some pretty somber facts; then he suddenly concludes, "The Lord God is my strength, who makes my feet nimble as a hind's and sets me to range the heights." (Hab. 3:19 NEB) Picture that frisky deer, leaping, scampering, exulting along the hilltops, and you are seeing the life God intends for us.

Sermons can offer healing for sick attitudes. One of these is a morbid self-concern. Psychiatrists like Fritz Kunkel and Alfred Adler have declared that most personality illnesses and aberrations start with egocentricity. Jesus can reverse this and make the currents of our concern flow outward. He makes us want to love, to give, to serve.

Another sick attitude is the slant toward criticism. There are some people who are most aware of the faults in those around them, and there are others who are most inclined to see the virtues. Jesus' injunction, "Judge not," is the prescription for a healthy mind. Paul described the characteristic Christian slant when he said, "If there is any excellence, if there is anything worthy of praise, think about these things."

Some people think most about what has gone wrong. Feeling sorry for oneself is a characteristic attitude. A church service should make people most aware of what is good. It tilts minds toward gratitude.

The fear and dislike of those who are different is a quality of sick minds. It is the source of endless evil. It sets the sales and production people against each other, the flat nosed against the hook nosed, liberals against conservatives. Jesus' delight in the company of publicans, sinners, and aliens, his emphasis on caring for strangers, and Paul's scorn of barriers show the way to mental health.

Caring more for things than for people is the sickness of a materialistic age. "God created persons to be loved and things to be used." When we reverse this, we are misinterpreting the way life was designed to operate. The preaching of the gospel gets at this disorder.

To praise Jesus as a master therapist would do him no honor. His purpose was to relate human beings to eternal Reality. But this would be expected to be therapeutic; it brings people into harmony with the way things are. Dr. James T. Fisher, one of the country's foremost psychiatrists, in a popular summary of his experience, wrote, "If you were to take the sum total of all the authoritative articles ever written by the most qualified of psychologists and psychiatrists on the subject of mental hygiene, if you were to combine them and refine them and leave out the excess verbiage, if you were to take the whole of the meat and none of the parsley, and if you were to have these unadulterated bits of pure scientific knowledge concisely expressed by the most capable of living poets, you would have an awkward and incomplete summation of the Sermon on the Mount." *(A Few Buttons Missing.)*

As you glance through the Sermon on the Mount you see that it refers to at least two dozen of the common personality and emotional disorders, such as—distintegration, melancholia, hostility, anxiety, and aggression. Consider, for example, what the Sermon says about enmity. We might wonder why Jesus and the Psalms talk so much about enemies. Most of us could say we do not have an enemy in the world and, in the sense that there is not one we expect to insult us on the street, we probably do not. But we have tradesmen who defraud us, strangers who raise our gorge by their comments on our driving, and people in our homes or businesses with whom we find it difficult to get along. There are old resentments that still poison us. We are all in the midst of difficult relationships that can, if badly handled, damage our emotions and our health.

A young man in our church told me about his overbearing office manager. Every time his human dignity was offended by this man, into his mind was poured another vial of hate. He could not sleep, his nerves were on edge, he was losing weight, his work was impaired. Clearly, the commandment to forgive enemies was not for the benefit of the office manager, but of the young man.

The immediate application of much of the Sermon on the Mount is right in our own homes—in the relationship of husbands and wives, parents and children. Preaching on marriage needs to impress strongly what the Sermon on the Mount says about meekness, peacemakers, anger, insults, trying to worship during an estrangement, retaliation, turning the other cheek, judging, forgiveness. Those are urgent domestic matters. A friend told me that the secret of his very happy marriage is being able to admit he is wrong when he knows quite well he is right. On the face of it that seems like a plain untruth; but those we live with need love most when they deserve it least. Jesus gave the example of a loving God who sends his rain on the just and on the unjust. By that he offers us a way of escape from those vicious social circles two people can get trapped in, with neither knowing how to get out.

A preacher is not offering his congregation a fantasy world of theological constructions into which they can escape from their daily problems. The Christian solutions to personal problems are down-to-earth practicalities. Think of what the gospel has to say about disappointment, depression, pessimism, decisions, goals. To a person who is crushed by the loss of someone who is very dear, Jesus comes with his assurance that there are ties of love that even death can never break. To those who are discouraged because one door after another seems slammed against them comes the assurance that a God of love will never let all the doors to happiness be closed.

Obsessive fear, in all its ugly forms, can become a dreadful malady. As on an eroded hillside, a trickle of anxiety can start down some channel until it washes out a deep gully into which every thought and feeling has to drain. Martin Luther King wrote of the time when he was worn out by endless worry. Then there began, by letter and telephone, a mounting series of threats to him and to his family. He knew they were serious. One night, after an especially exhausting day, he had gone to bed when the phone rang and an angry voice promised violence soon. Dr. King got out of bed and walked the floor; he brewed coffee; with his courage almost gone he wondered how to quit. Then, at the kitchen table, he bowed his head on his hands and told God, "I am at the end of my powers, I have nothing left. I've come to the point where I can't face it alone." Then, "At that moment I experienced the presence of the Divine as I had never before experienced him. It seemed as though I could hear the quiet assurance of an inner voice. . . . Almost at once my fears began to pass from me. . . . God had given me inner calm." (*Strength to Love,* p. 107.) The preacher can confidently recommend faith and prayer to those who are crippled by fear because there is so much experience that confirms it.

When we preach about the sources of strength, we are not necessarily thinking of the feeble and tottering. It is not the weaklings in the Bible who give the most convincing demonstrations of God's help, it is Joshua, the dauntless general, and David, the giant-killer, and Paul, the hard-driving apostle. Those with cane and shawl do not need God's help nearly as much as does the vigorous battler in the thick of the struggle. The strongest and most heroic characters the world has ever known have been strong precisely because they found the sources of strength and greatly used them. That is the way we were designed to operate. There are certain winged insects that have no mouths and no digestive systems. They live until they use up the vitality they were born with, then they die. Human beings are intended to draw in strength as they use it up. So the minister tells his congregation where strength is to be found. Prayer and the sense of God's presence keep our reservoirs filled from a source outside ourselves. We do not offer "cleverly devised myths" when we talk about the divine reinforcement. "He restoreth my soul" is literally true.

The minister can tell about the attitudes that increase our strength. A burden is lighter when it is cheerfully borne; but self-pity, fear, boredom, guilt, and worry make a load heavier. When our faith removes these, it increases what we can carry. John Wesley's biographer reviewed his seemingly incredible exertions and concluded, "Wesley's career is a striking proof of the fact that work without worry never kills."

WHAT THE MINISTER DOES

A minister performs the same function in his private counseling and in the pulpit. Each depends upon the other. What he learns in face-to-face contacts brings reality into his sermons; what he says in sermons supports his counseling. If a minister's sermons show understanding, people will come to him for private help. The chaplain of a mental hospital, who is also a trained therapist, says that his most important service to the patients is his preaching. This lets the patients know who and what he is. When he sees them in private, they already feel a connection with him and understand his point of view.

Every church service should be a healing service. Worship can be medicine. Participation in a fellowship of singing, praying believers, the symbols, the suggestions of health and happiness, can lift people out of their unhealthy states. This meets directly such problems as loneliness, anxiety, a lost sense of God, a colorless daily routine. A church service can be group therapy. Many churches also find great benefit in special healing services.

A church service is intended to be preventive medicine. It can keep people built up so that healing is not necessary. By and large, the people who come regularly to church are a tough crowd; what they can endure often seems beyond belief. People with small inner resources may go all to pieces if they mislay a pencil; those who have been "strengthened with might through his Spirit in the inner man" may lose all the things they count on most and still come through smiling and triumphant.

It is a minister's incomparable good fortune to have very definite ways by which his sermons can help people with their personal problems.

1. He can preach the great supportive truths on which all of life depends. Strong doctrinal preaching is the basic therapy. It can integrate a personality, keep spirits high, and give life a meaning.

2. Sermons can implant in minds the brief, memorable assurances that are needed when things get difficult. Phrases from creeds, hymns, and the Bible can be a strong support—". . . and the life everlasting," "For I will be with thee, thy troubles to bless, and sanctify to thee thy deepest distress," "Underneath are the everlasting arms." It is not the rote learning of these that helps, it is having them interpreted, filled with meaning, and used repeatedly. A student told me that when he was going through the most severe crisis of his life, the words kept running through his mind, "for thou art with me."

3. Sermons can help people recognize their problems. When a minister explains that long-continued grief may be an indulgence, that overwork may be self-punishment, that being shocked may reveal envy, that total recall of a mate's mistakes may come from guilt, people may be helped to understand themselves. They may see their self-deceptions.

4. Sermons can give good counsel with the problems people face. They can be helped with family relationships, teenage problems, understanding alcoholics, the choice of vocation, sensitivity, shyness, worry, disappointment. A minister could not count on treating the mentally ill by sermons, but he can give great help with the normal problems of the members of the congregation. He can count on modern insights as well as on the wisdom Christians have long been acquiring. The min-

ister, both for his preaching and his pastoral care, needs clinical experience and study in psychotherapy; he needs to try to keep up by courses and reading in these subjects. Few preachers have the opportunity to become qualified professionals in therapy. The preacher stands between the professionals and the congregation. He has more chance for study and experience than most laymen do, but he must beware of sounding more authoritative than he is. Much of his knowledge will have to come from the popularizers, not from the technicians. But at this level, supplemented by all the resources of the Christian faith, his sermons can do a great deal of good. If his study and experience have given him any sort of qualifications, he will be the only trained advisor most of the people in the congregation ever hear.

5. People see themselves through others. True stories are valuable in preaching on personal problems. Testimonies are impressive. A minister's best source of true accounts will be his own pastoral experiences. These can be used if the cautions are observed that were mentioned in Chapters XVII and XVIII. Never make the stories better than they are. Never present fiction as truth. Never use an illustration that makes you look impressive. When you tell a story from your ministry, people will wonder whether you would betray a confidence, so make it clear that what they tell you will never, even in a well-disguised form, be used in a sermon in their church.

6. The preacher's greatest assurance as he tries to help people with their problems is that the Bible's promises are true. It is not a matter just of techniques and therapies, of good mental habits and affirmative thinking. Those are important, but beyond them is the fact of God. Prayer is not a method we use on ourselves, it is a contact with a strength and wisdom that comes to us from across the border of ourselves. Christ does strengthen us; the Holy Spirit exists. It is not changed circumstances but the transformation of ourselves that makes the difference.

There is no human accounting for the way people of faith react from blows that should be crushing. A priest who had been for many years at the healing shrine at Lourdes was asked by an interviewer, "What is the greatest miracle you have ever seen in your long time here?" The priest answered, "The look on the faces of those who found they were not going to get well." It is such evidence that lets us preach with the full assurance of God's help.

HAZARDS

Ministers who preach well on personal problems are tempted to make that their rut. They are egged on in this by their congregations. Such problems are a large part of everyone's life, and people are vocally grateful for any real help they get. A preacher cannot be as sure that his other sorts of sermons are doing that much good. During a period when I regularly passed the church of a well-known minister, I noticed the sermon topics. They were all on the general theme of how to be happy though human—"Why People Do Not Like You," "When You Have the Blues," "Jesus' Gift of Affirmation." The sermons and books of such a preacher may give many people what they need and want. This specialty is likely to distinguish laymen's preachers from preachers' preachers. It could be said of a noted leader in this field that no one likes him but the people; you rarely hear a good word about him from a minister, or a criticism from a layman. But preaching only on mental and emotional difficulties deprives the congregation of the other essentials. It throws away the rest of the gospel.

Preaching on personal problems is often superficial. Such preaching offers easy grace; it emphasizes self-help and autosuggestion. The techniques it proposes are definite and easy to grasp, but they do not get to the deep sources of personality difficulties. Such preaching may talk much of Jesus Christ, but it presents him as a Dale Carnegie in robe and sandals.

Sermons on successful living easily miss the line between the satisfactions of the life in Christ and the payoff. The proffered rewards may be materialistic. The advertisement of a book of sermons in my church magazine said, "These methods will bring you greater success in business, a happier marriage, improved physical and mental health, larger earnings, a better chance for advancement. We stand ready to back up that statement with this generous guarantee . . ." A former student of Professor Julius Beber sent him a sermon of which he was proud. Its title was "Religion Pays Handsome Dividends." Dr. Beber's comment was brief: "Do you know who first said that? See Job 1:9." That verse says, "Then Satan answered the Lord, 'Does Job fear God for nought?'"

The wrong sort of peace may be what is offered. Jesus promised peace, but also conflict: "I have not come to bring peace, but a sword. For I have come to set a man against his father." (Mt. 10:34–35) To be well-adjusted in a sinful world is wrong. Christians are supposed to be crossed up with many things. The gospel's call is not "Relax." John Stuart Mill said, "All human progress has been due to discontented characters."

But with all the dangers to which sermons on personal problems are exposed, they are still one of the most needed sorts of preaching. The mistrust of them can be misleading. Jesus often promised peace, and peace of mind is one of the most cherished gifts of the Christian faith— "The peace of God, which passes all understanding, will keep your hearts and your minds in Christ Jesus." (Phil. 4:7) Christian peace is not placidity, it is the peace of great forces in perfect harmony. At Boulder Dam, the guide balances a nickel on edge on the housing of a dynamo that is turning at full speed, generating enough current to run a city.

Jesus delivers us from the inner conflict that can make our breasts battlefields of warring desires. Ambitions, appetites, and ideals can be pulling off in different directions. Home, business, and pleasure can be in jangling discord. We are Jekyll and Hyde. Dr. Alfred Adler gave a two-word definition of a neurosis—"Yes, but—" We can see ourselves in the demoniac who was torn by a legion of devils. We can also understand the man of whom it was said, "He was just beside himself, and they both looked dreadful." It is to those in this condition that Jesus says, "Peace I leave with you. . . . Let not your hearts be troubled." (Jn. 14:27) He can pull our clashing selves together around the great loyalties and purposes he gives. He can end the inner struggles that keep us distraught and weak. He can conserve our wasted power as he gives us his peace.

Preaching on personal problems is important because a minister of Jesus Christ has so much help to give. A review of a book by Harold Blake Walker suggested that he seemed to want to replace the pews in his church with psychiatrists' couches. His reply was, "No, I'm trying to replace psychiatrists' couches with pews."

XXV

Preaching
on the
Christian Disciplines

A church is a school of Christian living, and the preacher does a great deal of the teaching. There are skills for Christians. There are practices that make spirits strong. There are habits by which great living is sustained. All religions that powerfully affect the lives of their adherents have definite rules for the practice of their faith. These are the ways by which the faith is joined to daily living. A Moslem who is powerfully affected by the Koran is likely to be one who faithfully observes the rules for prayers, fasts, and shrines. The Jewish law gave detailed prescriptions for feasts, holy days, and Kosher observances; when the Jews kept the law, the law kept the Jews. Protestant Christianity in our generation has taken the great risk of proposing little and requiring nothing. Leaving each Christian free to find the ways that are best could be a source of strength, but wherever this turns out to be freedom to have no practices at all, Protestant Christianity will disappear. There must be definite ways by which our characters are molded, our conduct influenced, and our spirits sustained. Weak Christians are the best that can be expected from weak observances. Disciplines make disciples.

A preacher's task is vastly more difficult than a mullah's. It would be much easier if a minister could give a set of rules and say, "Our Lord requires these. He tells you what you can eat, and when, where, and how to pray. Keep these laws and they will bless you. Break them, and you will be an outcast from our faith." That would also relieve the members of the strain of self-direction. A young engineer who left our church told me, "Your church says, 'We hope you will not drink too much; whatever you want to give is between you and God.' My new church says, 'Drink and you are out; ten percent of your income is required.' I like a church that believes in itself." A minister, unlike a mullah, has to propose a wide variety of possibilities, and the members have to compel themselves to try some of them.

We are not without clear guides. Even among free Protestants, some powerful traditions have grown up. These preserve what Christians across the years have discovered bring the greatest blessings. The early Methodists spoke of "holy habits." The word "disciplines" is a good one; it is a strong word that saves us from our flighty impulses. "Discipline" means that we pray when our whole souls are yearning up to God; and we pray, or grimly try to, when every thought and feeling seem chained to the world. It means that we do our devotional reading when it fascinates us; and we do it when we have to drag our attention by sheer strength from one sentence to the next. It means that we go to church when our souls are singing with the Psalmist, "How lovely is thy dwelling place, O Lord of hosts!" and we go when we cannot think of a single adequate reason for going. It means that we have a family blessing at the table when the feeling is loving and unhurried; and we have it when everyone is impatient and out of sorts. A soul is not a rigid thing, it is alive. It can shrivel or grow strong. The Bible, and centuries of Christian experience, have shown us some of the disciplines that make souls strong. Disciplines take religion from the marginal area of optional pastimes and put it as solidly into our lives as eating, sleeping, or working.

1. *Private prayer.* Prayer is the breath of life for Christians. Jesus described God as a Father who loves us, knows us individually, and wants to be in communication with us. To exist with such a God and not to talk with him would be as unnatural as living in a house with someone and pretending to be alone. As Christians we have gone beyond the stages where we think of God as *It* or *He* to where we know him as *You.* Our spirits were designed to be sustained and replenished directly from God. Apart from him we are cut off from our source, our living is contrary to nature.

The enjoyment of a sunset or an act of loving service may well be called "prayer" by those who like that use of the word. But those who pray only in these less definite ways will miss the great reality.

In the material world, prayer does seem strange. It is so different from our other activities that it appears to be unusual, like walking on our hands. As spiritual beings in a material world we are amphibians. It must seem unnatural to a fish for a man to be down under water and still breathing air, but it is not unnatural for the man; he is designed to operate that way. If only one person prayed, it would seem so preposterous we would be sure he was insane. But when we observe that millions of the most clear-minded and rational people in every generation have prayed, we cannot dismiss it as an aberration. Plato, who was intelligent, declared that anyone who has any wisdom at all will call upon God before he takes up a task. Many of today's most clear-thinking philosophers, statesmen, authors, and scientists agree with Plato.

Every human being can pray. It is the only fine art in which everyone can be an artist, though the talent may remain childish and undeveloped. For earth-dwellers, there will always be a baffling sense of unreality in talking to someone who does not appear to be there. Anyone who talks on television has the same difficulty. In the midst of smiling, gesturing, and earnestly talking to a piece of glass there can be an almost overwhelming feeling of doing something ridiculous. The television speaker has to have a powerful imagination, not to deceive himself, but to apprehend the reality.

The preacher's first task is to persuade people that prayer is possible. He has to get them past that sense of unreality and to the consciousness that the communication with God actually takes place. The natural assumption for many in our society is that prayer belongs to the child-hood of the race, or that it is a useful form of self-suggestion for those who need it. The minister can use testimonies. He can show, from Christian philosophy, that enlightened modern thinkers can reasonably be-lieve in the possibility of prayer. But this is like using arguments from physics to show that swimming is possible. The minister's best hope of persuading people that prayer is real is to get them to try it.

Christians at all levels of their maturity need help in praying. We are all born with the ability to pray, but we have to learn to do it better. We are all born with the ability to communicate with people, but in school and afterward we spend a great deal of time improving our ability to do it. Prayer can stay trivial; it can go dead; it may be selfish or super-stitious. Even at its finest it will still be too limited to receive the full flood of God's love.

In all prayer there is something wonderful and something missing. Even after the finest prayer there is still the baffling sense of incom-pleteness; we remain encumbered by the earth. There is a discouragement in the fact that our prayers are never exactly like the prayers we hear about. No two people have the same experience. We can learn from others, but we cannot expect to get from prayer just what they do. There is a problem in that our "I-thou" relationship takes place inside us, so that when our spirits meet God we are never sure of the boundary between them. The 'other' is truly other, but the encounter is so deep within that it is hard to be sure who is who.

For all these reasons, a congregation counts on sermons to help them with their praying. The disciples came to Jesus and begged, "Lord, teach us to pray." The members of the church look to their minister with that same great need. Jesus gave specific advice about the occasions for prayer, and the place, and what to pray about, and what to avoid. He gave a model prayer. Preachers have to pass on the best of Christian thought about the skills of prayer. People need to learn ways of getting into the state of mind for prayer. They need advice about the regular and special times and the external conditions that may be helpful. They need sug-gestions on what to talk to God about, and how to listen to God, and what results to expect, and how to keep their minds from wandering. Prayer sequences can be proposed—the collect form or such a path as: adoration, confession, thanksgiving, petition, intercession, dedication. People need help with the many baffling questions about prayer. They need to hear about faith-healing, and the connection between prayer and health. They need counsel about their times of spiritual dryness. When Jesus told the disciples "that they ought always to pray and not to lose heart," he was recognizing that there are difficulties and discouragements. The church service should often be a school of prayer, and the minister needs to learn so he can teach.

2. *Group prayer.* Midway between private prayer and public worship is a third sort of prayer Christians need. It is found in the devotional intimacy of small groups. The old-fashioned prayer meeting, the new-fashioned koinonia groups, and family worship are familiar forms. The glow that kindles from heart to heart in such a fellowship can restore the sense of God when other sorts of prayer go cold. Many people have first discovered the reality of prayer not in solitude, or with the congregation, but by sharing the adventure with one or two others who help make it real. There is the sense of being together and carrying each other along as they come close to God.

It is strange that this is the form of prayer that congregations are most likely to neglect. They encourage private prayer and public worship but have much less to say about prayer in intimate groups. This sort of prayer was of great importance in the ministry of Jesus and in the early Church. It has been at the heart of every upsurge of spiritual renewal across the centuries. Its neglect by many congregations is allied to their failure to have any way by which members can be known as they really are. They may participate in discussions of topics, but they do not talk about themselves. The things that are most on the hearts of many members cannot be mentioned at the church. The Church was intended to be a loving fellowship, where Christians can be open to each other and support each other. We sing "We share our mutual woes, our mutual burdens bear," but we do not make provision for it.

It is not a problem just of large churches. Often the small churches are the coldest, while large churches work harder to provide for spiritual fellowship. Ministers who try to arrange for it can report an unpredictable record of success and failure. Plans that seem just right often bring disappointment, while a warm and vital fellowship will appear where it was not expected. Churches may offer devotional experiences through neighborhood meetings, house churches, groups for prayer and Bible study, special-interest groups which give prayer a large part in their meetings, family camps, retreats, women's devotional meetings, men's Lenten breakfasts, meetings of people in the same profession. The "relational" style in church life offers possibilities. Whatever is done will need help from the pulpit.

The first devotional comradeship for the Christian is the family. Homes are intended by God to be subchurches, shrines where he is known and worshipped. A family is a fellowship in Christ. The old-fashioned family altar may be out of date, but it is available in many contemporary styles. In many homes the only time the family can be assembled is at meal time. Elton Trueblood says, "The table is really the family altar! Here those of all ages come together and help to sustain both their physical and their spiritual existence. . . . A meal together can be a spiritual and regenerating experience." Family worship at the table can be a memorized prayer, a free prayer, or several prayers. There can be a Bible reading or reading from another book and conversation about it. Advent, Christmas, Easter, and birthdays are good times for family worship.

Christian homes count on sermons for much of their inspiration and help. This has always been one of the preacher's most important themes. He can renew the great vision of the glory Christianity gives to homes. The Bible shows us how necessary it is to talk to congregations about marriage, about the responsibilities of parents and children, and about spiritual nurture in the home. Sermons can stir consciences and tell of methods.

3. *Public worship.* The Christians in Rome could have saved themselves by saying their prayers in private; it was when they came together that they were caught. But they assembled for worship because they had no choice. They had to have this experience of being the Church of the living Christ. When the Scottish Covenanters were being hunted down and killed, they still took the awful risk of Sunday meetings. They assembled in hidden glens, preferably where there were waterfalls whose noise would cover the sound of hymns. A religion whose theme is love cannot be fully experienced apart from company.

The weekly assembly for worship has always been regarded by the Church as divinely ordained. The thought of God could grow dim if it were not regularly renewed. All week long, material concerns clutter our minds; they tend to divert us from what it is that makes us human beings. The Man with the Hoe has a twin sister, the woman with the shopping list, and a twin brother, the man with the slide rule—"Who made him dead to rapture and despair, a thing that grieves not and that never hopes, stolid and stunned, a brother to the ox?" (*The Man with the Hoe,* Edwin Markham.) Regular public worship was established to keep souls in human beings, to keep believers close to each other and to God. What happens in church worship is a miracle; the succession of events could not account for it. When Christians keep their Sunday appointment with God, in a mysterious way he keeps his appointment with them. Even Martin Luther, with all his personal religious resources, admitted that "At home, in my house, there is no warmth or vigor in me, but in the church when the multitude is gathered together, a fire is kindled in my heart and it breaks its way through." The busier we are, the more we need this weekly pause for recovery and refreshment. The Sunday service is the pit stop in the race we run.

Ministers hesitate to promote an occasion in which so much of the time is used for listening to their voices. This modesty comes from the immodesty of thinking they are that important. The preacher is a transfer agent who is making the thoughts and prayers of many others available to the congregation; he is an instrument by which the Bible is transmitted; he is an enabler for people who come to have their own experiences with the Holy Spirit. He can with all good grace use his sermons to impress on people the importance of church attendance. It is up to the minister to explain what church worship is, and what it does.

4. *Church life.* From the beginning, Christian living has meant being

a part of the loving fellowship of believers. Those who attend church only as an audience attends a theater are missing many of the essentials for Christian health and growth. "We know that we have passed out of death into life, because we love the brethren." (I Jn. 3:14) The failure to make friends in the church is a chief reason for the appalling falling away from it. Members grow as Christians through classes, groups, and church work. The preacher tries to bring members into church participation not for the sake of activity, but so that they may build up one another in the Christian life.

5. *Serving.* In Dr. Fosdick's memorable expression, too many church people suffer from "a glut of unutilized grace." Rich eating with no exercise is deadly. All we get religiously may be damaging if we do not act on it. Christ calls us to serve him, and we never know him as we should until we get into his line of work.

We can serve through the church. It was never intended that the work of the church be done by professionals. Every Christian is called to be Christ's minister. Jerome gave the memorable expression, *"Sacerdotium laici id est baptisma"*—"baptism is the ordination of the laity." Everyone who is baptized has been ordained to the Christian ministry. The directory of a large church under "Staff" has the line, "This church has 3100 ministers who are trained by three clergymen." The *Golden Book,* the meditations of an anonymous Christian in the fourteenth century, has the beautiful saying, "I would fain be to the eternal God what a man's hand is to the man." A Christian should be able to look at his hands and think, "There is where the arms of God are ending, in me." A church that is not organized to use its members has two losses—its mission is not accomplished, and its members are spiritually starved. A church must also call its members to service for Christ that has no connection with the church's program.

The preacher is the one who can best bring church members into service. His sermons can stir in them a longing to be used where they are needed, and he can propose specific tasks to be done.

6. *Financial giving.* Stewardship is a means of grace. Jesus said, "Where your treasure is, there will your heart be also." We might have expected it to be the other way around, but it is the giving of the treasure that pulls the heart along. Every church has plenty of evidence of that. Those who give poorly are likely to get very little from the church. We want their treasure because we want their hearts. A preacher need not hesitate to tell where money is needed, or to give people a chance to express their dedication. This makes consecration real. Money is angelic; it is a messenger by which we can save lives or have the good news proclaimed anywhere on earth. Church members need to be shown the Christian attitude to money and to giving. Pleas for gifts to important causes offer people a way to make their lives significant. Sermons on giving can be great spiritual occasions for the church. In that moment when the pen is poised above the pledge card, a life-transforming decision may be in the balance.

7. *Bible reading.* Each Protestant has to know the Bible because it is his religious source—it is his authority. Two doctrines make it necessary for Protestants to read the Bible: The doctrine of *the priesthood of all believers* assures us that each Christian has his own access to God. No one can tell him what to believe. The doctrine of *the perspicuity of the Scriptures* means that each Christian can get God's truth directly from the Bible for himself. He does not have to have a church, a minister, or a theologian to tell him what the Bible says. The Holy Spirit is his interpreter. Second-hand knowledge will not do.

Everything we know about the elemental truths of our faith comes from the Bible. Only there do we find the record of God's acts for man's salvation, in Hebrew history and in the gospel. All we know of who Jesus is, and what he did and said, is in the words of the New Testament. We do not have a "paper pope," in the sense that we have to go thumbing through the Bible to find an infalible answer spelled out for every question; but we do have the Bible as the ultimate authority for our faith. Preachers and scholars can be helpful, but no one can supply the illumination each believer gets through direct contact with the word of God. If we come to a time when the average church member has little first-hand knowledge of the Bible, there will not be much vitality left in the Church.

One of the very important purposes of preaching is to increase the private reading of the Bible. The preacher has to recognize the difficulties that keep people from reading the Bible more. One of these is its permanent value. Temporary books and magazines are thrust on us by temporary excitements. You have to read this year's popular novel this year because by next year it will be of no interest. But the Bible is permanently so important that we can postpone looking at it. For most of us "sometime" is "never." The temporary always wins a contest with the timeless.

Some of the Bible is dull reading. A person who starts to read from Genesis through Revelation will lose interest halfway through Exodus and find little of immediate benefit for the next hundred chapters. That is why exhortations to read the Bible are not enough. Some reading plan should be proposed. A good start would be fifty great chapters. Beyond this the preacher might give a trail to follow—beginning with the Gospel of Luke, going on to the more pellucid Epistles, finishing the Gospels, turning back for Genesis and the Psalms, then circling on out to Acts, the harder Epistles, the Revelation, and the stirring passages from the prophets, until all the parts that are most important for the Christian have been reached. The American Bible Society offers reading plans, and a way of checking off what is read for those who like to skip around to whatever they find most interesting. A Christian needs to have read the whole Bible, but cover-to-cover is not the way to start.

The preacher has to deal with prejudices against the Bible. Most people who have not done much Bible reading expect it to be tiresome. They have heard the gossip about vengeful, offensive, absurd parts. They suspect that the Bible may be largely primitive Hebrew folklore. They know about the uncertainties with manuscripts and sources, and they wonder whether any of the Bible is authentic. The preacher can deal with these difficulties. He must teach a sound lay hermeneutics that will instill a reverence for the Bible and a longing for its riches. He can also trust the Bible to be its own defender. Anyone who is reading the thirteenth chapter of First Corinthians is not worrying about manuscripts. The Sermon on the Mount is clearly more than ancient folklore.

People need help. The preacher can propose books they ought to have —a one-volume commentary, a Bible dictionary, a concordance. He can give advice on what to look for, what sort of notes to make, when to find time for reading, and what edition to use. A church may offer a selection of Bibles for sale.

Sermons may be joined with private Bible reading. Before Lent a "penny-portion" edition of a Bible book might be mailed to each home, with a plan for reading that would go with the sermons during Lent. A list of suggested readings may be sent to church members in connection with a sermon series. Sermons which assume home reading must keep the connection close—"You may have wondered when you read this verse . . ." Bible classes and study groups can be coordinated with the preaching.

Sermons can arouse a love for the Bible and a longing to know more about it. They can keep it from seeming strange and remote. The preacher's love and enthusiasm for the Bible can be contagious. A sermon many will appreciate is a primer on the Bible, which tries to answer as many elementary questions as can be crowded in: What the words *Bible* and *Testament* mean, how chapter and verse divisions were made, the reason for the order of the books, the major groups of books, the authors, Hebrew and Greek, manuscript sources, translations, how the authors were inspired, the Apocrypha. With rapid-fire style a great deal can be said in one sermon.

All the reasons why an educated person must know the Bible can be stressed. It is the source of much of our civilization. Western art, literature, and politics cannot be understood without it. But most of all there must be impressed on people their own deep personal need for Bible knowledge.

If people are to "know the Bible," they must have a picture of the whole sweep of its sequence of books and sections. They must see God's purpose running through it. They need to know where to look for what they want to find. To know the Bible means to be familiar with the contents of the most important books and chapters. It also means to have absorbed the great words of the Bible until their faith has formed the pattern of our thinking and their cadences are in our inner rhythms.

8. *Sabbath observance.* One of the most important of all the Christian disciplines is Sabbath observance. It is established deep in our faith. God, the Creator, observed the day of rest. It is ordained by the Ten Commandments. The laws of Moses gave it much attention, and its transgres-

sion was one of the sins the prophets most condemned. Jesus observed the Sabbath, and ever since it has been a central source of strength for Christianity. The Christian faith has never been a powerful influence where the Sabbath was casually observed.

The most important guide for the Sabbath was Jesus' saying, "The Sabbath was made for man." This does not mean ". . . so it doesn't matter what you do." It means "God made the Sabbath for man, so it matters tremendously how you use it." It was not made for man at his most trivial, but at his highest. It is his day to be most fully human. It is not made for man as the housecleaner or the adding machine puncher, but for man as the child of God. If you are most completely yourself when you are lolling in a chair, watching the shadows of people who are using their brains and muscles flicker across the television screen, then that is the way for you to spend your Sundays.

Sunday is ordained as a day of rest. We cannot operate at our best without it. It is like the ancient City of Refuge, within which a fugitive could be safe from his pursuers. All week long your creditors, your teachers, your competitors may be hot upon your heels. But when Sunday morning dawns you wake up within a sheltering wall. The lines on your face can relax and your taut nerves can loosen as the cares which hounded you are shut away.

The Sabbath is our chance to repossess our souls in peace. For six days we are absorbed in things that we can see and touch, but on Sunday we are reminded that man does not live by bread alone. In our highly organized society we need to remember the irony of the Latin proverb, *"propter vitam vivendi perdere causas"*—"in the business of living to lose the reason for living." The Sabbath was made for man as God sees him, for the real and essential man in his grandeur and profundity, for the child of God and the candidate for heaven.

The Sabbath is the Lord's day. It is not the one holy day, but it is the one that makes all the others holy. It is the day when the rushing things that fill our lives can be pushed aside and we can have time for worship and for centering our thought on who God is, who we are, and what Christ does for us.

Sunday gives Christians a chance to get acquainted with the members of their families and to have leisurely conversations with their friends. It gives those whose weekdays are spent within walls a time to enjoy the healing beauty of the out-of-doors.

The Sabbath is a day for sheer delight. Those who picture the traditional Christian Sabbath as starched, prim, and boring have had no experience of it. The Sundays are the days many Christians remember as their happiest. When homework is forbidden, children get to read the things they want to read; when the father cannot go to work, he helps the children with their hobbies or joins the family orchestra.

Every rule for the observance of the Sabbath can be ridiculed as arbitrary—but if you have no rules, you have no Sabbath. There is nothing in the Bible or in logic that makes it all right to toss a ball on

Sunday but not to keep a score of misses, and all right to read Shakespeare for pleasure but not for an English class; but without some such distinctions there are no protective walls around the day. Unless there are some expected customs, Sundays get lost in shapeless disarray.

The traditions of the Church have weight, though they have to be updated to provide for new situations, such as those caused by urban living, modern transportation, and television. Though the ways of keeping the Sabbath cannot be imposed, they cannot be wholly individual. Without a general observance among people of the same faith, private practices would be very difficult. Sabbath customs are not private; they go back through history, and they are shared by Christians around the world. It is through the Church that the ways of keeping the Sabbath are agreed on and disseminated.

Many people have a weak sense of distinctions; they are indifferent to traditions; they are wary of any suggestion of legalism. The minister has these handicaps to overcome when he preaches on the Sabbath. But he has much more in his favor. He has the great reverence for the Sabbath in the Old and New Testaments, and all through Christian history. He has the record of how much the use of Sunday as a special day has done to make the gospel powerful in human life and in society. He has the compelling reasons why this day is especially needed in our time. The Sabbath is our precious birthright, and sermons can do much to preserve its blessings and its beauty for our generation.

XXVI

Special Occasions

There are occasions that require a sort of preaching that is different from the usual Sunday sermons.

I. FUNERALS

Funeral customs change. There was a time when American Protestant funerals almost always included a sermon. Then, early in this century, many ministers began to omit the "remarks." It was felt that a time of grief and strain was not suitable for preaching, and that eulogies tended to be fulsome and unnecessary. Young ministers were taught that all they needed for a funeral was in their Churches' prescribed liturgies. The much-loved Bible passages were trusted to be the perfect expression of the Christian faith and hope. Whatever more might need to be said in tribute to the person who had died and to comfort the distressed could be put into the prayer, which for many ministers was the only part of the service that was not taken from the service book.

But this also presents problems. For one thing, it uses an impersonal service for an occasion that ought to be very intimate and personal. There are many funerals which give no clue to whether the person who is being buried was young or old, male or female. To God and to those who grieve, that person was a very special and infinitely precious individual. To mark the close of that life with a standardized, all-purpose service does not seem adequate.

There is also the problem of discrimination. Ordinary people are allowed only a mass-produced service, but when the funeral is for someone deemed important, the mayor, a bishop, or any clergyman, even churches that are most insistent on their liturgies make prolonged additions to them.

Everything a congregation needs to hear cannot be thrust into the prayer. A prayer may rightly thank God for a person's virtues and accomplishments. It may beseech God for strength and comfort. When one talks to God in public, it is not wrong to think of the effect of the words on those on whose behalf they are said. But it is wrong to use the appearance of praying to say what could be intended only for human listeners.

A funeral sermon usually has to be shorter than a Sunday sermon. It may be less than half as long. People will listen intently for a little while, but some of them will be weary and emotionally distraught. They can be helped by a sermon that is clear, vivid, and succinct. They are not in the mood to settle back and follow the extended development of a sermon theme. If a funeral is too brief, it seems trivial; but when it goes on and on, it undoes the good it might have done.

A good way to say what needs to be said in a funeral is to bring it in as comment on the Scripture reading. When the minister has read, "He leads me beside the still waters; he restores my soul. He leads me in paths of righteousness for his name's sake," then something can be said about how beautifully this has been fulfilled in the life of the person they are thinking of. When he gets to the words "Surely goodness and mercy shall follow me all the days of my life; and I shall dwell in the house of the Lord for ever," the minister can pause again to point out the logic. The Psalmist is inferring the unknown from the known. He has known God's goodness and mercy in this world, so he extrapolates into the unknown world to get an understanding of what is ahead. When the minister comes to the soaring words of Paul, "Death is swallowed up in victory," he can speak of what it is that makes a life victorious. Several passages can be used in this way, or the minister may use only one passage and comment on it for several minutes, but still do it as a part of the Scripture reading, and not as a formal sermon.

A funeral can offer an unusually good opportunity to explain Christian truth and give help with human problems. People listen well. The occasion is unusual and they are wondering what the minister will say. He finds that the congregation is looking at him with more interest than he can expect on Sundays. Some of them may be longing for help—"Out of the depths I cry to thee, O Lord!" All are made thoughtful by confronting the stark inevitability of death for themselves and for those they love. They are ready to hear and consider what the Bible says about God, hope, and destiny.

A funeral gives a chance to proclaim the gospel to those whom a preacher does not reach at any other time. For most of his work, a minister is too much walled off in a religious enclave. Almost all of his contacts, in private and in public, are with convinced Christians. He knows he is called to bring the good news of Christ to those who have missed its blessings, but opportunities to do this do not come easily. At funerals, however, he gets a chance to speak to those who may have little religious faith or knowledge. Moreover, they come expecting to hear about the very subjects that can best convey the essence of the gospel—a God who knows and cares, salvation through Christ, the meaning of life. They come when an experience with death has made them thoughtful. One of the many reasons for having a funeral service in a church is that it introduces those who are rarely in a church to the place of Christian worship.

A funeral offers a minister a chance to talk about death. Every religion is, in part, a philosophy of death. It offers a way of coming to terms with the mayfly evanescence of a human life. The swift approach of death, with the bewilderment, anger, and dread it brings, have to be brought into the open, or they will fester in the unconscious and spread their poisons out of sight. The ancient Egyptians, when the festivities at a banquet were at their height, would have a coffin carried through the room to remind the revelers of a reality they did not dare forget. In the older American cemeteries, on many of the tombstones are a skull and crossbones or the words, *Memento Mori,* "remember death." The warning was intended to prevent the folly of a frivolous disregard of the fact that everyone is about to die. Our ancestors had more to keep death in their thoughts than we do. It came to most people at home, where it was a family event, not in a hospital. It came more frequently, with the shorter life expectancy and the large families in which many of the children did not survive to become adults. Our forebears were more preoccupied with death, as can be seen from their poetry, songs, and sermons.

Modern people are likely to think that there is something unwholesome in thinking about death at all. It is true that the thought can be a morbid obsession that blights a life. We may prefer to be casual about it—"Death is the last thing I want to think about." We may like the logic of the old Epicureans: "Where death is, thou art not." So why worry about it? If death is not the end, then you escape it; and if it is the end, you won't be there to care. Much thinking about death has been inspired by the eagerness to make a good deal; but greed for the future is no nobler than is greed for now. These are all good reasons for not having an unhealthy fixation on death, but that can best be avoided by seeing death clearly for what it is. There can be so many disastrously wrong views of death that we must, as Christians, look straight at it. A minister can help those at a funeral face death squarely from a Christian point of view. Then they may be freed from lurking bitterness and enabled to look ahead with high hearts, with gratitude for the wonder of God's plan.

THE PURPOSES OF FUNERAL SERMONS

1. *Comfort* can be given. To com-*fort* is to fortify, to strengthen, to console. The minister can promise God's sustaining care. Believers are never told that they will not have to go through deep waters, but the promise is, "When you pass through the waters I will be with you; and through the rivers, they shall not overwhelm you." (Is. 43.2) The minister can be the spokesman for the love and concern of the congregation. The funeral sermon can be a part of the grief therapy.

2. *Thanksgiving* should be a dominating theme. A funeral is a service of praise and adoration. We thank God for all he has given to us and to the world through the person who has gone. We thank God for his mercies to that person and for the assurance we have in Christ of an eternal love and keeping.

3. *Hope* gives reasons for Christian joy that even death cannot repress. A funeral service is a witness to the resurrection, and the resurrection demonstrates that a good God will not let what is good be thrown away. This is the truth the sermon can impress on those who are mourning the loss of what has been most precious to them. It can show them that "the sufferings of this present time are not worth comparing with the glory that is to be revealed to us." It can make this a lively hope, and not just an empty doctrine. Frederick Myers told how his host interrupted a dinner table conversation about the future life by saying, "I believe that we shall enter into eternal bliss; but I wish you would not talk about such disagreeable subjects." The bliss can be more real than that. We may be uncertain about harps and pearly gates, but there is much that we can know. The Bible is no Baedeker's guidebook to the realms of glory. It does not tell us all we would like to know, but it does tell us all we need to know. It tells us that our loving will continue, and love is all that really matters. Our love of God and of each other will remain. Our hope does not need specific details in order to be very clear. Dr. Cleland B. McAfee, a teacher and seminary president, had an intellect that could not have entertained crude picturings of heaven. He was nearly eighty when he told me with great ardor, "I look forward to the first five minutes after death as the most exciting adventure I have ever known."

I doubt whether many Americans are afraid of not existing. The old idea that people are brought to religion by the fear of death is probably not true. It is easy to say, "For all I know or care, it will all be over when I die." What really shocks us into long, hard thinking about whether or not things make sense is the death of those we love. It is not easy to stand by the grave of someone who has been unutterably precious and say, "For all I know or care, there's nothing left of you." If that is the way God runs this universe, we cannot help thinking that it is under pretty shabby management. If the minister can offer an escape from cosmic gloom, he will be listened to.

The sermon can also give hope for the life on earth. Those who, in their sorrow, are looking bleakly toward the days ahead and seeing only loneliness can be told that life can still be good. A God of love will never leave a single day without some source of happiness.

4. *Personal reference* to the one who has died can be included. Lynn Caine, in her book, *Widow*, advises those who write letters of condolence, "Praise is wonderfully welcome." The effusive praises of the old-fashioned eulogy should be avoided. It is more useful to tell about an incident, a hobby, or a conversation that will present the person as a real human being. It should recall something characteristic that will be a tribute. If the minister did not know the person well, he may talk to those who did until he gets what he needs. The reference can be attached to a Scripture reading; the last chapter of Proverbs has references to all sorts of good things a woman might have done.

5. *Evangelism,* as was seen, can be important. There may be a chance to tell of Christ to someone who has no right knowledge of him. Dangling sinners over hell used to be a major part of many old-time funeral ser-

vices. Warnings and reproofs, whether blunt or decorous, may not be the best source of good for most of those who come to funerals. But when a minister talks of what Christ can do, he must always be hoping that this will open up a glorious new sort of life to someone who had never dreamed that it was possible.

6. *Repentance,* in its original sense of "rethinking," can be the result of a funeral service. The thought of the brief time on earth can bring a new longing to use that time for what is worthwhile. Those who have been living superficially may be impelled by a funeral to take stock of themselves. Funerals are likely to make people wonder what life is for and to search for new meaning for their existence. They may be inspired to be more worthy of the examples of those whom they have lost. Repentance is not remorse, though it may lead to that; it is a new slant. The minister must recognize the opportunity a funeral gives to help people to repent—to find a new direction for their lives.

7. A *turning point* is marked by a funeral. Mircea Eliade calls it one of the "rites of passage," like birth, baptism, or marriage. He says that in ancient times, as among primitive people today, a person was not considered dead until the funeral rites confirmed it. He had to be conducted ritually into his new dwelling and officially received into the community of the dead. Among us, death is not emotionally accepted until the funeral has been held. When people come back from the cemetery, they first turn definitely to the new sort of life without the person who is gone. There is a feeling of things being in suspension until the service has been held.

The funeral sermon can help people pass this turning point. Much neurotic grief comes from a failure to accept the reality of death. The grieving person has not completely faced life on the new terms. The minister can make the ending of an earthly life seem final as a finished stage in God's unfolding plan. He can turn people from looking toward the past and help direct them toward the future.

UNDERSTANDING THE CHRISTIAN FUNERAL

A funeral is often thought of as a grim necessity, an unwelcome ancestral rite that tradition forces on us. It may seem to be one more ordeal that must be endured among the trials that accompany death, a harsh decency that has to be observed in the disposal of the bodies of the dead. But if that is what a funeral really is, then we have surely evolved culturally to where we can drop it as an outworn relic.

No one who understands a Christian funeral could think of it with dread. Many a family, out of the depths of shock and grief, look forward to the funeral as the great help they are counting on. It is a time when friends come to offer the support of their sympathy and love. The sorrowing find the comfort of the beautiful words that have strengthened and consoled God's people through the years. A funeral is a time for gratitude and precious memories. There is sorrow, of course, and pain, and loss.

But the dominant mood must not be somber. A doleful preacher mis-understands his function. The mood of a funeral should be serious, though an affectionate reference that will bring smiles is not inappropriate. It should be tender, intimate, spiritual, loving. There must be a sense of majesty. Even when few are present, it is not a haphazard little prayer meeting; it is the solemn ceremony that marks the ending of an earthly life. Above all, there is the awareness of an unconquerable joy.

There is no time when Christians have more reason to thank God for the wonders of his love or to celebrate the victory we have in Christ. In small towns, there are sometimes smiles about the people who go to all the funerals, but why shouldn't they? There is no place that better re-minds us of all that Christians prize the most. There we see our small affairs in the bright light of eternity. There our memories are blessed and our hope renewed. Herman Melville starts his novel, *Moby Dick*, by say-ing, "Whenever it is a damp, drizzly November in my soul; whenever I find myself involuntarily . . . bringing up the rear of every funeral I meet . . ." Looking for a good funeral is an excellent idea for someone who needs cheering up.

The best time to prepare people for the death of those they love is long in advance. When the rain is falling, and the floods have come, and the wind blows, it is too late to start getting the house built upon the rock. The funeral themes we have considered are needed also in the Sun-day preaching, and they do not need to be reserved for Easter Sundays. If a minister always preaches about death at funerals and on Easter, there will be some who think he has no other theme.

The regular preaching should also show the congregation what a Chris-tian funeral is. People need to make up their minds about funerals before the emergency is on them. They should have counsel about the content, time, place, arrangements, expenses, flowers, memorial gifts, cremation, gifts of a body or parts of it for research or transplant, whether to have a funeral followed by a burial or a burial followed by a memorial service. Some of the foolish, religiously dubious practices could be avoided if thought were given to them sooner.

A minister's advice about funerals may well be made available to the congregation in written form. It can be combined with information about weddings and the sacraments. This may be a publication of a committee of the church.

A minister's theological training and his experience with many funerals qualify him to give advice, but he must be reserved about imposing his private opinions. For example, it is hard to be sure whether it is taste or Christian belief that determines the regard that is shown for the bodies of the dead. Some people have little feeling for bodies. They do not want to see them; they rarely visit the family burial plot; they regard the lying in state, the viewing, the rising when the casket is taken from the church as more appropriate for ancient Egyptians than for Christians. On the other hand, there are equally enlightened Christians to whom the bodies of the dead are very precious. It is through these bodies that those they have loved have been known. Symbols deserve respect. Christianity is not so spiritual that it has no regard for material objects. The desecration of human bodies has been denounced by the Church throughout history not just as bad taste, but as wrong. When we preach about funerals, we need to leave room for a wide variety of emotional makeups among normal and consistent Christians. Ministers may disparage unrestrained displays of grief on grounds they think are theological, when they are really only cultural—and also anti-therapeutic. We can discuss and give advice, but before we announce what is Christian, we need to be quite sure.

There are special funeral situations a preacher must be prepared to meet. One of these is presented by people who want a nonreligious service. Both they and the minister are in a difficult position. They feel forced by custom to have a funeral service, and to have it conducted by a minister. Their request to him is, "Please don't make it too religious." Not wanting to make a show of a faith they do not have is to their credit. The minister sympathizes with their dilemma, and he wants to be as helpful as he can be—but he has problems. He knows that his only qualification for conducting a funeral at all is religious. He has no right to conduct a nonreligious service, and to do so would be a reverse hypocrisy—pretending not to have a faith he really has. He has to conduct the sort of service he believes in, and he can hope there will be some present for whom it has a meaning. But he cannot say anything which will imply that there is Christian faith where there is no reason to believe that it exists.

When the person who has died was a self-proclaimed nonbeliever, or of notoriously bad character, this has to influence what the minister can say. Dr. Andrew Blackwood, who did not permit himself many puns, said that in such a situation what a minister needs is not a committal but a noncommittal. There are ministers who believe that honesty requires them to pronounce God's judgment on unbelief or sin, and to use the bad example as a warning. I doubt whether that has brought many to the Kingdom. But the minister cannot, in what he says or in the liturgy, make Christian faith and living seem of no importance.

Suicide has been regarded by some branches of the Church as self-murder—a sin for which there is no time for repentance. Therefore a Christian funeral was forbidden, and the body could not be buried in a church cemetery. Protestantism, with no purgatory, in some cases offered less hope than did the Roman church. Many people, therefore, are hesitant and embarrassed when they ask a minister to conduct a funeral for someone who has committed suicide. The minister must reassure them that suicide brings no special disgrace, either for the person who has died or for the family. Often the person was in no way morally responsible. It had to be a once-in-a-lifetime act that is no indication of essential character. What is said in private and at the funeral should try to assuage the special pain of a family in this situation.

A minister needs to collect material for funeral services—scripture readings, verses, prayers, poetry, prose selections, committals, benedictions. The best source of these will be his book of services, but one book could not possibly supply the available wealth of the material that is needed. Services cannot be standardized, and to have the prayer or reading that is just right for a particular occasion requires having a considerable variety at hand. Funerals do not come when there is enough time to prepare for them, and a minister needs good parts for the service which he can pick up quickly. He can repeat what he has used before, even in his talks, more than he would in Sunday services; but the same people will be present for many of the funerals, and the minister should not repeat too much.

Scripture passages that are often used are: Psalms 23; 90; 91; 103; 121; 130; 139 (selected); Matthew 5:3–9; 18:1–4, 10–14 (for a child); 25:34–40; Mark 10:13–16 (for a child); John 14:1–7, 15–19, 25–27; Romans 8:10–39 (selected); I Cor. 13; 15 (selected); II Cor. 1:3–5; 4:16–5:9; I Thessalonians 4:13–14; II Timothy 4:6–8; Hebrews 11:1–12:2 (selected); I John 4:7–21; Revelations 7:9–17; 21:1–7, 22–25. Separate verses are: Deuteronomy 33:½27; Job 1: 21½; Psalm 46:1; 103:13; 124:8; Isaiah 26:3; 66:½13; John 6:68; 11:25–26; 14:27; 16:33; Romans 14:8.

The minister will need for his collection some of the great classic prayers of the church—invocations, collects, funeral prayers—as well as his own. The poetry has to be the kind whose meaning and feeling are immediately perceptible. Nineteenth-century poems are likely to fit that description better than do recent ones. Such poets as Tennyson, Browning, and Whittier are still much heard at funerals. Death does not make doggerel endurable.

Many ministers use a loose-leaf funeral notebook that is small enough to look like a pocket-size book. It will never have to hold more than a few pages at a time, so it can be thin. Material for funerals is written or pasted on these pages and filed under an index that shows special purposes—"Christmas time," "Youth." Notes for the minister's talks are carried in that notebook, and kept in the file.

The feel of tradition and the emotional power of old, familiar words can be helpful in a funeral. With the best- known Bible passages, it may be better to use the long-loved words, and not a new translation. There is no occasion for which there are more well-worn expressions—"blessed dead," "present with the Lord," "on the other side." These should be used only with restraint, but the attachment to tradition lets the disapproval of clichés be somewhat relaxed.

II. WEDDINGS

In some denominations, the homily is an expected part of every wedding; in others, it is exceptional. The custom can be encouraged, and it should be. A minister will not be asked to say anything at a wedding unless the bride and groom know that this is often done. If the minister hesitates to suggest it, the possibility can be mentioned in the material the church supplies to help those who are making wedding plans. Some ministers, whose denominations have no tradition of a wedding talk, still make it a regular part of the services they conduct.

There are good reasons for it. The Church has much to say about Christian marriage which people urgently need to hear. There is no better place to say it than at a wedding, where the scene and sentiments make people ready to listen and be impressed. The bride and groom and their families have a very timely reason for wanting what the minister can tell them. The young unmarried, who are usually a large proportion of those present, need counsel about their ideals for marriage. This will help them see what sort of people they need to become, and what sort of people they will want to marry. A wedding sets the husbands and wives who are present to thinking about their own marriages. They will be intensely interested in any insights the minister can bring.

The minister's talk can make a formal ritual come alive with meaning. The traditional words, which have been the same for countless weddings, can give the feel of stability; but each wedding also needs something personal that makes it different from every other one.

A wedding sermon has to be brief, especially if the bridal couple and their attendants remain standing. But in that brief time some profound and searching things can be said on one of the most important of all subjects. Many people go to enough weddings to enable them, in a year or two, to get a great deal of understanding of marriage from the wedding talks. Thus the church can use its weddings to build up Christian homes. It can open up the meaning of Christian marriage to many who do not attend a church, or who have missed the few sermons a year that are on this subject.

There is no problem about making the wedding too long. In most denominations, the services in the worship books seem scandalously short. In my denomination, the most used service takes four and a half minutes, not counting the coming in and going out. The newest service, without hymns and a sermon, is even shorter. The importance of an occasion cannot be measured by the time it takes, but less than five minutes for life's most decisive ceremony seems scarcely adequate.

The sermon usually comes just after the opening prayer, or just before the marriage vows. Sometimes the processional ends with the wedding party seated in the front pews. There can then be a service of worship, with hymns and Scripture, and a sermon before the marriage ceremony.

The sermon may be addressed to everyone, or it may be spoken to the bride and groom but for the benefit of all. It may be scriptural, or topical, or it may interpret some part of the wedding ceremony. The Bible says almost nothing about romantic love, outside of the Song of Solomon. There is nothing in the Bible about getting married, but much about being married. There are a few profoundly revealing texts on marriage, like those from the creation story. Jesus said, "Have you not read that he who made them from the beginning made them male and female, and said, 'For this reason shall a man leave his father and mother and be joined to his wife, and the two shall become one'? So they are no longer two but one. What therefore God has joined together, let no man put asunder." (Matt. 19:4–6) The Epistles have some great marriage texts—"You are joint heirs of the grace of life." (I Pet. 3:7) "This is the will of God . . . that each one of you know how to take a wife for himself in holiness and honor." (I Thess. 4:3–4) Many of the great teachings of the Bible can be applied to marriage and the home. There is the Psalmist's advice, "Unless the Lord builds the house, those who build it labor in vain." (Ps. 127:1) What the Sermon on the Mount says about forgiveness, turning the other cheek, and putting a home on a firm foundation is needed for marriage. First Corinthians 13:4–7 is packed with wisdom for marriage.

The minister may speak of marriage as a divine ordering, something let down from God out of heaven for human blessing. He may talk about why an all-wise God, who must have foreseen the trouble it would make, created humanity male and female. He may show how the direction to leave father and mother means that the married couple will have a new center for their lives and a new first loyalty. The minister may point out that marriage is a miracle by which two human beings are divinely transformed into a different sort of creature. He may make it clear that in a changing world there are unchanging supports for homes and families. He may speak of the ways by which God can be recognized in family life.

The minister may talk about the wedding service. He may tell why it is performed in a church instead of in the courthouse where, by all ordinary logic, it would seem to belong. He may explain the vows, the symbolism of the ring, or the meaning of the joining of hands before the declaration of the marriage. A great deal of enlightenment can come from interpreting words from the service—*love, troth, honor, duty, faith, tenderness, cherish, covenant, comfort, peace, temporal things, holy marriage.*

A preliminary talk can make the rehearsal a far more significant occasion. Whether there are many participants and relatives or only four or five people present, there are good reasons for this talk. It helps to set the right mood. There is often a good deal of nervous tension at a rehearsal, which may be revealed by irritability or by a hectic facetiousness. There may be strong differences of opinion about decisions that have to be made. Strangers who will soon be relatives may be uneasy with each other. The minister's manner and what he says may change a time of strain into a beautiful and happy part of the whole wedding experience. Those who think they have come just to learn where to stand and how to walk can be made to feel that they are sharing in a a sacred event. The minister does not restrain the gaity that is so right for a marriage, but he does make it a deeper joy than just compulsive jocularity. The rehearsal gives the minister a chance to talk of the deeper meanings of marriage to the very people who most need to know about them.

The minister can get ready for the rehearsal talk by asking everyone to sit in the front pews. A great deal can be said within ten minutes.

There are many possible things to say. For example, the minister might start by telling the participants why they are present. They are not in the wedding because they are needed to get people into the pews or to add beauty to the scene but because the bride and groom want those to whom they feel close to be around about them at the greatest moment in their lives. The word "rehearsal" can be misleading. It suggests getting ready to put on a show. The real reason they have come is just the opposite. They want to get the details of where to stand and what to do out of the way so that at the wedding they will not need to think about the show, but they can have their whole attention on the great thing that is happening. They need to understand what this is so that they can truly be a part of it. A wedding is not just a legal event, for which a license is required; it is an act of God. It is not a contract between two parties, it is a covenant among three, with God the third party to it. It is not just put together out of scattered items, it has a carefully designed progression, with a plot that develops from the opening words until the benediction sends the bride and groom out into their new life together with God's blessing on them. The meaning of various acts and symbols and of the most important words is explained. A wedding is described as one of the most deeply solemn and holy occasions, but also one of the most joyful. Pasted-on smiles are not needed; if those in the wedding feel happy, they can show it. If they want to smile at someone, they should. When the talk is finished there can be a prayer. Then the minister has everyone remain seated while he explains what they are to do. Any decisions that are still unmade are settled. Questions are answered. The ushers, who are the weakest link in any wedding, are given their instructions while they are still under control. An extra advantage of the rehearsal talk is that it gets the participants settled down so they can understand the directions.

Sometimes the bride and groom want to have Communion at their marriage. A private Communion in advance raises theological problems in some churches. Having only the bride and groom take Communion in the presence of the congregation raises even harder questions. The wedding might be a Communion service for the whole congregation except that a good proportion of those present may have no Christian faith, or have a faith that would not permit them to take the Sacrament. A Communion service at the time of the rehearsal may be beautiful and full of meaning unless in so small a company those who are not able to take Communion would be embarrassed. What the minister says and the prayers at a Communion service can be beautifully related to the marriage.

III. COMMUNION SERVICES

The Communion talk is a special form of sermon. It is designed to be a part of the celebration of the Sacrament. In churches where the Eucharist is a part of all the regular church services, Communion sermons are not expected with every celebration. What we will consider here has to do both with Communion talks and with sermons about Communion which might be preached at any time.

A Communion talk is likely to be shorter than other sermons in order to allow time for the Sacrament. It may be given from behind the Communion table instead of from the pulpit, unless this makes it difficult for the minister to be seen or heard. Its mood is usually devotional. The "meditation" style of preaching is often used for Communion sermons. This can be impressive. The preacher's manner is quiet. His descriptions may be unusually vivid and imaginative. He looks for deeply spiritual meanings and for beauty of expression. This can be overdone. The preacher may be so hushed, deliberate, and spiritual that he is artificial. As with all preaching, there should be a variety of styles for Communion.

The first Communion sermon is in the 14th, 15th, and 16th chapters of the Gospel of John. Here the Gospel gives what Jesus said to the disciples when he gave them the Lord's Supper in the Upper Room, or immediately afterwards. These chapters are a rich source of texts for our Communion sermons.

The first purpose of a Communion sermon is to prepare people to receive the Sacrament. To take Communion is so different from all our other activities that we cannot do it with a casual, every-day state of mind. This holiest of all Christian observances is spiritually demanding. The people in the church may be far from a Communion state of mind. They may have been rushing around trying to get the children ready for Sunday School or chafing at traffic delays. They may sit in the pews counting the organ pipes or thinking of what they have to do on Monday. Without a complete change in their mental and emotional bearing they will not be able truly to receive the body and blood of Christ. Churches that practice "closed Communion" ask those who do not belong to the church to leave the room when the Lord's Supper is celebrated. But in every church there is a form of closed Communion. There may be some who are shut out by their lack of readiness. They bar themselves. They may receive some bread and grape juice, but that is all; they never really get to the Lord's table. The Communion tries to open up the way for those who are mentally and spiritually outside. The preacher during fifteen minutes tries to take them by the hand and lead them past all the barriers and mental blocks until they are longing for the Communion and prayerfully trying to receive it.

In some churches there are mid-week preparatory services before a Communion Sunday. In every church the people should be reminded on the preceding Sunday that the Lord's Supper will be celebrated. When people have been thinking about it, it will mean more to them.

A second purpose of the Communion sermon is to enlarge people's understanding of the Sacrament and of what it can do for them. The Communion is too great for us. We never get all we should from it. It is like prayer—even in our finest experiences of it there is the double sense of great gratitude for what we are getting and of bafflement because of what we do not get.

Many fine Christians do not get very much from the Communion. An older woman in our church, who had for many years been one of the most devoted members and a beautiful example of the Christian virtues, told me sadly, "The Lord's Supper never means much to me." There was a younger member, who in some ways seemed much less mature spiritually, who said to me after a service, "Communion is the most wonderful thing that ever happens." "What does it do for you?" I asked her. "It makes me feel like I never want to do anything bad again," she answered.

Some people dislike Communion services. They may feel what those who do not like difficult music feel when they have to attend a performance of it. They cannot really believe that all the intelligent-looking people who seem to be enjoying the music are putting on an act—but they are puzzled and suspicious. Those who do not get much from the Communion are likely to resent what seems to them the forced solemnity, the awe, and the reverence of the traditional service, and they are no more impressed by the foot-stomping jollity of the newer ones. Some who have never gotten deeply into the Communion service may conclude unhappily that they are just not the spiritual type.

The Lord's Supper is a mystery, in the double Greek sense of a *mysterion,* which is a secret that is hidden from all except those who are initiated, and also a truth too profound to be fully grasped by human understanding. The knights who sought the Holy Grail, the fabled chalice Jesus used, caught glimpses of its shining beauty, but it was always partly veiled. The full meanings of the Sacrament will always be beyond our reach, but we can keep coming closer, and keep growing in our thankfulness for all we do get.

When the minister stands up to deliver his Communion sermon he knows that some of those listening will have little feeling for the service. Some practical people will be thinking, "Since even the theologians cannot explain the Eucharist, it is foolish to waste time on something no one understands." There will be some who are growing into a fuller experience of the Sacrament, and some who are devoted to the Sacrament because of all it does for them. The minister knows that Christ is ready to give himself and his blessings through the Sacrament in greater measure than anyone is ready to receive. So the minister's great desire is to reveal more of what the Communion can be, to increase the faith and expectancy, and to remove the obstacles.

At its plainest level, the preacher can explain the Lord's Supper as the gospel presented in acts instead of words. Goethe said, "The highest cannot be spoken; it can only be acted." Jesus was incarnated to dramatize on our stage divine truth that could not be presented in any other form. At the Lord's supper we have all the deepest Christian truths in pantomime. There at the table are portrayed the relationship of Deity to humanity, and of human beings to each other. The whole sweep of essential theology is there—love, the Church, atonement, new life—all of it.

But if that were all the Communion is, there would be no special advantage in receiving it ourselves. Those who are watching the ceremony from the balcony would be learning just as much as would those who are participating in the service. The Sacrament would be the most beautiful of all audio-visual aids to teaching, but no more than that. The preacher must go beyond this easier explanation of the Sacrament as a symbol. He must go on to the awesome truth that the Sacrament not merely represents Christ's blessings, but actually conveys them. At the Lord's Table we are offered not merely the knowledge of Christ—we are offered Christ.

Various understandings of how Christ is really present in the Eucharist have been a major source of division among Christians. The Roman Catholic teaching of Transubstantiation says that by a miracle the bread and the wine become literally his real body and blood. But we could almost say that the difference between Protestants and Catholics is a matter of locations. Catholics believe that the miracle takes place on the altar; Protestants believe that it occurs in the bodies of believers who receive the bread and wine in faith. "Now you are the body of Christ," Paul says, after he has talked about the Communion. "It is no longer I who live, but Christ who lives in me," is the way he explains himself. We can believe that Christ becomes a physical reality in the flesh of those who receive him with full faith in what the Sacrament conveys.

The relationship between the spiritual result and the physical elements can never be precisely stated. To ascribe spiritual working to material objects is magic. It heads inevitably into absurdities like the old arguments about whether a man who had been baptized while wearing a wig could have received baptismal grace, or whether a mouse that had nibbled the consecrated wafer was a part of the body of Christ. We can be sure that the Communion miracle is a wholly spiritual event, but we can also know that the bread and wine connect it with the realm of tangible, temporal reality.

A third purpose of a Communion sermon is to apply the meanings of the Sacrament to every area of life. It has a clear connection with almost everything a Christian does and thinks. When Luther was tempted he would write on anything in reach, *Baptizatus sum,* "I am baptized," to remind himself that he was a special sort of creature. The knowledge, "I have had Communion" gives a different bearing toward everything in life. Sermons can apply the Communion meanings to home, church, vocation, money, to all our human and divine relationships.

TOPICS FOR COMMUNION SERMONS

A young minister might wonder how it would be possible, in a lifetime of preaching often on Communion, to keep from running dry. The possible topics here are just a beginning of all that might be listed. They may give some indication that the Communion is an exhaustless sermon subject, and they may serve as a reminder of some of the meanings of the

Sacrament. The topics are put in groups under the main subjects to which they are related:

INCARNATION: Advent—Getting our hands on God—The material as the bearer of the holy—Christian materialism—The commonplace made gloriously uncommon—The glory of the human body—Faith is no abstraction.

CHRIST'S SACRIFICE: The cross—The saving blood—Sin—Atonement—Redemption—Salvation—Maundy Thursday—Good Friday—God's love.

FORGIVENESS: God's forgiveness—Our forgiveness—Enmity—Reconciliation.

COVENANT: The divine promises—Our promises—The Communion pledge—The Roman *sacramentum* oath—Whose we are.

DEDICATION: Discipleship—Living for others—Self-sacrifice—Vocation.

FELLOWSHIP: Christian love—The Communion of Saints—*Koinoneia*—Friendship—Brotherhood—The Congregation—Barriers—Factions—My body broken by you—Ecumenism—World Wide Communion—Missions—Ties with those in the Church in heaven.

UNION WITH CHRIST: His life in us—Channels of his mercy—Members of his body.

CHRIST'S PRESENCE: The Friend—No loneliness—Guide—In our homes.

CHURCH: The body of Christ—The present form of the incarnation—The Church's mission—The sacramental fellowship.

THANKSGIVING: "Thanks" in modern Greek is *eucharisto*—What we are thankful for—The thankful slant toward life.

HOPE: Advent—Eternal life—His coming again—Joy—Fulfillment—Consummation.

MEMORIAL: A tangible connection with Christ—His actuality in history—Jesus' earthly life—Recalled by the table fellowship he loved.

NOURISHMENT: Food—Inner strength—Refreshment—Renewal—Vitality—Discouragement—Weakness—Transfusion.

MEDICINE: Antidote to death—Tonic—Spiritual sickness.

HUNGER AND THIRST: For love, beauty, joy, goodness, God, accomplishment, security—Satisfaction—Longing.

THEOLOGICAL TOPICS: Baptism and Communion—Faith—Grace—the Kingdom.

OTHER TOPICS: The names (Eucharist, Holy Communion, Lord's Supper, The Sacrament)—The table (One of the most eloquent religious symbols; the dining tables in our homes are extensions of the Communion Table)—Excommunicated (What bars us from the Sacrament)—Companions (From *com* + *panis*—eating from the same loaf, so physically kin)—Christophers (Means "Christ-bearer"; we go from the table to carry Christ to the world)—Table, Pew and Rail (We need what all three ways of receiving Communion represent).

OTHER FORMS FOR THE COMMUNION MESSAGE

A Communion sermon can be given entirely in the Bible's words. The minister outlines his sermon, but he fills in the outline with quotations from the Bible. The sermon might be on God's promises to us, with great passages quoted to declare each sort of promises. The sermon might be on preparing for the Sacrament, with such stages as examining our hearts, recalling God's mercies, being at peace with our neighbors, looking for Christ's blessings, and renewing our promises. These would be the subjects for the Scripture selections.

Congregations are likely to find this the most inspiring and helpful sort of talk. This can be especially impressive if the minister gives what the Bible says without reading it. Memorizing enough for a fifteen minute talk is not too difficult. Some of the passages will probably already be known almost well enough to give from memory. The minister benefits by storing in his mind some of the grandest portions of the Scriptures. This sort of talk can be repeated better than can our own sermons. The same Bible Communion sermon can be used every year or so, and people will look forward to it.

The Bible sermon might have such a sequence as this:

THE INVITATION: Psalm 107:8–9; Revelation 22:17; Isaiah 55; Isaiah 40:29–31; Hebrews 4:14–16.

THE PREPARATION: James 4:8; Joel 2:13; Isaiah 1:16–18; I Corinthians 5:7–8; Matthew 5:23–24; I John 4:7–21.

EIGHT BLESSINGS THE SACRAMENT CONVEYS:

1. *Christ's Death for Us:* Isaiah 53:4–7; Hebrews 9:13–14.
2. *His Love for Us:* Romans 8:35, 37–39.
3. *Our Union with Christ:* John 15:1–11; Galatians 2:20; Romans 8:10–11; Ephesians 3:14–19.
4. *Our Union with each Other:* I Corinthians 10:16–17; John 15:12–17; Romans 12:10; I Corinthians 12:27.
5. *Christ's Promises:* John 6:32–35, 47–51; Matthew 11:28–30; Matthew 5:6; John 3:14–17.
6. *His Control:* John 14:15, 21; Matthew 22:37–40; II Corinthians 10:5; James 1:22; Hebrews 5:8–9; Romans 12:1.
7. *His Presence:* Revelation 3:20; Matthew 18:20; Matthew 28:20½; Luke 24:35½.
8. *The Future with Him:* John 14:1–3; Revelation 22:20½.
   (All of this would take twenty-five minutes, which is too long. The extra is given here to provide a wider variety of examples.)

Musical parts from the Mass can provide an inspiring preparation for Communion. The word, "Mass," need not bother Protestants. These ancient canticles come out of our common heritage from long before the Reformation. The *Kyrie eleison* was used in the fourth century and the *Agnus Dei* in the seventh. These express penitence, petition, adoration, and belief in words that echo the Scriptures and join us to the timeless outpouring of the Christian heart. There is no standard listing of these parts. The Kyrie, Gloria, Miserere, Nicene Creed, Sanctus, Benedictus, and Agnus Dei are much used. The music for some of the Masses belongs more to the concert hall than to the church, and some of them are too long for a church service. Others, however, are deeply worshipful and do not require more than twenty minutes. Using words that are not in English is no handicap. Both languages can be in the Church bulletin. The worshippers, in following the two-language text, may be more aware of what it says than they would be if the words were sung in English.

There may be a brief Communion talk that comments on the old words, or the talk might tell of our union in Christ with fellow Christians of many churches throughout the world and across the centuries. Such a service brings people to the Lord's Table with the sense of a great heritage and a timeless faith.

Franz Schubert's "Mass in G" is beautiful and moving. It is not too difficult for the average choir and it is not too long. In recent years there has been a flood of new Masses, with a wide variety of musical styles and written for almost every sort of instrument except, possibly, kazoos and calliopes. Many of these may not survive long, but some are opening the way to valuable and untried experiences of worship. New Masses from other cultures are important. The haunting and lovely *Missa Criolla* (Creole Mass) by Ariel Ramírez uses the folk music and instruments of Argentina. Most choirs could not sing it without a good deal of Latin American help but the recording of it could be used, in whole or in part, for special Communion services, as on a retreat or with young people. There is a new appreciation of the Kyrie when one has heard the Hispanic choir sing, "Señor, ten piedad de nosotros." The same is true of the Congolese *Missa Luba*. Americans at first may hear only a complicated shouting and drum beating, but the knowledge that this is how Christians who share our faith praise Christ can deepen our spiritual understanding. We can be grateful for the present efforts to get more of what the Communion might mean to us, both by the recovery of the experience of the past and by moving on to new experiences.

XXVII

The Preacher

It is an awesome thought for preachers that the effect of their sermons depends very much on who they are. Every preacher is giving two messages at the same time: one is what his words say, the other is what his personality is saying. If the congregation has the feeling that the preacher is in earnest, that he deeply believes what he says, that he cares about the people he is talking to, and that he is essentially a happy man, this will all be a part of the sermon. Exactly the same words would have an entirely different effect if the preacher gave the impression of being pompous, egotistical, melancholy, or soft.

CHARACTER

Aristotle taught that the speaker's ethos (character) has most to do with the effect of a speech. He believed the three essential qualities for persuasive oratory to be manliness, kindliness, and wisdom. (Aristotle had no chance to know the power of womanliness in public speech.) In no other profession is personality so important. Your dentist performs very personal services for you and you need to trust your banker, but their value to you does not depend on whether they seem to enjoy their work or are at peace with themselves.

Woodrow Wilson said, "The only profession that consists in *being* something is the ministry of our Lord and Savior—and it does not consist of anything else." Are not the ministers who have done the most for you those you felt were the best persons, quite apart from whether they were the ablest? Bishop Quayle said that preaching is not the art of making and delivering a sermon, it is the art of making and delivering a preacher.

There might seem to be contradiction here with what Paul meant when he said, "What we preach is not ourselves, but Jesus Christ as Lord." (II Cor. 4:5) The chief aim of the preacher is to conceal himself so that Christ may be seen. Dr. Jowett liked a prayer that was offered just before he preached at a city mission: "O Lord, we thank thee for our brother. Now blot him out! Reveal thy glory to us in such blazing splendor that he shall be forgotten." But over against this is the fact that preaching is "truth through personality." In every sort of communication the medium colors the message. The character of the preacher will be part of what he says. The only way of reconciling Paul's "What we preach is not ourselves" with the actual process of communication is for the preacher to have the sort of personality that will least distort the message—in other words, to be as Christlike as possible. A minister longs to be a better man so that his nonverbal communication will not be noticed because it blends in with what he says.

Almost every book on preaching stresses the importance of the preacher's character; as you look through such books, a composite picture of the preacher emerges. It can be seen in the descriptive words the authors use. Here are some of them: As to *character*—honest, straightforward, sincere, patient, grave, courageous, manly, self-disciplined, on good terms with himself, living truly and deeply, wise. In relation to *God*—passionately seeking God, submitting to his will, striving to please him, depending on his grace, devoted without reserve, knowing God, in communion with him, penitent, aware of the need to be forgiven. In relation to *man*—kind, loving, tactful, friendly, eager to help, eager to understand, sensitive to needs, approving, enjoying people. In *disposition*—cheerful, hopeful, delighted, pleasant, buoyant, enthusiastic, enjoying his work.

Words the writers use to describe what a preacher should not be are: As to *character*—insincere, sham, aggressive, flabby, baffled, hazy, fearful, mild, gray, dusty, no spiritual force, defensive, uneasy, hard-hearted, callous. In relation to *self*—smug, conceited, complacent, pretentious, self-indulgent, self-conscious, preoccupied with his own problems. In *disposition*—melancholy, morbid, hypochondriacal, solemn, censorious, severe, narrow, unkind, exaggerating evil, inclined to criticize. In *depth* superficial, facile, blandly buoyant, stereotyped, clever, counting on a knack for preaching, with staged emotions.

With such a definite checklist before him, how can the preacher fail? He need only pay attention to the manuals to become the perfect minister. By intelligent design, he can put on the personality that will best serve the church, though it may take some tinkering and adjusting to get it right. From this best of motives comes the unfortunate effect the minister's planned personality sometimes creates. It is not a minister's shamming that can make him a too-carefully designed work of art, but his sincerity. He wants to be a living epistle that will tell of Christ. He earnestly wants to "walk worthy of the vocation" to which he has been called. But the public image he so carefully puts on for its effect may carry over into his private life until the real man is lost. The Bible ceaselessly emphasizes that the inner and the outer man must be as one. Isaiah hears God condemn those who "honor me with their lips, while their hearts are far from me"—which is a pulpit condition ministers will recognize. Jesus called those whose outer appearance was designed for its effect "whitewashed tombs." Even when it is done for the best of reasons, a minister's attempt to acquire the bearing that will do most for his work may leave him unsure of who he really is.

MANNER AND MANNERISMS

With all our desire to be what we appear to be, no one who works before the public can be entirely unself-conscious. It is impossible to cross a stage before an audience just as one would walk through an empty room. The joints and muscles operate differently. Politicians, actors, and ministers have to think of the effect of their public manner.

All sorts of elements enter into the impression we give. We live by semaphores. The way we walk, gesture, and wear our clothes gives signals by which we reveal ourselves. Body language is eloquent. The relationship between the symbol and the significance may be mysterious. There is no logical reason why a woman who smokes a cigarette without using either hand looks tough, or why a pipe that slants upward suggests jauntiness. We have to plan our signs for what we want to communicate. A salesman puts on the tie that will say about him what he wants to say. A lawyer makes his gestures slow, to show the jury that what he says has been carefully thought out. Justice would be impeded if a judge were to dress sloppily. When we are arrested for speeding, we can take it with better grace if the officer looks neat.

A doctor's beside manner has a great deal to do with his ability to heal; so does a minister's pulpit manner. All the mannerisms that speak for him affect his ability to comfort and inspire. His intonations, the way he leans, and something that flickers behind his eyeballs can help or obstruct the gospel.

Between the need to display those qualities that will assist his mission, and the need to be genuine, the minister has several choices:

First, he can play the role all the way. Just as a naked archbishop is wrapped around by his robes of office, so the person who is ordained a minister can disappear behind what he thinks is the image of Christ's Man. He will walk as to the strains of "Onward Christian Soldiers." Majestic sweetness will sit enthroned upon his brow. In the pulpit he will be the very model of all those qualities the books describe for preachers. The jokes about the ministerial manner indicate that most of us are not good enough impersonators to make this seem wholly natural. The mellow bass does not quite ring true.

Or a minister can go to the opposite extreme and work hard at the pose of not having a pose. Artlessness will be the object of his art. Everything he does will be designed to say, "That's the way I am, and it's too bad if you don't like it." He will strain at being fresh and original. He will constantly rehearse in his mind for the role he pictures as the authentic, unpious character. But some of the most typical and objectionable ministerial mannerisms come from the determination to be genuine. The bluff camaraderie, the hearty earthiness, the artful *Damns* and *Hells,* the unconventionality all turn out to be an act, and not a very good one. Complete honesty is impossible, because complete honesty is complete selfishness. To be blunt and undisguised will always hurt others. Kindness requires putting on an act. So does good workmanship.

Or a minister can consciously try to act better than he is not to win admiration for himself, but for the benefit of others. He will try to seem more interested in someone than he feels; his kindly, earnest manner in the pulpit will be planned—but he will never forget that he is not as good as he pretends to be. Though he cannot be completely honest with the world, he will be honest with himself. He will catch himself thinking about the ventilation as he stands before the congregation as though bowed in silent prayer, and he will be ashamed of it. William James' assertion that the inner state tends to match the action applies here. If you throw your shoulders back you become more assured; if you sing a cheerful song you will become more cheerful. A minister who acts loving, reverent, or sympathetic has made a start to becoming so.

Externals have something to do with the impression a sermon makes. An Anglican church paper says, "The depth of a clergyman's collar is inversely proportional to the height of his churchmanship." White bands and red neckties convey different messages to the congregation. In churches where cassocks, surplices, dickies, tabs, or stoles are traditional, the minister's indifference to them is a message. In churches where they are not expected, the minister's caring for them tells something about him. The Protestant minister's black robe has academic origins, which is important if the minister wants to identify himself as a scholar. There is a question whether somber black evokes the right mood for the preaching of the gospel.

A friend told me that the first time his little girl saw him in a preaching robe, she said he looked like a window with the shade pulled down. The impression of light and color would be helpful, though the psychedelic patterns of some of the newest robes may scream too loudly. Some ministers relieve the somberness of their robes with academic hoods, though one may wonder whether the minister's advertising of his school and the level of his schooling has any place in a church service. Beards and mustaches have decided meanings. It is important for the sermon whether the preacher's appearance is making the congregation think of Sigmund Freud, Captain Kidd, Santa Claus, or a Gay Nineties bartender. It says something if a minister is slumped in the pulpit chair. The tradition that a person sitting before an audience should not cross his knees has some reason. The minister can use the pulpit to give signals; it may be the prop that holds him up, the fence he leans across to give a confidence, the counter on which he spreads his wares, the perch from which he takes flight, or the barrier that shelters him from the congregation.

A distinctive personality adds interest. A preacher's manner and style should express his individual self, and not be standardized. This may be a temptation to eccentricity. A minister who wants to be distinctive may turn out to be merely odd in his delivery, mannerisms, or dress. Only preachers who lack real originality need to be sensational. Preachers

sometimes pick mannerisms that are wrong for them by imitating someone they admire. One of the very popular preachers near a seminary had
long hair he would toss out of his eyes. Many of the seminary's graduates
are said to have punctuated their sermons by tossing their heads that
way, with or without hair.

QUALITIES

A minister's pulpit manner should reveal a genuine liking for the
people in front of him. You can assume he loves them—that is his duty;
it is liking them that has to be established. Anyone who works with
people in the mass will get some hard blows from those with emotional
peculiarities and some painful criticisms from those of excellent judgment. This may make him so sensitive that when he stands before the
congregation his apprehension may give people the impression that he
dislikes them. A minister must cultivate a real affection for his people,
first in his heart, and then in his attitude in the pulpit.

This is important because the surest way to make people like you,
in private or in public, is to like them, and the emotional response to a
sermon is closely connected with the emotional response to the preacher.
If people like him, they are inclined to like what he says. The thought
of the man in the pulpit hoping wistfully that he will be liked, or even
well-liked, is not appealing. But the qualities that will make the congregation like the minister are those he should be cultivating anyway,
and the qualities that will turn hearers against him are the very defects
he is needing to get rid of.

A minister has to have a deep respect for the people he is preaching
to, and a strong appreciation of their worth. Because he is better schooled
than they are in the subjects of which he speaks, he may come to think
of them as retarded in their knowledge and primitive in their views.
He needs to be humbly aware of their real abilities and character. If in
private he thinks of them as clods or deficient Christians, he is sure to
give it away. They will catch the patronizing tone—"You might see
nothing wrong . . ." "It may not have occurred to you . . ." The attitude of Sir Oracle telling the uninformed can slip in. A preacher must
identify with those to whom he speaks. He does not point his finger
across to them; he stands among them. He makes it clear that their
vulnerability is his too.

Ministers who berate their congregations cut themselves off from them
and incite them to disagree. Often a minister scolds his congregation
because he is discouraged. When he sees little good from his efforts he
blames the congregation, and reveals his resentment in the pulpit. Some
young ministers upbraid because they are impatient; they overrate the
value of direct attack, or they are too much charmed by sarcasm and
innuendo as art forms. A hostile minister makes it hard for a congregation not to be against whatever he is for.

Those who speak in public most effectively almost always seem to be enjoying it. Their delight makes the hearers happy to be there. A preacher's natural nervousness can give a congregation the feeling that he is tense and unhappy. Even a charming person can be so hemmed in by his reverence for the pulpit that dignity and propriety will make him deadly dull. Another hazard may be the consuming determination to do something important for people. A tense, hard-driven preacher is not what tense, hard-driven parishoners are needing.

Strong preaching is confident. A minister has to believe in what he is doing. If his manner says, "There is really no reason why people who know so much more than I do should waste their time listening to me," the congregation will be inclined to agree with him. Well-mannered people do not act superior, they underplay their importance. Christians should be humble. A brash, pompous manner shows that a preacher is thinking of himself. But a minister of the gospel can have assurance without being self-assured. When he thinks of all he has been given, his manner can imply with all humility, "Listen to this! This is going to be good. Here is something you want to hear." No one would want a surgeon whose bearing seemed to say, "I'm not really very good at this sort of thing." The minister must never seem to think that he is wiser or better than others in the room, but he can always know that he is the only one in the room who has been assigned and commissioned by the church to preach that sermon. He is relying on God's word and promises. If he shows that he is expecting something wonderful to happen, the people will expect it to.

There is a spiritual force and vitality which empowers all arresting preaching. It has an electric quality which is communicated to the hearers. It is more than physical vitality. A preacher may have it when he is tired, and lack it when he is fresh. The sources of this psychic potency are not easy to understand. Politicians and labor leaders may have it. For preaching, the condition for it is a lively sense of God's purpose and of the people's need. It usually makes a vast difference if the minister, not long before he preaches, can call vividly to mind, by prayer and reflection, why God wants that sermon preached and the actual difference it could make in human lives.

A minister's pastoral experiences make his sermons real. He does not preach to his congregation as a technician who is an expert in religion, but as a pastor and a loving friend who knows his members and cares about them and enjoys them. The saying "A home-going minister makes a church-going congregation" offers a very inefficient promotional device, but it is true in the sense that a home-going minister knows what to preach about, so that people will want to be church-going. A minister gets close to people in their homes as he cannot in any other setting. Whether or not he follows the old custom of a call in every home every year will depend on his situation, but he has to recognize the obvious fallacy in the insistence, "I'm like the doctor; anyone who wants to see me can call for an appointment." A preacher has to seek every possible way of getting to know his people as human beings, not just as those with functions in church programs. The sermons of a minister who is not a pastor grow bookish and theoretical. It works both ways. Pastoral experience improves preaching, and his preaching makes a pastor more effective.

Tactlessness is a serious defect for a preacher. It is the result of a lack of feeling for someone else's point of view. The typical tactless remark is made by someone who wants to seem considerate, but is not bothering to think of the other person at all:

> When I look at you I think, "What a beautiful girl she must have been."
> I can't think of anyone who has done more with less.
> We keep telling each other we ought to have you over.
> You are lovely; I always say that beauty comes from within.
> When my uncle had your illness he was hopeful right up to the end.
> You shouldn't work so hard; you look tired all the time.
> I used to think I didn't like you.
> Your children are so bright—it's just amazing.
> I don't care what anybody says; I think you're great.
> I hope I seem as young as you do when I'm your age.
> Your husband seems so sort of human—not a bit like I expected.

Sermons offer endless opportunities to fail to think of what is said from the point of view of the many different sorts of people who are listening. There may be a reference to some defect or peculiarity, or an unfavorable observation about a profession or country. When a minister said, "A mule can't kick when he is pulling," several members of the congregation thought it was meant for them. The statement "Those who elope show they do not love their parents," can embarrass some couples in the church. The introduction of guest speakers, whether jocular or not, is often more satisfying to the host than to the guest. I heard a minister congratulate his guest preacher on having made it to such a distinguished pulpit. The "born tactless" probably have no missing brain function; they have fallen into the careless habit of not taking the trouble to think of other people's feelings.

Religious doubts are part of being religious. As Browning put it,

> With me faith means perpetual unbelief
> Kept quiet like the snake 'neath Michael's foot
> Who stands calm just because he feels it writhe.

When a minister works through his doubts at one level, he moves on to those at another one. When the problems of religion and science are no longer much in mind, the problems of religion and language can come up. There is no level at which we can take God for granted. Every Christian has to live with doubt, but the minister not only has to live with it, he has to preach with it. There are several ways he may try to do this. He may decide to preach just the basic, unshakable certainties. Paul backed away from less certain matters when he said, "I decided to know nothing among you except Jesus Christ and him crucified." (I Cor. 2:2) That is probably the way most preachers take; it works until the new doubts begin to undercut the basic certainties. Another way is for the preacher to regard himself as the spokesman for the Church's long tradition of faith which he can preach in spite of his present uncertainties. That puts him in the dubious position of trying to graft technical belief on actual skepticism. Still another way is to let the congregation know about the beliefs he has rejected. This is honest and open, but it collides with the practical difficulty that many in the congregation may not understand his thinking. If he admits he has misgivings about the Apostles' Creed, they may assume he does not believe in God the Father Almighty. If he tells them about Bultmann, they may quit reading the Bible.

A preacher's firmly held convictions are important for his congregation; the phase he is working his way through is not. His current searchings can be shared with his friends, or with a church group that is able to deal with them. A minister preaches what he is passionately eager to communicate. If there is not enough of this to supply sermon themes, he has no way to preach. What saves many ministers is the requirement of having to remind themselves every week of the things they believe. By this they are kept in healthy contact with a core of certainty around which their faith-shaking speculations circle.

When we do not live up to what we preach, we have to feel unworthy, but not dishonest. Sincerity does not require us to keep the summons to the life in Christ within the modest limits of our own attainments. The church is entitled to more than that! We need Archbishop Temple's reassaurance: "Practice what you preach. That is a very wholesome prod for the preacher's conscience, but if the preacher in fact preaches nothing more than he can practice, he is preaching very badly."

WOMEN

The Church has lost a great deal by not using more of its women as preachers. The reason is not lack of ability. Some of the qualities in which women are supposed to excel are the very ones that preachers need. Neither scientific research nor common opinion has ever determined whether the mental and emotional differences between men and women are inborn or acquired, but it is usually assumed that women are more aware of human feelings, more concerned with interpersonal relationships, more understanding of human character, more interested in the life of the spirit. They have high rank as novelists, dramatists, and poets. In the history of the Church, women are among the greatest saints, martyrs, mystics, and leaders in ministries of compassion. It is only in the preaching of God's word that the contributions of women to the Church have been small because their way to the pulpit has been barred.

Thomas Gray amid the rustic tombstones mourned at how many a "mute, inglorious Milton" had been lost to the world through lack of opportunity. Countee Cullen reproached God, "Yet do I marvel at this curious thing: To make a poet black and bid him sing." (*Yet Do I Marvel,* from *Color,* p. 3.) The Church has been impoverished by not using for its preaching the mental and spiritual endowments of half its members. The Christian cause cannot afford to be that wasteful.

The presumed differences between men and women give each some advantages in preaching. There is a good deal of evidence that women have a greater aptitude in the use of words. Professor Kagan and his colleagues at Harvard have found "clinical evidence that, in general, females are more proficient in verbal skills than males." John Watson, at Berkeley, recently discovered that . . . baby girls respond more often to auditory stimulation, boys to visual." (*The Atlantic Monthly,* March, 1970.) A century ago, Dr. John Broadus, in his classic book on preaching, wrote, "Women, of equal culture and practice, will oftener read well than men; and this is not surprising when we note that women are usually quicker in apprehension, more sensitive in feeling and sympathy, have greater flexibility of voice, and oftener read to each other." (*The Preparation and Delivery of Sermons,* p.515.)

Sermons are largely concerned with the relationships of human beings to each other and to God. Women are generally thought to have a better understanding of personal relations. This is often explained by the abused word, "intuition," which implies some mysterious knack. The explanation is probably that women pay more attention to what goes on among people. They will be better sources of information about inter-office frictions or family stress. In their sermons they show a sensitivity to motives and an understanding of the human heart that men often do not have.

My women students present more exceptionally good sermons than do the men, and the average quality is higher. This does not prove that women are naturally better preachers. There are fewer women students, so they may be a more select group. Being a minority may impel them to work harder on their sermons than do the men. But they do reveal some remarkable insights into human character and some profound spiritual perceptions. Their graceful and interesting style confirms what was said a century and a half ago by Thomas De Quincey, one of the greatest stylists, "Would you desire at this day to read our noble language in its native beauty, picturesque from idiomatic propriety, racy in its phraseology, delicate yet sinewy in its composition—steal the mail-bags, and break open all the letters in female handwriting."

The one handicap the women students have is their delivery. The reason for this is obvious—they have no models. Boys from their early years have models of how to speak in public in their ministers, lecturers to school assemblies, politicians, and the recollection of the Daniel Websters. Ability in public speech does not come naturally; much of it has to be learned by imitation of those who do it well. Girls usually have only male models, and most of them know it would be a mistake to use them as patterns.

One could exaggerate the difference in male and female styles of public speech. There is much that men and women speakers can learn from each other. But there is also a great deal that has to be different. If a woman tries to be emphatic in the same way a man does, she is likely to sound strident. They both have to show charm, and grace, and a range of emotional expression, but it is a disaster when a man tries to do this in a female way, or when a woman tries to do it like a man. Foreign students often start to show a comic effeminacy in the way they speak. If they are learning their new language from dates or women hostesses they will begin to use expressions and mannerisms that are appropriate only for females.

A public speaker has to be able to take command of an audience. This requires the quality that speech instructors call, "presence." It is the self-assurance that tells a room full of people that they are supposed to listen. It does not require effrontery or heavy-handedness; gentleness is no handicap. Physical strength is not essential; a weak man can keep a crowd under powerful control. The volume of sound is not the problem. A good speaker can project a whisper; women's voices in a theater reach the far balconies as well as do the men's. In a church the amplifier can always be turned up. But there is a force of personality that is needed to take control and women often do not know how to use it. Some of my women students deliver their remarkably fine sermons as though they are having a casual conversation, and the hearers do not discover how good the sermon is. A conversational style is not wrong; it is more likely to be right for a modern audience than is oratory. But even a conversational style requires a special attitude to seize the attention of a crowd of listeners.

Aristotle is a valuable guide through the perplexing questions of male and female speaking styles. His statement that the first requirement for public speech is *manliness* might seem to be an affront to women, but it was not. Ancient Athens had no women orators. If Aristotle had been speaking of women he would have said that the first requirement is womanliness. Public speakers need the full force of what is most distinctively themselves. A woman speaker needs the whole power of her womanhood, and a man of his manhood. An androgynous public speaker could not be impressive. Women must be clearly feminine, and men distinctly masculine. This does not mean that men should work at being robustly challenging, or that women should turn on their female wiles, but both should use all the resources of what they specially are.

Some women have perfected for semi-public use a skill that women public speakers need to study. They use it to hold the attention of a social gathering. There is something they want to tell everyone about—an unusual occurrence or some inside information. They have worked out with some art how they are going to tell it, but they have to make people listen. They have to be good because this is a very competitive activity. It is done with a combination of grace, humor, charm, and dramatic sense. One of my students, a girl from the South, has taken this skill into the pulpit. She could make a congregation listen gratefully to the city ordinances. No man could possibly do it in the same way—or, at least, he shouldn't.

Women can learn something about public speech from the theater; as much, at least, as men preachers can learn from actors. The way a woman delivers from the stage a long Elizabethan monologue can be a good model. There are many very able women speakers in American public life. It is important for woman preachers to get to hear them.

As churches call more women to be preachers, the problem of the lack of good women models for preaching will diminish. It is probably uncertainty about the other functions of the ministry that is now the chief reason for hesitation in calling women. When a church has only one minister it has to consider whether men or women are equally able to do all a ministry requires. This depends so much on the qualities of each individual that advance judgments are impossible. It was not the women's lack of abilities that caused most Churches to wait so many years before they elected women to their chief lay offices. We can hope that we are going through the transition to the time when any follower of Christ who can preach his gospel well will be called upon to do it.

CRITICISM

A preacher finds it very hard to evaluate his own work. His efforts receive no applause and no expressions of disapproval; they are only loosely connected with the gate receipts. There is no supervisor, no sales record, no performance chart, no ratings committee to tell the preacher whether or not his sermons are effective. His own appraisals may be quite inaccurate.

He needs most of all the evaluation of the congregation. It is a senseless thing that is often said to congregations, "Don't tell the preacher you liked his sermon. He is not trying to please you, he is trying to please God, and God will tell him." The truth is that the preacher very much needs to know whether people found the sermon helpful or not, whether it was interesting, whether they understood it or agreed with it, whether anything in it hit them hard. If the hearers do not tell him, the minister will remain in the dark about what he needs to know.

The preacher will understand that for many kindly people, "Nice sermon" is the way you say "Good morning" to a minister. He knows that a compliment observes the good custom of reassuring those who do something difficult in public; it expresses thanks for the hard work. These good words warm the preacher's heart, but he will not take them as information. Many comments, however, will be significant. Even the "Nice sermon" may come out with difficulty, or be unusually enthusiastic. Those who comment only once a month, or twice a year, have to have a reason for it. There will be critics who serve by mentioning only what they disagree with. People who speak of something special in the sermon are good guides. Those who say they could not hear should make the minister think about his delivery or the acoustics; even those in the remote corners should not be expected to strain to hear a sermon. Bad sound projection makes bad preaching, no matter how good the sermons are. Sometimes, when a sermon has been obviously disappointing, the considerate will go out of their way to speak kindly of it. The minister knows they mean "Poor as it was, we are still with you," which is what he most needs just then. Being in a church where a good many people comment on the sermons does not force anyone to perjure himself; I remain puzzled by the man who seized my hand and exclaimed, "Well, you did it again!" Comments that come between Sundays are specially important. When people write notes about a sermon, the preacher knows they reveal real thought and feeling. The grateful notes will be among the most treasured rewards of his ministry, and the critical ones will give useful information and an opening for discussion.

It is difficult for a minister to ask for comments without implying he thinks of the sermon as a performance; he does not want to encourage people to be sermon-tasters. If he seems interested in remarks about the sermon, there will be more of them. Sermon reaction meetings (Chapter VII) can be very helpful. A minister may ask for advice about his preaching in a meeting of the official board or the worship committee. A youth group can give him valuable suggestions, and asking for them may increase interest in the preaching. If a minister in any group explains his philosophy of preaching, the discussion will show him what those who are there think about it. When it is known that sermons will be mimeographed if enough people ask for them, the minister has a weekly score through the requests. Sermon copies are valuable for people to study and to give to their friends. Church members with secretarial skills may do the work.

A minister needs to be careful about giving too much weight to a single comment. The deaf person on the back pew who tells him he should speak louder may turn him into a strident shouter. If someone early in his ministry mentions his charming smile, he may beam through forty years of preaching. Someone's remark that he talks too fast may make him tedious. Any crushing criticism needs to be checked with those who can be trusted to be candid.

A minister has some direct perception of the response of the congregation. He can feel interest, pleasure, apathy, or disapproval. But such feelings are too subjective to be reliable. They may be determined by one sour or one delighted face, or by the minister's own mood. If he thinks the sermon was weak, he may be too impressed by any kind word. He is tempted to think poorly of his critics—they must have been inattentive or too obtuse to understand. It is useful to discuss with critics, but not to argue with them. A minister who disagrees with adverse comments will cut himself off from anything but praise. If the preacher has had to take an unpopular position, disapproval can be praise and unanimous approval a sign of failure. The minister must remember he is not striving for perfection; the faultless performance of a television announcer is not his goal. Art is not perfection. All the best preachers have some faults a critic would try to cure. A minister needs to be human, not a polished preaching machine.

A wife's or husband's opinions are important, but there are handicaps. If the advice is not taken, it can lead to tensions, or to what the preacher may interpret as nagging. If the mate wants the role of critic, it may suggest too much enjoyment of fault-finding. A couple's other disagreements may link up with differences about the sermons. Criticism is hardest to take right after preaching, which may make the Sunday dinner painful. A spouse is not a normal critic. Love is blind, and may approve of what should be condemned. It may be useful for a couple to review the sermons together, but there is no reason to assume that it will be. Some spouses believe that their best help is to pronounce each sermon the greatest masterpiece since Savonarola. After that, a few more comments may be very useful.

A minister is wise to employ someone to criticize his preaching every five or six years. There are advantages in employing a member of the church who has some background in public speech or who simply has unusually good judgment. A member's criticism will be based on the actual preaching situation, with more than one observation from which to make the judgments. A church member critic will know something of what other members think. Counseling sessions over five or six weeks can provide advice on many aspects of the preaching and on the conduct of the whole service. A professional speech teacher can give good help with delivery, but voice projection in a studio is very different from speaking in a church. A seminary summer school may have a good refresher course on preaching. Members of a church staff may help each other with their public speaking.

THE PREACHER'S SPIRITUAL LIFE

The preacher, who tries to speak for God to the people and for the people to God, must be well connected on both sides. Unless his friendship with God is kept close and growing, his friendship with man will be disappointing. All his trying to be a good and helpful friend of man requires more than he has in himself. In all our endeavors to help people with their problems, we feel like a blacksmith who is trying to repair a wrist watch. Our only hope in any of the work of the ministry, which is so far beyond our powers, is in staying close to God.

It might seem shocking to suggest that a minister can have spiritual problems. He is supposed to be living at the fountain source. To tell him he needs to cultivate his awareness of God might seem like a doctor's advising a postman to take a walk every day. But the minister has his special problems. He must know the warning in the words, "They made me keeper of the vineyards; but, my own vineyard I have not kept!" (Song of Sol. 1:6)

Being a religious technician is a spiritual hazard for a minister. When he attends a worship service, he has a notebook where his heart should be, and even in his private prayer a homiletical self is looking over his shoulder, watching for thoughts and phrases for the Sunday service. His Bible is a working tool, to be read with one eye out for likely texts. His devotional reading easily becomes more appraisal than appreciation. His Sabbath is a day for work. It is hard to see a rose as a poet does while you are studying for a botany exam. It is hard to take the kingdom of heaven as a little child if you are schooled in ancient heresies, modern structures, and the manipulations of ecclesiastics. A geologist may be less awed by the Grand Canyon than are most visitors.

The minister has the problem of familiarity; he gets so used to sacred things he may scarcely notice them. His failure is not that of the hypocrite, who lives contrary to his pretensions, but of the professional, who lives alongside them. His religious reactions are conditioned reflexes that no longer require thought or will. It is quite possible to handle the truth of God in a way that will be helpful for other people without being aware of it for oneself. A telegraph office was thrown into consternation by hearing the paperboys outside crying the news that President Lincoln had been shot. Then it was recognized that the only way the news could have gotten to the paper was through that office. The dispatch, which had been received and delivered without being thought about, was found in the files. We can handle the gospel like that.

Psychologically, God is of two sorts. He can be just God, or he can be the *living God,* and the two are quite different. The Epistle to the Hebrews makes the distinction plain when it says, "It is a fearful thing to fall into the hands of the living God." (Heb. 10:31) In our wrongdoing we might not be too much worried at the thought of falling into the hands of God; but to fall into the hands of the living God, that is what is fearful. When Hagar was forsaken in the wilderness, it might not have greatly helped her to believe that God was with her; that sort of comfort may not have much benefit. But when she had the direct discovery of God's actual presence, then in astonishment and awe she thankfully named the oasis "Beerlahairoi," "the well of the living One who seeth me." That is the hurdle ministers have to get over. In church we can talk on and on about God, and not be much affected. But when it comes to us that he is the *living* God, that is different.

Dr. Dale had for several years been preaching to large and grateful congregations in his London church. One morning, as he was preparing his Easter sermon, he suddenly sprang from his chair and exclaimed to himself, "Christ is alive! He is *alive!*" Dr. Dale walked excitedly around the room, saying, "Can that really be true! Living as really as I myself am?" He said later, "It was to me a new discovery, and I thought I had believed it all along." (*The Life of R. W. Dale,* A. W. Dale, p. 632.)

Something like that was in Paul's mind when he warned himself and us that the preacher who persuades others may not persuade himself, "lest after preaching to others I myself should be disqualified." (I Cor. 9:27)

The minister has been likened to the clerk in the tourist office who talks glowingly to others about faraway places in order to induce them to go where she has never been. Dr. Jowett said that "We may become mere guide-posts when we were intended to be guides. . . . We may assume that fine talk is fine living, that expository skill is deep piety." The great danger for ministers is that they will assume they are of course religious because they are thinking and talking of religion all the time; thus they will not recognize the difference between handling and having.

Repetition may make a minister lose his sensitivity. We get used to experiences that for nonprofessionals are still fresh and exciting. This was the fault that Jesus saw in the ecclesiastics, and he was "grieved at the hardness of their hearts." *Hardness,* in the New Testament Greek, is *porosis,* which means to be covered with a callous. The Pharisees had with time become insensitive; the frequent rubbing caused them to grow a hard covering. There is always danger that our hearts will lose their feeling and our brains will become machines for turning out sermons. Our preaching not only puts our hearers to sleep, it puts us to sleep.

Absorption in routines can dim our spiritual sensitivity. The roads where we lost sight of God are not deliberately chosen. The lost sheep in the parable did not put his head in the air and purposefully march off into the wilderness. He simply turned his eyes to the ground and grazed from tuft to tuft, and clump to clump. Then, when at last he raised his head and looked around, the shepherd and the sheepfold were nowhere in sight.

What can the minister do to defend himself against the spiritual hazards of his calling? The most important answers to that are obvious. He especially needs all those ways of keeping spirits strong that he urges on his congregation—Bible reading for his own soul's good, private prayer, group prayer, public worship. But there are also some special means of grace for him. He has more ministers than most Christians have. The people of the church minister to him; they pray for him; they are related to him in ways that keep him supported by their goodness and their love. He is constantly dealing with them on a spiritual level, and what flows from them to him sustains his soul. The times of prayer he has with the church officers, prayer groups, and the young people on their retreats are precious to him. Ministers' conferences offer him spiritual fellowship. He may belong to a club in which ministers share their personal problems, thoughts, and prayers.

A minister can get a great deal or very little from the church services. He may be completely the officiant, thinking only of what he will be doing next. The anthems may be only background music for last-minute thinking about the sermon, and the readings only exercises in elocution. But when the minister does put his attention on what is happening, he may be more alert and more affected by it than he would be in a pew.

A minister is likely to miss that spiritual quickening which comes from telling someone, face to face, about the Christian faith. Most of a minister's contacts are with church pepole. He never catches up with his duties to those who are already in the church. He has to devise a special time and occasion if he ever mentions religion to anyone who is not a professing Christian. It may be surprising that if a minister does only what is there for him to do every day, he will be very practiced in talking about Christianity in public and very inexperienced in talking about it privately. But if he submits to this natural course, he will lose that renewal of faith and experience with Christ that comes only from talking about him with another person. The minister who misses this will know that he has broken the faith, and something in him will die.

Because a minister is overoccupied with theological complexities, he has to cultivate a certain artlessness. What Jesus said about having to be like children to be fit for the kingdom of heaven applies specially to the religiously sophisticated. Ministers need to make their prayers as simple and direct as possible. They need to love Jesus with the rapt, uncluttered devotion of the pure in heart.

Like all Christians, ministers need to be spiritually revived. The ardor which brought them into the ministry has to be renewed in their thirties, forties, and fifties, or they will be dragging through an occupation from which the glory has departed. An astronomer who is studying a star has to keep re-aiming his telescope or the turning of the earth will put the star out of range. At each succeeding stage of our lives we need to get fresh bearings on God; in each changed situation we need to feel in a new way our love for Jesus Christ and our longing to make life better for those around us.

Paul wrote to Timothy, who had come into the full course of his ministry, "I now remind you to stir up that inner fire which God gave you at your ordination through my hands." (II Tim. 1:6 Phillips) That fire needs to be stirred up periodically in all of us. There may be something special—a course of study, a retreat, a devotional practice—through which the Holy Spirit can set new fires to blazing in our hearts.

In a London church there is a bronze tablet which says, "Here God laid his hands on William Booth." One day a man came there and stood long before the tablet. At last the caretaker asked him to leave so that the church could be closed. "Just one minute more," the visitor begged. The impatient caretaker stayed nearby, and he heard the man's prayer. He was pleading, "O God, do it again!" It was William Booth.

XXVIII

The Hearer

The hearers play the leading role in the preaching drama. Everything depends on what they do. They come for the great adventure of experiencing more of eternal truth, and they leave for the even greater adventure of living by that truth. No occupation could be more important.

The sheer number of the hearers makes them imposing. Millions assemble in this country every week to consider how to make themselves and the whole human race more Christian. Not much else ever brings so many people together except spectator sports—and the sermon event is decidedly not a spectator sport. It is cooperative, and its whole success depends on the ability of the preacher and the congregation to do their parts. It is a game in which the players are in the stands.

The skills of the hearers are more important than the skills of the preacher. They need their own instruction in homiletics, and a knowledge of the sorts of subjects that are touched on in this book will help them understand their part. They need to know what the whole idea of preaching is, and how the minister sees his task, and how he goes about it. Concertgoers do not have to be musicians, but they will get more if they know something about how music is put together and performed. Church goers need to know what the various sorts of sermons are getting at and why they are important.

The skills of the hearers can be taught in various ways. An occasional sermon on such a subject as "Partners In Preaching" can be useful. A class can offer a course on homiletics for hearers. This is important in the instruction of those who join the church. The minister can explain in writing how he looks at preaching and what he hopes the church members will do to participate in it. Here are some of the things they need to know:

1. *Hearers have to get ready for sermons in advance.* How much people get from a sermon depends very much on how much they already know about Christianity and the Bible. As their knowledge grows, so does their ability to think religiously. Religious illiteracy forces preaching to stay elementary. Christians need to be able to understand the day's events theologically, to read their newspapers by the light the Bible

sheds on them. Those with this sort of understanding can have a lively share in what happens from the preaching.

The state of mind in which hearers come to church determines what they get. An eager hope of getting something good is the precondition for listening to a sermon. Not much is likely to happen to the person who is merely sitting in the church out of habit, checking off the weekly duty. A person has to be in the right mental and emotional state to receive what a sermon has. Every mental activity—studying the stock market, talking with children—requires the appropriate mind-set. Someone who has just scraped his car on a post in the church parking lot or who sat through the Call to Worship reviewing his engagement calendar will not be ready to receive the word. The church service may be over before we begin to react to it unless we are getting ready before it starts. The worship before the sermon should be making us receptive, but it is not automatic. We cannot collapse into a pew and expect very much to happen. Real worship is hard work; it sometimes requires a fierce effort of attention. It is the sort of work that leaves us refreshed afterwards, but if we think of other things during the hymns, readings, and prayers, we will not be ready for the sermon.

2. *Church members help with the sermons.* A preacher needs to talk much with people about their needs and what is on their minds; this is the background from which good preaching comes. The better the church people know their minister and the more they confide in him, the more his sermons will come, not just from books, but from life. Their friendship makes the preaching far more of a heart-to-heart communication. Talking to strangers is completely different from talking to friends.

There are definite ways of bringing church members into sermon preparation. They may be asked to submit subjects or questions they would like to have the preacher deal with. Some ministers get members together to work on sermons. It is usually up to the minister to put the result of their labors into final form, but the sermon comes from all of them. Browne Barr, at Berkeley, invited a group to come each Wednesday evening to work on the next Sunday's sermon. They were told the subject and the text before they came. The preacher started the meetings by some explanation of the text and its Bible background. He might propose a question or two. Then the company dispersed to tables where eight or ten worked together on the sermon. The preacher circulated among them but did not participate. When they reassembled, the ideas from each table were reported and discussed. The sermon came from this.

Church members can help with sermons by giving the minister time to prepare them. They can respect the hours he hopes to reserve for sermon work, and not press him for Saturday engagements, and save him from interruptions on Sunday mornings. In the final preparation for preaching, each hour or minute is more important than the one before.

A preacher needs his people's prayers during the week while he is working on the sermon and on Sunday when he is preaching it. A statement by the Church of England says, "A preaching ministry to have effect requires the co-operation of an expectant and praying congregation. No one has earned the right to criticize the sermon who has not first prayed for the preacher." A sermon is not a tied-up literary package that can be handed over, as a scientific treatise might be. A sermon is simply an occasion for something to happen. Whether it does happen or not depends very literally on the praying of the congregation.

3. *Hearers have a great deal to do during the sermon.* Kierkegaard said that many people go to church as they would go to the theater, expecting to hear a performance by the minister, and to judge how well he does. But in reality, he declared, the roles are quite different. In church it is the hearer who is on the stage, under the spotlight. The preacher is the prompter who is just off the scene, whispering the lines to the players. If they forget their parts, he is there to remind them. The hearer, out on the stage, is supposed to catch the prompter's lines and work them into his act. The audience, who is watching the players and judging how well they do their parts, is Almighty God.

Listening is an activity, and a strenuous one. Tests have shown that when a listener is concentrating there is "increased heart action, faster circulation of the blood, and even slightly increased bodily temperature." The hearer must be willing to endure the strain and put out the energy his task requires. The Swedish government sent an expert to advise Laplanders on better housing. A large crowd assembled at the meeting hall, but refused to go in. Their spokesman explained, "They want to know what you will pay them." "Do you mean I should pay them for hearing me talk?" the government man asked. "Of course," the Laplander said. "It's easy to talk, but listening is hard work."

The listeners' work is not only that of following, but of creating. Only a part of their minds is needed for receiving what is said. A listener can grasp what is said at from 400 to 700 words a minute, but no speaker can talk that fast. 100 words a minute is tedious, more than 200 words a minute is unintelligible. So a mind uses its extra capacity and does other things while someone is talking. If these others things have to do with the sermon, the time is well used; if not, the sermon will accomplish much less.

There is another reason why hearers can do their own creative thinking during preaching. Our minds are working on several levels all the time. If you could put all your mind on just one thing, you would never dare drive a car. As you drive, you have to be thinking of a dozen things at once—interpreting the traffic lights, estimating the speed, deciding where to turn. Your mind does not dart from one of these to another; they are being worked on simultaneously. As a minister reads the Scripture, with no irreverence or lack of feeling, he can at the same time be thinking of the exegetical questions it raises, of his voice quality, of the latecomers who are disturbing the service, and of what sort of reading light would be better. He may read beautifully, and have the new light picked out before he finishes.

When the minister is preaching on the Good Samaritan, you may already have thought of all the applications he makes. But as he speaks, your mind can be playing around his words, relating them to your present problems, following up a new line of thought they suggest. You may be remembering a Sunday School picture of the Samaritan, wondering whether pouring on oil and wine has any medical value, recalling someone you should have helped, deciding how much to give to the Community Chest—and all this without missing a word the minister is saying. This working of your mind, along with and around the words from the pulpit, is the real sermon. It is the one that is being preached to you by the Holy Spirit, if you are receptive to him. That is what you are doing on your stage, with God looking on. The preacher is prompting you with the lines, but the performance takes place between you and God.

Many of our thoughts, as we listen to a sermon, may be completely trivial. They are like sledge dogs, ready at every instant to slip the harness and go dashing off after rabbits. The rabbit may be the noise of a passing fire engine, an urge to count the choir, or the thought of swinging from a light fixture. The minister may say a word that triggers our emotions—"mugging," "apple." We slide away from the sermon to relax. Scampering is a relief from pulling. It partly comes from habit; we can get used to listening to sermons, or we may be conditioned to start wool-gathering when we see the preacher rise. We cannot entirely blame the sermon for not holding our interest. It has been well said that "there are no uninteresting subjects, there are only uninterested people."

At the preacher's end, too, the real sermon goes far beyond the words. Preaching is like whistling a symphony. The words cannot possibly say all that is in the preacher's mind and heart. He can only hope that the hearers are adding the full orchestration to the little tune he gives.

One of the tricks of good sermon listening is to have some definite queries in mind. The listener may be asking: What need is this sermon trying to meet? What solution does it offer? What action does it ask for? The questions might be more personal: What does this sermon chiefly say to me? What difference will it make in my life? Some churches put cards in the pews with questions like these and spaces to be filled in under them. A minister may put in the Sunday bulletin questions that fit that Sunday's sermon. John R. Mott was said to scribble through every sermon he heard. He did it partly to record thoughts he wanted to keep and partly just to force himself to keep thinking along with the preacher.

There are wrong ways to listen to a sermon. The Pharisees demonstrated one of them. They were among Jesus' most faithful listeners; whenever he spoke in public, they wanted to be present. What a privilege might have been theirs! But the only reason they listened was "to entrap him in his talk," "to catch at something he might say." Sermons offer a great deal of opportunity for this sport. Some listeners are alert for any hint of heresy, whether the orthodoxy they require be theological or sociological. Distortions of the faith should not be taken lightly, but those who judge every sermon by whether it uses their phrases or fits their narrow standards will miss the good they should be getting. A preacher's grammar may be confused, his facts shaky, and his illustrations trite. Those who hope to think of themselves as discriminating can be reassured by all they can find wrong with sermons. But if this is what the hearer is looking for, and what determines his opinion of the sermon, he is not likely to get much else. Anyone who aspires to be a connoisseur of preaching does not know what preaching is.

The one time when Christians are supposed to think of themselves first is while they are listening to sermons. Then the rule is "Self first, others second." It is good to hope that others will get some benefit, but to say, "He told them off today" may indicate too much nimbleness in ducking. People can get calloused from all the sermons they let bounce off them to hit someone else.

4. *Good listening makes good preaching.* What Plutarch says on this is so timely it is hard to believe it comes from almost nineteen centuries ago: "There are some that think that the speaker has a function to perform, and the hearer none. They think it is only right that the speaker should come with his discourse carefully thought out and prepared, while they, without consideration and thought of their obligations, rush in and take their seats exactly as though they had come to dinner, to have a good time while others toil. And yet even a well-bred guest at dinner has a function to perform, much more a hearer; for he is a participant in the discourse, and a fellow-worker with the speaker, and he ought not rigorously to examine the speaker's little slips, applying his criticism to every word and action, while he himself, without being subject to any criticism, acts unhandsomely and commits many gross improprieties in the matter of listening. On the contrary, just as in playing ball it is necessary for the catcher to adapt his movements to those of the thrower and to be actively in accord with him, so with discourses, there is a certain accord between the speaker and the hearer, if each is heedful of his obligation."

Every minister who preaches often away from home is struck by the totally different effect on him that different congregations have. Some make him feel as though he is slogging through mud up to his waist, and he can guess that this is what they are doing to their minister every Sunday. (It may be the result of what their minister has done to them.) When he rises to preach, scarcely a pair of eyes will be turned in his direction. He gets the depressing feeling that the people in this church do not like him, and he becomes tentative and fumbling, or he hopelessly tries to stir some life by overemphasis and pounding. But in other churches the preacher has the impression that everyone is leaning toward him, looking pleased and expectant. A wave of interest picks him up and carries him along.

Some years ago I was with a group that held meetings around the country. The addresses were the same in every city, but in some they were enthusiastically successful and in others the whole three-day meeting was a dismal failure. There was nothing mysterious about it. A group photograph would have shown part of the reason. At one meeting it would be clear the attenders were delighted to be there and were looking for something great—and the speakers would outdo themselves. At another, everyone would seem bored and sorry to have come, and the preaching would be dispirited. A speaker is undone when he sees people paying no attention, reading, whispering, coming late, leaving early, looking listless or cynical. Communications theorists talk about *feedback,* but sometimes it is *drainback.*

Every responsive face is like a tonic. Alertness and sympathy in the pews lift the sermon higher and higher. Some listeners look troubled when the subject is distressing, and they start smiling before something amusing has been fully told. Listeners get back what they give. Gladstone said that a speaker has the "power of receiving from his audience in a vapor what he pours back upon them in a flood."

In some churches, this supportive interaction with the preacher is audible. In the New Testament churches and afterwards, the congregations spoke out. Litanies were first used in an attempt to bring order into the spontaneous exclamations. In less inhibited groups of modern Christians, the partnership, which all preaching is supposed to have, is vocal. The response may be a whispered "Yes, Lord," or an occasional decorous "Amen," or a chorus of outbursts that drown out the sermon. In my experience, audible responses are exciting and supportive. The preacher feels that his hearers are with him and helping him, and he can know when he is striking fire. Calls like "Glory!" "That's right!" "Help him, Lord!" mean something. They can give advice. One frequent call used to be "Pull away from the shore, Brother, pull away from the shore!" Silent congregations can interact with the preacher by the way they look back and how they sit.

A church member who uses the sermon time to scowl over his business troubles may not know he is torpedoing the preacher. One who is laying every word of the sermon to heart while he frowns at the floor may not think of the impression he is radiating. We should not ask people to put on a show for the preacher's benefit, but they do need to know that what seems to be happening to them has a great deal to do with what happens in the pulpit. The members should not exhibit what they are not feeling. The politely fixed expression of rapt attention, behind which the mind can wander freely, misleads the preacher. Dogs raise their ears when they are listening, and drop them when they lose interest. In congregations with rigid ears, the preacher has to count on other indications to know when he should become more lively, or should get to his conclusion.

Members help the preacher by sitting close to each other and to him. Twelve people on a front pew offer an excellent preaching situation. With the same twelve scattered through a big room, the preaching is almost like talking in an empty church. Physical proximity makes for mental and spiritual cohesion. Dim lighting gives a sense of remoteness; turning up the lights brings people closer. Some dimming of the lights just before the sermon may be helpful, especially for those in a balcony; but a spooky effect is not what preaching needs.

Steel needles turn and point in the same direction in a magnetic field. The lines of force that flow from each one through the others line them up. The members of a congregation become responsive when something points them in the same direction in that way. A united action, such as rising, kneeling, singing, or saying "Amen" can do it. So can a shared emotion like laughter, indignation, or sadness. A few obviously responsive individuals have the effect of cheerleaders in uniting those around them. This common feeling is important for a preacher because it magnifies the effect of what he says. In a united crowd, a little pathos becomes deeply moving; what is slightly funny becomes uproarious; an ordinary appeal for faith becomes soul-shaking.

5. *The church members supply hearers for the word.* First, they make the preaching effective by bringing themselves. Dependable attendance is one of the most important aids to preaching. Each person who comes improves the setting for the worship and the sermon; each one who misses impairs it. Preachers need to know whom they may expect to see in church. They prepare the sermons, not "for whom it may concern," but with definite people in mind. If there is no way to know who will be present, preaching becomes impersonal; the preacher cannot have anyone in particular to whom the sermon is addressed. Those imagined conversations with the expected listeners that are a part of good sermon preparation become impossible. Ministers plan important sermons for Sundays when they expect a good attendance. If that depends on the weather or the fortunes of the city's football team, sermon-planning becomes tentative. Hit-and-miss church attendance makes for hit-and-miss preaching. Church members have to decide whether the weekly assembly for worship is an important engagement. The Scottish beadle explained, "If it's wet they'll no' come out, and if it's dry they'll no' come in." The weekend migration to recreation areas dissipates a church's power; Sunday capriciousness debilitates a church.

Second, church members supply hearers for the word by bringing others. Their enthusiastic comments to their friends are the church advertising that is most successful; the best of all is, "Can I pick you up on Sunday?" In a Washington, D.C., church some years ago, the average attendance almost doubled when the members decided to tell at every chance how much they were getting from the services. Grateful Christians who want to tell others about how much Christ can do for life, and find it difficult, can make a start by bringing others to the church where they can hear the gospel. The evangelistic note has died out in many a pulpit because only the members of the church could be expected to be present.

6. *Hearers need to know what they can expect of their preacher.* They

cannot expect that he have an exceptional brain. Since the beginning of the Christian Church, members have gathered each week to listen gratefully to preachers who were their mental inferiors. They came because the benefit of the gospel does not depend on the cleverness of the one who preaches it. A preacher may not have an especially interesting mind, but he does have an especially interesting subject. All the average congregation can expect to have is an average preacher. But it is entitled to a preacher who takes his sermons very seriously, who works hard at them, and who preaches more than his own ideas.

A hearer cannot demand that the minister be right, but he can demand that he be thoughtfully trying to be right. An instant pundit, who preached his latest notions as eternal truth, would have no place in the pulpit. But it can be assumed that the most deliberative and conscientious minister will differ on important subjects with every member of the church. No two people occupy the same space. From everyone's point of view, the minister will be either too far to the right or too far to the left, too straight-laced or too unconventional, too mystical or too rational. That is one thing that makes going to church such a sure source of interest. There would be no use going to hear what you already think.

A pulpit that was not free, including free to be wrong, would not be worth having. Much of a preacher's influence in making a better world, and in making better Christians, comes from his being able to say what people do not want to hear. When he is right, he may persuade the dissenters; when he is wrong, he can impel them to hold more firmly to the truth. He has no access to divine wisdom that is not available to everyone else in the church. His study and experience give him some advantages; the people in the pews have some advantages. The minister has been assigned to speak the truth as he sees it, and the church should rejoice when he does that, courageously and plainly.

A church member who disagrees should give the minister's views serious consideration, and then make up his mind in the light of this new thinking. He can make a date to talk with the minister. This does not have to be a major encounter, just a chance for interesting discussion they will both enjoy. An exchange of letters may be useful. This is one way the listeners improve the preaching. It is a hard-headed minister who does not often have his thinking clarified by the wisdom he gets from the members of the church.

If a critical matter of faith or moral convictions is at issue, the discussion becomes more serious. Members should always talk over such a matter with the minister before making much of it with other people. If other good church members do not seem much concerned, the objector has to suspect that he has a personal bias that has magnified the problem.

7. *Hearers have a great deal to do after the sermon.* They can help the preacher by their comments. He needs to know whether he is meeting their needs. (Chapter XXVII) Neither praise nor criticism should be given carelessly, or the preacher will be misled. There is no value in

hit-and-run criticism that leaves the minister unhappy and uninformed. A remark like, "I could not go along with you today," has no point unless the reasons are given. A preacher cannot hope always to please people, but he does need to know whether they were interested, and helped. A preacher can have no greater satisfaction than to know of the good a sermon did. Some weeks after I had preached on family worship, the parents of a lively family told me they had been trying what I recommended, and had found real joy in it. They invited me to their home to join the family circle. That evening is a very happy memory.

Congregations teach their preachers; a minister learns more from his church members than he ever learned from his seminary. They best of all teach him the meaning of faith, the secrets of the human heart, and the skills of his profession. Devoted, loving, wise congregations make devoted, loving, wise ministers.

The indispensable instruction for sermon hearers is the parable of the Sower. In it, Jesus tells the hearers what to do and what not to do. It is their great responsibility to hear the word and let it grow in them until it bears rich fruit. A member of Dr. Jowett's church boasted to a friend of the great privilege of hearing the famous preacher every Sunday. The friend's startling reply was, "What a terrible responsibility!" Bringing forth the harvest is the awesome responsibility of all who hear the gospel preached. They are put in trust to take the sermon to the world where it belongs. Sermons are delivered to the church on Sunday so they can be delivered to the world on Monday. Out there is where the harvest will be reaped. Jesus ended this parable for hearers with the words, "He who has ears to hear, let him hear."

Bibliography

Many of the books named here are in print. Those that are not have been included for readers who have access to a theological library.

FIRST LIST

These books are recommended for a first round of reading about preaching. They all have quite striking and differing approaches.

BLACK, JAMES, *The Mystery of Preaching*. London: James Clarke & Co., 1934. Intelligent, comprehensive, Biblical, Scottish, superb writing.

BROOKS, PHILLIPS, *Lectures On Preaching*. New York: E. P. Dutton, 1877. (Paperback edition, New York: The Seabury Press, 1964.) America's great classic on homiletics by one of its most noted preachers. After a century, these lectures still seem warm, clear, spiritual, and fascinating because they tell of the timeless realities of Christianity and of the human heart.

GRASSO, DOMENICO, *Proclaiming God's Message*. Notre Dame, Indiana: University of Notre Dame Press, 1965. A Roman Catholic treatment of the theology of preaching. Theoretical, but good.

JONES, ILION T., *Principles and Practice of Preaching*. Nashville: Abingdon Press, 1956. Much useful material.

LUCCOCK, HALFORD E., *In The Minister's Workshop*. Nashville: Abingdon Press, 1944. (Also in Apex paperback.) Clever, charming style, excellent on common problems.

STEWART, JAMES S., *Heralds of God*. New York: Charles Scribner's Sons, 1946. (Paperback edition, Grand Rapids, Mich.: Baker Book House, 1972.) Contemporary, practical, sensitive, wise, timely, beautifully expressed; by one of the most admired preachers of our time.

SECOND LIST

These books each have some special emphasis that is important.

BARR, BROWNE, *Parish Back Talk*. Nashville: Abingdon Press, 1964. Some good ideas on the theology of preaching.

BARTH, KARL, *The Preaching of the Gospel*. Philadelphia: The Westminster Press, 1963. This almost restricts preaching to Bible paraphrasing, but it is a good corrective to Bible neglect. Barth's sermons are not Barthian.

BREED, DAVID R., *Preparing to Preach*. New York: George H. Doran Co. 1911. Sometimes quaintly out-of-date but scholarly, comprehensive, useful.

BROADUS, JOHN A., *Preparation and Delivery of Sermons*. New York: George H. Doran Co., 1870. (Many later editions with various publishers.) For sixty years America's most used seminary textbook. Sound, massive, still very helpful.

COFFIN, HENRY SLOANE, *What to Preach*. New York: George H. Doran Co., 1926. Not a basic book, but five good lectures on expository, doctrinal, ethical, pastoral, and evangelistic preaching.

DODD, C. H., *The Apostolic Preaching*. London: Hodder & Staughton, 1936. (New edition New York: Harper & Bros., 1962.) Much quoted, academic, biblical, theological, not always realistic.

FORSYTH, P. T., *Positive Preaching and the Modern Mind*. London: The Independent Press, 1907. Difficult, but sharp sentences. Much admired. You may have reservations.

HALL, THOR, *The Future Shape of Preaching*. Philadelphia: The Fortress Press (paperback) 1971. Contemporary, provocative, good on communication theories. You may not agree, but you will be stimulated.

HOWE, REUEL, *Partners in Preaching*. New York: Seabury Press, 1967. Has an important emphasis on the congregation's part in preaching.

JOWETT, J. H., *The Preacher: His Life and Work*. London: Hodder & Stoughton, 1912. A good man says obvious things well.

KENNARD, J. S., *Psychic Power in Preaching*. Philadelphia: G. W. Jacobs & Co., 1901. Old-time religion, sensible advice. The "psychic power" concept deserves reflection.

KNOX, JOHN, *Contemporary Preaching*. Nashville: Abingdon Press, 1957. Only 94 pages, but clear help with sermon content.

McGREGOR, W. M., *The Making of a Preacher*. Philadelphia: The Westminster Press, 1946. Ninety-two pages, some interesting ideas.

MACLEOD, DONALD, ed., *Here Is My Method*. Westwood, N.J.: Fleming H. Revell Co., 1952. Thirteen well-known preachers tell how they prepare their sermons. Dr. Coffin, pp. 52–60, is specially good.

MACLEOD, DONALD, *Word and Sacrament*. Englewood Cliffs, N.J.: Prentice-Hall, Inc., 1960. Good on the need for preaching, and its relation to worship.

MILLER, DONALD H., *Fire in Thy Mouth*. Nashville: Abingdon Press, 1954. A primer. Simple things are put clearly.

MITCHELL, HENRY H., *Black Preaching*. Philadelphia, New York: J. B. Lippincott, 1970. Specializes on preaching to black congregations. Scholarly, clear, graceful, revealing, well illustrated. Emphasis on keeping black style. Excellent adive on how to use Bible stories, pp. 126–147.

PARKER, T. H. L., *Oracles of God*. London: Lutterworth Press, 1947. On Calvin's preaching. Chapter I a brief, clear history of preaching. Last chapter good on the theory of preaching.

Reid, Clyde, *The Empty Pulpit.* New York: Harper & Row, 1967. Sharp criticism. Touches on communication theory.

Sangster, W. E., *The Craft of Sermon Illustration.* London: The Epworth Press, 1946. (Reprint, Grand Rapids, Mich.: Baker Book House, 1972.) Some good sense.

Scherer, Paul, *For We Have This Treasure.* New York: Harper & Bros., 1944. Wise, memorable, flashing ideas, beautiful sentences.

Thielicke, Helmut, *The Trouble With the Church.* New York: Harper & Row, 1965. On why dull sermons drive off hearers. Negative, but some arresting ideas.

Thompson, W. D., and G. C. Bennett, *Dialogue Preaching.* Valley Forge, Pa.: The Judson Press, 1969. Theory and advice, with examples.

THIRD LIST

These books are suggested for general reading. Some you will consider great, some will not fit your taste or interests. All have been widely praised. When you get to a library, you may wish to dip into these, reading some for concentrated value, skimming others for scattered benefits.

Abbey, Merrill R., *Preaching to the Contemporary Mind.* Nashville: Abingdon Press, 1963.

Blackwood, Andrew W., *The Preparation of Sermons.* Nashville: Abingdon Press, 1948.

Bowie, Walter R., *Preparing to Preach.* Nashville: Abingdon Press, 1954.

Buttrick, George A., *Jesus Came Preaching.* New York: Chas. Scribner's Sons, 1932.

Caemmerer, Richard R., *Preaching for the Church.* St. Louis: Concordia Publishing House, 1959.

Caldwell, Frank H., *Preaching Angles.* Nashville: Abingdon Press, 1954.

Coffin, Henry Sloane, *Communion Through Preaching.* New York: George H. Doran Co., 1932.

Davis, H. Grady, *Design for Preaching.* Philadelphia: Fortress Press, 1958.

Davis, Ozora S., *Principles of Preaching.* Chicago: University of Chicago Press, 1924.

Farmer, H. H., *The Servant of the Word.* London: Nisbet & Co., 1941.

Ferris, Theodore, *Go Tell the People.* New York: Charles Scribner's Sons, 1951.

Ford, D. W. Cleverley, *Preaching Today.* London: Epworth Press, 1969.

Garrison, Webb B., *The Preacher and His Audience.* Westwood, N.J.: Fleming H. Revell Co., 1954.

Horne, Sylvester, *The Romance of Preaching.* Westwood, N.J.: Fleming H. Revell Co., 1914.

Jones, Edgar D., *The Royalty of the Pulpit.* New York: Harper & Bros., 1949. (Brief comments on the 75 Yale lectures on preaching.)

KRAEMER, HENDRICK, *The Communication of the Christian Faith*. Philadelphia: The Westminster Press, 1956.

LISKE, T. V., *Effective Preaching*. New York: The Macmillan Co., 1953.

MCCRACKEN, ROBERT J., *The Making of the Sermon*. New York: Harper & Brothers, 1956.

MACLENNAN, DAVID A., *A Preacher's Primer*. New York: Oxford University Press, 1950.

MACLENNAN, DAVID A., *Pastoral Preaching*. Philadelphia: Westminster Press, 1955.

MIEGGE, GIOVANNI, *Christian Affirmation in a Secular Age*. New York: Oxford University Press, 1958.

NILES, D. T., *The Preacher's Task and the Stone of Stumbling*. New York: Harper & Bros., 1958.

———, *The Preacher's Calling to Be Servant*. London: Lutterworth Press, 1959.

OMAN, JOHN, *Concerning the Ministry*. New York: Harper & Brothers, 1937.

READ, DAVID H. C., *The Communication of the Gospel*. London, SCM Press, 1952.

RITSCHL, DIETRICH, *A Theology of Proclamation*. Atlanta: John Knox Press, 1960.

SANGSTER, W. E., *The Craft of Sermon Construction*. London, The Epworth Press, 1949. (Reprint Grand Rapids, Mich.: The Baker Book House, 1972).

SCHERER, PAUL, *The Word God Sent*. New York: Harper & Row, Publishers, 1965.

SEMMELROTH, OTTO, *The Preaching Word*. New York: Herder & Herder, 1965.

SITTLER, JOSEPH, *The Ecology of Faith*. Philadelphia: The Muhlenberg Press, 1961.

SLEETH, R., *Persuasive Preaching*. New York: Harper & Bros., 1956.

STEWART, JAMES S., *A Faith to Proclaim*. New York: Chas. Scribner's Sons, 1953.

THOMPSON, E. T., *Changing Emphases in American Preaching*. Philadelphia: The Westminster Press, 1943.

WEDEL, THEODORE, *The Pulpit Rediscovers Theology*. Greenwich, Conn.: The Seabury Press, 1956.

———, *The Gospel in a Strange New World*. Philadelphia: The Westminster Press, 1963.

WHITE, R. E. O., *A Guide to Preaching*. London: Pickering & Inglis, 1973.

ON COMMUNICATION STUDIES

ABBEY, MERRILL R., *Communication in Pulpit and Parish*. Philadelphia: The Westminster Press, 1973. Excellent application of communication theory to preaching. Wise, contemporary, easy to read, original.

BERLO, DAVID K., *The Process of Communication*. New York: Holt, Rinehart and Winston, Inc., 1960. Not specifically on preaching. A clear, concise, comprehensive introduction.

MCLAUGHLIN, RAYMOND W., *Communication for the Church*. Grand Rapids,

Mich.: Zondervan Publishing House, 1968. Conservative theology and extensive communications training underlie interesting, untechnical, practical advice. Good on group techniques.

CORBETT, EDWARD P. J., *Classical Rhetoric for the Modern Student.* New York: Oxford University Press, 1971. Massive, technical, surprisingly interesting. Value for preachers in explanations of logic, fallacies, persuasion, style.

McCROSKEY, JAMES C., *An Introduction to Rhetorical Communication.* Englewood Cliffs, N.J.: Prentice-Hall, Inc., 1972. Common-sense, untechnical, much useful council. Good communications bibliography pp. 15–16.

"Fallacy," *Encyclopaedia Britannica* IX, (1967), 50–51.

"Logic," *Encyclopaedia Britannica* XIV, (1967), 209–37.

"Rhetoric," *Encyclopaedia Britannica* XIX, (1967), 257–60.

STYLE

STRUNK, WILLIAM, JR., and E. B. WHITE, *The Elements of Style.* New York: The Macmillan Co., 1959 (paperback). Gives common mistakes in writing and speaking. Brief and important.

FLESCH, RUDOLPH, *The Art of Plain Talk.* New York: Harper & Brothers, 1946. A light style and a dubious scoring system cleverly present highly important qualities for good expression.

FOWLER, H. W., *A Dictionary of Modern English Usage.* New York: Oxford University Press, 1926 (revised 1965). Called "the best book of its kind ever written in any European language." Analyzes and solves the difficult problems of grammar, style, and taste we worry over. Opinionated, but wise. British slant.

NICHOLSON, MARGARET, *A Dictionary of American English Usage.* New York: Oxford University Press, 1957. A useful supplement to Fowler (above).

Roget's International Thesaurus, 3rd ed. New York: Thomas Y. Crowell Co., 1962. An invaluable aid for finding precisely the right word, and for avoiding word repetitions.

QUOTATIONS

STEVENSON, BURTON, *The Home Book of Quotations.* New York: Dodd, Mead & Co., 1934 (revised 1967). Larger than Bartlett, and lists by topics instead of authors, which is more useful for preachers. Looking through a topic may give just the right quotation, and is likely to stimulate the preacher's thinking. Intemperate use could be disastrous.

BARTLETT, JOHN, *Familiar Quotations,* 14th ed. Boston: Little, Brown and Co., 1968. Less expensive and easier to handle than Stevenson (above).

SERMONS

Preachers learn to preach by studying those who do it well. They also read sermons for their spiritual good and growth in understanding.

Preachers from other centuries and traditions may not be good models, but they are still important.

When preachers have published many books of sermons, the titles are not listed here. The chief publisher, if any, will be given.

ARMSTRONG, JAMES, *The Urgent Now*. Nashville: Abingdon Press, 1970. Sermons with an intentionally contemporary mood and style.

BARTH, KARL, *Come Holy Spirit*. New York: Round Table Press, 1934.
  Deliverance to the Captives. New York: Harper & Brothers, 1961. Included here because of the author's fame as a theologian, but providing interesting examples of simple, Biblical, European preaching.

BLACK, HUGH, *According to My Gospel*. Westwood, N.J.: Fleming H. Revell Co., 1913. An arch example of the great Scottish preaching tradition.
  Listening to God. Same publisher, 1906.

BROOKS, PHILLIPS. His published sermons take several feet of shelf space. E. P. Dutton & Co., New York, published them from 1878 to 1910. Profoundly simple, clear, original, strong illustrations. One of the greatest preachers.

BRUNNER, EMIL, *The Great Imitation*. London: The Lutterworth Press, 1955.
  ———, *I Believe in the Living God*. Philadelphia: The Westminster Press, 1961. Sermons of a famous Swiss theologian.

BUSHNELL, HORACE. Many volumes published by Chas. Scribner's & Sons. New York, in the last half of the last century. A pioneer in theology and education.

BUTTRICK, GEORGE A., *Sermons Preached in a University Church*. Nashville: Abingdon Press, 1959. English-born New York preacher, author, teacher.

CHAPPELL, CLOVIS G. Many volumes published by Abingdon Press, Nashville, during the last thirty years. Simple, popular, heart-warming.

COFFIN, HENRY SLOANE, *The Creed of Jesus*. New York: Chas. Scribner's Sons, 1907.
  ———, *University Sermons*. New Haven: Yale University Press, 1914.
  ———, *God's Turn*. New York: Harper & Brothers, 1934. Beautifully clear wording, splendid construction.

DOCHERTY, GEORGE M., *One Way of Living*. New York: Harper & Brothers, 1958. To Washington, D.C. from Scotland. Forceful, original, contemporary.

FERRIS, THEODORE P., *The Image of God*. New York: Oxford University Press, 1965. Rich content with deceptive simplicity. Good example of clarity.

FOSDICK, HARRY EMERSON. Many volumes published by Harper & Row, New York. Remarkable for clarity, interest, range of subjects, illustrations. Famed New York preacher 1920 to 1950.

GOSSIP, ARTHUR J., *The Galilean Accent*. Edinburgh: T.&T. Clark, 1927.
  ———, *Experience Worketh Hope*. New York: Chas. Scribner's Sons, 1945.
  ———, *From the Edge of the Crowd*. Edinburgh: T.&.T. Clark, 1924.
  ———, *The Hero in Thy Soul*. New York: Chas. Scribner's Sons, 1930. A colorful British preacher and an eloquent stylist.

JOWETT, JOHN HENRY. His books of sermons had various publishers. An early twentieth-century New York preacher from England. Elegant literary polish.

KING, MARTIN LUTHER, *Strength to Love*. New York: Harper & Row, 1963. One of America's greatest preachers in clarity, depth, structure, power to move. An excellent example of style. Black freedom martyr.

LUCCOCK, HALFORD E., *Five-Minute Shop Talks*. Westwood, N.J.: Fleming H. Revell Co., 1916.

———, *Marching Off the Map*. New York: Harper & Brothers, 1952. Inventive, unconventional, interesting, lively.

McCRACKEN, ROBERT J., *Questions People Ask*. New York: Harper & Brothers, 1951. Dr. Fosdick's successor at Riverside Church. From Canada. Simple, clear.

MacLENNAN, DAVID A., *Joyous Adventure*. New York: Harper & Brothers, 1952.

———, *No Coward Soul*. New York: Oxford University Press, 1949.

———, *Sermons from Thanksgiving to Easter*. Valley Forge, Pa.: The Judson Press, 1968. Fresh approaches and illustrations from a popular preacher, author, and teacher.

• MARNEY, CARLYLE, *The Carpenter's Son*. Nashville: Abingdon Press, 1967.

———, *The Crucible of Redemption*. Same publisher, 1968. Original, unconventional.

MARSHALL, PETER, *Mr. Jones, Meet the Master*. Westwood, N.J.: Fleming H. Revell Co., 1949. From Scotland to America. Lilting, easy style. Interesting page layout.

MORGAN, G. CAMPBELL. Many volumes published by Fleming H. Revell Co., Westwood, N.J. British master of Bible exposition in first third of the twentieth century.

READ, DAVID H. C., His books have various publishers. New York preacher from Britain and a popular radio preacher.

ROBERTSON, F. W., *The Preaching of F. W. Robertson*. Philadelphia: Fortress Press, 1964.

———, *Sermons and Outlines on the Seven Words*. Grand Rapids, Mich.: Baker Book House, 1954. His published sermons fill a shelf. Mid-nineteenth-century British preacher of spiritual sensitivity and theological clarity. Brilliant illustrations. Died young.

SCHERER, PAUL, *Facts That Undergird Life*. New York: Harper & Brothers, 1938.

———, *The Place Where Thou Standest*. Same publisher, 1942. Original, a master stylist. A Manhattan pastor and teacher of preaching.

SHOEMAKER, SAMUEL K., *Confident Faith*. Westwood, N.J.: Fleming H. Revell Co., 1932.

———, *Religion that Works*. Westwood, N.J.: Fleming H. Revell Co., 1928.

———, *And Thy Neighbor*. Waco, Texas: Word Books, 1968. Pointed, practical sermons by a pioneer of "relational" practices.

SIZOO, JOSEPH, *Make Life Worth Living*. New York: The Macmillan Co., 1938.

———, *Not Alone*. New York: The Macmillan Co., 1940.

———, *The Way of Faith*. New York: Harper & Brothers, 1935. His interesting, incisive personality is much in his sermons.

SOCKMAN, RALPH W., *Suburbs of Christianity*. Nashville: The Abingdon Press, 1924.

———, *The Unemployed Carpenter*. New York: Harper & Brothers, 1933.

———, *Whom Christ Commended*. Nashville: The Abingdon Press, 1963. From a long Manhattan and radio ministry. Popular, useful.

SPEAKMAN, FREDERICK B., *Love Is Something You Do*. Westwood, N.J.: Fleming H. Revell Co., 1959.

———, *The Salty Tang*. Same publisher, 1954. Unusual skill in basing a sermon on a story or incident.

STEIMLE, EDMUND A., *Are You Looking for God?* Philadelphia: Muhlenberg Press, 1957.

———, *Disturbed By Joy*. Philadelphia: Fortress Press, 1967. Clear, pointed, interesting, important.

STEWART, JAMES S. His sermons have various publishers. Edinburgh pastor and professor. Perhaps the most admired and imitated contemporary preacher in English. Spiritual, biblical, moving, beautiful expression.

THIELICKE, HELMUT. Eerdmans, Harper, and Fortress have each published two books of his sermons. A German preacher and professor, and a prolific writer. Dynamic. A remarkably un-European style. Bible intrepreter and theologian.

THURMAN, HOWARD, *The Growing Edge*. New York: Harper & Brothers, 1956. Black preacher and teacher. Devotional, original. A much-read writer.

TRUETT, GEORGE W. Several books of sermons published by William B. Eerdmans of Grand Rapids, Mich. A mid-twentieth-century Southern preacher and evangelist.

WEATHERHEAD, LESLIE D. Most of his many books are published by Abingdon Press of Nashville. A mid-twentieth-century London pastor and writer. Brilliant, many-sided. A model for interest, clarity, and illustrations.

Collections of Sermons:

FANT, CLYDE E., and WILLIAM M. PINSON, JR., eds., *Twenty Centuries of Great Preaching*. Twelve volumes plus an index volume. Waco, Texas: Word Books, 1971.

MCCARTNEY, CLARENCE E., ed., *Great Sermons of the World*. Boston: The Stratford Co., 1926. Thirty-five well-selected classics.

HOLLAND, DEWITTE, ed., *Sermons In American History*. Nashville: Abingdon Press, 1971. Gives sermons on both sides, or three sides, of twenty theological, ecclesiastical, or social issues that have divided American Christians. The sermons range from great to poor, but all show the place of preaching in history.

Recommended Bible Commentaries

This list combines the selections of professors of Bible in two theological seminaries who were asked to recommend the commentaries that are most helpful for preaching. Most of these books can be bought new; a few classics may have to be bought second-hand. Those marked (Int) are only a part of a volume in the series.

PUBLISHERS

Allenson—Naperville, Ill.: Alec R. Allenson, Inc.
Anchor—*The Anchor Bible*. Garden City, N.Y.: Doubleday & Co.
Cam—New York: Cambridge University Press
CBS—*The Cambridge Bible for Schools and Colleges*. Cambridge University Press
Eerdmans—Grand Rapids, Mich.: William B. Eerdmans Publishing Co.
Fortress—Philadelphia: Fortress Press
Harper—New York: Harper & Row, Publishers, Inc.
ICC—*The International Critical Commentary*. Naperville, Ill.: Allenson
Int—*The Interpreter's Bible*. Nashville: The Abingdon Press
LBC—*The Layman's Bible Commentary*. Atlanta: John Knox Press
Mac—New York: The Macmillan Co.
Magnes—Jerusalem, Israel: The Magnes Press
New Century—New York: The Oxford University Press
OTL—*The Old Testament Library*. Philadelphia: The Westminster Press
Oxford—New York: Oxford University Press
Pelican—*The Pelican Gospel Commentaries*. New York: The Seabury Press
St. Martin's—New York: St. Martin's Press
West—Philadelphia: The Westminster Press

OLD TESTAMENT

Genesis	Skinner (ICC); von Rad (OTL); Fritsch (LBC)
Exodus	Driver (CBS); Noth (OTL); Cassuto (Magnes)
Leviticus	Kennedy (New Century)
Numbers	Gray (ICC); Noth (OTL); Marsh (Int)

Deuteronomy	Driver (ICC); Wright (Int); Smith (CBS); von Rad (OTL)
Joshua	Bright (Int)
Judges & Ruth	Moore (ICC); Smith (Int)
I & II Samuel	Kirkpatrick (CBS); Caird (Int); Hertzberg (OTL)
I & II Kings	Montgomery (ICC); Gray (OTL)
I & II Chronicles	Elmslie (CBS); Meyers (Anchor)
Ezra & Nehemiah	Bowman (Int); Meyers (Anchor)
Esther	Anderson (Int)
Job	Terrien (Int)
Psalms	Weiser (OTL)
Proverbs	Fritsch (Int); Scott (Anchor)
Ecclesiastes	Gordis, "Koheleth" (New York: Schocken Books)
Song of Solomon	Meek-Kerr (Int); Gordis (New York: The Jewish Theol. Sem. of America)
Isaiah	Scott-Muilenberg (Int); Skinner (CBS)
Jeremiah and Lamentations	Hyatt (Int); Welch (Allenson); Bright (Anchor)
Ezekiel	May (Int); Eichrodt (OTL); Cook (ICC)
Daniel	Montgomery (ICC)
Minor Prophets	*Hosea*—Ward (Harper); Mauchline (Int). *Amos*—Mays (OTL); Cripps (London: SPCK). *Joel, Amos*—Driver (CBS). *Nahum through Malachi*—Driver (New Century). *All 12*—G. A. Smith—2 vols. (Garden City, N.Y.: Doubleday, Doran & Co.)

NEW TESTAMENT

Matthew	A. H. M'Neile (St. Martin's); A. Plummer (Allenson)
Mark	V. Taylor (St. Martin's); Cranfield (Cam); Schweizer (Atlanta: John Knox Press); Nineham (Pelican)
Luke	Leaney (Allenson); Caird (Pelican); Geldenhuys (Eerdmans)
John	Dodd (Cam); Hoskyns (Allenson); Lightfoot (Oxford); Brown—2 vols. (Anchor); Morris (Eerdmans); Bultmann (West)
Acts	Williams (Harper); Bruce (Eerdmans)
Romans	Barrett (Harper); Nygren (Fortress); Sanday-Headlam (ICC)
I Corinthians	Barrett (Harper); Robertson-Plummer (ICC)
II Corinthians	Hughes (Eerdmans); Plummer (ICC)
Galatians	Burton (ICC); Bring (Fortress)
Ephesians	Abbott (ICC); Allan (Allenson)
Philippians	Beare (Allenson)
Colossians	Lightfoot (Zondervan); Radford (West); Moule (CBS); Lohse (Fortress)
I & II Thessalonians	Frame (ICC); Milligan (Mac); Best (Harper)
Pastoral Epistles	Barrett (Oxford); Kelly (Harper); Dibelius-Conzelmann (Fortress)
Philemon	Knox (Int)

Hebrews	Westcott (Eerdmans); Moffatt (ICC); Bruce (Eerdmans); Montefiore (Harper)
James	Ropes (Allenson); Reicke (Anchor)
I Peter	Beare (ICC); Selwyn (St. Martin's)
II Peter	Cranfield (Allenson)
Jude	Bigg (ICC)
I, II, & III John	Westcott (Eerdmans); Findlay (London: Hodder & Stoughton); Dodd (Allenson); Bultmann (Fortress)
Revelations	Swete (Mac); Caird (Harper); Minear (Washington, D.C.: Corpus Books); Bowman (West)

BRIEFER COMMENTARIES

DUMMELOW, J. R., ed., *A Commentary on the Holy Bible.* New York: The Macmillan Co., 1909 & 1961.

The Interpreter's One-Volume Commentary. Nashville: The Abingdon Press, 1971.

The Jerome Bible Commentary. Englewood Cliffs, N.J.: Prentice-Hall, Inc., 1968.

REDACTIONAL STUDIES

These comment on the Bible author's views and intentions.

BLAIR, E. P., *Jesus in the Gospel of Matthew.* Nashville: The Abingdon Press, 1960.

STENDAHL, K., *The School of Matthew.* Philadelphia: Fortress Press, 1954.

MARXSEN, W., *Mark the Evangelist.* Nashville: The Abingdon Press, 1969.

CONZELMANN, H., *The Theology of St. Luke.* London: Faber and Faber, 1961.

KECK, L., and J. L. MARTYN, eds., *Studies in Luke—Acts.* Nashville: The Abingdon Press, 1966.

DICTIONARY AND WORDBOOK

The Interpreter's Dictionary of the Bible, 4 vols. Nashville: The Abingdon Press, 1962.

RICHARDSON, ALAN, *A Theological Wordbook of the Bible.* New York: The Macmillan Co., 1960.

Index

V

Valentine, Father, 185-86
van Dyke, Henry, 140
Variety, 73, 82, 91-92, 95, 102, 120, 140-41, 144, 162
Visualize hearers, 52, 122, 316
Vitalize for delivery, 123-24
Vocabulary, 132, 148-53
Voelkel, Harold, 259
Voice, 94-95
Voltaire, 145

W

Walker, Harold B., 266
Walsh, James J., 205
War, 239, 251, 254
Warren, Earl, 238
Watson, John, 302
Weatherhead, Leslie D., 103
Webster, Daniel, 100, 129
Weddings, 284-87
  bible for, 285-86
  homily, 284-86
  rehearsal, 286-87

Wesley, John, 18, 262
Westminster Assembly, 76
What to preach, 57-69
White, E. B., 158
White, Governor, 109
Whittier, John Greenleaf, 219
Wilkie, Wendell, 220
Wilson, Woodrow, 251, 294
Wittgenstein, Ludwig, 46
Women, 2, 36, 127, 156-57, 301-4
Words, 3, 19, 49-50, 52, 89-90, 129, 140, 147-60, 193, 236
  to avoid, 157-60, 216
  to favor, 153-55
  have character, 147-48
  many modern languages, 149-50
  right language, 131, 132, 143, 148-53
Work, 45, 105, 107-8, 112-13, 272
Working schedule, 105-9, 113
World, mission to, 3-4, 6, 318
Worship, public, 4, 14, 40, 61, 234, 263, 271, 277-78, 308, 311
Write out sermon?, 117-20
Writing, mechanics of, 120-21
Writing and speaking styles, 127-28
Wyeth, Andrew, 139